THE LIVES AND OPINIONS OF EMINENT PHILOSO[PHERS]
DIOGENES LAERTIUS

Publisher's Note

The book descriptions we ask booksellers to display prominently warn that the book may have numerous typos, missing text, images and indexes.

We scanned this book using character recognition software that includes an automated spell check. Our software is 99 percent accurate if the book is in good condition. However, we do understand that even one percent can be a very annoying number of typos! And sometimes all or part of a page is missing from our copy of a book. Or the paper may be so discolored from age that you can no longer read the type. Please accept our sincere apologies.

After we re-typeset and design a book, the page numbers change so the old index and table of contents no longer work. Therefore, we often remove them.

We would like to manually proof read and fix the typos and indexes, manually scan and add any illustrations, and track down another copy of the book to add any missing text. But our books sell so few copies, you would have to pay up to a thousand dollars for the book as a result.

Therefore, whenever possible, we let our customers download a free copy of the original typo-free scanned book. Simply enter the barcode number from the back cover of the paperback in the Free Book form at www.general-books.net. You may also qualify for a free trial membership in our book club to download up to four books for free. Simply enter the barcode number from the back cover onto the membership form on the same page. The book club entitles you to select from more than a million books at no additional charge. Simply enter the title or subject onto the search form to find the books.

If you have any questions, could you please be so kind as to consult our Frequently Asked Questions page at www.general-books.net/faqs.cfm? You are also welcome to contact us there.
General Books LLC®, Memphis, USA, 2012. ISBN: 9781458928160.

➛ ➛ ➛ ➛ ➛ ➛ ➛ ➛

PREFACE.
Diogenes, the author of the following work, was a native (as is generally believed) of Laerte, in Cilicia, from which circumstance he derived the cognomen of Laertius. Little is known of him personally, nor is even the age in which he lived very clearly ascertained. But as Plutarch, Sextus Empiricus, and Satuminus are among the writers whom he quotes, he is generally believed to have lived near the end of the second century of our era: although some place him in the time of Alexander Severus, and others as late as Constantine. His work consists of ten books, variously called: The Lives of Philosophers, A History of Philosophy, and The Lives of Sophists. From internal evidence (iii. 47, 29), we learn that he wrote it for a noble lady (according to some, Arria; according to others, Julia, the Empress of Severus), who occupied herself with the study of philosophy, and especially of Plato..

Diogenes Laertius divides the philosophy of the Greeks into the Ionic, beginning with Anaximander, and ending with Theophrastus (in which class, he includes the Socratic philosophy and all its various ramifications); and the Italian, beginning with Pythagoras, and ending with Epicurus, in which he includes the Eleatics, as also Heraclitus and the, Sceptics. From the minute consideration which he devotes to Epicurus and his system, it has been supposed that he himself belonged to that school.

His work is the chief source of information we possess

B concerning the history of Greek philosophy, and is the foundation of nearly all the modern treatises on that subject; some of the most important of which are little more than translations or amplifications of it. It is valuable, as containing a copious collection of anecdotes illustrative of the life and manners of the Greeks; but he has not always been very careful in his selection, and in some parts there is a confusion in his statements that makes them scarcely intelligible. These faults have led some critics to consider the work as it now exists merely a mutilated abridgment of the original. Breslaeus, who in the thirteenth century, wrote a Treatise on the Lives and Manners of the Philosophers, quotes many anecdotes and sayings, which seem to be derived from Diogenes, but which are not to be found in our present text; whence Schneider concludes that he had a very different and far more complete copy than has come down to us.

The text used in the following translation is chiefly that of Huebner, as published at Leipsic, A.d. 1828.

LIVES AND OPINIONS OF EMINENT PHILOSOPHERS. BOOK I. INTRODUCTION. I. Some say that the study of philosophy originated with the barbarians. In that among the Persians there existed the Magi, and among the Babylonians or Assyrians the Chaldaei,t among the Indians the Gymnosophistae.J and among the Celts and Gauls men who were called Druids § and " The religion of the ancient Persians was the worship of fire or of the elements, in which fire was symbolical of the Deity. At a later period, in the time of the Greeks, the ancient worship was changed into the adoration of the stars (Sabaeism), especially of the sun and of the morning star. This religion was distinguished by a simple and majestic character. Its priests were called Magi."—*Tennemaris Manual of the History of Philosophy, lidrod.* §70.

t " The Chaldeans were devoted to the worship of the stars and to astrology; the nature of their climate and country disposing them to it. The worship of the stars was revived by them and widely disseminated even subsequently to the Christian era."—*Ibid.* § 71. X " Cicero speaks of those who in India are accounted philosophers, living naked and enduring the greatest severity of winter without betraying any feeling of pain, and displaying the same insensibility when exposed to the flames."—*Tusc. Quest.* v. 27.

§ " The religion of the Britons was one of the most considerable parts of their government, and the Druids who were their priests, possessed great authority among them. Besides ministering at the altar, and directing all religious duties, they presided over the education of youth; they possessed both the civil and criminal jurisdiction, they decided all controversies among states as well as among private persons, and whoever refused to submit to their decree was exposed to the most severe penalties. The sentence of excommunication was pronounced Semnothei. as Aristotle relates in his book on Magic, and Sotion in the twenty-third book of his Succession of Philosophers. Besides those men there were the Phoenician Ochus, the Thracian Zamolxis, and the Libyan Atlas. For the against him; he was forbidden access to the sacrifices of public worship; he was debarred all intercourse with his fellow citizens even in the common affairs of life: his company was universally shunned as profane and dangerous, he was refused the protection of law, and death itself became an acceptable relief from the misery and infamy to which he was exposed. Thus the bonds of government, which were naturally loose among that rude and turbulent people, were happily corroborated by the terrors of their superstition.

" No species of superstition was ever more terrible than that of the Druids; besides the several penalties which it was in the power of the ecclesiastics to inflict in this world, they inculcated the eternal transmigration of souls, and thereby extended their authority as far as the fears of their timorous votaries. They practised their rites in dark groves or other secret recesses, and in order to throw a greater mystery over their religion, they communicated their doctrines only to the initiated, and strictly forbade the committing of them to writing, lest they should at any time be exposed to the examination of the profane and vulgar. Human sacrifices were practised among them; the spoils of war were often devoted to their divinities, and they punished with the severest tortures whoever dared to secrete any part of the consecrated offering. These treasures they kept secreted in woods and forests, secured by no other guard than the terrors of their religion; and their steady conquest over human avidity may be regarded as more signal than their prompting men to the most extraordinary and most violent efforts. No idolatrous worship ever attained such an ascendant over mankind as that of the ancient Gauls and Britons. And the Romans after their conquest, finding it impossible to reconcile those nations to the laws and institutions of their masters while it maintained its authority, were at last obliged to abolish it by penal statutes, a violence which had never in any other instance been resorted to by those tolerating conquerors."—*Hume's History of England,* chap. 1. § 1.

Zamolxis, or Zalmoxis, so called from the bear-skin (?dX;toc) in which he was wrapped as soon as he was born, was a Getan, and a slave cf Pythagoras at Samos; having been emancipated by his master, he travelled into Egypt; and on his return to his own country he introduced the ideas which he had acquired in his travels on the subject of civilisation, religion, and the immortality of the soul. He was made priest of the chief deity among the Getae, and was afterwards himself worshipped as a divine person. He was said to have lived in a subterraneous cavern for three years, and after that to have re-appeared among his countrymen. Herodotus, however, who records these stories (iv. 95), expresses his disbelief of them, placing him before the time of Pythagoras by many years, and seems to incline to the belief that he was an indigenous Getan deity.

Egyptians say that Vulcan was the son of Nilus, and that he was the author of philosophy, in which those who were especially eminent were called his priests and prophets.

II. From his age to that of Alexander, king of the Macedonians were forty-eight thousand eight hundred and sixty-three years, and during this time there were three hundred and seventy-three eclipses of the sun, and eight hundred and thirty-two eclipses of the moon.

Again, from the time of the Magi, the first of whom was Zoroaster the Persian, to that of the fall of Troy, Hermodorus the Platonic philosopher, in his treatise on Mathematics, calculates that fifteen thousand years elapsed. But Xanthus the Lydian says that the passage of the Hellespont by Xerxes took place six thousand years after the time of Zoroaster, and that after him there was a regular succession " The real time of Zoroaster is, as may be supposed, very uncertain, but he is said by some eminent writers to have lived in the time of Darius Hystaspes; though others, apparently on better grounds, place him at a very far earlier date. He is not mentioned by Herodotus at all. His native country too is very uncertain. Some writers, among whom are Ctesias and Ammian, call him a Bactrian, while Porphyry speaks of him as a Chaldeean, and Pliny as a native of Proconnesus;—Niebuhr considers him a purely mythical personage. The great and fundamental article of the system (of the Persian theology) was the celebrated doctrine of the two principles; a bold and injudicious attempt of Eastern philosophy to reconcile the existence of moral and physical evil with the attributes of a beneficent Creator and governor of the world. The first and original being, in whom, or by whom the universe exists, is denominated, in the writings of Zoroaster, *Time without bounds* From either the bund or the intelligent operation of this infinite Time, which bears but too near an affinity to the Chaos of the Greeks, the two secondary but active principles of the universe were from all eternity produced; Ormusd and Ahriman, each of them possessed of the powers of creation, but each disposed by his invariable nature to exercise them with different designs; the principle of good is eternally absorbed in light, the principle of evil is eternally buried in darkness. The wise benevolence of Ormusd formed man capable of virtue, and abundantly provided his fair habitation with the materials of happiness. By his vigilant providence the motion of the planets, the order df the seasons, and the temperate mixture of the elements are preserved. But the maker of Ahriman has long since pierced *OrmusoVs Egg,* or in other words, has violated the harmony of his works. Since that fatal irruption, the most minute articles of good and evil are intimately intermingled and agitated together; the rankest poisons spring up among the most salutary plants; deluges, earthquakes, and conflagrations attest the conflict of of Magi under the names of Ostanes and Astrampsychos and Gobryas and Pazatas, until the destruction of the Persian empire by Alexander.

III. But those who say this, ignorantly impute to the barbarians the merits of the Greeks, from whom not only all philosophy, but even the whole human race in reality originated. For Musseus was born among the Athenians, and Linus among the Thebans; and they say that the former, who was the son of Eumolpus, was the first person who taught the system of the genealogy of the gods, and who invented the spheres; and that he taught that all things originated in one thing, and when dissolved returned to that same thing; and that he died at Phalerum, and that this epitaph was inscribed on his tomb: —

Phalerum's soil beneath this tomb contains
Musaeus dead, Eumolpus' darling son.

And it is from the father of Musaeus that the family called Eumolpidae among the Athenians derive their name. They say too that Linus was the son of Mercury and the Muse Urania; and that he invented a system of Cosmogony, and of the motions of the sun and moon, and of the generation of animals and fruits; and the following is the beginning of his poem,

There was a time when all the present world
Uprose at once.

From which Anaxagoras derived his theory, when he said that nature, and the little world of man is perpetually shaken by vice and misfortune. While the rest of mankind are led away captives in the chains of their infernal enemy, the faithful Persian alone reserves his religious adoration for his friend and protector Ormusd, and fights under his banner of light, in the full confidence that he shall, in the last day, share the glory of his triumph. At that decisive period, the enlightened wisdom of goodness will render the power of Ormusd superior to the furious malice of his rival; Ahriman and his followers, disarmed and subdued, will sink into their native darkness, and virtue will maintain the eternal peace and harmony of the universe...... As a legislator, Zoroaster " discovered a liberal concern for the public and private happiness seldom to be found among the visionary schemes of superstition. Fasting and celibacy, the common means of purchasing the divine favour, he condemns *wit* abhorrence, as a criminal rejection of the best gifts of Providence."—*Gibbon, Decline and Fall of the Roman Empire,* c. viii.
all things had been produced at the same time, and that then intellect had come and arranged them all in order.

They say, moreover, that Linus died in Euboea, having been shot with an arrow by Apollo, and that this epitaph was set over him: —

The Theban Linus sleeps beneath this ground,
Urania's son with fairest garlands crown'd.

IV. And thus did philosophy arise among the Greeks, and indeed its very name shows that it has no connection with the barbarians. But those who attribute its origin to them, introduce Orpheus the Thracian, and say that he was a philosopher, and the most ancient one of all. But if one ought to call a man who has said such things about the gods as he has said, a philosopher, I do not know what name one ought to give to him who has not scrupled to attribute all sorts of human feelings to the gods, and even such discreditable actions as are but rarely spoken of among men; and tradition relates that he was murdered by women; but there is an inscription at Dium in Macedonia, saying that he was killed by lightning, and it runs thus:—

Here the bard buried by the Muses lies,
The Thracian Orpheus of the golden lyre;
Whom mighty Jove, the Sovereign of the skies,
Removed from earth by his dread lightning's fire.

V. But they who say that philosophy had its rise among the barbarians, give also an account of the different systems prevailing among the various tribes. And they say that the Gymnosophists and the Druids philosophize, delivering their apophthegmns in enigmatical language, bidding men worship the gods and do no evil, and practise manly virtue.

This is the account given by Virgil—
Spretfc Ciconum quo munere matres
Inter sacra Deum nocturnique orgia Bacchi,
Disceptumlatos juvenemsparsere per agros.—Gboro.iv.520.

Which Dryden translates—

The Thracian matrons who the youth accus'd,
Of love diadain'd and marriage rites refus'd;
With furies and nocturnal orgies fird,
At length against his sacred life conspir'd;
Whom ev'n the savage beasts had spar'd they kill'd,
And strew'd his mangled limbs about the field.

VI. Accordingly Clitarchus, in his twelfth book, says that the Gymnosophists despise death, and that the Chaldaeans study astronomy and the science of soothsaying—that the Magi occupy themselves about the service to be paid to the gods, and about sacrifices and prayers, as if they were the only people to whom the deities listen: and that they deliver accounts of the existence and generation of the gods, saying that they are fire, and earth, and water; and they condemn the use of images, and above all things do they condemn those who say that the gods are male and female; they speak much of justice, and think it impious to destroy the bodies of the dead by fire; they allow men to marry their mothers or their daughters, as Sotion tells us in his twenty-third book; they study the arts of soothsaying and divination, and assert that the gods reveal their will to them by those sciences. They teach also that the air is full of phantoms, which, by emanation and a sort of evaporation, glide into the sight of those who have a clear perception; they forbid any extravagance of ornament, and the use of gold; their garments are white, their beds are made of leaves, and vegetables are their food, with cheese and coarse bread; they use a rush for a staff, the top of which they run into the cheese, and so taking up a piece of it they eat it. Of all kinds of magical divination they are ignorant, as Aristotle asserts in his book on Magic, and Dinon in the fifth book of his Histories. And this writer says, that the name of Zoroaster being interpreted means, a sacrifice to the stars; and Hermodorus makes the same statement. But Aristotle, in the first book of his Treatise on Philosophy, says, that the Magi are more ancient than the Egyptians; and that according to them there are two principles, a good demon and an evil demon, and that the name of the one is Jupiter or Oromasdes, and that of the other Pluto or Arimanius. And Hermippus gives the same account in the first book of his History of the Magi; and so does Eudoxus in his Period; and so does Theopompus in the eighth book of his History of the Affairs of Philip; and this last writer tells us also, that according to the Magi men will have a resurrection and be immortal, and that what exists now will exist hereafter under its own present name; and Eudemus of Rhodes coincides in this statement. But Hecataeus says, that according to their doctrines the gods also are beings who have been born. But Clearchus the Solensian, in his Treatise on Education says, that the Gymnosophists are descendants of the Magi; and some say that the Jews also are derived from them. Moreover, those who have written on the subject of the Magi condemn Herodotus; for they say that Xerxes would never have shot arrows against the sun, or have put fetters on the sea, as both sun and sea have been handed down by the Magi as gods, but that it was quite consistent for Xerxes to destroy the images of the gods.

VII. The following is the account that authors give of the philosophy of the Egyptians, as bearing on the gods and on justice. They say that the first principle is matter; then that the four elements were formed out of matter and divided, and that some animals were created, and that the sun and moon are gods, of whom the former is called Osiris and the latter Isis, and they are symbolised under the names of beetles and dragons, and hawks, and other animals, as Manetho tells us in his abridged account of Natural Philosophy, and Hecataeus confirms the statement in the first book of his History of the Philosophy of the Egyptians. They also make images of the gods, and assign them temples because they do not know the form of God. They consider that the world had a beginning and will have an end, and that it is a sphere; they think that the stars are fire, and that it is by a combination of them that the things on earth are generated; that the moon is eclipsed when it falls into the shadow of the earth; that the soul is eternal and migratory; that rain is caused by the changes of the atmosphere; and they enter into other speculations on points of natural history, as Hecataeus and Aristagoras inform us.

They also have made laws about justice, which they attribute to Mercury, and they consider those animals which are useful to be gods. They claim to themselves the merit of having been the inventors of geometry, and astrology, and arithmetic. So much then for the subject of invention.

VIII. But Pythagoras was the first person who invented the term Philosophy, and who called himself a philosopher; when he was conversing at Sicyon with Leon, who was tyrant of the Sicyonians or of the Phliasians (as Heraclides Ponticus relates in the book which he wrote about a dead woman); for he said that no man ought to be called wise, but only God. For formerly what is now called philosophy *(piXoeopla)* was called wisdom *(eopla)*, and they who professed it were called wise men *(eopol)*, as being endowed with great acuteness and accuracy of mind; but now he who embraces wisdom is called a philosopher *(pi'Aotsopog.)*

But the wise men were also called Sophists. And not only they, but poets also were called Sophists: as Cratinus in his Archilochi calls Homer and Hesiod, while praising them highly.

IX. Now these were they who were accounted wise men. Thales, Solon, Periander, Cleobulus, Chilo, Bias, Pittacus. To these men add Anacharsis the Scythian, Myson the Chenean, Pherecvdes the Syrian, and Epimenides the Cretan; and some add, Pisistratus, the tyrant: These then are they who were called the wise men.

X. But of Philosophy there arose two schools. One derived from Anaximander, the other from Pythagoras. Now, Thales had been the preceptor of Anaximander, and Pherecydes of Pythagoras. And the one school was called the Ionian, because Thales, being an Ionian (for he was a native of Miletus), had been the tutor of Anaximander;—but the other was called the Italian from Pythagoras, because he spent the chief part of his life in Italy. And the Ionic school ends with Clitomachus, and Chrysippus, and Theophrastus; and the Italian one with Epicurus; for Anaximander succeeded Thales, and he was succeeded again by Anaximenes, and he by Anaxagoras, and he by Archelaus, who was the master of Socrates, who was the originator of moral philosophy. And he was the master of the sect of the Socratic philosophers, and of Plato, who was the founder of the old Academy; and Plato's pupils were Speusippus and Xenocrates; and Polemo was the pupil of Xenocrates, and Crantor and Crates of Polemo. Crates again was the master of Arcesilaus, the founder of the Middle Academy, and his pupil was Lacydes, who gave the new Academy its distinctive principles. His pupil was Carneades, and he in his turn was the master of Clitomachus. And this school ends in this way with Clitomachus and

Chrysippus.

Antisthenes was the pupil of Socrates, and the master of Diogenes the Cynic; and the pupil, of Diogenes was Crates the Theban; Zeno the Cittiaean was his; Cleanthes was his; Chrysippus was his. Again it ends with Theophrastus in the following manner:—

Aristotle was the pupil of Plato, Theophrastns the pupil of Aristotle; and in this way the Ionian school comes to an end.

Now the Italian school was carried on in this way. Pythagoras was the pupil of Pherecydes; his pupil was Telauges his son; he was the master of Xenophanes, and he of Parmenides; Parmenides of Zeno the Eleatic, he of Leucippus, he of Democritus: Democritus had many disciples, the most eminent of whom were Nausiphanes and Nausicydes, and they were the masters of Epicurus.

XI. Now, of Philosophers some were dogmatic, and others were inclined to suspend their opinions. By dogmatic, I mean those who explain their opinions about matters, as if they could be comprehended. By those who suspend their opinions, I mean those who give no positive judgment, thinking that these things cannot be comprehended. And the former class have left many memorials of themselves; but the others have never written a line; as for instance, according to some people, Socrates, and Stilpo, and Philippus, and Menedemus, and Pyrrho, and Theodorus, and Carneades, and Bryson; and, as some people say, Pythagoras, and Aristo of Chios, except that he wrote a few letters. There are some men too who have written one work only, Melissus, Parmenides, and Anaxagoras; but Zeno wrote many works, Xenophanes still more; Democritus more, Aristotle more, Epicurus more, and Chrysippus more.

XII. Again, of philosophers some derived a surname from cities, as, the Elians, and Megaric sect, the Eretrians, and the Cyrenaics. Some from the places which they frequented, as the Academics and Stoics. Some from accidental circumstances, as the Peripatetics; or, from jests, as the Cynics. Some again from their dispositions, as the Eudaemonics; some from an opinion, as the Elenctic, and Analogical schools. Some from their masters, as the Sooratic and Epicurean philosophers; and so on. The Natural Philosophers were so called from their study of nature; the Ethical philosophers from their investigation of questions of morals *(vngl r & ttfjj).* The Dialecticians are they who devote themselves to quibbling on words. XIII. Now there are three divisions of philosophy. Natural, Ethical, and Dialectic. Natural philosophy occupies itself about the world and the things in it; Ethical philosophy about life, and the things which concern us; Dialectics are conversant with the arguments by which both the others are supported.

Natural philosophy prevailed till the time of Archelaus; but after the time of Socrates, Ethical philosophy was predominant; and after the time of Zeno the Eleatic, Dialectic philosophy got the upper hand.

Ethical philosophy was subdivided into ten sects; the Academic, the Cyrenaic, the Elian, the Megaric, the Cynic, the Eretriau, the Dialectic, the Peripatetic, the Stoic, and the Epicurean. Of the old Academic school Plato was the president; of the middle, Arcesilaus; and of the New, Lacydes:—the Cyrenaic school was founded by Aristippus the Cyrenian; the Elian, by Phaedo, of Elis; the Megaric, by Euclid, of Megara; the Cynic, by Antisthenes, the Athenian; the Eretrian, by Menedemus, of Eretria; the Dialectic by Clitomachus, the Carthaginian; the Peripatetic, by Aristotle, the Stagirite; the Stoic, by Zeno, the Cittiaean; the Epicurean school derives its name from Epicurus, its founder.

But Hippobotus, in his Treatise on Sects, says that there are nine sects and schools: first, the Megaric; secondly, the Eretrian; thirdly, the Cyrenaic; fourthly, the Epicurean; fifthly, the Annicerean; sixthly, the Theodorean; seventhly, the sect of Zeno and the Stoics; eighthly, that of the Old Academy; and ninthly, the Peripatetic;—not counting either the Cynic, or the Eliac, or the Dialectic school. That also which is called the Pyhrronean is repudiated by many writers, on account of the obscurity of its principles. But others consider that in some particulars it is a distinct sect, and in others not. For it does appear to be a sect—for what we call a sect, say they, is one which follows, or appears to follow, a principle which appears to it to be the true one; on which principle we correctly call the Sceptics a sect. But if by the name sect we understand those who incline to rules which are consistent with the principles which they profess, then the Pyrrhonean cannot be called a sect, for they have no rules or principles.

These, then, are the beginnings,'these are the successive masters, these are the divisions, and schools of philosophy.

XIV. Moreover, it is not long ago, that a new Eclectic school was set up by Potamo, of Alexandria, who picked out of the doctrines of each school what pleased him most. And as he himself says, in his Elementary Instruction, he thinks that there are certain criteria of truth: first of all the faculty which judges, and this is the superior one; the other that which is the foundation of the judgment, being a most exact appearance of the objects. And the first principles of everything he calls matter, and the agent, and the quality, and the. place. For they show out of what, and by what, and how, and where anything is done. The end is that to which everything is referred; namely, a life made perfect with every virtue, not without the natural and external qualities of the body.

But we must now speak of the men themselves; and first of all about Thales.

LIFE OF THALES.

I. Thales, then, as Herodotus and Duris and Democritus say, was the son of Euxamius and Cleobule; of the family of the Thelidae, who are Phoenicians by descent, among the most noble of all the descendants of Cadmus and Agenor, as Plato testifies. And he was the first man to whom the name of Wise was given, when Damasius was Archon at Athens, in whose time also the seven wise men had that title given to them, as

Demetrius Phalereus records in his Catalogue of the Archons. He was enrolled as a citizen at Miletus when he came thither with Neleus, who had been banished from Phoenicia; but a more common statement is that he was a native Milesian, of noble extraction.

II. After having been immersed in state affairs he applied himself to speculations in natural philosophy; though, as some people state, he left no writings behind him, For the book on Naval Astronomy, which is attributed to him is said in reality to be the work of Focus the Samian. But Callimachus was aware that he was the discoverer of the Lesser Bear; for in his Iambics he speaks of him thus:

And, he, 'tis said, did first compute the stars
Which beam in Charles's wain, and guide the bark
Of the Phoenician sailor o'er the sea.

According to others he wrote two books, and no more, about the solstice and the equinox; thinking that everything else was easily to be comprehended. According to other statements, he is said to have been the first who studied astronomy, and who foretold the eclipses and motions of the sun, as Eudemus relates in his history of the discoveries made in astronomy; on which account Xenophanes and Herodotus praise him greatly; and Heraclitus and Democritus confirm this statement.

III. Some again (one of whom is Chaerilus the poet) say that he was the first person who affirmed that the souls of men were immortal; and he was the first person, too, who discovered the path of the sun from one end of the ecliptic to the other; and who, as one account tells us, defined the magnitude of the sun as being seven hundred and twenty times as great as that of the moon. He was also the first person who called the last day of the month the thirtieth. And likewise the first to converse about natural philosophy, as some say. But Aristotle and Hippias say that he attributed souls also to lifeless things, forming his conjecture from the nature of the magnet, and of amber. And Pamphile relates that he, having learnt geometry from the Egyptians, was the first person to describe a right-angled triangle in a circle, and that he sacrificed an ox in honour of his discovery. But others, among whom is Apollodorus the calculator, say that it was Pythagoras who made this discovery. It was Thales also who carried to their greatest point of advancement the discoveries which Callimachus in his iambics says were first made by Euphebus the Phrygian, such as those of the scalene angle, and of the triangle, and of other things which relate to investigations about lines. He seems also to have been a man of the greatest wisdom in political matters. For when Croesus sent to the Milesians to invite them to an alliance, he prevented them from agreeing to it, which step of his, as Cyrus got the victory, proved the salvation of the city. But Clytus relates, as Heraclides assures us, that he was attached to a solitary and recluse life. IV. Some assert that he was married, and that he had a son named Cibissus; others, on the contrary, say that he never had a wife, but that he adopted the son of his sister; and that once being asked why he did not himself become a father, he answered, that it was because he was fond of children. They say, too, that when his mother exhorted him to marry, he said, " No, by Jove, it is not yet time." And afterwards, when he was past his youth, and she was again pressing him earnestly, he said, " It is no longer time."

V. Hieronymus, of Rhodes, also tells us, in the second book of his Miscellaneous Memoranda, that when he was desirous to show that it was easy to' get rich, he, foreseeing that there would be a great crop of olives, took some large plantations of olive trees, and so made a great deal of money.

VI. He asserted water to be the principle of all things, and that the world had life, and was full of daemons: they say, too, that he was the original definer of the seasons of the year, and that it was he who divided the year into three hundred and sixty-five days. And he never had any teacher except during the time that he went to Egypt, and associated with the priests. Hieronymus also says that he measured the Pyramids: watching their shadow, and calculating when they were of the same size as that was. He lived with Thrasybulus the tyrant of Miletus, as we are informed by Minyas.

VII. Now it is known to every one what happened with respect to the tripod that was found by the fishermen and sent to the wise men by the people of the Milesians. For they say that some Ionian youths bought a cast of their net from some Milesian fishermen. And when the tripod was drawn up in the net there was a dispute about it; until the Milesians sent to Delphi: and the God gave them the following answer:—

You ask about the tripod, to whom you shall present it;
'Tis for the wisest, I reply, that fortune surely meant it.

Accordingly they gave it to Thales, and he gave it to some one, who again handed it over to another, till it came to Solon. But he said that it was the God himself who was the first in wisdom; and so he sent it to Delphi. But Callimachus gives a different account of this in his Iambics, taking the tradition which he mentions from Leander the Milesian; for he says that a certain Arcadian of the name of Bathydes, when dying, left a goblet behind him with an injunction that it should be given to the first of the wise men. And it was given to Thales, and went the whole circle till it came back to Thales, on which he sent it to Apollo Didymaeus, adding (according to Callimachus,) the following distich:—

Thales, who's twice received me as a prize,
Gives me to him who rules the race of Neleus.

And the prose inscription runs thus —

Thales the son of Examius, a Milesian, offers this to Apollo Didymaeus, having twice received it from the Greeks as the reward for virtue.

And the name of the sou of Bathydes who carried the goblet about from one to the other, was Thyrion, as Eleusis tells us in bis History of Achilles. And Alexander the Myndian agrees with him in the ninth book of his Traditions. But

Eudoxus of Cnidos, and Evanthes of Miletus, say that one of the friends of Croesus received from the king a golden goblet, for the purpose of giving it to the wisest of the Greeks; and that he gave it to Thales, and that it came round to Chilo, and that he inquired of the God at Delphi who was wiser than himself; and that the God replied, Myson, whom we shall mention hereafter. (He is the man whom Eudoxus places among the seven wise men instead of Cleobulus; but Plato inserts his name instead of Periander.) The God accordingly made this reply concerning him:—

I say that Mysou, the *Mt&&n* sage,
The citizen of Chen, is wiser far
In his deep mind than you.

The person who went to the temple to ask the question was Anacbarsis; but again Daedacus, the Platonic philosopher, and Clearchus, state that the goblet was sent by Croesus to Pittacus, and so was carried round to the different men. But Andron, in bis book called The Tripod, says that the Argives offered the tripod as a prize for excellence to the wisest of the Greeks; and that Aristodemus, a Spartan, was judged to deserve it, but that he yielded the palm to Chilo; and Alcseus mentions Aristodemus in these lines:—.

And so they say Aristodemus once
Uttered a truthful speech in noble Sparta:
'Tis money makes the man; and he who's none,
Is counted neither good nor honourable.

But some say that a vessel fully loaded was sent by Periander to Thrasybulus the tyrant of the Milesians; and that as the ship was wrecked in the sea, near the island of Cos, this tripod was afterwards found by some fishermen, Phanodicus says that it was found in the sea near Athens, and so brought into the city; and then, after an assembly had been held to decide on the disposal, it was sent to Bias—and the reason why we will mention in our account of Bias. Others say that this goblet had been made by Vulcan, and presented by the Gods to Pelops, on his marriage; and that subsequently it came into the possession of Menelaus, and was taken away by Paris c when he carried off Helen, and was thrown into the sea near Cos by her, as she said that it would become a cause of battle. And after some time, some of the citizens of Lebedos having bought a net, this tripod was brought up in it; and as they quarrelled with the fishermen about it, they went to Cos; and not being able to get the matter settled there, they laid it before the Milesians, as Miletus was their metropolis; and they sent ambassadors, who were treated with neglect, on which account they made war on the Coans; and after each side had met with many revolutions of fortune, an oracle directed that the tripod should be given to the wisest; and then both parties agreed that it belonged to Thales: and he, after it had gone the circuit of all the wise men, presented it to the Didymamn Apollo. Now, the assignation of the oracle was given to the Coans in the following words:—

The war between the brave Ionian race
And the proud Meropes will never cease,
Till the rich golden tripod which the God,
Its maker, cast beneath the briny waves,
Is from your city sent, and justly given
To that wise being who knows all present things,
And all that's past, and all that is to come.

And the reply given to the Milesians was—

You ask about the tripod: and so on, as I have related it before. And now we have said enough on this subject.

But Hermippus, in his Lives, refers to Thales what has been by some people reported of Socrates; for he recites that he used to say that he thanked fortune for three things:—first of all, that he had been born a man and not a beast; secondly, that he was a man and not a woman; and thirdly, that he was a Greek and not a barbarian.

VIII. It is said that once he was led out of his house by an old woman for the purpose of observing the stars, and he fell into a ditch and bewailed himself, on which the old woman said to him—" Do you, 0 Thales, who cannot see what is under your feet, think that you shall understand what is in heaven?" Timon also knew that he was an astronomer, and in his Silli he praises him, saying:—
Like Thales, wisest of the seven sages,
That great astronomer.

And Lobon, of Argos, says, that which was written by him extends to about two hundred verses; and that the following inscription is engraved upon his statue:—.

Miletus, fairest of Ionian cjties,
Gave birth to Thales, great astronomer,
Wisest of mortals in all kinds of knowledge.

IX. And these are quoted as some of his lines:—

It is not many words that real wisdom proves;
Breathe rather one wise thought,
Select one worthy object,
So shall you best the endless prate of silly men reprove.—

And the following are quoted as sayings of his:—" God is the most ancient of all things, for he had no birth: the world is the most beautiful of things, for it is the work of God: place is the greatest of things, for it contains all things: intellect is the swiftest of things, for it runs through everything: necessity is the strongest of things, for it rules everything: time is the wisest of things, for it finds out everything."

He said also that there was no difference between life and death. " Why, then," said some one to him, " do not you die?" "Because," said he, "it does make no difference." A man asked him which was made first, night or day, and he replied, " Night was made first by one day." Another man asked him whether a man who did wrong, could escape the notice of the Gods. " No, not even if he thinks wrong," said he. An adulterer inquired of him whether he should swear that he had not committed adultery. "Perjury," said he, "is no worse than adultery." When he was asked what was very difficult, he said, " To know one's self." And what was easy, "To advise another." What was most pleasant? "To be successful." To the question, "What is the divinity?" he replied, "That which has neither beginning nor end." When asked what hard thing he had seen, he said, "An old man a tyrant." When the question was put to him how a man might most easily endure misfortune, he said, "If he saw his enemies more unfortunate still." When asked how men might live most virtuously and most justly, he said, "If we never do ourselves what we blame in others." To the question, "Who was c 2 happy?" he made answer. "He who is healthy in his body, easy in his circumstances, and well-instructed as to his mind." He said that men ought to remember those friends who were absent as well as those who were present, and not to care about adorning their faces, but to be beautified by their studies. "Do not," said he, "get rich by evil actions, and let not any one ever be able to reproach you with speaking against those who partake of your friendship. All the assistance that you give to j'our parents, the same you have a right to expect from your children." He said that the reason of the Nile overflowing was, that its streams were beaten back by the Etesian winds blowing in a contrary direction.

X. Apollodorus, in his Chronicles, says, that Thales was born in the first year of the thirty-fifth Olympiad; and he died at the age of seventy-eight years, or according to the statement of Sosicrates, at the age of ninety, for he died in the fifty-eighth Olympiad, having lived in the time of Croesus, to whom he promised that he would enable him to pass the Halys without a bridge, by turning the course of the river.

XI. There have also been other men of the name of Thales, as Demetrius of Magnesia says, in his Treatise on People and Things of the same name; of whom five are particularly mentioned, an orator of Calatia of a very affected style of eloquence; a painter of Sicyon, a great man; the third was one who lived in very ancient times, in the age of Homer and Hesiod and Lycurgus; the fourth is a man who is mentioned by Duris in his work on Painting; the fifth is a more modern person, of no great reputation, who is mentioned by Dionysius iD his Criticisms. XII. But this wise Thales died while present as a spectator at a gymnastic contest, being worn out with heat and thirst and weakness, for he was very old, and the following inscription was placed on his tomb: —
You see this tomb is small—but recollect,
The fame of Thales reaches to the skies.

I have also myself composed this epigram on him in the first book of my epigrams or poems in various metres: —
O mighty sun, our wisest Thales sat Spectator of the games, when you did seize upon him;
But you were right to take him near yourself,
Now that his aged sight could scarcely reach to heaven.

XIII. The apophthegm, "know yourself," is his; though Antisthenes in his Successions, says that it belongs to Phemonoe, but that Chilo appropriated it as his own. XIV. Now concerning the seven, (for it is well here to speak of them all together,) the following traditions are handed down. Damon the Cyrenaean, who wrote about the philosophers, reproaches them all, but most especially the seven. Aud Anaximenes says, that they all applied themselves to poetry, But Dicamrchus says, that they were neither wise men nor philosophers, but merely shrewd men, who had studied legislation. And Archetimus, the Syracusian, wrote an account of their having a meeting at the palace of Cypselus, at which he says that he himself was present. Ephorus says that they all except Thales met at the court of Croesus. And some say that they also met at the Pandionium and at Corinth, and at Delphi. There is a good deal of disagreement between different writers with respect to their apophthegms, as the same one is attributed by them to various authors. For instance there is the epigram: —
Chilo, the Spartan sage, this sentence said:
Seek no excess— all timely things are good.

There is also a difference of opinion with respect to their number. Leander inserts in the number instead of Cleobulus and Myson, Leophantus Gorsias, a native of either Lebedos or Ephesus; and Epimenides, the Cretan; Plato, in his Protagoras, reckons Myson among them instead of Periander. And Ephorus mentions Anacharsis in the place of Myson; some also add Pythagoras to the number. Dicaearchus speaks of four, as universally agreed upon, Thales, Bias, Pittacus, and Solon; and then enumerates six more, of whom we are to select three, namely, Aristodemus, Pamphilus, Chilo the Lacedaemonian, Cleobulus, Anacharsis, and Periander. Some add Acusilaus of Argos, the son of Cabas, or Scabras. But Hermippus, in his Treatise on the Wise Men says that there were altogether seventeen, out of whom different authors selected different individuals to make up the seven. These seventeen were Solon, Thales, Pittacus, Bias, Chilo, Myson, This was the temple of the national diety of the Ionians, Neptune Heliconius, on Mount Mycale. "—Vide *Smith, Diet. Or. and Mom. Antiq.* Cleobulus, Periander, Anacharsis, Acusilaus, Epimenides, Leophantus, Pherecydes, Aristodemus, Pythagoras, Lasus the son of Charmantides, or Sisymbrinus, or as Aristoxenus calls him the son of Chabrinus, a citizen of Hermione, and Anaxagoras. But Hippobotus in his Description of the Philosophers enumerates among them Orpheus, Linus, Solon, Periander, Anacharsis, Cleobulus, Myson, Thales, Bias, Pittacus, Epicharmus, and Pythagoras.

XV. The following letters are preserved as having been written by Thales:—
THALES TO PHEF.ECYDES.
I hear that you are disposed, as no other Ionian has been, to discourse to the Greeks about divine things, and perhaps it will be wiser of you to reserve for your own friends what you write rather than to entrust it to any chance people, without any advantage. If therefore it is agreeable to you, I should be glad to become a pupil of yours as to the matters about which you write; and if you invite me I will come to you to Syros;

for Solon' the Athenian' and I must be out of our senses if we sailed to Crete to investigate the history of that country, and to Egypt for the purpose of conferring with the priests and astronomers who are to be found there, and yet are unwilling to make a voyage to you; for Solon will come too, if you will give him leave, for as you are fond of your present habitation you are not likely to come to Ionia, nor are you desirous of seeing strangers; but you rather, as I hope, devote yourself wholly to the occupation of writing. We, on the other hand, who write nothing, travel over all Greece and Asia.

THALES TO SOLON. XVI. If you should leave Athens it appears to me that you would find a home at Miletus among the colonists of Athens more suitably than anywhere else, for here there are no annoyances of any kind. And if you are indignant because we Milesians are governed by a tyrant, (for you yourself hate all despotic rulers), still at all events you will find it pleasant to live with us for your companions. Bias has also written to invite you to Priene, and if you prefer taking up your abode in the city of the Prieneans, then we ourselves will come thither and settle near you. LIFE OF SOLON.

I. Solon the son of Execestides, a native of Salamis, was the first person who introduced among the Athenians, an ordinance for the lowering of debts; for this was the name given to the release of the bodies and possessions of the debtors. For men used to borrow on the security of their own persons, and many became slaves in consequence of their inability to pay; and as seven talents were owed to him as a part of his paternal inheritance when he succeeded to it, he was the first person who made a composition with his debtors, and who exhorted the other men who had money owing to them to do likewise, and this ordinance was called *eueddiia;* and the reason why is plain. After that he enacted his other laws, which it would take a long time to enumerate; and he wrote them on wooden revolving tablets.

II. But what was his most important act of all was, when there had been a great dispute about his native land Salamis, between the Athenians and Megarians, and when the Athenians had met with many disasters in war, and had passed a decree that if any one proposed to the people to go to war for the sake of Salamis he should be punished with death, he then pretended to be mad and putting on a crown rushed into the market place, and there he recited to the Athenians by the agency of a crier, the elegies which he had composed, and which were all directed to the subject of Salamis, and by these means he excited them; and so they made war again upon the Megarians and conquered them by means of Solon. And the elegies which had the greatest influence on the Athenians were these: —

Would that I were a man of Pholegandros,t
Or small Sicinna,i rather than of Athens:
Vide Thirlwall, Hist, of Greece, ii. p. Zi.
t One of the Sporades. J An island near Crete.

For Boon this will a common proverb be,
That's an Athenian who won't fight for Salamis.

And another was: —

Let's go and fight for lovely Salamis,
And wipe off this our present infamy.

He also persuaded them to take possession of the Thracian Chersonesus, and in order that it might appear thatthe Athenians had got possession of Salamis not by force alone, but also with justice, he opened some tombs, and showed that the corpses buried in tbem were all turned towards the east, according to the Athenian fashion of sepulture; likewise the tombs themselves all looked east, and the titles of the boroughs to which the dead belonged were inscribed on them, which was a custom peculiar to the Athenians. Some also say that it was he 'who added to the catalogue of Homer, after the lines: —

With these appear the Salaminian bands,
Whom Telamon's gigantic son commands—

These other verses: —

In twelve black ships to Troy they steer their course,
And with the great Athenians join their force.

III. And ever after this time the people was willingly obedient to him, and was contented to be governed by him; but he did not choose to be their ruler, and moreover, as Sosicrates relates, he, as far as in him lay, hindered also his relative Pisistratus from being so, when he saw that he was inclined to such a step. Rushing into one of the assemblies armed with a spear and shield, he forewarned the people of the design of Pisistratus, and not only that but told them that he was prepared to assist them; and these were his words: " Ye men of Athens, I am wiser than some of you, and braver than others. Wiser than those of you who do not perceive the treachery of Pisistratus; and braver than those who are aware of it, but out of fear hold their peace." But the council, being in the interest of Pisistratus, said that he was mad, on which he spoke as follows: —

A short time will to all my madness prove,
When stern reality presents itself.
Horn. II. 2. 671. Dryden's Version.

And these elegiac verses were vfritten by him about the tyranny of Pisistratus, which he foretold,

Fierce snow and hail are from the clouds borne down,
And thunder after brilliant lightning roars;
And by its own great men a city falls,
The ignorant mob becoming slaves to kings.

IV. And when Pisistratus had obtained the supreme power, he, as he would not influence him, laid down his arms before the chief council-house, and said, " 0 my country, I have stood by you in word and deed." And then he sailed away to' Egypt, and Cyprus, and came to Croesus. And while at his court being asked by him, " Who appears to you to be happy?" He replied, " Tellus the Athenian, and Cleobis and Biton," and enumerated other commonly spoken of instances. But some people say, that once Croesus adorned himself in every possible manner, and took his seat upon his throne, and then asked Solon whether he had ever seen a more beautiful sight. But he said, " Yes, I have seen cocks and pheasants, and peacocks; for they are adorned with natural colours, and such as are ten thousand times more beautiful." Afterwards leaving Sardis he went to Cilicia, and there he founded a city which he called Soli after his own name; and he placed in it a few Athenians as colonists, who in time departed from the strict use of their native language, and were said to speak *Solecisms*; and the inhabitants of that city are called Solensians; but those of Soli in Cyprus are called Solians.

V. And when he learnt that Pisistratus continued to rule in Athens as a tyrant, he wrote these verses on the Athenians:—

If through your vices you afflicted are, Lay not the blame of your distress on God;
You made your rulers mighty, gave them guards,
So now you groan 'neath slavery's heavy rod—
Each one of you now treads in foxes' steps,
Bearing a weak, inconstant, faithless mind,
Trusting the tongue and slippery speech of man;
Though in his acts alone you truth can find.

This, then, he said to them.

VI. But Pisistratus, when he was leaving Athens, wrote him a letter in the following terms: — PISISTRATUS TO SOLON.
I am not the only one of the Greeks who has seized the sovereignty of his country, nor am I one who had no right whatever to do so, since I am of the race of Codrus; for I have only recovered what the Athenians swore that they would give to Codrus and all his family, and what they afterwards deprived them of. And in all other respects I sin neither against men nor against gods, but I allow the Athenians to live under the laws which you established amongst them, and they are now living in a better manner than they would if they were under a democracy; for I allow no one to behave with violence: and I, though I am the tyrant, derive no other advantage beyond my superiority in rank and honour, being content with the fixed honours which belonged to the former kings. And every one of the Athenians brings the tithe of his possessions, not to me, but to the proper place in order that it may be devoted to the public sacrifices of the city; and for any other public purposes, or for any emergencies of war which may arise.

But I do not blame you for laying open my plans, for I know that you did so out of regard for the city rather than out of dislike to me; and also because you did not know what sort of government I was about to establish; since, if you had been acquainted with it, you would have been content to live under it and would not have fled. Now, therefore, return home again; believing me even without my swearing to you that Solon shall never receive any harm at the hands of Pisistratus; know also that none of my enemies have suffered any evil from me; and if you will consent to be one of my friends, you shall be among the first; for I know that there is no treachery or faithlessness in you. Or if you wish to live at Athens in any other manner, you shall be allowed to do so; only do not deprive yourself of your country because of my actions.

Thus wrote Pisistratus.

VII. Solon also said, that the limit of human life was seventy years, and he appears to have been a most excellent lawgiver, for he enjoined, " that if any one did not support his parents he should be accounted infamous; and that the man who squandered his patrimony should be equally so, and the inactive man was liable to prosecution by any one who choose to impeach him. But Lysias, in his speech against Nicias, says that Draco first proposed this law, but that it was Solon who enacted it. He also prohibited all who lived in debauchery from ascending the tribunal; and he diminished the honours paid to Athletes who were victorious in the games, fixing the prize for a victor at Olympia at five hundred drachmae, and for one who conquered at the Isthmian games at one hundred; and in the same proportion did he fix the prizes for the other games, for he said, that it was absurd to give such great honours to those men as ought to be reserved for those only who died in the wars; and their sons he ordered to be educated and bred up at the public expense. And owing to this encouragement, the Athenians behave themselves nobly and valiantly in war; as for instance, Polyzelus, and Cynaegirus, and Callimachus, and all the soldiers who fought at Marathon, and Harmodius, and Aristogiton, and Miltiades, and numberless other heroes.

But as for the Athletes, their training is very expensive, and their victories injurious, and they are crowned rather as conquerors of their country than of their antagonists, and when they become old, as Euripides says: —

They're like old cloaks worn to the very woof.

IX. So Solon, appreciating these facts, treated them with moderation. This also was an admirable regulation of his, that a guardian of orphans should not live with their mother, and that no one should be appointed a guardian, to whom tho orphans' property would come if they died. Another excellent law was, that a seal engraver might not keep an impression of any ring which had been sold by him, and that if a person struck out the eye of a man who had but one, he should lose both his own, and that no one should claim what he had not deposited, otherwise death should be his punishment. If an archon was detected being drunk, that too was a capital crime And he compiled the poems of Homer, so that they might be recited by different bards, taking the cue from one another, so that where, one had left off the next one might take him up, so that it was Solon rather than Pisistratus who brought Homer to light, as Dieuchidas says, in the fifth book of his History of Megara, and the most celebrated of his verses . drachma was something less than ten pence.

Full fifty more from Athena stem the main. And the rest of that passage— " And Solon was the first person who called the thirtieth day of the month Evjj *xal via."* He was the first person also who assembled the nine archons together to deliver their opinions, as Apollodorus tells us in the second book of his Treatise on Lawgivers. And once, when there was a sedition in the city, he took part neither with the citizens, nor with the inhabitants of the plain, nor with the men of the sea-coast.

X. He used to say, too, that speech was the image of actions, and that the king was the mightiest man as to his power; but that laws were like cobwebs—for that if any trifling or powerless thing fell into them, they held it fast; but if a thing of any size fell into them, it broke the meshes and escaped. He used also to say that discourse ought to be sealed by silence, and silence by opportunity.. It was also a saying of his, that those who had influence with tyrants, were like the pebbles which are used in making calculations; for that every one of those pebbles were sometimes worth more, and sometimes less, and so that the tyrants sometimes made each of these men of consequence, and sometimes neglected them. Being asked why he had made no law concerning parricides, he made answer, that he did not expect that any such person would exist. When he was asked how men could be most effectually deterred from committing injustice, he said," If those who are not injured feel as much indignation as those who are." Another apophthegm of his was, that satiety was generated by wealth, and insolence by satiety.

XI. He it was who taught the Athenians to regulate their days by the course of the moon; and he also forbade Thespis to perform and represent his tragedies, on the ground of falsehood being unprofitable; and when Pisistratus wounded himself, he said it all came of Thespis's tragedies. ""*evij xal via* the last day of the month: elsewhere *rptaviag*. So called for this reason. The old Greek year was lunar; now the moon's monthly orbit is twenty-nine and a half days. So that if the first month began with the sun and moon together at sunrise, at the month's end it would be sunset; and the second month would begin at sunset. To prevent this irregularity, Solon made the latter half day belong to the first month; so that this thirtieth day consisted of two halves, one belonging to the old, the other to the new moon. And when the lunar month fell into disuse, the last day of the calendar month was still called "Evq *xal via."—Z, is S. Greek Lexicon,* in v. tvoc. XII. He gave the following advice, as is recorded by Apollodorus in his Treatise on the Sects of Philosophers:—"Consider your honour, as a gentleman, of more weight than an oath. '—Never speak falsely.—Pay attention to matters of importance.—Be not hasty in making friends; and do not cast off those whom you have made.—Rule, after you have first learnt to submit to rule.—Advise not what is most agreeable, but what is best.—Make reason your guide.—Do not associate with the wicked.—Honour the gods; respect your parents." XIII. They say also that when Mimnermus had written:—
Happy's the man who 'scapes disease and care,
And dies contented in Ms sixtieth year:
Solon rebuked him, and said:—
Be guided now by me. erase this verse,
Kor envy me if I'm more wise than you.
If you write thus, your wish would not be worse,
May I be eighty ere death lays me low.
The following are some lines out of his poems:—
Watch well each separate citizen,
Lest having in his heart of hearts
A secret spear, one still may come
Saluting you with cheerful face,
And utter with a double tongue
The feigned good wishes of his wary mind.
As for his having made laws, that is notorious; he also composed speeches to the people, and a book of suggestions to himself, and some elegiac poems, and five thousand verses about Salamis and the constitution of the Athenians; and some iambics and'epodes.
XV. And on his statue is the following inscription—
Salamis that checked the Persian insolence,
Brought forth this holy lawgiver, wise Solon.

He flourished about the forty-sixth Olympiad, in the third year of which he was archon at Athens, as Sosicrates records; and it was in this year that he enacted his laws; and he died in Cyprus, after he had lived eighty years, having given charge to his relations to carry his bones to Salamis, and there to burn them to ashes, and to scatter the ashes on the ground. In reference to which Cratinus in his Chiron represents him as speaking thus:—

And as men say, I still this isle inhabit,
Sown o'er the whole of Ajax' famous city.

There is also an epigram in the before mentioned collection of poems, in various metres, in which I have made a collection of notices of all the illustrious men that have ever died, in every kind of metre and rhythm, in epigrams and odes. And it runs thus:—

The Cyprian flame devour'd great Solon's corpse, Far in a foreign land; but Salamis
Retains his bones, whose dust is turned to corn.
The tablets of his laws do bear aloft
His mind to heaven. Such a burden light
Are these immortal rules to th' happy wood.

XVI. He also, as some say, was the author of the apophthegm—" Seek excess in nothing." And Dioscorides, in his Commentaries, says, that, when he was lamenting his son, who was dead (with whose name I am not acquainted), and when some one said to him, " You do no good by weeping," he replied, " But that is the very reason why I weep, because I do no good." XVII. The following letters also are attributed to him:— SOLON TO PERIANDER.

You send me word that many people are plotting against you; but if you were to think of putting everyone of them out of the way, you would do no good; but some one whom you do not suspect would still plot against you, partly because he would fear for himself, and partly out of dislike to you for fearing all sorts of things; and he would think, too, that he would make the city grateful to him, even if you were not suspected.

It is better, therefore, to abstain from the tyranny, in order to escape from blame. But if you absolutely must be a tyrant, then you had better provide for having a foreign force in the city superior to that of the citizens; and then no one need be formidable to you, nor need you put any one out of the way.

SOLON TO EPIMENIDES. XVIII. My laws were not destined to be long of service to the Athenians, nor have you done any great good by purifying the city. For neither can the Deity nor lawgivers do much good to cities by themselves; but these people rather have this power, who, from time to time, can lead the people to any opinions they choose; so also the Deity and the laws, when the citizens are well governed, are useful; but when they are ill governed, they are no good. Nor are my laws nor all the enactments that I made, any better; but those who were in power transgressed them, and did great injury to the commonwealth, inasmuch as they did not hinder Pisistratus from ureurping the tyranny. Nor did they believe me when I gave them warning beforehand. But he obtained more credit than I did, who flattered the Athenians while I told him the truth: but I, placing my arms before the principal councilhouse, being wiser than they, told those who had no suspicion of it, that Pisistratus was desirous to make himself a tyrant; and I showed myself more valiant than those who hesitated to defend the state against him. But they condemned the madness of Solon. But at last I spoke loudly—" O, my country, I, Solon, here am ready to defend you by word and deed; but to these men I seem to be mad. So I will depart from you, being the only antagonist of Pisistratus; and let these men be his guards if they please." For you know the man, my friend, and how cleverly he seized upon the tyranny. He first began by being a demagogue; then, having inflicted wounds on himself, he came to the Heliaea, crying out, and saying, " That he had been treated in this way by his enemies.' And he entreated the people to assign him as guards four hundred young men; and they, disregarding my advice, gave them to him. And they were all armed with bludgeons. And after that he put down the democracy. They in vain hoped to deliver the poor from their state of slavery, and so now they are all of them slaves to Pisistratus.

" SOLON TO PISISTRATUS.

I am well assured that I should suffer no evil at your hands. For before your assumption of the tyranny I was a friend of yours, and now my case is not different from that of any other Athenian who is not pleased with tyranny. And whether it is better for them to be governed by one individual, or to live under a democracy, that each person may decide according to his own sentiments. And I admit that of all tyrants you are the best. But I do not judge it to be good for me to return to Athens, lest any one should blame me, for, after having established equality of civil rights among the Athenians, and after having refused to be a tyrant myself when it was in my power, returning now and acquiescing in what you are doing.

SOLON TO CB03SUS. XX. I thank you for your goodwill towards me. And, by Minerva, if I did not think it precious above everything to live in a democracy, I would willingly prefer living in your palace with you to living at Athens, since Pisistratus has made himself tyrant by force. But life is more pleasant to me where justice and equality prevail universally. However, I will come and see you, being anxious to enjoy your hospi. tality for a season. LIFE OF CHILO.

I, Chilo was a Lacedaemonian, the son of Damagetus. He composed verses in elegiac metre to the number of two hundred: and it was a saying of his that a foresight of future events, such as could be arrived at by consideration was the virtue of a man. He also said once to his brother, who was indignant at not being an ephor, while he himself was one, " The reason is because I know how to bear injustice; but you do not." And he was made ephor in the fifty-fifth Olympiad; but Pamphila says that it was in the fifty-sixth. And he was made first ephor in the year of the archonship of Euthydemus, as we are told by Sosicrates. Chilo was also the first person who introduced the custom of joining the ephors to the kings as their counsellors: though Satyrus attributes this institution to Lycurgus. He, as Herodotus says in his first book, when Hippocrates was sacrificing at Olympia, and the cauldrons began to boil of their own accord, advised him either to marry, or, if he were married already, to discard his wife, and disown his children.

II. They tell a story, also, of bis having asked *Æsop* what Jupiter was doing, and that lisop replied, " He is lowering what is high, and exalting what is low." Being asked in what educated men differed from those who were illiterate, he said, " In good hopes." Having had the question put to him, What was difficult, he said, " To be silent about secrets; to make good use of one's leisure, and to be able to submit to injustice." And besides these three things he added further, " To rule one's tongue, especially at a banquet, and not to speak ill of one's neighbours; for if one does so one is sure to hear what one will not like. " He advised, moreover, " To threaten no one; for that is a womanly trick. To be more prompt to go to one's friends in adversity than in prosperity. To make but a moderate display at one's marriage. Not to speak evil of the dead. To honour old age.—To keep a watch upon one's self.—To prefer punishment to disgraceful gain; for the one is painful but once, but the other for one's whole life.—Not to laugh at a person in misfortune.—If one is strong to be also merciful, so that one's neighbours may respect one rather than fear one.—To learn how to regulate one's own house well.—Not to let one's tongue outrun one's sense. —To restrain anger. —Not to dislike divination.—Not to desire what is impossible.—Not to make too much haste on one's road––When speaking not to gesticulate with the hand; for that is like a madman.—To obey the laws.—To love quiet."

And of all his songs this one was the most approved:—

Gold is beat tested by a whetstone hard,
Which gives a certain proof of purity;
And gold itself acts as the test of men,

By which we know the temper of their mir.ds.

III. They say, too, that when he was old he said, that he was not conscious of having ever done an unjust action in his life; but. that he doubted about one thing. For that once when judging in a friend's cause he had voted himself in accordance with the law, but had persuaded a friend to vote for his acquittal, in order that so he might maintain the law, and yet save his friend.

IV. But he was most especially celebrated among the Greeks for having delivered an early opinion about Cythera Mi island belonging to Laconia. For having become ac
D quainted with its nature, he said, " I wish it had never existed, or that, as it does exist, it were sunk at the bottom of the sea." And his foresight was proved afterwards. For when Demaratus was banished by the Lacedaemonians, he advised Xerxes to keep his ships at that island: and Greece would have been subdued, if Xerxes had taken the advice. And afterwards Nicias, having reduced the island at the time of the Peloponnesian war, placed in it a garrison of Athenians, and did a great deal of harm to the Lacedaemonians:

V. He was very brief in his speech. On which account Aristagoras, the Milesian, calls such conciseness, the Chilonean fashion; and says that it was adopted by Branchus, who built the temple among the Branchidae. Chilo was an old man, about the fifty-second Olympiad, when iEsop, the fable writer, flourished. And he died, as Hermippus says, at Pisa, after embracing his son, who had gained the victory in boxing at the Olympic games. The cause of his death was excess of joy, and weakness caused by extreme old age. All the spectators who were present at the games attended his funeral, paying him the highest honours. And we have written the following epigram on him:—

I thank you, brightest Pollux, that the son Of ChUo wears the wreath of victory;
Nor need we grieve if at the glorious sight
His father died. May such my last end be!

And the following inscription is engraved on his statue:—

The warlike Sparta called this Chilo son,
The wisest man of all the seven sages.

One of his sayings was, "Suretyship, and then destruction." The following letter of his is also extant:— CHILO TO PEEIANDEK.

You desire me to abandon the expedition against the emigrants, as you yourself will go forth. But I think that a sole governor is in a slippery position at home; and I consider that tyrant a fortunate man who dies a natural death in his own house.

LIFE OF PITTACUS.

I. Pittacus was a native of Mitylene, and son of Hyrradius. But Duris says, that his father was a Thracian. He, in union with the brothers of Alcaeus, put down Melanchrus the tyrant of Lesbos. And in the battle which took place between the Athenians and Mitylenaeans on the subject of the district of Achilis, he was the Mitylenaean general; the Athenian commander being Phrynon, a Pancratiast, who had gained the victory at Olympia. Pittacus agreed to meet him in single combat, and having a net under his shield, he entangle. Phrynon without his being aware of it beforehand, and so, having killed him, he preserved the district in dispute to his countrymen. But Apollodorus, in his Chronicles, says, that subsequently, the Athenians had a trial with the Mitylenaeans about the district, and that the cause was submitted to Periander, who decided it in favour of the Athenians.

II. In consequence of this victory the Mitylenaeans held Pittacus in the greatest honour, and committed the supreme power into his hands. And he held it for ten years, and then, when he had brought the city and constitution into good ordej, he resigned the government. And he lived ten years after that, and the Mitylenaeans assigned him an estate, which he consecrated to the God, and to this day it is called the Pittacian land. But Sosicrates says that he cut off a small portion of it, saying that half was more than the whole; and when Croesus offered him some money he would not accept it, as he said that he had already twice as much as he wanted; for that he had succeeded to the inheritance of his brother, who had died without children. III. But Pamphila says, in the second book of his Commentaries, that he had a son named Tyrrhseus, who was killed while sitting in a barber's shop, at Cyma, by a brazier, who threw an axe at him; and that the Cymaeans sent the murderer to Pittacus, who when he had learnt what had been done, dismissed the man, saying, " Pardon is better than repentance." But Heraclitus says that the true story is, that he had got Alcaeus into his power, and that he released him, saying, " Pardon is better than punishment." He was also a lawgiver; and he made a law that if a man committed a crime while drunk, he should have double punishment; in the hope of deterring men from getting drunk, as wine was very plentiful in the island. IV. It was a saying of his that it was a hard thing to be good, and this apophthegm is quoted by Simonides, who says, " It was a saying of Pittacus, that it is a hard thing to be really a good man." Plato also mentions it in his Protagoras. Another of his sayings was, " Even the Gods cannot strive against necessity." Another was, " Power shows the man." Being once asked what was best, he replied, " To do what one is doing at the moment well." When Croesus put the question to him, " What is the greatest power?" " The power," he replied, " of the variegated wood," meaning the wooden tablets of the laws. He used to say too, that there were some victories without bloodshed. He said once to a man of Phocaea, who was saying that we ought to seek out a virtuous man, " But if you seek ever so much you will not find one." Some people once asked him what thing was very grateful? and he replied, "Time."—What was uncertain? "The future."—What was trusty? " The land."—What was treacherous? " The sea " Another saying of his was, that it was the part of wise men, before difficult circumstances arose, to provide for their not arising; but that it was the part of brave men to make the best of existing circumstances. He used to say too, " Do not say before hand what you are going to do; for if you fail, you will be laughed at." " Do not reproach a man with his misfortunes, fearing lest Nemesis may overtake you." " If you have received a deposit, restore it." " Forbear to speak evil not only of your friends, but also of your enemies. " " Practise piety, with temperance." " Cultivate truth, good faith, experience, cleverness, sociability, and industry."

V. He wrote also some songs, of which the following is the most celebrated one:—

The wise will only face the wicked man',

With bow in hand well bent,

And quiver full of arrows—

For such a tongue as his says nothing true,

Prompted by a wily heart

To utter double speeches.

He also composed six hundred verses in elegiac metre; and . he wrote a treatise in prose, on Laws, addressed to Lis countrymen.

VI. He flourished about the forty-second Olympiad; and he died when Aristomenes was Archon, in the third year of the fifty-second Olympiad; having lived more than seventy years, being a very old man. And on his tomb is this inscription:—

Lesbos who bore him here, with tears doth bury

Hyrradius' worthy son, wise Pittaous.

Another saying of his was, " Watch your opportunity." VII. There was also another Pittacus, a lawgiver, as Favorinus tells us in the first book of his Commentaries; and Demetrius says so too, in his Essay on Men and Things of the same name. And that other Pittacus was called Pittacus the less.

VIII. But it is said that the wise Pittacus once, when a young man consulted him on the subject of marriage, made him the following answer, which is thus given by Callimachus in his Epigrams.

Hyrradius' prudent son, old Pittacus

The pride of Mitylene, once was asked

By an Atarnean stranger; " Tell me, sage,

I have two marriages proposed to me;

One maid my equal is in birth and riches;

The other's far above me;—which is best?

Advise me now which shall I take to wife P

Thus spoke the stranger; but the aged prince,

Raising his old man's staff before his face,

Said, " These will tell you all you want to know;"

And pointed to some boys, who with quick lashes

Were driving whipping tops along the street.

" Follow their steps," said he; so he went near them

And heard them say, " Let each now mind his own."—

So when the stranger heard the boys speak thus,

He pondered on their words, and laid aside

Ambitious thoughts of an unequal marriage.

As then he took to shame the poorer bride,

So too do you, 0 reader, mind thy own.

And it seems that he may have here spoken from experience, for his own wife was of more noble birth than himself, since she was the sister of Draco, the son of Penthilus; and she gave herself great airs, and tyrannized over him.

IX. Alcaeas calls Pittacus *eagdirovg* and *eagccirog,* because he was splay-footed, and used to drag his feet in walking; he also called him *eigo!r6drig,* because he had scars on his feet which were called *iiddeg.* And *yavgri%,* implying that he gave himself airs without reason. And *pvextnv* and *yaergwv,* because he was fat. He also called him *fypoBogiridag,* because he had weak eyes, and *ayaevgrog,* because he was lazy and dirty. He used to grind corn for the sake of exercise, as Clearchus, the philosopher, relates.

X. There is a letter of his extant, which runs thus:— PITTACUS TO CR03SUS.

You invite me to come to Lydia in order that I may see your riches; but I, even without seeing them, do not doubt that the son of Alyattes is the richest of monarchs. But I should get no good by going to Sardis; for I do not want gold myself, but what I have is sufficient for myself and my companions. Still, I will come, in order to become acquainted with you as a hospitable man.

LIFE OF BIAS.

I. Bias was a citizen of Priene, and the son of Teutamus, and by Satyrus he is put at the head of the seven wise men. Some writers affirm that he was one of the richest men of the city; but others say that he was only a settler. And Phanodicus says, that he ransomed some Messenian maidens who had been taken prisoners, and educated them as his own daughters, and gave them dowries, and then sent them back to Messina to their fathers. And when, as has been mentioned before, the tripod was found near Athens by some fishermen, the brazen tripod I mean, which bore the inscription—"For the Wise;" then Satyrus says that the damsels (but others, such as Phanodicus, say that it was their father,) came into the assembly, and said that Bias was the wise man—recounting what he had done to them: and so the tripod was sent to him. But Bias, when he saw it, said that it was Apollo who was " the Wise," and would not receive the tripod.

II. But others say that he consecrated it at Thehes to Hercules, because he himself was a descendant of the Thebans, who had sent a colony to Priene, as Phanodicus relates. It is said also that when Alyattes was besieging Priene, Bias fattened up two mules, and drove them into his camp; and that the king, seeing the condition that the mules were in, was astonished at their being able to spare food to keep the hrute beasts so well, and so he desired to make peace with them, and sent an ambassador to them. On this Bias, having made some heaps of sand, and put corn on the top, showed them to the convoy; and Alyattes, hearing from him what he had seen, made peace with the people of Priene; and then, when he sent to Bias, desiring him to come quickly to him, " Tell Alyattes, from me," he replied, "

to eat onions;"—which is the same as if he had said, " go and weep." III. It is said that he was very energetic and eloquent when pleading causes; but that he always reserved his talents for the right side. In reference to which Demodicus of Alerius uttered the following enigmatical saying—" If you are a judge, give a Prienian decision." And Hipponax says, " More excellent in his decisions than Bias of Priene." Now he died in this manner:— IV. Having pleaded a cause for some one when he was exceedingly old, after he had finished speaking, he leaned back with his head on the bosom of his daughter's son; and after the advocate on the opposite side had spoken, and the judges had given their decision in favour of Bias's client, when the court broke up he was found dead on his grandson's bosom. And the city buried him in the greatest magnificence, and put over him this inscription—
Beneath this stone lies Bias, who was born
In the illustrious Prienian land,
The glory of the whole Ionian race.

And we ourselves have also written an epigram on him—
Here Bias lies, whom, when the hoary snow
Had crowned his aged, temples, Mercury
Unpitying led to Pluto's darken'd realms.
He pleaded his friend's cause, and then reclin'd
In his child's arms, repos'd in lasting sleep.

Y. He also wrote about two thousand verses on Ionia, to show in what matter a man might best arrive at happiness; and of all his poetical sayings these have the greatest reputation:—
Seek to please all the citizens, even though
Your house may be in an ungracious city.
For such a course will favour win from all:
But haughty manners oft produce destruction.
And this one too:—
Great strength of body is the gift of nature;
But to be able to advise whate'er
Is most expedient for one's country's good,
Is the peculiar work of sense and wisdom.
Another is:—
Great riches come to many men by chance.

He used also to say that that man was unfortunate who could not support misfortune; and that it is a disease of the mind to desire what was impossible, and to have no regard for the misfortunes of others. Being asked what was difficult, he said—" To bear a change of fortune for the worse with magnanimity." Once he was on a voyage with some impious men, and the vessel was overtaken by a storm; so they began to invoke the assistance of the Gods; on which he said, " Hold your tongues, lest they should find out that you are in this ship." When he was asked by an impious man what piety was, he made no reply; and when his questioner demanded the reason of his silence, he said, " I am silent because you are putting questions about things with which you have no concern." Being asked what was pleasant to men, he replied, "Hope." It was a saying of his that it was more agreeable to decide between enemies than between friends; for that of friends, one was sure to become an enemy to him; but that of enemies, one was sure to become a friend. When the question was put to him, what a man derived pleasure while he was doing, he said, " While acquiring gain." He used to say, too, that men ought to calculate life both as if they were fated to live a long and a short time: and that they ought to love one another as if at a future time they would come to hate one another; for that most men were wicked. He used also to give the following pieces of advice:—
" Choose the course which you adopt with deliberation; but when you have adopted it, then persevere in it with firmness.—Do not speak fast, for that shows folly.— Love prudence.—Speak of the Gods as they are.— Do not praise an undeserving man because of his riches.—Accept of things, having procured them by persuasion, not by force.—Whatever good fortune befalls you, attribute it to the gods. —Cherish wisdom as a means of travelling from youth to old age, for it is more lasting than any other possession." VI. Hipponax also mentions Bias, as has been said before; and Heraclitus too, a man who was not easily pleased, has praised him; saying, in Priene there lived Bias the son of Teutamus, whose reputation is higher than that of the others; and the Prienians consecrated a temple to him which is called the Teutamium. A saying of his was, " Most men are wicked." LIFE OF CLEOBULUS.

I. Cleobdlus was a native of Lindus, and the son of Evagoras; but according to Duris he was a Carian; others again trace his family back to Hercules. He is reported to have been eminent for personal strength and beauty, and to have studied philosophy in Egypt; he had a daughter named Cleobulina, who used to compose enigmas in hexameter verse, and she is mentioned by Cratinus in his play of the same name, except that the title is written in the plural number. They say also that he restored the temple of Minerva which had been built by Danaus.

II. Cleobulus composed songs and obscure sayings in verse to the number of three thousand lines, and some say that it was he who composed the epigram on Midas.
I am a brazen maiden lying here Upon the tomb of Midas. And as long As water flows, as trees are green with leaves, As the sun shines and eke the silver moon, As long as rivers flow, and billows roar, So long will I upon this much wept tomb, Tell passers by, " Midas lies buried here." And as an evidence of this epigram being by him they quote a song of Simonides, which runs thus:—
What men possessed of sense
Would ever praise the Lindian Cleobulus?
Who could compare a statue made by man
To overflowing streams,
To blushing flowers of spring,
To the sun's rays, to beams o' the golden morn,

And to the ceaseless waves of mighty Ocean?
All things are trifling when compared to God.
While men beneath their hands can crush a stone;
So that such sentiments can only come from fools.

And the epigram cannot possibly be by Homer, for he lived many years, as it is said, before Midas.

III. There is also the following enigma quoted in the Commentaries of Pamphila, as the work of Cleobulus:—

There was one father and he had twelve daughters,
Each of his daughters had twice thirty children.
But most unlike in figure and complexion;
For some were white, and others black to view,
And though immortal they all taste of death.

And the solution is, " the year." IV. Of his apophthegms, the following are the most celelebrated. Ignorance and talkativeness bear the chief sway among men. Opportunity will be the most powerful. Cherish not a thought. Do not be fickle, or ungrateful. He used to say too, that men ought to give their daughters in marriage while they were girls in age, but women in sense; as indicating by this that girls ought to be well educated. Another of his sayings was, that one ought to serve a friend that he may become a greater friend; and an enemy, to make him a friend. And that one ought to guard against giving one's friends occasion to blame one, and one's enemies opportunity of plotting against one. Also, when a man goes out of his house, he should consider what he is going to do: and when he comes home again he should consider what he has done. He used also to advise men to keep their bodies in health by exercise.—To be fond of hearing rather than of talking.—To be fond of learning rather than unwilling to learn.—To speak well of people.—To seek virtue and eschew vice.—To avoid injustice.—To give the best advice in one's power to one's country.—To be superior to pleasure.—To do nothing by force.—To instruct one's children, —To be ready for reconciliation after quarrels.—Not to caress one's wife, nor to quarrel with her when strangers are present, for that to do the one is a sign of folly, and to do the latter is downright madness.—Not to chastise a servant while elated with drink, forso doing one will appear to be drunk one's self.— To marry from among one's equals, for if one takes a wife of a higher rank than one's self, one will have one's connexions for one's masters.—Not to laugh at those who are being reproved, for so one will be detested by them.—Be not haughty when prosperous.—Be not desponding when in difficulties.—Learn to bear the changes of fortune with magnanimity.

V. And he died at a great age, having lived seventy years, and this inscription was put over him:—

His country, Lindus, this fair sea-girt city
Bewails wise Cleobulus here entombed.

VI. One of his sayings was, " Moderation is the best thing." He also wrote a letter to Solon in these terms:— CLEOBULUS TO SOLON.

You have many friends, and a home everywhere, but yet I think that Lindus will be the most agreeable habitation for Solon, since it enjoys a democratic government, and it is a maritime island, and whoever dwells in it has nothing to fear from Pisistratus, and you will have friends flock to you from all quarters.

LIFE OF PERIANDER.

I. Periander was a Corinthian, the son of Cypselus, of the family of the Heraclidae. He married Lyside (whom he himself called Melissa), the daughter of Procles the tyrant of Epidaurus, and of Eristhenea the daughter of Aristocrates, and sister of Aristodemus, who governed nearly all Arcadia, as Heraclides Ponticus says in his Treatise on Dominion and had by her two sons Cypselus and Lycophron, the younger of whom was a clever boy, but the elder was deficient in intellect. At a subsequent period he in a rage either kicked or threw his wife down stairs when she was pregnant, and so killed her, being wrought upon by the false accusations of his concubines, whom he afterwards burnt alive. And the child, whose name was Lycophron, he sent away to Corcyra because he grieved for his mother.

II. But afterwards, when he was now extremely old, he sent for him back again, in order that he might succeed to the tyranny. But the Corcyreans, anticipating his intention, put him to death, at which he was greatly enraged, and sent their children to Corcyra to be made eunuchs of; and when the ship came near to Samos, the youths, having made supplications to Juno, were saved by the Samians. And he fell into despondency and died, being eighty years old. Sosicrates says that he died forty-one years before Croesus, in the last year of the fortyeighth Olympiad. Herodotus, in the first book of his History, says that he was connected by ties of hospitality with Thrasybulus the tyrant of Miletus. And Aristippus, in the first book of his Treatise on Ancient Luxury, tells the following story of him; that his mother Cratea fell in love with him, and introduced herself secretly into his bed; and he was delighted; but when the truth was discovered he became very oppressive to all his subjects, because he was grieved at the discovery. Ephorus relates that he made a vow that, if he gained the victory at Olympia in the chariot race, he would dedicate a golden statue to the God. Accordingly he gained the victory; but being in want of gold, and seeing the women at some national festival beautifully adorned, he took away their golden ornaments, and then sent the offering which he had vowed. III. But some writers say that he was anxious that his tomb should not be known, and that with that object he adopted the following contrivance. He ordered two young men to go out by night, indicating a particular road by which they were to go, and to kill the first man they met, and bury him; after them he sent out four other men who were to kill and bury them. Again he sent out a still greater number against these four, with similar instructions. And in this manner he put himself in the way of the first pair, and was slain, and the Corinthians erected a cenotaph over

him with the following inscription:—
The sea-beat land of Corinth in her bosom,
Doth here embrace her ruler Periander,
Greatest of all men for his wealth and wisdom.

We ourselves have also written an epigram upon him:—
Grieve not when disappointed of a wish,
But be content with what the Gods may give you—
For the great Periander died unhappy,
At failing in an object he desired.

IV. It was a saying of his that we ought not to do anything for the sake of money; for that we ought only to acquire such gains as are allowable. He composed apophthegms in verse to the number of two thousand lines; and said that those who wished to wield absolute power in safety, should be guarded by the good will of their countrymen, and not by arms. And once, being asked why he assumed tyrannical power, he replied, " Because, to abdicate it voluntarily, and to have it taken from one, are both dangerous." The following sayings also belong to him:—Tranquillity is a good thing.—Rashness is dangerous.—Gain is disgraceful.—Democracy is better than tyranny. —Pleasures are transitory, but honour is immortal.—Be moderate when prosperous, but prudent when unfortunate.— Be the same to your friends when they are prosperous, and when they are unfortunate.—Whatever you agree to do, observe —Do not divulge secrets.—Punish not only those who do wrong, but those who intend to do so.

V. This prince was the first who had body-guards, and who changed a legitimate power into a tyranny; and he would not allow any one who chose to live in his city, as Euphorus and Aristotle tell us.

VI. And he flourished about the thirty-eighth Olympiad, and enjoyed absolute power for forty years. But Sotion, and Heraclides, and Pamphila, in the fifth book of her Commentaries, says that there were two Perianders; the one a tyrant, and the other a wise man, and a native of Ambracia. And Neanthes of Cyzicus makes the same assertion, adding, that the two men were cousins to one another. And Aristotle says, that it was the Corinthian Periander who was the wise one; but Plato contradicts him. The saying—" Practice does everything," is his. He it was, also, who proposed to cut through the Isthmus. VII. The following letter of his is quoted:—
PERIANDER TO THE WISE MEN.
I give great thanks to Apollo of Delphi that my letters are able to determine you all to meet together at Corinth; and I will receive you all, as you may be well assured, in a manner that becomes free citizens. I hear also that last year you met at Sardis, at the court of the King of Lydia. So now do not hesitate to come to me, who am the tyrant of Corinth; for the Corinthians will all be delighted to see you come to the house of Periander.
VIII. There is this letter too:— PERIANDER TO PROCLES.
The injury of my wife was unintended by me; and you have done wrong in alienating from me the mind of my child. I desire you, therefore, either to restore me to my place in his affections, or I will revenge myself on you; for I have myself made atonement for the death of your daughter, by burning in her tomb the clothes of all the Corinthian women.
IX. Thiasybulus also wrote him a letter in the following terms:—
I have given no answer to your messenger; but having taken him into a field, I struck with my walking-stick all the highest ears of corn, and cut off their tops, while he was walking with me. And he will report to you, if you ask him, everything 'which he heard or saw while with me; and do you act accordingly if you wish to preserve your power safely, taking off the most eminent of the citizens, whether he seems an enemy to you or not, as even his companions are deservedly objects of suspicion to a man possessed of supreme power.
LIFE OF ANACHARSIS, THE SCYTHIAN.
I. Anacharsis the Scythian was the son of Gnurus, and the brother of Caduides the king of the Scythians; but his mother was a Grecian woman; owing to which circumstance he understood both languages.

II. He wrote about the laws existing among the Scythians, and also about those in force among the Greeks, urging men Herodotus mentions the case of Periander's children, iii. 50, and the death of his wife, and his burning the clothes of all the Corinthian women, v. 92. to adopt a temperate course of life; and he wrote also about war, his works being in verse, and amounting to eight hundred lines. He gave occasion for a proverb, because he used great freedom of speech, so that people called such freedom the Scythian conversation. III. But Sosicrates says that he came to Athens in the forty-seventh Olympiad, in the archonship of Eucrates. And Hermippus asserts that he came to Solon's house, and ordered one of the servants to go and tell his master that Anacharsis was come to visit him, and was desirous to see him, and, if possible, to enter into relations of hospitality with him. But when the Bervant had given the message, he was ordered by Solon to reply to him that, " Men generally limited such alliances to their own countrymen. " In reply to this Anacharsis entered the house, and told the servant that now he was in Solon's country, and that it was quite consistent for them to become connected with one another in this way. On this, Solon admired the readiness of the man, and admitted him, and made him one of his greatest friends. IV. But after some time, when he had returned to Scythia, and shown a purpose to abrogate the existing institutions of his country, being exceedingly earnest, in his fondness for Grecian customs, he was shot by his brother while he was out hunting, and so he died, saying, " That he was saved on account of the sense and eloquence which he had brought from Greece, but slain in consequence of envy in his own family." Some, however, relate that he was slain while performing some Grecian sacrificatory rites. And we have written this epigram on him:—
When Anacharsis to his land returned,
His mind was turn'd, so that he wished to make
His countrymen all live in Grecian fash-

ion—
So, ere his words had well escaped his lips,
A winged arrow bore him to the Gods.

V. He said that a vine bore three bunches of grapes. The first, the bunch of pleasure; the second, that of drunkenness; the third, that of disgust. He also said that he marvelled that among the Greeks, those who were skilful in a thing contend together; but those who have no such skill act as judges of the contest. Being once asked how a person might be made not fond of drinking, he said, "If he always keeps in view the indecorous actions of drunken men." He used also to say, that he marvelled how the Greeks, who make laws against those who behave with insolence, honour Athletae because of their beating one another. When he had been informed that the side3 of a ship were four fingers thick, he said, " That those who sailed in one were removed by just that distance from death. He used to say that oil was a provocative of madness, ' because Athletae, when anointed in the oil, attacked one another with mad fury. "

" How is it," he used to say, " that those who forbid men to speak falsely, tell lies openly in their vintners' shops?" It was a saying of his, that he " marvelled why the Greeks, at the beginning of a banquet, drink out of small cups, but when they have drunk a good deal, then they turn to large goblets." And this inscription is on his statues—" Restrain your tongues, your appetites, and your passions." He was once asked if the flute was known among the Scythians; and he said, " No, nor the vine either." At another time, the question was put to him, which was the safest kind of vessel? and he said, " That which is brought into dock." Ho said, too, that the strangest things that he had seen among the Greeks was, that " They left the smoke in the mountains, and carried the wood down to their cities." Once, when he was asked, which were the more numerous, the living or the dead? he said, " Under which head do you class those who are at sea." Being reproached by an Athenian for being a Scythian, he said, " Well, my country is a disgrace to me, but you are a disgrace to your country." When he was asked what there was among men which was both good and bad, he replied, " The tongue." He used to say " That it was better to have one friend of great value, than many friends who were good for nothing." Another saying of his was, that " The forum was an established place for men to cheat one another, and behave covetously." Being once insulted by a young man at a drinking party, he said, " O, young man, if now that you are young you cannot bear wine, when you are old you will have to bear water. " VI. Of things which are of use in life, he is said to have been the inventor of the anchor, and of the potter's wheel.

Some propose to read *Kapirbv, fruit,* instead of *icairvbv, tmole,* here; others explain this saying as meaning that the Greeks avoided houses on the hills in order not to be annoyed with the smoke from the low cottages, and yet did not use coal, but wood, which made more smoke. VII. The following letter of his is extant:— ANACHABSIS TO CB03SUS. 0 king of the Lydians, I am come to the country of the Greeks, in order to become acquainted with their customs and institutions; but 1 have no need of gold, and shall be quite contented if I return to Scythia a better man than I left it. However I will come to Sardis, as I think it very desirable to become a friend of yours. LIFE OF MYSON.

I. Myson, the son of Strymon, as Sosicrates states, quoting Hermippus as his authority, a Chenean by birth, of some Etaean or Laconian village, is reckoned one of the seven wise men, and they say that his father was tyrant of his country. It is said by some writers that, when Anacharsis inquired if any one was wiser than he, the priestess at Delphi gave the answer which has been already quoted in the life of Thales in reference to Chilo:—

I say that Myson the Eta;an sage,
The citizen of Chen, is wiser far
In his deep mind than you.

And that he, having taken a great deal of trouble, came to the village, and found him in the summer season fitting a handle to a plough, and he addressed him, " 0 Myson, this is not now the season for the plough." " Indeed," said he, " it is a capital season for preparing one;" but others say, that the words of the oracle are the Etean sage, and they raise the question, what the word Etean means." So Parmenides says, that it is a borough of Laconia, of which Myson was a native; but Sosicrates, in his Successions says, that he was an Etean on his father's side, and a Chenean by his mother's. But Euthyphron, the son of Heraclides Ponticus, says that he was a Cretan, for that Etea was a city of Crete.

II. And Anaxilaus says that he was an Arcadian. Hipponax also mentions him, saying, " And Myson, whom Apollo stated

E to be the most prudent of all men. " But Aristoxenus, in his Miscellanies, says that his habits were not very different from those of Timon and Apemantus, for that he was a misanthrope. And that accordingly he was one day found in Lacedaemon laughing by himself in a solitary place, and when some one came up to him on a sudden and asked him why he laughed when he was by himself, he said, " For that very reason." Aristoxenus also says thflt he was not thought much of, because he was not a native of any city, but only of a village, and that too one of no great note; and according to him, it is on account of this obscurity of his that some people attribute his sayings and doings to Pisistratus the tyrant, but he excepts Plato the philosopher, for he mentions Myson in his Protagoras, placing him among the wise men instead of Periander.

III. It used to be a common saying of his that men ought not to seek for things in words, but for words in things; for that things are not made on account of words, but that words are put together for the sake of things. IV. He died when he had lived ninety-seven years. LIFE OF EPIMENIDES.

I. Epimentdes, as Theopompus and many other writers tell us, was the son of a man named Phaedrus, but some call him the son of Dosiadas; and others of Agesarchus. He was a Cretan by birth, of the city of Gnossus; but because he let his hair grow long, he did not look like a Cretan.

II. He once, when he was sent by his father into the fields to look for a sheep, turned out of the road at mid-day and lay down in a certain cave and fell asleep, and slept there fiftyseven years; and after that, when he awoke, he went on looking for the sheep, thinking that he had been taking a short nap; but as he could not find it he went on to the field and there he found everything changed, and the estate in another person's possession, and so he came back again to the city in great perplexity, and as he was going into his own house he met some people who asked him who he was, until at last he found his younger brother who had now become an old man, and from him he learnt all the truth. III. And when he was recognized he was considered by the Greeks as a person especially beloved by the Gods, on which account when the Athenians were afflicted by a plague, and the priestess at Delphi enjoined them to purify their city, they sent a ship and Nicias the son of Niceratus to Crete, to invite Epimeuides to Athens; and he, coming there in the fortysixth Olympiad, purified the city and eradicated the plague for that time; he took some black sheep and some white ones and led them up to the Areopagus, and from thence he let them go wherever they chose, having ordered the attendants to follow them, and wherever any one of them lay down they were to sacrifice him to the God who was the patron of the spot, and so the evil was stayed; and owing to this one may even now find in the different boroughs of the Athenians altars without names, which are a sort of memorial of the propitiation of the Gods that then took place. Some said that the cause of the plague was the pollution contracted by the city in the matter of Cylon, and that Epimenides pointed out to the Athenians how to get rid of it, and that in consequence they put to death two young men, Cratinus and Ctesilius, and that thus the pestilence was put an end to. III. And the Athenians passed a vote to give him a talent and a ship to convey him back to Crete, but he would not accept the money, but made a treaty of friendship and alliance between the Gnossians and Athenians. IV. And not long after he had returned home he died, as Phlegon relates in his book on long-lived people, after he had lived a hundred and fiftyseven years; but as the Cretans report he had lived two hundred and ninetynine; but as Xenophones the Colophonian, states that he had heard it reported, he was a hundred and fifty-four years old when he died.

V. He wrote a poem of five thousand verses on the Generation and Theogony of the Curetes and Corybantes, and another poem of six thousand five hundred verses on the building of the Argo and the expedition of Jason to Colchis.

VI. He also wrote a treatise in prose on the Sacrifices in Crete, and the Cretan Constitution, and on Minos and Rhodamanthus, occupying four thousand lines. » VI. Likewise he built at Athens the temple which is there dedicated to the venerable goddesses, as Lobon the Augur says in his book on Poets; and he is said to have been the first person who purified houses and lands, and who built temples. VII. There are some people who assert that he did not sleep for the length of time that has been mentioned above, but that he was absent from his country for a considerable period, occupying himself with the anatomisation and examination of roots. VIII. A letter of his is quoted, addressed to Solon the lawgiver, in which he discusses the constitution which Minos gave the Cretans. But Demetrius the Magnesian, in his treatise on Poets and Prose writers of the same name as one another, attempts to prove that the letter is a modern one, and is not written in the Cretan but in the Attic dialect, and the new Attic too. IX. But I have also discovered another letter of his which runs thus:— EPIMENIDES TO SOLON.

Be of good cheer, my friend; for if Pisistratus had imposed his laws on the Athenians, they being habituated to slavery and not accustomed to good laws previously, he would have maintained his dominion for ever, succeeding easily in enslaving his fellow countrymen; but as it is, he is lording it over men who are no cowards, but who remember the precepts of Solon and are indignant at their bonds, and who will not endure the supremacy of a tyrant. But if Pisistratus does possess the city to-day, still I have no expectation that the supreme power will ever descend to his children. For it is impossible that men who have lived in freedom and in the enjoyment of most excellent laws should be slaves permanently; but as for yourself, do not you go wandering about at random, but come and visit me, for here there is no supreme ruler to be formidable to you; but if while you are wandering about any of the friends of Pisistratus should fall in with you, I fear you might suffer some misfortune.

He then wrote thus: —

X. But Demetrius says that some writers report that he used to receive food from the nymphs and keep it in a bullock's hoof; and that eating it in small quantities he never required any evacuations, and was never seen eatiug. And Timaeus mentions him in his second book.

XI. Some authors say also that the Cretans sacrifice to him as a god, for they say that he was the wisest of men: and accordingly, that when he saw the port of Munychia, at Athens, he said that the Athenians did not know how many evils that place would bring upon them: since, if they did, they would tear it to pieces with their teeth; and he said this a long time before the event to which he alluded. It is said also, that he at first called himself Eacus; and that he foretold to the Lacedaemonians the defeat which they should suffer from the Arcadians; and that be pretended that he had lived several times. But Theopompus, in his Strange Stories, says that when he was building the temple of the Nymphs, a voice burst forth from heaven; — " Oh! Epimenides, build this temple, not for the Nymphs but for Jupiter." He also foretold to the Cretans the defeat of the Lacedaemonians by the Arcadians, as has been said before. And, indeed, they were beaten at Orchomenos. XII. He pretended also, that he grew old rapidly, in the same number of days as he had been years asleep; at least, so Theopompus says. But Mysonianus, in his Coincidences, says, that the Cretans call him one of the Curetes. And the Lacedaemonians preserve his body among them, in obedience to some oracle, as Sosilius the Lacedaemonian says. XIII. There were also two other Epimenides, one the genealogist; the other, the man who wrote a history of Rhodes in the Doric dialect LIFE OF PHERECYDES.

I. Phf.recydes was a Syrian, the son of Babys, and, as Alexander says, in his Successions, he had been a pupil of Pittacus.

This refers to the result of the war which Antipater, who became regent of Macedonia on the death of Alexander the Great, carried on against the confederacy of Greek states, of which Athens was the head; and in which, after having defeated them at Cranon, he compelled the Athenians to abolish the democracy, and to admit a garrison into Munychia; II. Theopompus says that he was the first person who ever wrote among the Greeks on the subject of Natural Philosophy and the Gods. And there are many marvellous stories told of him. For it is said that he was walking along the sea-shore at Samos, and that seeing a ship sailing by with a fair wind, he said that it would soon sink; and presently it sank before their eyes. At another time he was drinking some water which had been drawn up out of a well, and he foretold that within three days there would be an earthquake; and there was one. And as he was going up to Olympia, and had arrived at Messene, he advised his entertainer, Perilaus, to migrate from the city with all his family, but that Perilaus would not be guided by him; and afterwards Messene was taken. III. And he is said to have told the Lacedaemonians to honour neither gold nor silver, as Theopompus says in his Marveh; and it is reported that Hercules laid this injunction on him in a dream, and that the same night he appeared also to the kings of Sparta, and enjoined them to be guided by Pherecydes; but some attribute these stories to Pythagoras. IV. And Hermippus relates that when there was a war between the Ephesians and Magnesians, he, wishing the Ephesians to conquer, asked some one, who was passing by, from whence he came? and when he said, " From Ephesus," " Drag me now," said he, " by the legs, and place me in the terrritory of the Magnesians, and tell your fellow countrymen to bury me there after they have got the victory; and that he went and reported that Pherecydes had given him this order. And so they went forth the next day and defeated the Magnesians; and as Pherecydes was dead, they buried him there, and paid bim very splendid honours.

V. But some writers say that he went to Delphi, and threw himself down from the Corycian hill; Aristoxenus, in his History of Pythagoras and his Friends, says that Pherecydes fell sick and died, and was buried by Pythagoras in Delos; But others say that he died of the lousy disease; and when Pythagoras came to see him, and asked him how he was, he put his finger through the door, and said, " You may see by my skin." And from this circumstance that expression passed into a proverb among the philosophers, when affairs are going on badly; and those who apply it to affairs that are go ng on well, make a blunder. He used to say, also, that the Gods call their table 6u%lg. VI. But Andron, the Ephesian, says that there were two men of the name of Pherecydes, both Syrians: one an astronomer, and the other a writer on God and the Divine Nature; and that this last was the son of Babys, who was also the master of Pythagoras. But Eratosthenes asserts that there was but one, who was a Syrian; and that the other Pherecydes was an Athenian, a genealogist; and the work of the Syrian Pherecydes is preserved, and it begins thus:—" Jupiter, and Time, and Chthon existed externally." And the name of Cthonia became TeUus, after Jupiter gave it to her as a reward. A sun-dial is also preserved, in the island of Syra, of his making.

VII. But Duris, in the second book of his Boundaries, says that this epigram was written upon him:—
The limit of all wisdom is in me;
   And would be, were it larger. But report
To my Pythagoras that he's the first
Of all the men that tread the Grecian soil;
   I shall not speak a falsehood, saying this.
   And Ion, the Chian, says of him:—
   Adorned wiih valour while alive, and modesty,
Now that he's dead he still exists in peace;
   For, like the wise Pythagoras, he studied
The manners and the minds of many nations.
   And I myself have composed an epigram on him in the Pherecratean metre:—
   The story is reported,
   That noble Pherecydes
   Whom Syros calls her own,
   Was eaten up by lice;
   And so he bade his friends,
   Convey his corpse away
   To the Magnesian land,
   That he might victory give
   To holy Ephesus.
   For well the God had said, (Though he alone did know
   Th' oracular prediction),
   That this was fate's decree.
   So in that land he lies.
   This then is surely true,
   That those who're really wise
   Are useful while alive,
   And e'en when breath has left them.

VIII. And he flourished about the fifty-ninth Olympiad. There ia a letter of his extant in the following terms:— PHEKECYDES TO THALES.

May you die happily when fate overtakes you. Disease has seized upon me at the same time that I received your letter. I am all over lice, and suffering likewise under a low fever. Accordingly, I have charged my servants to convey this book of mine to you, after they have buried me. And do you, if you think fit, after consulting with the other wise men, publish it; but if you do not approve of doing so, then keep it unpublished, for I am not entirely pleased with it myself. The subject is not one about which there is any certain knowledge, nor do I undertake to say that I have arrived at the truth; but I have advanced arguments, from which any one who occupies himself with speculations on the divine nature, may make a selection; and as to other points, he must exercise his intellect, for I speak obscurely throughout. I, myself, as I am afflicted more severely by this disease every day, no longer admit any physicians, or any of my friends. But when they stand at the door, and ask me how I am, I put out my finger to them through the opening of the door, and show them how I am eaten up with the evil; and I desired them to come to-morrow to the funeral of Pherecydes.

These, then, are they who were called wise men; to which list some writers add the name of Pisistratus. But we must also speak of the philosophers. And we will begin first with the Ionic philosophy, the founder of which school was Thales, who was the master of Anaximander.

BOOK II. i LIFE OF ANAXIMANDER.

I. Anaximandkr, the son of Praxiadas, was a citizen of Miletus.

II. He used to assert that the principle and primary element of all things was the Infinity, giving no exact definition as to whether he meant air or water, or anything else. And he said that the parts were susceptible of change, but that the whole was unchangeable; and that the earth lay in the middle, being placed there as a sort of centre, of a spherical shape. The moon, he said, had a borrowed light, and borrowed it from the sun; and the sun he affirmed to be not less than the earth, and the purest possible fire. III. He also was the first discoverer of the gnomon; and he placed some in Lacedaemon on the sun-dials there, as Pharorinus says in his Universal History, and they showed the solstices and the equinoxes; he also made clocks. He was the first person, too, who drew a map of the earth and sea, and he also made a globe; and he published a concise statement of whatever opinions he embraced or entertained; and this treatise was met with by Apollodorus, the Athenian. IV. And Apollodorus, in his Chronicles, states, that in the second year of the fifty-eighth Olympiad, he was sixty-four years old. And soon after he died, having flourished much about the same time as Polycrates, the tyrant, of Samos. They say that when he sang, the children laughed; and that he, hearing of this, said, "We must then sing better for the sake of the children."

V. There was also another Anaximander, a historian; and he too was a Milesian, and wrote in the Ionic dialect.

LIFE OF ANAXIMENES.

I. Anaximenes, the son of Eurystratus, a Milesian, was a pupil of Anaximander; but some say that he was also a pupil of Parmenides. He said that the principles of everything were the air, and the Infinite; and that the stars moved not under the earth, but around the earth. He wrote in the pure unmixed Ionian dialect. And he lived, according to the statements of Apollodorus, in the sixty-third Olympiad, and died about the time of the taking of Sardis.

II. There were also two other persons of the name of Anaximenes, both citizens of Lampsacus; one an orator and the other a historian, who was the son of the sister of the orator, and who wrote an account of the exploits of Alexander.

III. And this philosopher wrote the following letters:— ANAXIMENES TO PYTHAGORAS.

Thales, the son of Euxamias, has died in his old age, by an unfortunate accident. In the evening, as he was accustomed to do, he went forth out of the vestibule of his house with his maid-servant, to observe the stars: and (for he had forgotten the existence of the place) while he was looking up towards the skies, he fell down a precipitous place. So now the astronomer of Miletus has met with this end. But we who were his pupils cherish the recollection of the man, and so do our children and our own pupils: and we will lecture on his principles. At all events, the beginning of all wisdom ought to be attributed to Thales.

IV. And again he writes:— ANAXIMENES TO PYTHAGORAS.

You are more prudent than we, in that you have migrated from Samos to Crotona, and live there in peace. For the descendants of iEacus commit unheard-of crimes, and tyrants never cease to oppress the Milesians. The king of the Medes too is formidable to us: unless, indeed, we choose to become tributary to him. But the Ionians are on the point of engaging in war with the Medes in the cause of universal freedom. For if we remain quiet there is no longer any hope of safety for us. How then can Anaximenes apply his mind to the contemplation of the skies, while he is in perpetual fear of death or slavery? But you are beloved by the people of Crotona, and by all the rest of the Italians; and pupils flock to you, even from Sicily.

LIFE OF ANAXAGORAS.

I. Anaxagoras, the son of Hegesibulus, or Eubulus, was a citizen of Clazomenae. He was a pupil of Anaximenes, and was the first philosopher who attributed mind to matter, beginning his treatise on the subject in the following manner (and the whole treatise is written in a most beautiful and magnificent style): " All things were mixed up together; then Mind came and arranged them all in distinct order." On which account he himself got the same name of Mind. And Timon speaks thus of him in his Silli:—

They say too that wise Anaxagoras
Deserves immortal fame; they call him Mind,
Because, as he doth teach, Mind came in season,
Arranging all which was confus'd before.

II. He was eminent for his noble birth and for his riches, and still more so for his magnanimity, inasmuch as he gave up all his patrimony to his relations; and being blamed by them for his neglect of his estate, " Why, then," said he, " do not you take care of it?" And at last he abandoned it entirely, and devoted himself to the contemplation of subjects of natural philosophy, disregarding politics. So that once when some said to him, " You have no affection for your country," " Be silent," said he, " for I have the greatest affection for my country," pointing up to heaven.

III. It is said, that at the time of the passage of the Hellespont by Xerxes, he was twenty years old, and that he lived to the age of seventy-two. But Apollodorus, in his Chronicles says that he flourished in the seventieth Olympiad, and that he died in the first year of the seventy-eighth. And he began to study philosophy at Athens, in the archonship of Callias, being twenty years of age, as Demetrius Phalerius tells us in his Catalogue of the Archons, and they say that he remained at Athens thirty years.

IV. He asserted that the sun was a mass of burning iron, greater than Peloponnesus; (that some attribute this doctrine to Tantalus), and that the moon contained houses, and also hills and ravines: and that the primary elements of everything were similarities of parts; for as we say that gold consists of a quantity of grains combined together, so too is the universe formed of a number of small bodies of similar parts. He further taught that Mind was the principle of motion: and that of bodies the heavy ones, such as the earth, occupied the lower situations; and the light ones, such as fire, occupied the higher places, and that the middle spaces were assigned to water and air. And thus that the sea rested upon the earth, which was broad, the moisture being all evaporated by the sun. ' And he said that the stars originally moved about in irregular confusion, so that at first the pole star, which is continually visible, always appeared in the zenith, but that afterwards it acquired a certain declination. And that the milky way was a reflection of the light of the sun when the stars did not appear. The comets he considered to be a concourse of planets emitting rays: and the shooting stars he thought were sparks as it were leaping from the firmament. The winds he thought were caused by the ratification of the atmosphere, which was produced by the sun. Thunder, he said, was produced by the collision of the clouds; and lightning by the rubbing together of the clouds. Earthquakes, he said, were produced by the return of the air into the earth. All animals he considered were originally generated out of moisture, and heat, and earthy particles: and subsequently from one another. And males he considered were derived from those on the right hand, and females from those on the left.

V. They say, also, that he predicted a fall of the stones which fell near iEgospotami, and which he said would fall from the sun: on which account Euripides, who was a disciple of his, said in his Phaethon that the sun was a golden clod of earth. He went once to Olympia wrapped in a leathern cloak as if it were going to rain; and it did rain. And they say that he once replied to a man who asked him whether the mountains at Lampsacus would ever become sea, " Yes, if time lasts long enough."

VI. Being once asked for what end he had been born, he said, " For the contemplation of the sun, and moon, and heaven." A man once said to him, "You have lost the Athenians;" " No," said he, " they have lost me." When he beheld the tomb of Mausolus, he said, "A costly tomb is an image of a petrified estate." And he comforted a man who was grieving because he was dying in a foreign land, by telling him, " The descent to hell is the same from every place."

VII. He appears to have been the first person (according to the account given by Pharorinus in his Universal History), who said that the Poem of Homer was composed in praise of virtue and justice: and Metro, of Lampsacus, who was a friend of his, adopted this opinion, and advocated it energetically, and Metrodorus was the first who seriously studied the natural philosophy developed in the writings of the great poet.

VIII. Anaxagoras was also the first man who ever wrote a work in prose; and Silenus, in the first book of his Histories, says, that in the archonship of Lysanias a large stone fell from heaven; and that in reference to this event Anaxagoras said, that the whole heaven was composed of stones, and that by its rapid revolutions they were all held together; and when those revolutions get slower, they fall down.

IX. Of his trial there are different accounts given. For Sotion, in his Succession of the Philosophers, says, that he was persecuted for impiety by Cleon, because he said that the sun was a fiery ball of iron. And though Pericles, who had been his pupil, defended him, he was, nevertheless, fined five talents and banished. But Satyrus, in his Lives, says that it was Thucydides by whom he was impeached, as Thucydides was of the opposite party to Pericles; and that he was prosecuted not only for impiety, but also for Medison; and that he was condemned to death in his absence. And when news was brought him of two misfortunes—his condemnation, and the death of his children; concerning the condemnation he said, " Nature has long since condemned both them and me." But about his children, he said, " I knew that I had become the father of mortals. " Some, however, attribute this saying to Solon, and others to Xenophon. And Demetrius Phalereus, in bis treatise on Old Age, says that Anaxagoras buried them with his own hands. But Hermippus, in his Lives, says that he was thrown into prison for the purpose of being put to death: but that Pericles came forward and inquired if any one brought any accusation against him respecting his course of life. And as no one alleged anything against him: " I then," said he, " am his disciple: do not you then be led away by calumnies to put this man to death; but be guided by me, and release him." And he was released. But, as he was indignant at the insult which had been offered to him, he left the city.

But Hieronymus, in the second book of his Miscellaneous Commentaries, says that Pericles produced him before the court, tottering and emaciated by disease, so jthat he was released rather out of pity, than by any deliberate decision on the merits of his case. And thus much may be said about his trial. Some people have fancied that he was very hostile to Democritus, because he did not succeed in getting admission to him for the purposes of conversation.

X. And at last, having gone to Lampsacus, he died in that city. And it is said, that when the governors of the city asked him what he would like to have done for him, he replied, " That they would allow the children to play every year during the month in which he died. " And this custom is kept up even now. And when he was dead, the citizens of Lampsacus buried him with great honours, and wrote this epitaph on him:—

Here Anaxagoras lies, who reached of truth
The farthest bounds in heavenly speculations.

We ourselves also have written an epigram on him:— Wise Anaxagoras did call the sun
A mass of glowing iron; and for this
Death was to be his fate. But Pericles
Then saved his friend; but afterwards he died
I A victim of a weak philosophy.

XI. There were also three other people of the name of Anaxagoras; none of whom combined all kinds of knowledge; But one was an orator and a pupil of Isocrates; another was a statuary, who is mentioned by Antigonus; another is a grammarian, a pupil of Zenodotus.

LIFE OF ARCHELAUS.

I. Archklaus was a citizen of either Athens or Miletus, and his father's name was Apollodorus; but, as some say, Mydon. He was a pupil of Anaxagoras, and the master of Socrates.

II. He was the first person who imported the study of natural philosophy from Ionia to Athens, and he was called the Natural Philosopher, because natural philosophy terminated with him, as Socrates introduced ethical philosophy. And it seems probable that Archelaus too meddled in some degree with moral philosophy; for in his philosophical speculations he discussed laws and what was honourable and just. And Socrates borrowed from him; and because he enlarged his principles, he was thought to be the inventor of them.

III. He used to say that there were two primary causes of generation, heat and cold; and that all animals were generated out of mud: and that what are accounted just and disgraceful are not so by nature, but only by law. And his reasoning proceeds in this way. He says, that water being melted by heat, when it is submitted to the action of fire, by which it is solidified, becomes earth; and when it is liquefied, becomes air. And, therefore, the earth is surrounded by air and influenced by it, and so is the air by the revolutions of fire. And he says that animals are generated out of hot earth, which sends up a thick mud something like milk for their food. So too he says that it produced men.

And he was the first person who said that sound is produced by the percussion of the air; and that the sea is filtered in the hollows of the earth in its passage, and so is condensed; and that the sun is the greatest of the stars, and that the universe is boundless.

IV. But there were three other people of the name of Archelaus: one, a geographer, who described the countries traversed by Alexander; the second, a man who wrote a poem on objects which have two natures; and the third, an orator, who wrote a book containing the precepts of his art. LIFE OF SOCRATES.

I. Socrates was the son of Sophroniscus, a statuary, and of Phaenarete, a midwife; as Plato records in his Miaetetus; he was a citizen of Athens, of the borough of Alopece.

II. Some people believed that he assisted Euripides in his poems; in reference to which idea, Moresimachus speaks as follows:—

The Phrygians are a new play of Euripides,
But Socrates has laid the main foundation.

ipvyava, sticks or faggots.

And again he says:—

Euripides: patched up by Socrates.
And Callias, in his Captives, says:— *A.* Are you so proud, giving yourself such airs *t B.* And well I may, for Socrates is the cause.

And Aristophanes says, in his Clouds:—

This is Euripides, who doth compose
Those argumentative wise tragedies.

III. But, having been a pupil of Anaxagoras, as some people say, but of Damon as the other story goes, related by Alexander in his Successions, after the condemnation of Anaxagoras, he became a disciple of Archelaus, the natural philosopher. And, indeed, Aristoxenus says that he was very intimate with him.

IV. But Duris says that he was a slave, and employed in carving stones. And some say that the Graces in the Acropolis are his work; and they are clothed figures. And that it is in reference to this that Timon says, in his Silli:—

From them proceeded the stone polisher,
The reasoning legislator, the enchanter
Of all the Greeks, makifeg them subtle arguers,
A cunning pedant, a shrewd Attic quibbler.

V. For he was very clever in all rhetorical exercises, as Idomeneus also assures us. But the thirty tyrants forbade him to give lessons in the art of speaking and arguing, as Xenophon tells us. And Aristophanes turns him into ridicule in his Comedies, as making the worse appear the better reason. For he was the first man, as Pharorinus says in his Universal History, who, in conjunction with his disciple iEschines, taught men how to become orators. And Idomeneus makes the same assertion in his essay on the Socratic School. He, likewise, was the first person who conversed about human life; and was also the first philosopher who was condemned to death and executed. And Aristoxenus, the son of Spintharas, says that he lent money in usury; and that he collected the interest and principal together, and then, when he had got the interest, he lent it out again. And Demetrius, of Byzantium, says that it was Criton who made him leave his workshop and instruct men, out of the admiration which he conceived for his abilities.

VI. He then, perceiving that natural philosophy had no immediate bearing on our interests, began to enter upon moral speculations, both in his workshop and in the marketplace. And he said that the objects of his search were—

Whatever good or barm can man befall
In his own house.

And very often, while arguing and discussing points that arose, he was treated with great violence and beaten, and pulled about, and laughed at and ridiculed by the multitude. But he bore all this with great equanimity. So that once, when he had been kicked and buffeted about, and had borne it all patiently, and some one expressed his surprise, he said, " Suppose an ass had kicked me, would you have had me bring an action against him ʄ And this is the account of Demetrius.

VII. But he had no need of travelling (though most philosophers did travel), except when he was bound to serve in the army. But all the rest of his life he remained in the same place, and in an argumentative spirit he used to dispute with all who would converse with him, not with the purpose of taking away their opinions from them, so much as of learning the truth, as far as he could do so, himself. And they say that Euripides gave him a small work of Heraclitus to read, and asked him afterwards what he thought of it, and he replied, " What I have understood is good; and so, I think, what I have not understood is; only the book requires a Delian diver to get at the meaning of it." He paid great attention also to the training of the body, and was always in excellent condition himself. Accordingly, he joined in the expedition to Amphipolis, and he it was who took up and saved Xenophon in the battle of Delian, when he had fallen from his horse; for when all the Athenians had fled, he retreated quietly, turning round slowly, and watching to repel any one who attacked him. He also joined in the expedition to Potidara, which was undertaken by sea; for it was impossible to get there by land, as the war impeded the communication. And they say that on this occasion he remained the whole night in one place; and that though he had deserved the prize
F of pre-eminent valour, he yielded it to Alcibiades, to whom Aristippus, in the fourth book of his treatise on the Luxury of the Ancients, says that he was greatly attached. But Ion, of Chios, says, that while he was a very young man he left Athens, and went to Samos with Archelaus. And Aristotle says, that he went to Delphi; and Phaioripus also, in the first book of his Commentaries, says that he went to the Isthmus.

VIII. He was a man of great firmness of mind, and very much attached to the democracy, as was plain from his not submitting to Critias, when he ordered him to bring Leon of Salamis, a very rich man, before the thirty, for the purpose of being murdered. And he alone voted for the acquittal of the ten generals; and when it was in his power to escape out of prison he would not do it; and he reproved those who bewailed his fate, and even while in prison, he delivered those beautiful discourses which we still possess. IX. He was a contented and venerable man. And once, as Pamphila says, in the seventh book of her Commentaries, when Alcibiades offered him a large piece of ground to build a house upon, he said, " But if I wanted shoes, and you had given me a piece of leather to make myself shoes, I should be laughed at if I took it." And often, when he beheld the multitude of things which were being sold, he would say to himself, " How many things are there which I do not want." And he was continually repeating these iambics:—
For silver plate and purple useful are
For actors on the stage, but not for men.

And he showed his scorn of Archelaus the Macedonian, and Scopas the Crononian, and Eurylochus of Larissa, when he refused to accept their money, and to go and visit them. And he was so regular in his way of living, that it happened more than once when there was a plague at Athens, that he was the only person who did not catch it.

X. Aristotle says, that he had two wives. The first was Xanthippe, by whom he had a son named Lamprocles; the second was Myrto, the daughter of Aristides the Just; and he took her without any dowry, and by her he had two sons, Sophroniscus and Menexenus. But some say that Myrto was After the battle of Arginusae.
his first wife. And some, among whom are Satyrus, and Hieronymus, of Rhodes, say that he had them both at the same time. For they say that the Athenians, on account of the scarcity of men, passed a vote, with the view of increasing the population, that a man might marry one citizen, and might also have children by another who should be legitimate; on which account Socrates did so. XI. And he was a man able to look down upon any who mocked him. And he prided himself upon the simplicity of his way of life; and never exacted any pay from his pupils. And he used to say, that the man who ate with the greatest appetite, had the least need of delicacies; and that he who drank with the greatest appetite, was the least inclined to look for a draught which is not at hand; and that those who want fewest things are nearest to the Gods. And thus much, indeed, one may learn from the comic poets; who, without perceiving it, praise him in the very matters for which they ridicule him. Aristophanes speaks thus:—

Prudent man, who thus with justice long for mighty wisdom,

Happiness will be your lot in Athens, and all Greece too;

For you've a noble memory, and plenty of invention,

And patience dwells within your mind, and you are never tired,

Whether you're standing still or walking; and you care not for cold,

Nor do you long for breakfast time, nor e'er give in to hunger;

But wine and gluttony you shun, and all such kind of follies.

And Ameipsias introduces him on the stage in a cloak, and speaks thus of him:—

O Socrates, among few men the best,,

And among many vainest; here at last

You come to us courageously—but where,

Where did you get that cloak? so strange a garment,

Some leather cutter must have given you

By way of joke: and yet this worthy man,

Though ne'er so hungry, never flatters any one.

Aristophanes too, exposes his contemptuous and arrogant disposition, speaking thus:—

You strut along the streets, and look around you proudly,

And barefoot many ills endure, and hold your head above us.

And yet, sometimes he adapted himself to the occasion and dressed handsomely. As, for instance, in the banquet of Plato, where he is represented as going to find Agathon.

XII. He was a man of great ability, both in exhorting men to, and dissuading them from, any course; as, for instance, having discoursed with Theaetetus on the subject of knowledge, he sent him away almost inspired, as Plato says. And when Euthyphron had commenced a prosecution against his father for having killed a foreigner, he conversed with him on the subject of piety, and turned him from his purpose: and by his exhortations he made Lysis a most moral man. For he was very ingenious at deriving arguments from existing circumstances. And so he mollified his son Lamprocles when he was very angry with his mother, as Xenophon mentions somewhere in his works; and he wrought upon Glauson, the brother of Plato, who was desirous to meddle with affairs of state, and induced him to abandon his purpose, because of his want of experience in such matters, as Xenophon relates. And, on the contrary, he persuaded Charmidas to devote himself to politics, because he was a man very well calculated for such business. He also inspired Iphicrates, the general, with courage, by showing him the gamecocks of Midias the barber, pluming themselves against those of Callias; and Glauernides said, that the state ought to keep him carefully, as if he were a pheasant or a peacock. He used also td say, that it was a strange thing that every one could easily tell what property he had, but was not able to name all his friends, or even to tell their number; so careless were men on that subject. Once when he saw Euclid exceedingly anxious about some dialectic arguments, he said to him, " 0 Euclid, you will acquire a power of managing sophists, but not of governing men." For he thought that subtle hair-splitting on those subjects was quite useless; as Plato also records in the Euthydemus. XIII. And when Charmidas offered him some slaves, with the view to his making a profit of them, he would not have them; and, as some people say, he paid no regard to the beauty of Alcibiades. XIV. He used to praise leisure as the most valuable of possessions, as Xenophon tells us in his Banquet. And it was a saying of his that there was one only good, namely, knowledge; and one only evil, namely ignorance; that riches and high birth had nothing estimable in them, but that, on tho contrary, they were wholly evil. Accordingly, when some one told him that the mother of Antisthenes was a Thracian woman, " Did you suppose," said he, " that so noble a man must be born of two Athenians?" And when Phaedo was reduced to a state of slavery, he ordered Crito to ransom him, and taught him, and made him a philosopher. XV. And, moreover, he used to learn to play on the lyre when he had time, saying, that it it was not absurd to learn anything that one did not know; and further, he used frequently to dance, thinking such an exercise good for the health of the body, as Xenophon relates in his Banquet. XVI. He used also to say that the daemon foretold the future to him; and that to begin well was not a trifling thing, but yet not far from a trifling thing; and that he knew nothing, except the fact of his ignorance. Another saying of his was, that those who bought things out of season, at an extravagant price, expected never to live till the proper season for them. Once, when he was asked what was the virtue of a young man, he said, " To avoid excess in everything." And he used to say, that it was necessary to learn geometry only so far as might enable a man to measure land for the purposes of buying and selling. And when Euripides, in his Augur, had spoken thus of virtue:—

Tis best to leave these subjects undisturbed; he rose up and left the theatre, saying that it was an absurdity to think it right to seek for a slave if one could not find him, but to let virtue be altogether disregarded. The question was once put to him by a man whether he would advise him to marry or not? And he replied, " Whichever you do, you will repent it." He often said, that he wondered at those who made stone statues, when he saw how careful they were that the stone should be like the man it was intended to represent, but how careless they were of themselves, as to guarding against being like the stone. He used also to recommend young men to be constantly looking in the glass, in order that, if they were handsome, they might be worthy of their beauty; and if they were ugly, they " This is not quite correct. Socrates believed that the daemon which attended him, limited his warnings to his own conduct; preventing him from doing what was wrong, but not prompting him to do right."— *See Grote's admirable chapter on Socrates. Hist, of Greece,* vol v.

might conceal their unsightly appearance by their accomplishments. He once invited some rich men to dinner, and when Xanthippe was ashamed of their insufficient appointments, he said, "Be of good cheer; for if our guests are sensible men, they will bear with us; and if they are not, we need not care about them." He used to say, " That other men lived to eat, but that he ate to live." Another saying of his was, " That to have a regard for the worthless multitude, was like the case of a man who refused to take one piece of money of four drachmas as if it were bad, and then took a heap of such coins and admitted them to be good." When iEschines said, "Iama poor man, and have nothing else, but I give you myself;" " Do you not," he replied, " perceive that you are giving me what is of the greatest value?" He said to some one, who was expressing indignation at being.overlooked when the thirty had seized on the supreme power, " Do you, then, repent of not being a tyrant too?" A man said to him, " The Athenians have condemned you to death." "And nature," he replied, "hascondemned them." But some attribute this answer to Anaxagoras. When his wife said to him, " You die undeservedly." " Would you, then," he rejoined, " have had me deserve death?" He thought once that some one appeared to him in a dream, and said:—

On the third day you'll come to lovely Phthia.

And so he said to Eschines, " In three days I shall die." And when he was about to drink the hemlock, Apollodorus presented him with a handsome robe, that he might expire in it; and he said, " Why was my own dress good enough to live in, and not good enough to die in?" When a person said to him, " Such an one speaks ill of you;" " To be sure," said he, " for he has never learnt to speak well." When Antisthenes turned the ragged side of his cloak to the light, be said, " I see your silly vanity through the holes in your cloak." When some one said to him, " Does not that man abuse you?" " No," said he, " for that does not apply to me. It was a saying of his, too, " That it is a good thing for a man to offer himself cheerfully to the attacks of the comic writers; for then, if they say anything worth hearing, one will be able to mend; and if they do not, then all they say is unimportant." XVII. He said once to Xanthippe, who first abused him, and then threw water at him, " Did I not say that Xanthippe was thundering now, and would soon rain?" When Alcibiades said to him, " The abusive temper of Xanthippe is intolerable;" " But I," he rejoined, " am used to it, just as I should be if I were always hearing the noise of a pulley; and you yourself endure to hear geese cackling." To which Alcibiades answered, " Yes, but they bring me eggs and goslings." " Well," rejoined Socrates, " and Xanthippe brings me children." Once, she attacked him in the marketplace, and tore his cloak off; his friends advised him to keep her off with his hands; " Yes, by Jove," said he, " that while we are boxing you may all cry out,' Well done, Socrates, well done, Xanthippe."' And he used to say, that one ought to live with a restive woman, just as horsemen manage violent-tempered horses; " and as they," said he, " when they have once mastered them, are easily able to manage all others; so I, after managing Xanthippe, can easily live with any one else whatever." XVIII. And it was in consequence of such sayings and actions as these, that the priestess at Delphi was witness in his favour, when she gave Chaerephon this answer, which is so universally known:—

Socrates of all mortals is the wisest.

In consequence of which answer, he incurred great envy; and he brought envy also on himself, by convicting men who gave themselves airs of folly and ignorance, as undoubtedly he did to Anytus; and as is shown in Plato's Meno. For he, not being able to bear Socrates'jesting, first of all set Aristophanes to attack him, and then persuaded Melitus to institute a prosecution against him, on the ground of impiety and of corrupting the youth of the city. Accordingly Melitus did institute the prosecution; and Polyeuctus pronounced the sentence, as Pharorinus records in his Universal History. And Polycrates, the sophist, wrote the speech which was delivered, as Hermippus says, not Anytus, as others say. And Lycon, the demagogue, prepared everything necessary to support the impeachment; but Antisthenes in his Successions of the Philosophers, and Plato in his Apology, say that these men brought the accusation:—Anytus, and Lycon, and Melitus; A.nytus, acting against him on behalf of the magistrates, and because of his political principles; Lycon, on behalf of the orators; and Melitus on behalf of the poets, all of whom Socrates used to pull to pieces. But Pharorinus, in the first book of his Commentaries, says, that the speech of Polycrates against Socrates is not the genuine one; for in it there is mention made of the walls having been restored by Conon, which took place six years after the death of Socrates; and certainly this is true.

XIX. But the sworn informations, on which the trial proceeded, were drawn up in this fashion; for they are preserved to this day, says Pharorinus, in the temple of Cybele:—" Melitus, the son of Melitus, of Pittea, impeaches Socrates, the son of Sophroniscus, of Alopece: Socrates is guilty, inasmuch as he does not believe in the Gods whom the city worships, but introduces other strange deities; he is also guilty, inasmuch as he corrupts the young men, and the punishment he has incurred is death." XX. But the philosopher, after Lysias had prepared a defence for him, read it through, and said—" It is a very fine speech, Lysias, but is not suitable for me; for it was manifestly the speech of a lawyer, rather than of a philosopher." And when Lysias replied, " How is it possible, that if it is a good speech, it should not be suitable to you?" he said, " Just as fine clothes and handsome shoes would not be suitable to me." And when the trial was proceeding, Justus, of Tiberias, in his Garland, says that Plato ascended the tribune and said, " I, men of Athens, being the youngest of all those who have mounted the tribune... and that he was interrupted by the judges, who cried out $xarafiavrcdv,$ that is to say, ' Come down.' XXI. So when he had been condemned by two hundred and eighty-one votes, being six more than were given in his favour, and when the judges were making an estimate of what punishment or fine should be inflicted on him, he said that he ought to be fined five and twenty drachmas; but Eubulides says that he admitted that he deserved a fine of one hundred. And when the judges raised an outcry at this proposition, he said, " My real opinion is, that as a return for what has been done by me, I deserve a maintenance in the Prytaneum for the rest of my life. " So they condemned him to death, by eighty votes more than they had originally found him guilty. And he was put into prison, and a few days afterwards he drank the hemlock, having held many admirable conversations in the meantime, which Plato has recorded in the Phaedo. XXII. He also, according to some accounts, composed a paean, which begins—

Hail Apollo, King of Delos,
Hail Diana, Leto's child.

But Dionysidorus says that this paean is not his. He also composed a fable, in the style of iEsop, not very artistically, and it begins— iEsop one day did this sage counsel give To the Corinthian magistrates: not to trust 1 The cause of virtue to the people's judgment.

XXIII. So he died; but the Athenians immediately repented of their action, so that they closed all the palaestra and gymnasia; and they banished his accusers, and condemned Melitus to death; but they honoured Socrates with a brazen statue, which they erected in the place where the sacred vessels are kept; and it was the work of Lysippus. But Anytus had already left Athens; and

the people of Heraclea banished him from that city the day of his arrival. But Socrates was not the only person who met with this treatment at the hands of the Athenians, but many other men received the same: for, as Heraclides says, they fined Homer fifty drachmas as a madman, and they said that Iystaeus was out of his wits. But they honoured Astydamas, before Eschylus, with a brazen statue. And Euripides reproaches them for their conduct in his Palamedes, saying—
Ye have slain, ye have slain, 0 Greeks, the all-wise nightingale,
The favourite of the Muses, guiltless all.

And enough has been said on this head.

But Philochorus says that Euripides died before Socrates; and he was born, as Apollodorus in his Chronicles asserts, in the archonship of Apsephion, in the fourth year of the seventyseventh Olympiad, on the sixth day of the month Thargelion, when the Athenians purify their city, and when the citizens of Delos say that Diana was born. And he died in the first Grote gives good reasons for disbelieving this.
year of the ninety-fifth Olympiad, being seventy years of age. And this is the calculation of Demetrius Phalereus, for some say that he was but sixty years old when he died. XXIV. Both he and Euripides were pupils of Anaxagoras; and Euripides was born in the first year of the seventy-fifth Olympiad, in the archonship of Calliades. But Socrates appears to me to have also discussed occasionally subjects of natural philosophy, since he very often disputes about prudence and foresight, as Xenophon tells us; although he at the same time asserts that all his conversations were about moral philosophy. And Plato, in his Apology, mentions the principles of Anaxagoras and other natural philosophers, which Socrates denies; and he is in reality expressing his own sentiments about them, though he attributes them all to Socrates. And Aristotle tells us that a certain one of the Magi came from Syria to Athens, and blamed Socrates for many parts of his conduct, and also foretold that he would come to a violent death. And we ourselves have written this epigram on him—
Drink now, 0 Socrates, in the realms of Jove,
For truly did the God pronounce you wise,
And he who said so is himself all wisdom:
You drank the poison which your country gave,
But they drank wisdom from your godlike voice.

XXV. He had, as Aristotle tells us in the third book of his Poetics, a contest with a man of the name of Antiolochus of Lemnos, and with Antipho, an interpreter of prodigies, as Pythagoras had with Cylon of Crotona; and Homer while alive with Sagaris, and after his death with Xenophanes the Colophonian: and Hesiod, too, in his lifetime with Cereops, and after his death with the same Xenophanes; and Pindar with Aphimenes of Cos; and Thales with Pherecydes; and Bias with Salamis of Priene; and Pittacus with Antimenides; and Cellars and Anaxagoras with Sosibrius; and Simonides with Timocrea.

XXVI. Of those who succeeded him, and who are called the Socratic school, the chiefs were Plato, Xenophon, and Antisthenes: and of the ten, as they are often called, the four most eminent were Eschines, Phaedo, Euclides, and Aristippus. But we must first speak of Xenophon, and after him of Antisthenes among the Cynics. Then of the Socratic school, and so about Plato, since he is the chief of the ten sects, and the founder of the first Academy. And the regular series of them shall proceed in this manner. XXVII. There was also another Socrates, a historian, who wrote a description of Argos; and another, a peripatetic philosopher, a native of Bithynia; and another a writer of epigrams; and another a native of Cos, who wrote invocations to the Gods. LIFE OF XENOPHON.

I. Xenophon, the son of Gryllus, a citizen of Athens, was of the borough of Erchia; and he was a man of great modesty, and as handsome as can be imagined.

II. They say that Socrates met him in a narrow lane, and put his stick across it, and prevented him from passing by, asking him where all kinds of necessary things were sold. And when he had answered him, he asked him again where men where made good and virtuous. And as he did dot know, he said, " Follow me, then, and learn." And from this time forth, Xenophon became a follower of Socrates. III. And he was the first person who took down conversations as they occurred, and published them among men, calling them memorabilia. He was also the first man who wrote a history of philosophers. IV. And Aristippus, in the fourth book of his treatise on Ancient Luxury, says that he loved Clinias; and that he said to him, " Now I look upon Clinias with more pleasure than upon all the other beautiful things which are to be seen among men; and I would rather be blind as to all the rest of the world, than as to Clinias. And I am annoyed even with night and with sleep, because then I do not see him; but I am very grateful to the sun and to daylight, because they show Clinas to me."

V. He became a friend of Cyrus in this manner He had an acquaintance, by name Proxenus, a Boeotian by birth, a pupil of Gorgias of Leontini, and a friend of Cyrus. He being iu Sardis, staying at the court of Cyrus, wrote a letter to Athens to Xenophon, inviting him to come and be afriend of Cyrus. And Xenophon showed the letter to Socrates, and asked his advice. And Socrates bade him go to Delphi, and ask counsel of the God. And Xenophon did so, and went to the God; but the question he put was, not whether it was good for him to go to Cyrus or not, but how he should go; for which Socrates blamed him, but still advised him to go. Accordingly he went to Cyrus, and became no less dear to him than Proxenus. And all the circumstances of the expedition and the retreat, he himself has sufficiently related to us.

VI. But he was at enmity with Menon the Pharsalian, who was the commander of the foreign troops at the time of the expedition; and amongst other reproaches, he says that he was much addicted to the worst kind of debauchery. And he reproaches a man of the name of Apollonides with having his ears bored. VII. But after the expedition, and the disasters which took place in Pontus, and the violations of the truce by Seuthes, the king of the Odrysae, he came into Asia to Agesilaus, the king of Lacedaemon, bringing with him the soldiers of Cyrus, to serve for pay; and he became a very great friend of Agesilaus. And about the same time he was condemned to banishment by the Athenians, on the charge of being a favourer of the Lacedaemonians. And being in Ephesus, and having a sum of money in gold, he gave half of it to Megabyzus, the priest of Diana, to keep for him till his return; and if he never returned, then he was to expend it upon a statue, and dedicate that to the Goddess; and with the other half he sent offerings to Delphi. From thence he went with Agesilaus into Greece, as Agesilaus was summoned to take part in the war against the Thebans. And the Lacedaemonians made him a friend of their city. VIII. After this he left Agesilaus and went to Scillus, which is a strong place in the district of Elis, at no great distance from the city. And a woman followed him, whose name was Philesia, as Demetrius the Magnesian relates; and his sons, Gryllus and Diodorus, as Dinarchus states in the action against Xenophon; and they were also called Dioscuri. And when The Greek is, *iv 7rpbg EevoQutvTa AiroaTaoiov—" ctiroGTatrLov Iutj,* an action against a freedman for having forsaken or slighted his *irpoaTarrig.*"—L. & S.

Megabyzus came into the country, on the occasion of some public assembly, he took back the money and bought a piece of ground, and consecrated it to the Goddess; and a river named Selinus, which is the same name as that of the river at Ephesus, flows through the land. And there he continued hunting, and entertaining his friends, and writing histories. But Dinarchus says that the Lacedaemonians gave him a house and land. Theysayalso that Philopides,the Spartan, sent him there, as a present, some slaves, who had been taken prisoners of war, natives of Dardanus, and that he located them as he pleased. And that the Eleans, having made an expedition against Scillus, took the place, as the Lacedaemonians dawdled in coming to its assistance.

IX. But then his sons escaped privily to Lepreum, with a few servants; and Xenophon himself fled to Elis before the place fell; and from thence he went to Lepreum to his children, and from thence he escaped in safety to Corinth, and settled in that city.

X. In the meantime, as the Athenians had passed a vote to go to the assistance of the Lacedaemonians, he sent his sons to Athens, to join in the expedition in aid of the Lacedaemonians; for they had been educated in Sparta, as Diocles relates in his Lives of the Philosophers. Diodorus returned safe back again, without having at all distinguished himself in the battle. And he had a son who bore the same name as his brother Gryllus. But Gryllus, serving in the cavalry, (and the battle took place at Mantinea,) fought very gallantly, and was slain, as Ephorus tells us, in his twenty-fifth book; Cephisodorus being the Captain of the cavalry, and Hegesides the commander-in-chief. Epaminondas also fell in this battle. And after the battle, they say that Xenophon offered sacrifice, wearing a crown on his head; but when the news of the death of his son arrived, he took off the crown; but after that, hearing that he had fallen gloriously, he put the crown on again. And some say that he did not even shed a tear, but said, " I knew that I was the father of a mortal man." And Aristotle says, that innumerable writers wrote panegyrics and epitaphs upon Gryllus, partly out of a wish to gratify his father. And Hermippus, in his Treatise on Theophrastus, says that Isocrates also composed a panegyric on Gryllus. But Timon ridicules him in these words:—

A silly couplet, or e'en triplet of speeches,
Or longer series still, just such as Xenophon
Might write, or Meagre_-35schines.

Such, then, was the life of Xenophon.

XI. And he flourished about the fourth year of the ninetyfourth Olympiad; and he took part in the expedition of Cyrus, in the archonship of Xenaenetus, the year before the death of Socrates. And he died, as Stesiclides the Athenian states in his List of Archons and Conquerors at Olympia, in the first year of the hundred and fifth Olymiad, in the archonship of Callidemides; in which year, Philip the son of Amyntas began to reign over the Macedonians. And he died at Corinth, as Demetrius the Magnesian says, being of a very advanced age. XII. And he was a man of great distinction in all points, and very fond of horses and of dogs, and a great tactician, as is' manifest from his writings. And he was a pious man, fond of sacrificing to the Gods, and a great authority as to what was due to them, and a very ardent admirer and imitator of Socrates. XIII. He also wrote near forty books; though different critics divide them differently. He wrote an account of the expedition of Cyrus, to each book of which work he prefixed a summary, though he gave none of the whole history. He also wrote the Cyropaedia, and a history of Greece, and Memorabilia of Socrates, and a treatise called die Banquet, and an essay on (Economy, and one on Horsemanship, and one on Breaking Dogs, and one on Managing Horses, and a Defence of Socrates, and a Treatise on Revenues, and one called Hiero, or the Tyrant, and one called Agesilaus; one on the Constitution of the Athenians and Lacedaemonians, which, however, Demetrius the Magnesian says is not the work of Xenophon. It is said, also, that he secretly got possession of the books of Thucydides, which were previously unknown, and himself published them. XIV. He was also called the Attic Muse, because of the sweetness of his diction, in respect of which he and Plato felt a spirit of rivalry towards one another, as we shall relate further in our life of Plato. And we ourselves have composed an epigram on him, which runs thus:—

Not only up to Babylon for Cyrus
Did Xenophon go, but now he's mounted up
The path which leads to Jove's eternal realms—

For he, recounting the great deeds of Greece,
Displays his noble genius, and he shows
The depth of wisdom of his master Socrates.

And another which ends thus:—

O Xenophon, if th' ungrateful countrymen Of Cranon and Cecrops, banished you,
Jealous of Cyrus' favour which he show'd you,
Still hospitable Corinth, with glad heart, Received you, and you lived there happily,
And so resolved to stay in that fair city.

XV. But I have found it stated in some places that he flourished about the eighty-ninth Olympiad, at the same time as the rest of the disciples of Socrates. And Ister says, that he was banished by a decree of Eubulus, and that he was recalled by another decree proposed by the same person. XVI. But there were seven people of the name of Xenophon. First of all, this philosopher of ours; secondly, an Athenian, a brother of Pythostratus, who wrote the poem called the Theseid, and who wrote other works too, especially the lives of Epaminondas and Pelopidas; the third was a physician of Cos; the fourth, a man who wrote a history of Alcibiades; the fifth, was a writer who composed a book full of fabulous prodigies; the sixth, a citizen of Paros, a sculptor; the seventh, a poet of the Old Comedy. LIFE OF SCHINES.

I. eschines was the son of Charinus, the sausage-maker, but, as some writers say, of Lysanias; he was a citizen of Athens, of an industrious disposition from his boyhood upwards, on which account he never quitted Socrates.

II. And this induced Socrates to say, the only one who knows how to pay us proper respect is the son of the sausage-seller. Idomeneus asserts, that it was he who, in the prison, tried to persuade Socrates to make his escape, and not Crito. But that Plato, as he was rather inclined to favour Aristippus, attributed his advice to Crito. III. And Eschines was calumniated on more than one occasion; and especially by Menedemus of Eretria, who states that he appropriated many dialogues of Socrates as his own, having procured them from Xanthippe. And those of them which are called "headless," are exceedingly slovenly performances, showing nothing of the energy of Socrates. And Pisistratus, of Ephesus, used to say, that they were not the work of Eschines. There are seven of them, and most of them are stated by Persaeus to be the work of Pasiphon, of Eretria, and to have been inserted by him among the works of iEscbines. And he plagiarised from the Little Cyrus, and the Lesser Hercules, of Antisthenes, and from the Alcibiades, and from the Dialogues of the other philosophers. The Dialogues then of schines, which profess to give an idea of the system of Socrates are, as I have said, seven in number. First of all, the Miltiades, which is rather weak; the Callias, the Axiochus, the Aspasia, the Alcibiades, the Jelanges, and the Rhino. And they say that he, being in want, went to Sicily, to Dionysius, and was looked down upon by Plato, but supported by Aristippus, and that he gave Dionysius some of his dialogues, and received presents for them. IV. After that he came to Athens, and there he did not venture to practise the trade of a sophist, as Plato and Aristippus were in high reputation there. But he gave lectures for money, and wrote speeches to be delivered in the courts of law for persons under prosecution. On which account, Timon said of him, "The speeches of iEschines which do not convince any one." And they say that when he was in great straights through poverty, Socrates advised him to borrow of himself, by deducting some part of his expenditure in his food.

V. And even Aristippus suspected the genuineness of some of his Dialogues; accordingly, they say that when he was reciting some of them at Megara, he ridiculed him, and said to him, "Oh! you thief; where did you get that?" VI. And Polycritus, of Menda, in the first book of his History of Dionysius, says that he lived with the tyrant till he was deposed, and till the return of Dion to Syracuse; and he says that Caramis, the tragedian, was also with him. And there is extant a letter of Eschines addressed to Dionysius.

VII. But he was a man well versed in rhetorical art, as is plain from the defence of his father Phoeax, the general; and from the works which he wrote in especial imitation of Gorgias, of Leontini. And Lysias wrote an oration against him; entitling it, On Sycophancy; from all which circumstances it is plain that he was a skilful orator. And one man is spoken of as his especial friend, Aristotle, who was surnamed The Tahle. VIII. Now Panaetius thinks that the Dialogues of the following disciples of the Socratic school are all genuine,— Plato, Xenophon, Antisthenes, and Eschines; but he doubts about those which go under the names of Phsedon, and Euclides; and he utterly repudiates all the others.

IX. And there were eight men of the name of JSschines. The first, this philosopher of ours; the second was a man who wrote a treatise on Oratorical Art; the third was the orator who spoke against Demosthenes; the fourth was an Arcadian, a disciple of Isocrates; the fifth was a citizen of Mitylene, whom they used to call the Scourge of the Orators; the sixth was a Neapolitan, a philosopher of the Academy, a disciple and favourite of Melanthius, of Rhode; the seventh was a Milesian, a political writer; the eighth was a statuary. LIFE OF ARISTIPPUS.

I. Aristippus was by birth a Cyrenean, hut he came to Athens, as iEschines says, having been attracted thither by the fame of Socrates.

II. He, haying professed himself a Sophist, as Phaniaa, of Eresus, the Peripatetic, informs us, was the first of the pupils of Socrates who exacted money from his pupils, and who sent money to his master. And once he sent him twenty drachmas, but had them sent back again, as Socrates said that his daemon would not allow him to accept them; for, in fact, he was indignant at having them offered to him. And Xenophon used to hate him; on which account he wrote his book against pleasure as an attack upon Aristippus, and assigned the main argument to Socrates. Theodorus also, in his Treatise on Sects, has attacked him severely, and so has Plato in his book on the Soul, as we have mentioned in another place. III. But he was a man very quick at adapting himself to every kind of place, and time, and person, and he easilj supported every change of fortune. For which reason he was in greater favour with Dionysius than any of the others, as he always made the best of existing circumstances. For he enjoyed what was before him pleasantly, and he did not toil to procure himself the enjoyment of what was not present. On which account Diogenes used to call him the king's dog. And Timon used to snarl at him as too luxurious, speaking somewhat in this fashion:—

Like the effeminate mind of Aristippus,
Who, as he said, by touch could judge of falsehood.

They say that he once ordered a partridge to be bought for him at the price of fifty drachmas; and when some one blamed him, " And would not you," said he, " have bought it if it had cost an obol?" And when he said he would, " Well," replied Aristippus, "fifty drachmas are no more to me." Dionysius once bade him select which he pleased of three beautiful courtesans; and he carried off all three, saying that even Paris did not get any good by prefering one beauty to the rest. However, they say, that when he had earned them as far as the vestibule, he dismissed them; so easily inclined was he to select or to disregard things. On which account Strato, or, as others will have it, Plato, said to him, " You are the only man to whom it is given to wear both a whole cloak and rags." Once when Dionysius spit at him, he put up with it; and when some one found fault with him, he said, " Men endure being wetted by the sea in order to catch a tench, and shall not I endure to be sprinkled with wine to catch a sturgeon?" IV. Once Diogenes, who was washing vegetables, ridiculed him as he passed by, and said, " If you had learnt to eat these vegetables, you would not have been a slave in the palace of a tyrant." But Aristippus replied, " And you, if you had known how to behave among men, would not have been washing vegetables." Being asked once what advantage he had derived from philosophy, he said, " The power of associating confidently This is exactly the character that Horace gives of him:—

Omnia Aristippum decuit color et status et res;
Tentantem majora, fere praesentibus aequum.—
Ep. i. 23, 24.

with every body." When he was reproached for living extravagantly, he replied, " If extravagance had been a fault, it would not have had a place in the festivals of the Gods." At another time he was asked what advantage philosophers had over other men; and he replied, " If all the laws should be abrogated, we should still live in the same manner as we do now." Once, when Dionysius asked him why the philosophers haunt the doors of the rich, but the rich do not frequent / those of the philosophers, he said, " Because the first know what' they want, but the second do not."

On one occasion he was reproached by Plato for living in an expensive way; and he replied, " Does not Dionysius seem to you to be a good man?" And as he said that he did; " And yet," said he, " he lives in a more expensive manner than I do, so that there is no impossibility in a person's living both expensively and well at the same time." He was asked once in what educated men are superior to uneducated men; and answered, "Just as broken horses are superior to those that are unbroken." On another occasion he was going into the house of a courtesan, and when one of the young men who were with him blushed, he said, " It is not the going into such a house that is bad, but the not being able to go out." Once a man proposed a riddle to him, and said, " Solve it." " Why, you silly fellow," said Aristippus, " do you wish me to loose what gives us trouble, even while it is in bonds?" A saying of his was, " that it was better to be a beggar than an ignorant person; for that a beggar only wants money, but an ignorant person wants_humanity." Once when he was abusecT, he was going away, and as his adversary pursued him and said, " Why are you going away?" " Because," said he, " you have a license for speaking ill; but I have another for declining to hear ill." When some one said that he always saw the philosophers at the doors of the rich men, he said, " And the physicians also are always seen at the doors of their patients; but still no one would choose for this reason to be an invalid rather than a physician."

Once it happened, that when he was sailing to Corinth, he was overtaken by a violent storm; and when somebody said. " We common individuals are not afraid, but you philosophers are behaving like cowards;" he said, " Very likely, for we i have not both of us the same kind of souls at stake." Seeing a man who prided himself on the variety of his learning and accomplishments, he said, " Those who eat most, and who take the most exercise, are not in better health than they who eat just as much as is good for them; and in the same way it is not those who know a great many things, but they who know what is useful who are valuable men." An orator had pleaded a cause for him and gained it, and asked him afterwards, "Now, what good did you ever get from Socrates?" " This good," said he, " that all that you have said in my ' behalf is true." He gave admirable advice to his daughter Aretes, teaching her to despise superfluity. And being asked by some one in what respect his son would be better if he I received a careful education, he replied, " If he gets no other good, at all events, when he is at the theatre, he will not be one stone sitting upon another." Once when some one brought his son to introduce to him, he demanded five hundred drachmas; and when the father said, "Why, for such a price as that I can buy a slave." " Buy him then," he replied, " and you will have a pair."

It was a saying of his that he took money from his acquaintances not in order to use it himself, but to make them aware in what they ought to spend their money. On one occasion, being reproached for having employed a hired advocate in a cause that he had depending: " Why not," said he; " when I have a dinner, I hire a cook." Once he was compelled by Dionysius to repeat some philosophical sentiment; " It is an absurdity," said he, " for you to learn of me how to speak, and yet to teach me when I ought to speak:" and as Dionysius was offended at this, he placed him at the lowest end of the table; on which Aristippus said, " You wish to make this place more respectable." A man was one day boasting of his skill as a diver; " Are you not ashamed," said Aristippus, " to pride yourself on your performance of the duty of a dolphin?" On one occasion he was asked in what respect a wise man is superior to one who is not wise; and his answer was, " Send them both naked among strangers, and you will find out." A man was boasting of being able to drink a great deal without being drunk; and he said, " A mule can do the very same thing." When a man reproached him for living with a mistress, he said, " Does it make any difference whether one takes a house in which many others have lived before one, or one where no one has ever lived?" and his reprover said, " No." " Well, does it make any difference whether one sails in a ship in which ten thousand people have sailed before one, or whether one sails in one in which no one has ever embarked?" " By no means," said the other. " Just in the same way," said he, " it makes no difference whether one lives with a woman with whom numbers have lived, or with one with whom no one has lived." When a person once blamed him for taking money from his pupils, after having been himself a pupil of Socrates: " To be sure I do," he replied, " for Socrates too, when some friends sent their corn and wine, accepted a little, and sent the rest back; for he had the chief men of the Athenians for his purveyors. But I have only Eutychides, whom I have bought with money." And he used to live with Lais the courtesan, as Sotion tells us in the Second Book of his Successions. Accordingly, when some one reproached him on her account, he made answer, "I possess her, but I am not possessed by her; since the best thing is to possess pleasures without being their slave, not to be devoid of pleasures." When some one blamed him for the expense he was at about his food, he said, " Would you not have bought those things yourself if they had cost three obols?" And when the other admitted that he would, " Then," said he, " it is not that I am fond of pleasure, but that you are fond of money." On one occasion, when Simus, the steward of Dionysius, was showing him amagnificent house, paved with marble (but Simus was a Phrygian, and a great toper), he hawked up a quantity of saliva and spit in his face; and when Simus was indignant at this, he said, " I could not find a more suitable place to spit in. "

Charondas, or as some say, Phaedon, asked him once, " Who are the people who use perfumes ?" " I do," said he, "wretched man that'I am, and the king of the Persians is still more wretched than I; but, recollect, that as no animal is the worse for having a pleasant scent, so neither is a man; but plague take those wretches who abuse our beautiful unguents." On another occasion, he was asked how Socrates died; and he made answer, " As I should wish to die myself." When Polyxenus, the Sophist, came to his house and beheld his women, and the costly preparation that was made for dinner, and then blamed him for all this luxury, Aristippus after a while said, " Can you stay with me to day?" and when Polyxenus consented, " Why then," said he, " did you blame me? it seems that you blame not the luxury, but the expense of it." When his servant was once carrying some money along the road, and was oppressed by the weight of it (as Bion relates in his Dissertations), he said to him, "Drop "what is beyond your strength, and only carry what you can." Once he was at sea, and seeing a pirate vessel at a distance, he began to count his money; and then he let it drop into the sea, as if unintentionally, and began to bewail his loss; but others say that he said besides, that it was better for the money to be lost for the sake of Aristippus, than Aristippus for the sake of his money. On one occasion, when Dionysius asked him why he had come, he said, to give others a share of what he had, and to receive a share of what he had not; but some report that his answer was, " When I wanted wisdom, j I went to Socrates; but now that I want money, I have come to you." He found fault with men, because when they are at sales, they examine the articles offered very carefully, but yet they approve of men's lives without any examination. Though some attribute this speech to Diogenes. They say that once at a banquet, Dionysius desired all the guests to dance in purple garments; but Plato refused, saying:—

" I could not wear a woman's robe, when I
Was born a man, and of a manly race."

But Aristippus took the garment, and when he was about to dance, he said very wittily:—

" She who is chaste, will not corrupted be
By Bacchanalian revels."

He was once asking a favour of Dionysius for a friend, and when he could not prevail, he fell at his feet; and when some one reproched him for such conduct, he said, " It is not I who am to blame, but Dionysius who has his ears in his feet." When he was staying in Asia, and was taken prisoner by Artaphernes the Satrap, some one said to him, " Are you still cheerful and sanguine?" " When, you silly fellow," he replied, " can I have more reason to be cheerful than now when I am on the point of conversing with Artaphernes?" It used to be a saying of his, that those who had enjoyed the encyclic course of education, but who had omitted philosophy, were like the suitors of Penelope; for that they gained over Melantho and Polydora and the other maid-servants, and found it easier to do that than to marry the mistress. And Ariston said in like manner, that Ulysses when he had gone to the shades below, saw and conversed with nearly all the dead in those regions, but could not get a sight of the Queen herself.

On another occasion, Aristippus being asked what were the most necessary things for well-born boys to learn, said, " Those things which they will put in practice when they become men." And when some one reproached him for having come from Socrates to Dionysius, bis reply was, " I went to Socrates because I wanted instruction *(ireudsTas),* and I have come to Dionysius because I want diversion *(imidi&i).* As he had made money by having pupils, Socrates once said to him, " Where did you get so much?" and he answered, " Where you got a little." When his mistress said to him, " I am in the family way by you," he said, " You can no more tell that, than you could tell, after you had gone through a thicket, which thorn had scratched you." And when some one blamed him for repudiating his son, as if he were not really his, he said, " I know that phlegm, and I know that lice, proceed from us, but still we cast them away as useless." One day, when he had received some money from Dionysius, and Plato had received a book, he said to a man who jeered him, " The fact is, money is what I want, and books what Plato wants." When he was asked what it was for which he was reproached by Dionysius, "The same thing," said he, "for which others reproach me." One day he asked Dionysius for some money, who said, " But you told me that a wise man would never be in want;" " Give me some," Aristippus rejoined, " and then we will discuss that point;" Dionysius gave him some, " Now then," said he, " you see that I do not want money." When Dionysius said to him;—

" For he who does frequent a tyrant's court,
Becomes his slave, though free when first he came:"

He took him up, and replied: —

" That man is but a slave who comes as free." This story is told by Diocles, in his book on the Lives of the Plutarch, in his life of Pompey, attributes these lines to Sophocles, but does not mention the play in which they occurred.

Philosophers; but others attribute the rejoinder to Plato. He once quarrelled with Machines, and presently afterwards said to him, " Shall we not make it up of our own accord, and cease this folly; but will you wait till some blockhead reconciles us over our cups?" " With all my heart," said Eschines. " Recollect, then," said Aristippus, " that I, who am older than you, have made the first advances." And iEschines answered, " You say well, by Juno, since you are far better than I; for I began the quarrel, but you begin the friendship." And these are the anecdotes which are told of him.

V. Now there were four people of the name of Aristippus; one, the man of whom we are now speaking; the second, the man who wrote the history of Arcadia; the third was one who, because he had been brought up by his mother, had the name of /i»irgo5/5aw-oj given to him; and he was the grandson of the former, being his daughter's son; the fourth was a philosopher of the New Academy.

VI. There are three books extant, written by the Cyrenaic philosopher, which are, a history of Africa, and which were sent by him to Dionysius; and there is another book containing twenty-five dialogues, some written in the Attic, and some in the Doric dialect. And these are the titles of the Dialogues— Artabazus; to the Shipwrecked Sailors; to the Exiles; to a Beg gar; to Lais; to Porus; to Lais about her Looking-glass; Mercury; the Dream; to the President of the Feast; Philomelus; to his Domestics; to those who reproached him for possessing old wine and mistresses; to those who reproached him for spending much money on his eating; a Letter to Arete his daughter; a letter to a man who was training himself for the Olympic games; a book of Questions; another book of Questions; a Dissertation addressed to Dionysius; an Essay on a Statue; an Essay on the daughter of Dionysius; a book addressed to one who thought himself neglected; another to one who attempted to give him advice. Some say, also, that he wrote six books of dissertations; but others, the chief of whom is Sosicrates of Rhodes, affirm that he never wrote a single thing. According to the assertions of Sotion in his second book; and of Panoetius, on the contrary, he composed the following books, — one concerning Education; one concerning Virtue; one called An Exhortation; Artabazus; the Shipwrecked Men; the Exiles; six books of Dissertations; three books of Apoph thegms; an essay addressed to Lais; one to Porus; one to Socrates; one on Fortune. And he used to define the chief good as a gentle motion tending to sensation. VII. But since we have-written his life, let us now speak of the Cyrenaics who came after him; some of whom called

' themselves Hegesiaci, some Annicerci, others Theodorei. And let us also enumerate the disciples of Phaedo, the chief of whom were the Eretrians. Now the pupils of Aristippus were his own daughter Arete, and iEthiops of Ptolemais, and Antipater of Cyrene. Arete had for her pupil the Aristippus who was surnamed */itirgodidan-og,* whose disciple was Theodorus the atheist, but who was afterwards called *hbg.* Antipater had for a pupil Epitimedes of Cyrene, who was the master of Pyraebates, who was the master of Hegesias, who was surnamed *KeieiQavaTog* (persuading to die), and of Anniceris who ransomed Plato.

VIII. These men then who continued in the school of Aristippus, and were called Cyrenaics, adopted the following opinions.—They said that there were two emotions of the mind, pleasure and pain; that the one, namely pleasure, was a moderate emotion; the other, namely pain, a rough one. And that no one pleasure was different from or more pleasant than another; and that pleasure was praised by all animals, but pain avoided. They said also that pleasure belonged to the body, and constituted its chief good, as Paraetius also tells us in his book on Sects; but the pleasure which they call the chief good, is not that pleasure as a state, which consists in the absence of all pain, and is a sort of undisturbedness, which is what Epicurus admits as such; for the Cyrenaics think that there is a distinction between the chief good and a life of happiness, for that the chief good is a particular pleasure, but that happiness is a state consisting of a number of particular pleasures, among which, both those which are past, and those which are future, are both enumerated. And they consider that particular pleasure is desirable for its own sake; but that happiness is desirable not for its own sake, but for that of the particular pleasure. And that the proof that pleasure is the chief good is that we are from our childhood attracted to it without any deliberate choice of our own; and that when we have obtained it, we do not seek anything further, and also that there is nothing which we avoid so much as we do its opposite, which is pain. And they assert, too, that pleasure is a good, even if it arises from the most unbecoming causes, as Hippobotus tells us in his Treatise on Sects; for even if an action be ever so absurd, still the pleasure which arises out of it is desirable, and a good.

Moreover, the banishment of pain, as it is called by Epicurus, appears to the Cyrenaics not to be pleasure; for neither is the absence of pleasure pain, for both pleasure and pain consist in motion; and neither the absence of pleasure nor the absence of pain are motion. In fact, absence of pain is a condition like that of a person asleep. They say also that it is possible that some persons may not desire pleasure, owing to some perversity of mind; and that all the pleasures and pains of the mind, do not all originate in pleasures and pains of the body, for that pleasure often arises from the mere fact of the prosperity of one's country, or from one's own; but they deny that pleasure is caused by either the recollection or the anticipation of good fortune—though Epicurus asserted that it was—for the motion of the mind is put an end to by time. They say, too, that pleasure is not caused by simple seeing or hearing. Accordingly we listen with pleasure to those who give a representation of lamentations; but we are pained when we see men lamenting in reality. And they called the absence of pleasure and of pain intermediate states; and asserted that corporeal pleasures were superior to mental ones, and corporeal sufferings worse than mental ones. And they argued that it was on this principle that offenders were punished with bodily pain; for they thought that to suffer pain was hard, but that to be pleased was more in harmony with the nature of man, on which account also they took more care of the body than of the mind.

And although pleasure is desirable for its own sake, still they admit that some of the efficient causes of it are often troublesome, and as such opposite to pleasure; so that they think that an assemblage of all the pleasures which produce happiness, is the most difficult thing conceivable. But they admit that every wise man does not live pleasantly, and that every bad man does not live unpleasantly, but that it is only a general rule admitting of some exceptions. And they think it sufficient if a person enjoys a happy time in consequence of one pleasure which befalls him. They say that prudence is a good, but is not desirable for its own sake, but for the sake of those things which result from it. That a friend is desirable for the sake of the use which we can make of him; for that the parts of the body also are loved while they are united to the body; and that some of the virtues may exist even in the foolish. They consider that bodily exercise contributes to the comprehension of virtue; and that the wise man will feel neither envy, nor love, nor superstition; for that the3e things originate in a fallacious opinion. They admit, at the same time, that he is liable to grief and fear, for that these are natural emotions. They said also that wealth is an efficient cause of pleasure, but that it is not desirable for its own sake. That the sensations are things which can be comprehended; but they limited this assertion to the sensations themselves, and did not extend it to the causes which produce them. They left out all investigation of the subjects of natural philosophy, because of the evident impossibility of comprehending them; but they applied themselves to the study of logic, because of its utility.

Meleager, in the second book of his Treatise on Opinions, and Clitomachus in the first book of his Essay on Sects says, that they thought natural philosophy and dialectics useless, for that the man who had learnt to understand the question of good and evil could speak with propriety, and was free from super- l stition, and escaped the fear of death, without either. They also taught that there was nothing naturally and intrinsically just, or honourable, or disgraceful; but that things were considered so because of law and fashion. The good man will do nothing out of the way, because of the punishments which are imposed on, and the discredit which is attached to, such actions: and that the good man is a wise man. They admit, too, that there is such a thing as improvement in philosophy, and in other good studies. And they say that one man feels grief more than another; and that the sensations are not always to be trusted as faithful guides.

IX. But the philosophers who were called Hegesiaci, adopted the same chief goods, pleasure and pain; and they denied that there was any such thing as gratitude, or friendship, or beneficence, because we do not choose any of those things for their own sake, but on account of the use of which they are, and on account of tbese other things which cannot subsist without them. But they teach that complete happiness cannot possibly exist; for that the body is full of many sensations, and that the mind sympathizes with the body, and is troubled when that is troubled, and also that fortune prevents many things which we cherished in anticipation; so that for all these reasons, perfect happiness eludes our grasp. Moreover, that both life and death are desirable. They also say that there is nothing naturally pleasant or unpleasant, but that owing to want, or rarity, or satiety, some men are pleased and some vexed; and that wealth and poverty have no influence at all on pleasure, for that rich men are not affected by pleasure in a different manner from poor men. In the same way they say that slavery and freedom are things indifferent, if measured by the standard of pleasure, and nobility and baseness of birth, and glory and infamy. They add that, for the foolish man it is expedient to Jive, but to the wise man it is a matter of indifference; and i that the wise man will do everything for his own sake; for that he will not consider any one else of equal importance with himself; and he will see that if he were to obtain ever such great advantages from any one else, they would not be equal i to what he could himself bestow. They excluded the sensations, inasmuch as they had no certain knowledge about them; but they recommended the doing of everything which appeared consistent with reason.

They asserted also that errors ought to meet with pardon; for that a man did not err intentionally, but because he was influenced by some external circumstance; and that one ought not to hate a person who has erred, but only to teach him better. They likewise said that the wise man would not be so much absorbed in the pursuit of what is good, as in the attempt to avoid what is bad, considering the chief good to be living free from all trouble and pain: and that this end was attained best by those who looked upon the efficient causes of pleasure as indifferent.

X. The Annicereans.in many respects, agreed with these last; but they admitted the existence in life of friendship and gratitude and respect forone's parents.and the principle of endeavouring to serve one's country. On which principle, even if the wise man should meet with some annoyance, he would be no less happy, even though he should have but few actual pleasures. They thought that the happiness of a friend was not to be desired by us for its own sake; for that in fact such happiness was not capable of being felt by the person's neighbour; and that reason is hot sufficient to give one confidence, and to authorise one to look down upon the opinions of the multitude; but that one must learn a deference for the sentiments of others by custom, because the opposite bad disposition being bred up with infirm and early age. They also taught that one ought not to make friends solely on account of the advantage that we may derive from them, and not discard them when these hopes or advantages fail; but that we ought rather to cultivate them on account of one's natural feelings of benevolence, in compliance with which we ought also to encounter trouble for their sakes, so that though they consider pleasure the chief good, and the deprivation of it an evil, still they think that a man ought voluntarily to submit to this deprivation out of his regard for his friend, XI. The Theodereans, as they are called, derived their name from the Theodorus who has been already mentioned, and adopted all his doctrines.

XII. Now Theodorus utterly discarded all previous opinions about the Gods: and we have met with a book of his which is entitled, On Gods, which is not to be despised; and it is i from that that they say that Epicurus derived the principall I portions of his sentiments. But Theodorus had been a pupil of Anniceris, and of Dionysius the Dialectician, as Antisthenes tells us in his Successions of Philosophers. XIII. He considered joy and grief as the chief goods: and that the former resulted from knowledge, and the latter from ignorance. And he called prudence and justice goods: the contrary qualities evils, and pleasure and pain something j " intermediate. He discarded friendship from his system, because it could not exist either in foolish men or in wise men. For that, in the case of the former, friendship / was at an end the moment that the advantage to be derived from it was out of sight. And that wise men were sufficient / for themselves, and so had no need of friends. He used also to say that it was reasonable for a good man not to expose himself to danger for the sake of his country, for that he ought not to discard his own prudence for the sake" of I benefiting those who had none. And he said that a wise man's country was the World. He allowed that a wise man might steal, and commit adultery and sacrilege, at proper seasons: for that none of these actions were disgraceful by nature, if one only put out of sight the common opinion about them, which owes its existence to the consent of fools. And he said that the wise man would indulge his passions openly, without any regard to circumstances: on which principle he used to ask the following questions: " Is a woman who is well instructed in literature of use just in proportion to the amount of her literary knowledge?" " Yes," said the person questioned. " And is a boy, and is a youth, useful in proportion to his acquaintance with literature?" " Yes." " Is not then, also, a beautiful woman useful in proportion as she is beautiful;, and a boy and a youth useful in proportion to their beauty?" " Yes. " " Well, then, a handsome boy and a handsome youth must be useful exactly in proportion as they are handsome 7" "Yes." "Now the use of beauty is, to be embraced." And when this was granted he pressed the argument thus:— If then a man embraces a woman just as it is useful that he should, he does not do wrong; nor, again, will he be doing wrong in employing beauty for the purposes for which it is useful. And with such questions as these he appeared to convince his hearers. XIV. But he appears to have got the uame of *tth* from Stilpo one day asking him, " Are you, Theodorus, what you say you are?" And when he said he was, " And you said that you are *hbg*" continued his questioner; he admitted that also. " Then," continued the other, " you are *hhg."* And as he willingly received the title, the other laughed and said, " But you, wretched man, according to this principle, you would also admit that you were a raven, or a hundred other things." One day Theodorus sat down by Euryclides the hierophant, and said to him, " Tell me now, Euryclides, who are they who behave impiously with respect to the mysteries?" And when Euryclides answered, " Those who divulge them to the uninitiated; " Then," said he, " you also are impious, for you divulge them to those who are not initiated." XV. And indeed he was very near being brought before the Areopagus if Demetrius of Phalereus had not saved him. But Amphicrates in his Essay on Illustrious Men, says that he was condemned to drink hemlock. XVI. While he was staving at the court of Ptolemy, the son of Lagus, he was sent once by him to Lysimachus as an ambassador. And as he was talking very freely, Lysimachus said to him, " Tell me, Theodorus, have not you been banished from Athens?" And he replied, you have been rightly informed; for the city of the Athenians could not bear me, just as Semele could not bear Bacchus; and so we were both cast out." And when Lysimachus said again, " Take care that you do not come to me again;" " I never will," he replied, " unless Ptolemy sends me." And as Mythras, the steward of Lysimachus was present, and said, " You appear to me to be the only person who ignores both Gods and Sovereigns;"

How," rejoined Theodorus, " can you say that I ignore the Gods, when I look upon you as their enemy? " XVII. They say also that on one occasion he came to Corinth, bringing with him a great many disciples; and that Metrocles the Cynic, who was washing leeks said so him, " You, who are a Sophist, would not have wanted so many pupils, if you had washed vegetables." And Theodorus, talcing him up, replied, " And if you had known how to associate with men, you would not have cared about those vegetables." But this rejoinder, as I have said already, is attributed both to Diogenes and Aristippus.

XVIII. Such was Theodorus, and such were his circumstances and opinions. But at last he went away to Cyrene, and lived there with Megas, being treated by him with the greatest distinction. And when he was first driven away from Cyrene, he is reported to have said very pleasantly, " You do wrong, 0 men of Cyrene, driving me from Africa to Greece." XIX. But there were twenty different people of the name of Theodorus. The first was a Samian, the son of Bhoeus; he it was who advised the putting of coals under the foundations of the temple of Diana at Ephesus; for as the ground was very swampy, he said that the coals, having got rid of their ligneous qualities, would retain their solidity in a way that could not be impaired by water. The second was a Cyrenean, a geometrician, and had Plato for one of his pupils. The third was the philosopher whom we have been describing. The fourth was an author who wrote a very remarkable treatise on the art of exercising the voice. The fifth was a man who wrote a treatise on Musicial Composers, beginning with Terpander. The sixth was a Stoic. The seventh was the historian of Borne. The eighth was a Syracusan, who wrote an Essay on Tactics. The ninth was a citizen of Byzantium, who was a political orator. The tenth was another orator, who is mentioned by Aristotle in his Epitome of the Orators. The eleventh was a Theban, a statuary. The twelfth was a painter, who is mentioned by Polemo. The thirteenth was also a painter, who is spoken of by Menodotus. The fourteenth was an Ephesian a painter, mentioned by Theophanes in his Essay on Painting. The fifteenth was an epigrammatic poet. The sixteenth wrote an essay on Poets. The seventeenth was a physician, a pupil of Athenaeas. The eighteenth was a Chian, a Stoic philosopher. The nineteenth was a citizen of Miletus, another Stoic. The twentieth was a tragic poet. LIFE OF PHGEDO.

I. Phosdo the Elean, one of the Eupatridae, was taken prisoner at the time of the subjugation of his country, and was compelled to submit to the vilest treatment. But while he was standing in the street, shutting the door, he met with Socrates, who desired Alcibiades, or as some say, Crito, to ransom him. And after that time he studied philosophy as became a free man. But Hieronymus, in his essay on suspending one's judgment, calls him a slave.

II. And he wrote dialogues, of which we have genuine copies; by name—Zopyrus, Simon, and Nicias (but the genuineness of this one is disputed); Medius, which some people attribute to iEschines, and others to Polyaenus; Antimachus, or the Elders (this too is a disputed one); the Scythian discourses, and these, too, some attribute to schines.

III. But his successor was Phistamus of Elis; and the next in succession to him were Menedemus of Eretria, and Asclepiades of Philias, who came over from Stilpo. And down to the age of these last, they were called the Eliac school; but after the time of Menedemus, they were called the Eretrians. And we will speak of Menedemus hereafter, because he was the founder of a new sect. LIFE OF EUCLIDES.

I. EucuDESwas anative of Megara on the Isthmus, or of Gela, according to some writers, whose statement is mentioned by Alexander in his Successions. He devoted himself to the study of the writings of Parmenides; and his successors were called the philosophers of the Megaric school; after that they were called the Contentious school, and still later, the Dialecticians, which name was first given to them by Dionysius the Carthaginian; because they carried on their investigations by question and answer. Hermodorus says that after the death of Socrates, Plato and the other philosophers came to Euclides, because they feared the cruelty of the tyrants.

II. He used to teach that the olfigt good is unity; but that it is known by several names; for at one time people call it prudence; at another time God; at another time intellect, and so on. But everything which was contrary to good, he discarded, denying its existence. And the proofs which he used to bring forward to support his arguments, were not those which proceed on assumptions, butj conclusion He also rejected all that sort of reasoning which proceeds on comparison,: saying that it must be founded either on things which are like,'j or on things which are unlike. If on things which are like,' then it is better to reason about the things themselves, thanj about those which resemble them; and if on things which are unlike, then the comparison is quite useless. And on this account Timon uses the following language concerning him, where he also attacks all the other philosophers of the Socratic school:—

But I do care for none of all these triflere,
Nor for any one else; not for your Phaedon,
Whoever he may be; not for the quarrelsome
Euclides, who bit all the Megareans
With love of fierce contention.

III. He wrote six dialogues—the Lamprias, the J5schines, the Phoenix, the Crito, the Alcibiades, and the Amatory dialogue.

IV. Next in succession to Euclides, came Eubulides of Miletus, who handed down a great may arguments in dialec H tics; such as the Lying one; the Concealed one; the Electra; the Veiled one; the Sorites; the Horned one; the Bald one. And one of the Comic poets speaks of him in the following terms:—

Eubulides, that most contentious sophist,
Asking his horned quibbles, and preplexing
The natives with his false arrogant speeches,
Has gone with all the fluency of Demosthenes.

For it seems that Demosthenes had been his pupil, and" that being at first unable to pronounce the C, he got rid of that defect. Eubulides had a quarrel with Aristotle, and was constantly attacking him.

V. Among the different people who succeeded Eubulides, was Alexinus of Elis, a man very fond of argument, on which account he was nicknamed 'EXsyivog. He had an especial quarrel with Zeno; and Hermippus relates of him that he went from Elis to Olympia, and studied philosophy there; and that when his pupils asked him why he lived there, he said that he wished to establish a school which should be called the Olympic school; but that his pupils being in distress, througb want of means of support, and finding the situation unhealthy for them, left him; and that after that Alexinus lived by himself, with only one servant. And after that, when swimming in the The French translator gives the following examples, to show what is meant by these several kinds of quibbling arguments:—

The *lying* one is this:—Is the man a liar who says that he tells lies. If he is, then he does not tell lies; and if he does not tell lies, is he a liar?

The *concealed*, one:—Do you know this man who is concealed? If you do not, you do not know your own father; for he it is who is concealed.

The *veiled* one is much the same as the preceding.

The *electra* is a quibble of the same kind as the two preceding ones: Electra sees Orestes: she knows that Orestes is her brother, but does not know that the man she sees is Orestes; therefore she does know, and does not know, her brother at the same time.

The *Sorites* is universally known.

The *bald* one is a kind of Sorites; pulling one hair out of a man's head will not make him bald, nor two, nor three, and so on till every hair in his head is pulled out.

The *horned* one:—You have what you have not lost. You have not lost horns, therefore you have horns.
t From iXfyYWi to confute.
Alpheus, he was pricked by a reed, and the injury proved fatal, and he died. And we have written an epigram on him which runs thus:—

Then the report, alas! was true, That an unhappy man,
While swimming tore his foot against a nail;
For the illustrious sage,
Good Alexinus, swimming in the Alpheus, '
Died from a hostile reed.

And he wrote not only against Zeno, but he composed other works also, especially one against Ephorus the historian.

VI. One of the school of Eubulides was Euphantus of Olynthus, who wrote a history of the events of his own time; he also composed several tragedies, for which he got great distinction at the festivals. And he was the preceptor of Antigonus, the king to whom he dedicated a treatise on Monarchy, which had an exceedingly high reputation. And at last he died of old age. VII. There are also other pupils of Eubulides, among whom is Apollonius Cronus, who was the preceptor of Diodorus of Iasos, the son of Aminias; and he too was surnamed Cronus, and is thus mentioned by Callimachus in his epigrams:—
Momus himself did carve upon the walls,
Cronus is wise.

And he was a dialectician, and, as some believe, he was the first person who invented the Concealed argument, and the Horned one. When he was staying at the court of Ptolemy Soter, he had several dialectic questions put to him by Stilpo; and as he was not able to solve them at the moment, he was reproached by the king with many hard words, and among other things, he was nicknamed Cronus, out of derision. So he left the banquet, and wrote an essay on the question of Stilpo, and then died of despondency. And we have written the following epigram on him:— 0 Diodorus Cronus, what sad fate Buried you in despair?
So that you hastened to the shades below,
Perplexed by Stilpo's quibbles—
Tou would deserve your name of Cronus better,
If C and r were gone.
Kpovoe, take away K. p., leaves *ovog,* an ass. VIII. One of the successors of Euclides was Icthyas, the son of Metellus, a man of great eminence, to whom Diogenes the Cynic addressed a dialogue. And Clinomachus of Therium, who was the first person who ever wrote about axioms and categorems, and things of that kind. And Stilpo the Megarian, a most illustrious philosopher, whom we must now speak of. LIFE OF STILPO.

I. Stilpo, a native of Megara in Greece, was a pupil of some of Euclides' school. But some say that he was a pupil of Euclides himself. And also of Thrasymachus, the Corinthian, who was a friend of Icthyas, as He,raclides informs us.

II. And he was so much superior to all his fellows in command of words and in acuteness, that it may almost be said that all Greece fixed its eyes upon him, and joined the Megaric school. And concerning him Philippus o.f Megara speaks thus, word for word:—" For he carried off from Theophrastus, Metrodorus the speculative philosopher, and Timagoras of Gela; and Aristotle the Cyrenaic, he robbed of Clitarchus and Simias; and from the dialecticians' school also he won men over, carrying off Poeoneius from Aristides, and Dippilus of the Bosphorus from Euphantus, and also Myrmex of the Venites, who had both come to him to argue against him, but they became converts and his disciples." And besides these men, he attracted to his school Phrasidemus the Peripatetic, a natural philosopher of great ability; and Alcimus the rhetorician, the most eminent orator in all Greece at that time; and he won over Crates, and great numbers of others, and among them Zeno the Phoenician. III. And he was very fond of the study of politics. And he was married. But he lived also with a courtesan, named Nicarete, as Onetor tells us somewhere. And he had a licentious daughter, who was married to a friend of his named Simias, a citizen of Syracuse. And as she would not live in an orderly manner, some one told Stilpo that she was a disgrace to him. But he said, " She is not more a disgrace to me than I am an honour to her." IV. Ptolemy Soter, it is said, received him with great honour; and when he had made himself master of Megara, he gave him money, and invited him to sail with him to Egypt. But he accepted only a moderate sum of money, and declined the journey proposed to him, but went over to Egina, until Ptolemy had sailed. Also when Demetrius, the son of Antigonus had taken Megara, he ordered Stilpo's house to he saved, and took care that everything that had been plundered from him should be restored to him. But when he wished Stilpo to give him in a list of all that he had lost, he said that he had lost nothing of his own; for that no one had taken from him his learning, and that he still had his eloquence and his knowledge. And he conversed with Demetrius on the subject of doing good to men with such power, that he became a zealous hearer of his.

V. They say that he once put such a question as this to a man, about the Minerva of Phidias:—" Is Minerva the Goddess the daughter of Jupiter?" And when the other said, " Yes;" " But this," said he, " is not the child of Jupiter, but of Phidias." And when he agreed that it was so—" This then," he continued, " is not a God." And when he was brought before the Areopagus for this speech, he did not deny it, but maintained that he had spoken correctly; for that she was not a God *(hog)* but a Goddess *(ha)* ; for that Gods were of the male sex only. However the judges of the Areopagus ordered him to leave the city; and on this occasion, Theodorus, who was nicknamed *hbg,* said in derision, " Whence did Stilpo learn this? and how could he tell whether she was a God or a Goddess? " But Theodorus was in truth a most impudent fellow. But Stilpo was a most witty and elegant-minded man. Accordingly when Crates asked him if the Gods delighted in adoration and prayer; they say that he answered, " Do not ask these questions, you foolish man, in the road, but in private." And they say too that Bion, when he was asked whether there were any Gods, answered in the same spirit:—

" Will you not first, 0 I miserable old man,
Remove the multitude *V*

VI. But Stilpo was a man of simple character, and free from all trick and humbug, and universally affable. Accord The quibble here is, that *9tbg* is properly only masculine, though it is sometimes used as feminine.
ingly, when Crates the Cynic once refused to answer a question that he had put to him, and only insulted his questioner— " I knew," said Stilpo, " that he would say anything rather than what he ought. And once he put a question to him, and offered him a fig at the same time; so he took the fig and ate it, on which Crates said, " 0 Hercules, I have lost my fig." " Not only that," he replied, " but you have lost your question too, of which the fig was the pledge." At another time, he saw Crates shivering in the winter, and said to him, " Crates, you seem to me to want a new dress," meaning, both a new mind and a new garment; and Crates, feeling ashamed, answered him in the following parody:—

" There Stilpo too, through the Megarian bounds,
Pours out deep groans, where Syphon's voice resounds,
And there he oft doth argue, while a school
Of eager pupils owns his subtle rule,
And virtue's name with eager chase pursues."

And it is said that at Athens he attracted all the citizens to such a degree, that they used to run from their workshops to look at him; and when some one said to him, " Why, Stilpo, they wonder at you as if you were a wild beast," he replied, " Not so; but as a real genuine man." VII. And he was a very clever arguer; and rejected the theory of species. And he used to say that a person who spoke of man in general, was speaking of nobody; for that he was not speaking of this individual, nor of that one; for speaking in general, how can he speak more of this person than of that person? therefore he is not speaking of this person at all. Another of his illustrations was, " That which is shown to me, is not a vegetable; for a vegetable existed ten thousand years ago, therefore this is not a vegetable." And they say that once when he was conversing with Crates, he interrupted the discourse to go off and buy some fish; and as Crates tried to drag him back, and said, " You are leaving the argument; " " Not at all," he replied," " I keep the argument, but I am leaving you; for the argument remains, but the fish will be sold to some one else." VIII. There are nine dialogues of his extant, written in a frigid style: The Moschus; the Cnistippus or Callias; the The Greek is a parody on the descriptions of Tantalus and Sisyphus. Horn. Od. ii. 581, 592. See also, Dryden's Version, B. ii. 719.

Ptolemy; the Choerecrates; the Metrocles; the Anaximenes; the Epigenes; the one entitled To my Daughter, and the Aristotle.

IX. Heraclides affirms that Zeno, the founder of the Stoic school, had been one of his pupils.

X. Hermippus says that he died at a great age, after drinking some wine, in order to die more rapidly. And we have written this epigram upon him:—

Stranger, old age at first, and then disease,
A hateful pair, did lay wise Stilpo low.
The pride of Megara: he found good wine
The best of drivers for his mournful coach,
And drinking it, he drove on to the end.

And he was ridiculed by Sophibus the comic poet, in his play called Marriages:—

The dregs of Stilpo make the whole dicourse of this Charinus.

LIFE OF CEITO.

I. Crito was an Athenian. He looked upon Socrates with the greatest affection; and paid such great attention to him, that he took care that he should never be in want of anything.

II. His sons also were all constant pupils of Socrates, and their names were Critobulus, Hermogenes, Epigenes, and Ctesippus. III. Crito wrote seventeen dialogues, which were all published in one volume; and I subjoin their titles:—That men are not made good by Teaching; on Superfluity; what is Suitable, or the Statesman; on the Honourable; on doing ill; on Good Government; on Law; on the Divine Being; on Arts; on Society; Protagoras, or the Statesman; on Letters; on Polititical Science; on the Honourable; on Learning; on Knowledge; on Science; on what Knowledge is. LIFE OF SIMON.

I. Simon was an Athenian, a leather-cutter. He, whenever Socrates came into his workshop and conversed, used to make memorandums of all his sayings that he recollected.

II. And from this circumstance, people have called his dialogues leathern ones. But he has written thirty-three which, however, are all combined in one volume:—On the Gods; on the Good; on the Honourable; what the Honourable is; the first Dialogue on Justice; the second Dialogue on Justice; on Virtue, showing that it is not to be taught; the first Dialogue on Courage; the second; the third; on Laws; on the Art of Guiding the People; on Honour; on Poetry, on Good Health; on Love; on Philosophy: on Knowledge; on Music; on Poetry; on what the Honourable is; on Teaching; on Conversation; on Judgment; on the Existent; on Number; on Diligence; on Activity: on Covetousness; on Insolence; on the Honourable; Some also add to these dialogues; on taking Counsel; on Reason or Suitableness; on doing Harm. III. He is, as some people say, the first writer who reduced the conversations of Socrates into the form of dialogues. And when Pericles offered to provide for him, and invited him to come to him, he said that he would not sell his freedom of speech.

IV. There was also another Simon, who wrote a treatise on Oratorical Art. And another, who was a physician in the time of Seleucus Nicanor. And another, who was a statuary. LIFE OF GLAUCO.

Glauco was an Athenian; and there are nine dialogues of his extant, which are all contained in one volume. The Phidylus; the Euripides; the Amyntichias; the Euthias; the Lysithides; the Aristophanes; the Cephalus; the Anaxiphemus; the Minexenus. There are thirty-two others which go under his name, but they are spurious.

LIFE OF SIM1AS.

Simeas was a Theban; and tbere are twenty-three dialogues of his extant, contained in one single volume. On Wisdom; on Ratiocination; on Music; on Verses; on Fortitude; on Philosophy; on Truth; on Letters; on Teaching; on Art; on Government; on what is Becoming; on what is Eligible, and what Proper to be Avoided; on A Friend; on Knowledge; on the Soul; on Living Well; on what is Possible; on Money; on Life; on what the Honourable is; on Industry, and on Love.

LIFE OF CEBES.

Cebes was a Theban, and there are three dialogues of his extant. The Tablet; the Seventh, and the Phrynichus.

LIFE OF MENEDEMUS.

I. This Menedemus was one of those who belonged to the school of Phaedo; and he was one of those who are called Theoprobidae, being the son of Clisthenes, a man of noble family, but a poor man and a builder. And some say that he was a tent-maker, and that Menedemus himself learned both trades. On which account, when he on one occasion brought forward a motion for some decree, a man of the name of Alexinius attacked him, saying that a wise man had no need to draw a tent nor a decree.

II. But when Menedemus was sent by the Eretrians to Megara, as one of the garrison, he deserted the rest, and went to file Academy to Plato; and being charmed by him, he abandoned the army altogether. And when Asclepiades, the Phliasian, drew him over to him, he went and lived in Megara, near Stilpo, and they both became his disciples. And from thence they sailed to Elis, where they joined Anchipylus and Moschus, who belonged to Phaedo's school. And up to this time, as I have already mentioned in my account of Phaido, they were called Eleans; and they were also called Eretrians, from the native country of Menedemus, of whom I am now speaking. III. Now Menedemus appears to have been a very severe and rigid man, on which account Crates, parodying a description, speaks of him thus:—

And Asclepiades the sage of Phliua,
And the Eretrian bull.

And Timon mentions him thus:—

Rise up, you frowning, bristling, frothy sage.

And he was a man of such excessive rigour of principle, that when Eurylochus, of Cassandra, had been invited by Antigonus, to come to him in company with Cleippides, a youth of Cyzicus, he refused to go, for he was afraid lest Menedemus should hear of it; for he was very severe in his reproofs, and very free spoken. Accordingly, when a young man behaved with boldness towards him, he did not say a word, but took a bit of stick and drew on the floor an insulting picture"; until the young man, perceiving the insult that was meant in the presence of numbers of people, went away. And when Hierocles, the governor of the Piraeus, attacked him in the temple of Amphiaraus, and said a great deal about the taking of Eretria, he made no other reply beyond asking him what Antigonus's object was in treating him as he did.

On another occasion, he said to a profligate man who was giving himself airs, " Do not you know that the cabbage is not the only plant that has a pleasant juice, but that radishes have it also?" And once, hearing a young man talk very loudly, he said, " See whom you have behind you." When Antigonus consulted him whether he should go to a certain revel, he made no answer beyond desiring those who brought him the message, to tell him that he was the son of a king. When a stupid fellow once said something at random to him, he asked him whether he had a farm; and when he said that he had, and a large stock of cattle, he said, " Go then and look after them; lest, if you neglect them, you lose them, and that elegant rusticity of yours with them.'' He was once asked whether a good man should marry, and his reply was, " Do I seem to you to be a good man, or not?" and when the other said he did; " Well," said he, " and I am married." On one occasion a person said that there were a great many good things, so he asked him how many; and whether he thought that there were more than a hundred. And as he could not bear the extravagance of one man who used frequently to invite him to dinner, once when he was invited he did not say a single word, but admonished him of his extravagance in silence, by eating nothing but olives.

IV. On account then of the great freedom of speech in which he indulged, he was very near while in Cyprus, at the court of Nicorreon, being in great danger with his friend Asclepiades. For when the king was celebrating a festival at the beginning of the month, and had invited them as he did all the other philosophers; Menedemus said, " If the assemblage of such men as are met here to-day is good, a festival like this ought to be celebrated every day: but if it is not good, even once is too often." And as the tyrant made answer to this speech, " that he kept this festival in order to have leisure in it to listen to the philosophers," he behaved with even more austerity than usual, arguing, even while the feast was going on, that it was right on every occasion to listen to philosophers; and he went on in this way till, if a flute-player had not interrupted their discussion, they would have been put to death. In reference to which, when they were overtaken by a storm in a ship, they say that Asclepiades said, " that the fine playing of a flute-player had saved them, but the freedom of speech of Menedemus had ruined them.

V. But he was, they say, inclined to depart a good deal from the usual habits and discipline of a school, so that he never regarded any order, nor were the seats arranged around properly, but every one listened to him while lecturing, standing up or sitting down, just as he might chance to be at the moment, Menedemus himself setting the example of this irregular conduct.

VI. But in other respects, it is said that he was a nervous man, and very fond of glory; so that, as previously he and Asclepiades had been fellow journeymen of a builder, when Asclepiades was naked on the roof carrying mortar, Menedemus would stand in front of him to screen him when he saw any one coming. VII. When he applied himself to politics he was so nervous, that once, when setting down the incense, he actually missed the incense burner. Aud on one occasion, when Crates was standing by him, and reproaching him for meddling with politics, he ordered some men to put him in prison. But he, even then, continued not the less to watch him as he passed, and to stand on tiptoe and call him Agamemnon and Hegesipolis. VIII. He was also in some degree superstitious. Accordingly, once, when he was at an inn with Asclepiades, and had unintentionally eaten some meat that had been thrown away, when he was told of it he became sick, and turned pale, until Asclepiades rebuked him, telling him that it was not the meat itself which disturbed him, but only the idea that he had adopted. But in other respects he was a high minded man, with notions such as became a gentleman. IX. As to his habit of body, even when he was an old man he retained all the firmness and vigour of an athlete, with firm flesh, and a ruddy complexion, and very stout and fresh looking. In stature he was of moderate size; as is plain from the statue of him which is at Eretria, in the Old Stadium. For he is there represented seated almost naked, undoubtedly for the purpose of displaying the greater part of his body.

X He was very hospitable and fond of entertaining his friends; and because Eretria was unhealthy, he used to have a great many parties, particularly of poets and musicians. And he was very fond of Aratus and Lycophon the tragic poet, and Antagoras of Rhodes. And above all he applied himself to the study of Homer; and next to him to that of the Lyric poets; then to Sophocles, and also to Achaeus, to whom he assigned the second place as a writer of satiric dramas, giving iEschylus the first. And it is from Achaeus that he quoted these verses against the politicians of the opposite party:—

A speedy runner once was overtaken
By weaker men than he. An eagle too, i
Was beaten by a tortoise in a race.

And these lines are out of the satiric play of Achaeus, called Omphale; so that they are mistaken who say that he had never read anything but the Medea of Euripides, which is found, they add, in the collection of Neophron, the Sicyonian.

XI. Of masters of philosophy, he used to despise Plato and Xenocrates, and Paraebates of Cyrene; and admired no one but Stilpo. And once, being questioned about him, he said nothing more of him than that he was a gentleman.

XII. Menedemus was not easy to be understood, and in his conversation he was hard to argue against; he spoke on every subject, and had a great deal of invention and readiness. But he was very disputatious, as Antisthenes says in his Successions; and he used to put questions of this sort, " Is one thing different from another thing?" " Yes." " And is benefiting a person something different from the good?" " Yes." " Then the good is not benefiting a person." And he, as it Is said, discarded all negative axioms, using none but affirmative ones; and of these he only approved of the simple ones, and rejected all that were not simple; saying that they were intricate and perplexing. But Heraclides says that in his doctrines he was a thorough discipleof Plato,and that he scorned dialectics; so that once when Alexinus asked him whether he had left off beating his father, he said, " I have not beaten him, and I have not left off;" and when he said further that he ought to put an end to the doubt by answering explicitly yes or no, " It would be absurd," he rejoined, " to comply with your conditions, when I can stop you at the entrance."

When Bion was attacking the soothsayers with great perseverance, he said that he was killing the dead over again. And once, when he heard some one assert that the greatest good was to succeed in everything that one desires; he said, " It is a much greater good to desire what is proper." But Antigonus of Carystus, tells us that he never wrote or composed any work, and never maintained any principle tenaciously. But in cross-questioning he was so contentious as to get quite black in the face before he went away. But though he was so violent in his discourse, he was wonderfully gentle in his actions. Accordingly, though he used to mock and ridicule Alexinus very severely, still he conferred great benefits on him, conducting his wife from Delphi to Chalcis for him, as she was alarmed about the danger of robbers and banditti in the road.

XIII. And he was a very warm friend, as is plain from his attachment to Asclepiades; which was hardly inferior to the friendship of Pylades and Orestes. But Asclepiades was the elder of the two, so that it was said that he was the poet, and Meuedemus the actor. And they say that on one occasion, Archipolis bequeathed them three thousand pieces of money between them, they had such a vigorous contest as to which should take the smaller share, that neither of them would receive any of it. XIV. It is said that they were both married; and that Asclepiades was married to the mother, and Menedemus to the daughter; and when Asclepiades's wife died, he took the wife of Menedemus; and Menedemus, when he became the chief man of the state, married another who was rich; and as they still maintained one house in common, Menedemus entrusted the whole management of it to his former wife. Asclepiades died first at Eretria, being of a great age; having lived with Menedemus with great economy, though they had ample means. So that, when on one occasion, after the death of Asclepiades, a friend of his came to a banquet, and when the slaves refused him admittance, Menedemus ordered them to admit him, saying that Asclepiades opened the door for him, even now that he was under the earth. And the men who chiefly supported them were Hyporicus the Macedonian, and Agetor the Lamian. And Agetor gave each of them thirty minae, and Hipporicus gave Menedemus two thousand drachmas to portion his daughters with; and he had three, as Heraclides tells us, the children of his wife, who was a native of Oropus.

XV. And he used to give banquets in this fashion: —First of all, he would sit at dinner, with two or three friends, till late in the day; and then he would invite in any one who came to see him, even if they had already dined; and if any one came too soon, they would walk up and down, and ask those who came out of the house what there was on the table, and what o'clock it was; and then, if there were only vegetables or salt fish, they would depart; but if they heard it was meat, they would go in. And during the summer, mats of rushes were laid upon the couches, and in winter soft cushions; and each guest was expected to bring a pillow for himself. And the cup that was carried round did not hold more than a cotyla. And the second course consisted of lupins or beans, and sometimes fruits, such as pears, pomegranates, pulse, and sometimes, by Jove, dried figs. And all these circumstances are detailed by Lycophron, in his satiric dramas, which he inscribed with the name of Menedemus, making his play a panegyric on the philosopher. And the following are some of the lines:—

After a temperate feast, a small-sized cup
Is handed round with moderation due;
And conversation wise makes the dessert.

XVI. At first, now, he was not thought much of, being called cynic and trifler by the Eretrians; but subsequently, he was so much admired by his countrymen, that they entrusted him with the chief government of the state. And he was sent on embassies to Ptolemy and Lysimachus, and was greatly honoured everywhere. He was sent as envoy to Demetrius; and, as the city used to pay him two hundred talents a year, he persuaded him to remit fifty. And having been falsely accused to him, as having betrayed the city to Ptolemy, he defended himself from the charge, in a letter which begins thus:—

" Menedemus to king Demetrius.—Health. I hear that information has been laid before you concerning us.".. And the tradition is, that a man of the name of iEschylus, who was one of the opposite party in the state, was in the habit of making these false charges. It is well known too that he was sent on a. most important embassy to Demetrius, on the subject of Oropus, as Euphantus relates in his History.

XVII. Antigonus was greatly attached to him, and professed himself his pupil; and when he defeated the barbarians, near Lysimachia, Menedemus drew up a decree for him, in simple terms, free from all flattery, which begins thus:—

" The generals and councillors have determined, since king Antigonus has defeated the barbarians in battle, and has returned to his own kingdom, and since he has succeeded in all his measures according to his wishes, it has seemed good to the council and to the people. "... And from these circumstances, and because of his friendship for him, as shown in other matters, he was suspected of betraying the city to him; and being impeached by Aristodemus, he left the city, and returned to Oropus, and there took up his abode in the temple of Amphiaraus; and as some golden goblets which were there were lost, he was ordered to depart by a general vote of the Boeotians. Leaving Oropus, and being in a state of great despondency, he entered his country secretly; and taking with him his wife and daughters, he went to the court of Antigonus, and there died of a broken heart

But Heraclides gives an entirely different account of him; saying, that while he was the chief councillor of the Eretrians, he more than once preserved the liberties of the city from those who would have brought in Demetrius the tyrant; so that he never could have betrayed the city to Antigonus, and the accusation must have been false; and that he went to the court of Antigonus, and endeavoured to effect the deliverance of his country; and as he could make no impression on him, he fell into despondency, and starved himself for seven days, and so he died. And Antigonus of Carystus gives a similar account: and Persaeus was the only man with whom he had an implacable quarrel; for he thought that when Antigonus himself was willing to re-establish the democracy among the Eretrians for his sake, Persaeus prevented him. And on this account Menedemus once attacked him at a banquet, saying many other things, and among them, " He may, indeed, be a philosopher, but he is the worst man that lives or that ever will live." XVIII. And he died, according to Heraclides, at the age of seventy-four. And we have written the following epigram on him:—

I've heard your fate, 0 Menedemus, that of your own accord,
You starved yourself for seven days and died;
Acting like an Eretrian, but not much like a man,
For spiritless despair appears your guide.

These men then were the disciples of Socrates, and their successors; but we must now proceed to Plato, who founded the Academy; and to his successors, or at least to all those of them who enjoyed any reputation.

BOOK III. LIFE OF PLATO.
I. Plato was the son of Ariston and Perictione;or Petone, and a citizen of Athens; and his mother traced her family back to §olon; for Solon had a brother named Diopidas, who had a son named Critias, who was the father of Calloeschrus, who was the father of that Critias who was one of the thirty tyrants and also of Glaucon, who was the father cf Charmides and Perictione. And she became the mother of Plato by her husband Ariston, Plato being the sixth in descent from Solon. And Solon traced his pedigree up to Neleus and Neptune. They say too that on the father's side, he was descended from Codrus, the son of Melanthus, and they too are said by Thrasylus to derive their origin from Neptune. And Speusippus, in his book which is entitled the Funeral Banquet of Plato, and Clearchus in his Panegyric on Plato, and Anaxilides in the second book of his History of Philosophers, say that the report at Athens was that Perictione was very beautiful, and that Ariston endeavoured to violate her and did not succeed; and that he, after he had desisted from his violence saw a vision of Apollo in a dream, in consequence of which he abstained from approaching his wife till after her confinement.

II. And Plato was born, as Apollodorus says in his Chronicles, in the eighty-eighth Olympiad, on the seventh day of the month Thargelion, on which day the people of Delos say that Apollo also was born. And he died, as Hermippus says, at a marriage feast, in the first year of the hundred and eighth Olympiad, having lived eighty-one years. But Neanthes says that he was eighty-four years of age at his death. He is then younger than Isocrates by six years; for Isocrates was born in the archonship of Lysimacbus, and Plato in that of Aminias, in which year Pericles died. III. And he was of the borough of Colytus, as Antileon tells us in his second book on Dates. And he was born, according to some writers, in iEgina, in the house of Phidiades the son of Thales, as Pharqrinus affirms in his Universal History, as his father had been sent thither with several others as a settler, and returned again to Athens when the settlers were driven out by the Lacedaemonians, who came to the assistance of the JEginetans. And he served the office of choregus at Athens, when Dion was at the expense of the spectacle exhibited, as Theodorus relates in the eighth book of his Philosophical Conservations. IV. And he had brothers, whose names were Adimantus and Glaucon, and a sister called Petone, who was the mother of Speusippus.

V. And he was taught learning in the school of Dionysius, whom he mentions in his Eival Lovers. And he learnt gymnastic exercises under the wrestler Ariston of Argos. And it was by him that he had the name of Plato given to him instead of his original name, on account of his robust figure, as he had previously been called Aristocles, after the name of his' grandfather, as Alexander informs us in his Successions. But some say that he derived this name from the breadth *(irXiTvTrig)* of his eloquence, or else because he was very wide *(irXariig)* across the forehead, as Neanthes affirms There are some also, among whom is Dicaearchus in the first volume on Lives, who say that he wrestled at the Isthmian games.

VI. It is also said that he applied himself to the study of painting, and that he wrote poems, dithyrambics at first, and afterwards lyric poems and tragedies. VII. But haiada very weak voice, they say; and the same fact is stated by Timotheus the Athenian, in his book on Lives. And it is said that Socrates in a dream saw a cygnet on his knees, who immediately put forth feathers, and flew up on high, uttering a sweet note, and that the next day Plato came to him, and that he pronounced him the bird which he had seen. VIII. And he used to philosophize at first in the Academy, and afterwards in the garden near Colonus, as Alexander tells us in his Successions, quoting the testimony of Heraulitus; and subsequently, though he was about to contend for the prize in tragedy in the theatre of Bacchus, after he had heard the discourse of Socrates, he learnt his poems, saying:—
Vulcan, come here; for Plato wants your aid.

And from henceforth, as they say, being now twenty years old, he became a pupil of Socrates. And when he was gone, he attached himself to Crattlus, the disciple of Heraclitus, and to Hermogenes, who ha3adopted the principles of Parmenides. AfterwardsTwhen he was eight and twenty years of age, as Hermodorus tells us, he withdrew to Megara to Euclid, with certain others of the pupils of Socrates; and subsequently, he went to Cyrene to Xheodorus the mathematician; and from thence he proceeded to Italy to the Pythagoreans, Philolaus and Eurytus, and from thence he went to Eurytus to the priests there; and having fallen sick at that place, he was cured by the priests by the application of sea water, in reference to which he said:—

The sea doth wash away all human evils.

And he said too, that, according to Homer, all the Egyptians were physicians. Plato had also formed the idea of making the acquaintance of the Magi; but he abandoned it on account of the wars in Asia.

IX. And when he returned to Athens, he settled in the Academy, and that is a suburban place of exercise planted like a grove, so named from an ancient hero named Hecademus, as. Eupolis tells us in his Discharged Soldiers.
In the well-shaded walks, protected well
By Godlike Academus.

And Timon, with reference to Plato, says:—

A man did lead them on, a strong stout man,
A honeyed speaker, sweet as melody
Of tuneful grasshopper, who, seated high
On Hecademus' tree, unwearied sings.

For the word academy was formerly spelt with E. Now our philosopher was a friend of Isocrates; and Praxiphanes composed an account of a conversation which took place between them, on the subject of poets, when Isocrates was staying with Plato in the country.

X. And Aristoxenus says that he was three times engaged in military expeditions; once against Tanagra; the second time against Corinth, and the third time at Delium; and that in the battle of Delium he obtained the prize of pre-eminent valour. He combined the principles of the schools of Hera
' I 2 ". clitus, and Pythagoras and Socrates; for he used to philosophize on those things which are the subjects of sensation, according to the system of Heraclitus; on those with which intellect is conversant, according to that of Pythagoras; and on politics, according to that of Socrates.

XI. And some people, (of whom Satyrus is one,) say that he sent a commission to Sicily to Dion, to buy him three books c of Pythagoras from Philolaus for a hundred minae; for they say that he was in very easy circumstances, having received from Dionysius more than eighty talents, as Dnetor also asserts in his treatise which is entitled, Whether a wise Man ought to acquire Gains. XII. And he was much assisted by Epicharmus the comic poet, a great part of whose works he transcribed, as Alcinus says in his essays addressed to Amyntas, of which there are four. And in the first of them he speaks as follows:—" And Plato appears to utter a great many of the sentiments of Epicharmus. Let us just examine. Plato says that that is an object of sensation, which is never stationary either as to its quality or its quantity, but which is always flowing and changing; as, for instance, if one take from any objects all number, then one cannot affirm that they are either equal, or of any particular things, or of what quality or quantity they are. And these things are of such a kind that they are always being produced, but that they never have any invariable substances." But that is a subject for intellect from which nothing is taken, and to which nothing is added. And this is the nature of things eternal, which is always similar and the same. And, indeed, Epicharmus speaks intelligibly on the subject of what is perceived by the senses and by the intellect:— A. But the great Gods were always present, nor
Did they at any moment cease to be;
    And their peculiar likeness at all times
Do they-retain, by the same principles.
B. Yet chaos is asserted to have been
The first existent Deity.
A. How can that be?
For 'tis impossible that we should find
Any first principle arise from anything.
B. Is there then no first principle at all?
A. Nor second either in the things we speak of; But thus it is—if to an even number,
Or e'en an odd one, if you so prefer it,
You add a unit, or if you deduct one,
Say will the number still remain the same?
B. Certainly not.
A. So, if you take a measure
A cubit long, and add another cubit,
Or cut a portion off, the measure then
No longer is the same?
B. Of course it is not A. Now turn your eyes and thoughts upon mankind—
We see one grows, another perishes:
So that they all exist perpetually
In a condition of transition. That
Whose nature changes must be different
' At each successive moment, from the thing
It was before. So also, you and I
Are different people now from what we were
But yesterday; and then, again, to-morrow
We shall be different from what we're now;
So that, by the same rule, we're always different.

And Alcinus speaks as follows: —
" The wise men say that the soul perceives some things by means of the body, as for instance, when it hears and sees; but that it also perceives something by its own power, without availing itself at all of the assistance of the body. On which account existent things are divisible into objects of sensation and objects of understanding. On account of which Plato used to say, that those who wished to become acquainted with the principles of everything, ought first of all to divide the ideas as he calls them, separately, such as similarity, and unity, and multitude, and magnitude, and stationariness, and motion. And secondly, that they ought to form a notion of the honourable and the good, and the just, and things of that sort, by themselves, apart from other considerations. And thirdly, that they ought to ascertain the character of such ideas as are relative to one another, such as knowledge, or magnitude, or authority; considering that the things which come under our notice from partaking of their nature, have the same names that they have. I mean that one calls that just which partakes of the just; and that beautiful which partakes of the beautiful. And each of these primary species is eternal, and is to be understood by the intellect, and is not subject to the influence of external circumstances. On which account he says, that ideas exist in nature as models; and that all other things are

like them, and, as it were, copies of them. Accordingly Epicharmus speaks thus about the good, and about the ideas.

A. Tell me, ia flute-playing now a tiling at all? B. Of course it is. A. Is man then flute-playing? B. No, nothing of the sort. A. Well, let us see—.
What is a flute-player? what think you now
Of him—is he a man, or is he not?
B. Of course he is a man.
A. Think you not then
The case is just the same about the good.
That the good is something by itself, intrinsic,
And he who's learnt, does at once become
Himself a good man? just as he who's learnt
Flute-playing is a flute-player; or dancing,
A dancer; weaving, a weaver. And in short,
Whoever learns an art, does not become
The art itself, but just an artist in it.

Plato, in his theory of Ideas, says, " That since there is such a thing as memory, the ideas are in existent things, because memory is only conversant about what is stable and enduring; and that no other thing is durable except ideas, for in what way," he continues, " could animals be preserved, if they had no ideas to guide them, and if, in addition to them, they had not an intellect given to them by nature?" But as it is they recollect similitudes, and also their food, so as to know what kind of food is fit for them; which they learn because the notion of similarity is implanted naturally in every animal; owing to which notion they recognize those of the same species as themselves. What is it then that Epicharmus says?
Eumaeus' wisdom?—not a scanty gift
Appropriated to one single being;
But every animal that breathes and lives,
Has mind and intellect.—So if you will
Survey the facts attentively, youH find,
E'en in the common poultry yard, the hen
Brings not her offspring forth at first alive,
But sits upon her eggs, and by her warmth,
Cherishes them into life. And all this wisdom
She does derive from nature's gift alone,
For nature is her only guide and teacher.

And in a subsequent passage he says:—
There is no wonder in my teaching this,
That citizens please citizens, and seem
To one another to be beautiful:
For so one dog seems to another dog
The fairest object in the world; and so
One ox seems to another, ass to ass,
And swine to swine.

And these and similar speculations are examined and compared by Alcinus through four books, where he shows how much assistance Plato has derived from Epicharmus. And that Epicharmus himself was not indisposed to appreciate his own wisdom, one may learn from these lines, in which he predicts that there will arise some one to imitate him:—

But as I think, I surely foresee this,
That these my words will be preserved hereafter
In many people's recollection. And
Another man will come, who'll strip my reasons
Of their poetic dress, and, clothing them
In other garments and with purple broidery
Will show them off; and being invincible,
Will make all rivals bow the knee to him.

XIII. Plato also appears to have brought the books of.Sophron, the farce-writer, to Athens, which were previously neglected; and to have availed himself of them in his Speculations on Morals: and a copy of them was found under his head. XIV. And Plato made thjee voyages to Sicily, first of all for the purpose of seeing the island and the craters of volcanoes, when Dionysius, the son of Hermocrates, being the tyrant of Sicily, pressed him earnestly to come and see him; and he, conversing about tyranny, and saying that that is not the best government which is advantageous for one individual alone, unless that individual is pre-eminent in virtue, had a quarrel with Dionysius, who got angry, and said, " Your words are those of an old dotard." And Plato replied.j The Greek is row *itifioypaipov*. " A *mime* was a kind of prose drama, intended as a familiar representation of life and character, without any distinct plot. It was divided into /iTjuiot *dvlptloi* and *yvvaiKtioi*, also into *fiifjLOL tnrovSaiwv* and *ysXoitov*."—L. tk. S. in voc. p/iOC.

" And your language is that of a tyrant. " And on this the tyrant became very indignant, and at first was inclined to put him to death; but afterwards, being appeased by Deni and Aristimenes, he forebore to do that, but gave him to Pollis, the Lacedaemonian, who happened to have come to him on an embassy just at that time, to sell as a slave. And he took him to Egina and sold him; and Charmander, the son of Charmandrides, instituted a capital prosecution against him, in accordance with the law which was in force, in the island of Egina, that the first Athenian who landed on the island should be put to death without a trial; and he himself was the person who had originally proposed that law, as Pharorinus says, in his Universal History. But when some one said, though he said it only in joke, that it was a philosopher who had landed, the people released him. But some say that he was brought into the assembly and watched; and that he did not say a word, but stood prepared to submit to whatever might befall him; and that they determined not to put him to death, but to sell him after the fashion of prisoners of war. And it happened by chance thatAnniceriSj, the Cyrenean, was present, who ransomed him Tortwenty minae, or, as others say, for thirty, and, sent him to Athens, to his companions, and they immediately sent Anniceris his money: but he refused to receive it, saying that they were not the only people in the world who were entitled to have a regard for Plato. Some writers again say, that it was Deni who sent the money, and that he did not refuse it, but bought him the garden in the Academy. And with respect to

Pollis it is said that he was defeated by Chabrias, and that he was afterwards drowned in Helia, in consequence of the anger of the deity at his treatment of this philosopher. And this is the story told by Pharorinus in the first book of his Commentaries. Dionysius, however, did not remain quiet; but when he had heard what had happened he wrote to Plato not to speak ill of him, and he wrote back in reply that he had not leisure enough to think at all of Dionysius.

XV. But he went a second time to Sicily to the younger Dionysius, and asked him for some land and for some men whom he might make live according to his own theory of a constitution. And Dionysius promised to give him some, but never did it. And some say that he was in danger himself, having been suspected of exciting Dion and Thetas to attempt the deliverance of the island; but that Archytas, the Pythagorean, wrote a letter to Dionysius, and begged Plato off and sent him back safe to Athens. And the letter is as follows:—
ABCHYTAS TO DIONYSIUS, GREETING.
" All of us who are the friends of Plato, have sent to you Lamiscus and Photidas, to claim of you this philosopher in accordance with the agreement which you made with us. And it is right that you should recollect the eagerness which you had to see him, when you pressed us all to secure Plato's visit to you, promising to provide for him, and to treat him hospitably in every respect, and to ensure his safety both while he remained with you, and when he departed. Remember this too that you were very delighted indeed at his arrival, and that you expressed great pleasure at the time, such as you never did on any other occasion. And if any unpleasantness has arisen between you, you ought to behave with humanity, and restore the man unhurt; for by so doing you will act justly, and do us a favour." XVI. The third time that he went to Sicily was for the purpose of reconciling Dion to Dionysius. And as he could not succeed he returned back to his own country, having lost his labour.

XVII. And in his own country he did not meddle with state affairs, although he was a politician as far as his writings, went. And the reason was, that the people were accustomed to a form of government and constitution different from what he approved of. And Pamphile, in the twenty-fifth book of his I Commentaries, says that the Arcadians and Thebans, when they were founding a great city, appointed him its lawgiver; but that he, when he had ascertained that they would not con-! sent to an equality of rights, refused to go thither. XVIII. It is said also, that he defended Chabrias the general, when he was impeached in a capital charge; when no one else of the citizens would undertake the task: and as he was going up towards the Acropolis with his client, Crobylus the sycophant met him and said, "Are you come to plead for another, not knowing that the hemlock of Socrates is waiting also for you?" But he replied, " And also, when I fought for my country I encountered dangers; and now too I encounter them in the cause of justice and for the defence of a friend." XIX. He was the first authojLjrho.wrote treatises in the form of dialogues, as Pharorinus tells us in the eighth book of his Universal History. And he was also the first person who introduced the analytical metiKHLc£jbi£S.tigation, which he taught to Leodamas of Thasos. He was also the first person in philosophy who spoke of antipodes, and elements, and dialectics, and actions (wo/jj/iara), and oblong numbers, and plane surfaces, and the providence of God. He was likewise the first of the philosophers who contradicted the assertion of Lysias, the son of Cephalus, setting it out word for word in his Phaedrus. And he was also the first person who examined the subject of grammatical knowledge scientifically. And as he.argued against almost every one who had lived before his time, it is often asked why he has never mentioned Democritus. XX. Neanthes of Cyzicus says, that when he came to the Olympic games all the Greeks who were present turned to look at him: and that it was on that occasion that he held a conversation with Dion, who was on the point of attacking Dionysius. Moreover, in the first book of the Commentaries of Pharorinus, it is related that Mithridates, the Persian, erected a statue of Plato in the Academy, and put on it this inscription, " Mithridates, the son of Rhodobates, a Persian, consecrated an image of Plato to the Muses, which was made by Silanion." XXI. And Heraclides says, that even while a young man, he was so modest and well regulated, that he was never once seen to laugh excessively. XXII. But though he was of such a grave character himself, he was nevertheless ridiculed by the comic" poets. Accordingly, Theopompus, in his Pleasure-seeker, says:—
For one thing is no longer only one,
But two things now are scarcely one; as says
The solemn Plato.

And Anaxandrides in his Theseus, says:—
When he ate olives like our worthy Plato.

And Timon speaks of him in this way, punning on his name:—
As Plato placed strange platitudes on paper.

Alexis says in his Mesopis:—
You've come in time: since I've been doubting long,
And walking up and down some time, like Plato;
And yet have hit upon no crafty plan,
But only tir"d my legs.

And in his Analion, he says:—
You speak of what you do not understand,
Eunning about like Plato: hoping thus,
Tojggrn.the nature of saltpetre and onions.

Amphis says in his Amphicrates:—
A. ' But what the good is, which you hope to get
By means of her, my master, I no more
Can form a notion of, than of the good
Of Plato.
B. Listen now.

And in his Dexidemides he speaks thus:— 0 Plato! how your learning is confined
To gloomy looks, and wrinkling up your brows,
Like any cockle.

Cratinas in his Pseudripobolimaeus, says:—

You clearly are a man, endued with sense,
And so, as Plato says, I do not know;
But I suspect.

Alexis, in his Olympiodorus speaks thus:—

My mortal body became dry and withered:
But my immortal part rose to the sky.
Is not this Plato's doctrine?

And in his Parasite he says:—

Or to converse alone, like Plato.

Anaxilas also laughs at him in his Botrylion, and Circe, and his Rich Women.

XXIII. And Aristippus, in the fourth hook of his treatise upon Ancient Luxury, says that he was much attached to a youth of the name of Aster, who used to study astronomy with him; and also to Dion, whom we have already men The Greek is, 5c *aveirXaTTC UXarmv TtTtXaa/tiva Bat/tara itSwg* tioned. And some say that he was also attached to Phaedrus, and that the following epigrams which he wrote upon them are evidences of the love he felt for them:—

My Aster, you're gazing on the stars (aorepec),
; Would that I were the heavens, that so I might
iGaze in return with many eyes on thee.

Another of his epigrams is:—

Aster, you while among the living shone,
The morning star. But now that you are dead,
You beam like Hesperus in the shades below.

And he wrote thus on Dion:—

Onee, at their birth, the fates did destine tears
To be the lot of all the Trojan women.
And Heeuba, their Queen—to you, 0 Dion,
As the deserved reward for glorious deeds,
They gave extensive and illustrious hopes.
And now you lie beneath your native soil;
Honoured by all your countrymen, O Dion,

And loved by me with ardent, lasting love.

And they say that this epigram is inscribed upon his tomb at Syracuse. They say, also, that he was in lov« with Alexis, and with Phaedrus, as I have already mentioned, and that he wrote an epigram on them both, which runs thus:—

Now when Alexis is no longer aught,
Say only how beloved, how fair he was,
And every one does turn his eyes at once.
Why, my mind, do you show the dogs a bone?
You're but preparing trouble for yourself:
Have we not also lost the lovely Phaedrus!

There is also a tradition that he had a mistress named Archianassa, on whom he wrote the following lines:—

I have a mistress fair from Colophon,
Archianassa, on whose very wrinkles
Sits genial love: hard must have been the fate,
Of him who met her earliest blaze of beauty,
Surely he must have been completely scorched.

He also wrote this epigram on Agathon:—

While kissing Agathon, my soul did rise,
And hover'd o'er my lips; wishing perchance,
O'er anxious that it was, to migrate to him.

Another of his epigrams is:— I throw this apple to you. And if you
Love me who love you so, receive it gladly,
And let me taste your lovely virgin charms.
Or if that may not be, still take the fruit,
And in your bosom cherish it, and learn
How fleeting is all gracefulness and beauty.

And another:—

I am an apple, and am thrown to youy
By one who loves-you: but consent, Xanthippe;
For you and I shall both with time decay.

They also attribute to him the following epigram on the Eretrians who had been surprised in an ambuscade:—

We were Eretrians, of Eubaean race?
And now we lie near Susa, here entomb'd,
Far from my native land.

And this one also:—

Thus Venus to the muses spoke:
Damsels submit to Venus' yoke,
Or dread my Cupid's arms.
Those threats, the Virgins nine replied,
May weigh with Mars, but we deride
Love's wrongs, or darts, or charms.

Another is: —

A certain person found some gold.
Carried it off, and in its stead
Left a strong hatter neatly roll'd.
The owner found his treasure fled;
And powerless to endure his fortune's wreck,
Fitted the halter to his hapless neck.

XXIV. But Molon, who had a great dislike to Plato, says, " There is not so much to wonder at in Dionysius being at Corinth, as in Plato's being in Sicily. Xenophon, too, does _not appear to have been very friendlily disposeu towards him: and accordingly they have, as if in rivalry of one another, both written books with the same title, the Banquet, the Defence of Socrates, Moral Reminiscences. Then, too, the one wrote the Cyropaedia and the other a book on Politics; and Plato in his Laws says, that the Cyropsdia is a mere romance, for that Cyrus was not such a person as he is described in that book. And though they both speak so much of Socrates, neither oX them ever mentjonsthe other, except that Xenophon once "speaks of Platoin the third took of his Reminiscences. It is said also, that Antisthenes, being about to recite something that he had written, invited him to be present; and that Plato having asked what he was going to recite, he said it was an essay on the impropriety of contradicting. " How then," said Plato, " can you write on this subject?" and then he showed him that he was arguing in a circle. But Antisthenes was annoyed, and composed a dialogue against Plato, which he entitled Sothon; after which they were always enemies to one another; and they say that Socrates having heard Plato read the Lysis, said, " O Hercules! what a number of lies the young man has told about me." For he had set down a great many things as sayings of Socrates which he never said. Plato also was a great jmemy of Aristippus; accordingly, he speaks ill of him in his book on the Soul, and says that he was not with Socrates when he died, though he was in iEgina, at no great distance. He also had a great rivalry with iEschines, for that he had been held in great esteem by Dionysius, and afterwards came to want, and was despised by Plato, but supported by Aristippus. And Idomeneus says, that the speech which Plato attributes to Crito in the prison, when he counselled Socrates to make his escape, was really delivered by iEschines, but that Plato attributed it to Qrito because of his dislike to the other. And Plato never makes the slightest mention of him in any of his books, except in the treatise on the Soul, and the Defence of Socrates.

XXV. Aristotle sa3s, that the treatises of Plato are something between poems and prose; and Pharorinus says, when Plato read his treatise on the Soul, Aristotle was the only person who sat it out, and that all the rest rose up and went away. And some say that Philip the Opuntian copied out the whole of his books upon Laws, which were written on waxen tablets only. Some people also attribute the Epinomis to him. Euphorion and Panaetius have stated that the beginning of the treatise on the Republic was often altered and re-written; and that very treatise, Aristoxenus affirms, was found almost entire in the Contradictions of Protagoras; and that the first book he wrote at all was the Phaedrus; and indeed that composition has a good many indications of a young composer. But Dicae- archus blames the whole style of that work as vulgar. XXVI. A story is told, that Plato, having seen a man playing at dice, reproached him for it, and that he said he was playing for a trifle; " But the habit," rejoined Plato, " is not a trifle." On one occasion he was asked whether there would be any monument of him, as of his predecessors in philosophy? and he answered,

" A man must first make a name, and the monument will follow." Once, when Xenocrates came into his house, he desired him to scourge one of his slaves for him, for that he himself could not do it because he was in a passion; and that at another time he said to one of his slaves, " I should beat s you if I were not in a passion." Having got on horseback he dismounted again immediately, saying that he was afraid that he should be infected with horse-pride. He used to advise people who got drunk to look in the glass, and then they would abandon their unseemly habit; and he said that it was never decorous to drink to the degree of drunkenness, except at the festivals of the God who had given men wine. He also disapproved of much sleeping: accordingly in his Laws he says,

" No one while sleeping is good for anything." Another saying of his was, " That the pleasantest of all things to hear was the truth; but others report this saying thus, " That the sweetest of all things was to speak truth." And of truth he speaks thus in his Laws, " Truth, my friend, is a beautiful and a durable thing; but it is not easy to persuade men of this fact." XXVII. He used also to wish to leave a memorial of himself behind, either in the hearts of his friends, or in his books.

XXVIII. He also used to travel a good deal as some authors inform us. XXIX. And he died in the manner we have already mentioned, in the thirteenth year of tbe reign of Philip of Macedon, as Pharorinus mentions in the third book of his Commentaries; and Theopompus relates that Philip on one occasion reproached him. But Mysonianus, in his Resemblances, says that Philo mentions some proverbs that were in circulation about Plato's lice; implying that he had died of that disease. XXX. He was buried in the Academy, where he spent the greater part of his time in the practice of philosophy, from which his was called the Academic school; and hia funeral was attended by all the pupils of that sect. And he made his will in the following terms:—" Plato left these things, and has bequeathed them as follows:—

The farm in the district of the Hephaestiades, bounded on the north by the road from the temple of the Cephiciades, and on the south by the temple of Hercules, which is in the district of the Hephaestiades; and on the east by thc estate of Archestratus the Phreanian, and on the west by the farm of Philip the Challidian, shall be incapable of being sold or alienated, but shall belong to my son Ademantus as far as possible. And so likewise shall my farm in the district of the Eiresides, which I bought of Callimachus, which is bounded on the north by the property of Eurymedon the Myrrhinusian, on the south by that of Demostratus of Xypeta, on the east by that of Eurymedon the Myrrhinusian, and on the west by the Cephisus;— I also leave him three minae of silver, a silver goblet weighing a hundred and sixty-five drachms, a cup weighing forty-five drachms, a golden ring, and a golden ear-ring, weighing together four drachms and three obols. Euclides the stonecutter owes me three minae. I leave Diana her liberty. My slaves Sychon, Bictas, Apolloniades, and Dionysius, I bequeath to my son; and I also give him all my furniture, of which Demetrius has a catalogue. I owe no one anything. My executors shall be Tozthenes, Speusippus, Demetrius, Hegias, Eurymedon, Callimachus, andTEasippus." This was his will. And on his tomb the following epigrams were inscribed. First of all:—

Here, first of all men for pure justice famed, And moral virtue, Aristocles lies;

And if there e'er has lived one truly wise,

This man was wiser still; toojjreat for envy.

A second is:—

Here in her bosom does the tender earth

Embrace great Plato's corpse.—His soul aloft

Has ta'en its place among the immortal Gods.

Ariston's glorious son—whom all good men,

Though in far countries, held in love and honour,

Remembering his pure and god-like life.

There is another which is more modern:— *A.* Eagle, why fly you o'er this holy tomb f
Or are you on your way, with lofty wing,
To some bright starry domicile of the Gods? j *B.* I am the image of the soul of Plato,
And to Olympus now am borne on high; I
His body lies in his own native Attica.

We ourselves also have written one epigram on him, which is as follows:—

If fav'ring Phoebus had not Plato given
To Grecian lands, how would the learned God
Have e'er instructed mortal minds in learning?
But he did send him, that as Esculapius
His son's the best physician of the body,
So Plato should be of the immortal soul.

And others, alluding to his death:—

Phoebus, to bless mankind, became the father
Of.Esculapius, and of god-like Plato; *That* one to heal the body, *this* the mind.
Now, from a marriage feast he's gone to heaven.
To reajige the happy city there,
Which he has planned fit for the realms of Jove.

These then are the epigrams on him.

XXXI. His disciples were, Speusippus the Athenian, Zenocrates of Chalcedon, Aristotle the Stagirite, Philip of Opus, Histiaeus of Perinthus, Dion of Syracuse, Amyclus of Heraclea, Erastus and Coriscus of Sceptos, Timolaus of Cyzicus, Eudon of Lampsacus, Pithon and Heraclides of Emus, Hippo'thales and Callippus, Athenians, Demetrius of Amphipolis, Heraclides of Pontus, and numbers of others, among whom there were also two women, Lasthenea of Mantinea, and Axiothea of Phlius, who used even to wear man's clothes, as we are told by Dicaearchus. Some say that Theophrastus also was a pupil of his; and Chamaelion says that Hyperides the orator, and Lycurgus, were so likewise. Polemo also asserts that Demosthenes was. Sabinus adds Mnesistratus of Thasos to the number, quoting authority for the statement in the fourth book of his Meditative Matter; and it is not improbable. XXXII. But as you, O lady, are rightly very much attached to Plato, and as you are very fond of hunting out in every quarter all the doctrines of the philosopher with great eager
E ness, I have thought it necessary to subjoin an account of the general character of his lectures, and of the arrangement of his dialogues, and of the method of his inductive, argument; going back to their elements and first principles as far as I could, so that the collection of anecdotes concerning his life which I have been able to make, may not be curtailed by the omission of any statement as to his doctrines. For it would be like sending owls to Athens, as the proverb is, if I were to descend to particular details.

They say now, that Zeno, the Eleatic, was the first person who composed essays in the form of dialogue. But Aristotle, in the first book of his treatise on Poets, says that Alexander, a native of Styra, or Teos, did so before him, as Phavorinus also says in his Commentaries. But it seems to me that Plato gave this kind of writing the last polish, and that he has therefore, a just right to the first honour, not only as the improver, but also as inventor of that kind of writing, Now, the dialogue is a discourse carried on by way of question and answer, on some one of the subjects with which philosophy is conversant, or with which statesmanship is concerned, with a becoming attention to the characters of the persons who are introduced as speakers, and with a careful selection of language governed by the same consideration. And dialectics is the art of conversing, by means of which we either overturn 6i establish the proposition contended for, by means of the questions and answers which are put in the mouths of the parties conversing. Now, of the Platonic discourse there are two characteristics discernible on the very surface; one fitted for guiding, the other for investigating.

The first of these has two subordinate species, one speculative, the other practical; and of these two again, the speculative is divided into the natural and the logical, and the practical into the ethical and the political. Again, the kind fitted for investigating has also two primary divisions with their separate characteristics, one object of which is simply practice, the other being also disputatious: and the first of these two is again subdivided into two; one of which may be compared to the art of the midwife, and the other is at it were tentative; the disputatious one is also divided into the demonstrative and the distinctive.

I But we are not unaware that some writers distinguish the various dialogues in a different manner from what we do. For they say that some of them are dramatic, and others narrative, and others of a mixed nature. But they, in this division, are classifying the dialogues in a theatrical rather than in a philosophical manner. Some of the dialogues also refer to subjects of natural philosophy, such as the Timaeus. Of the logical class, there are the Politics, the Cratylus, the Parmenides, and the Sophist. Of the ethical kind there is the defence of Socrates, the Crito, the Phaedo, the Phsedrus, the Banquet, the Menexenus, the Clitiphon, the Epistles, the Philebus, the Hipparchus, and the Rival Lovers. Of the political class there is the Republic, the Laws, the Minos, the Epinomis, and the Atlanticus. Of the midwife description we have the two Alcibiades's, the Theages, the Lysis, the Laches. Of the tentative kind, there is the Euthyphro, the Meno. the Ion, the Charmides, and the Theaetetus. Of the demonstrative description, we have the Protagoras, and of the distinctive class the Euthydemus, the two Hippias's, and the Gorgias. And this is enough to say about the dialogues as to what they are, and what their different kinds are.

XXXIIL But since there is also a great division of opinion respecting them, from some people asserting that in them Plato dogmatizes in a positive manner, while others deny this, we had better also touch upon this part of the question. Now, dogmatizing is laying down dogmas, just as legislating is making laws. But the word dogma is used in two senses; to mean both that which we think, and opinion itself. Now of these, that which we think is the proposition, and opinion is the conception by which we entertain it in our minds. Plato then explains the opinions which he entertains himself, and refutes false ones; and about doubtful matters he suspends his judgment. His opinions of matters as they appear to him he puts into the mouth of four persons, Socrates, Timaeus, an Athenian poet, and an Eleatic stranger. But the strangers are not, as some people have supposed, Plato and Parmenides, but certain nameless imaginary characters. Since Plato asserts as undeniable axioms all the opinions which he puts into the mouth of Socrates or Timaeus. But when he is refuting false propositions, he introduces such characters as Thrasymachus, and Callicles, and Polus, and Gorgias, and Protagoras, Hippiastro, and Euthydemus, and men pf that stamp. But when he is demonstrating anything, then he chiefly uses the inductive form of argument, and that too not of one kind only, but of two. For induction is an argument, which by means of some admitted truths establishes naturally other truths which resemble them. But there are two kinds of induction; the one proceeding from contraries, the other from consequents. Now, the one which proceeds from contraries, is one in which from the answer given, whatever that answer may be, the contrary of the principle indicated in the question must follow. As for instance. My father is either a different person from your father, or he is the same person. If now your father is a different person from my father, then as he is a different person from a father, he cannot be a father. If, on the other hand, he is the same person as my father, then, since he is the same person as my father, he must be my father. And again, if man be not an animal, he must be either a stone or a piece of wood; but he is not a stone or a piece of wood, for he is a living animal, and capable of independent motion. Therefore, he is an animal. But, if he is an animal, and a dog or an ox is likewise an animal, then man must be an animal, and a dog, and an ox. — This then is the method of induction in contradiction and contention, which Plato was accustomed to employ, not for the purpose of establishing principles of his own, but with the object of refuting the arguments of others.

Now, the inductive kind of argument drawn from consequents is of a twofold character. The one proving a particular opinion by an admitted fact of an equally particular nature; or else going from particulars to generals. And the first of these two divisions is the oratorical one, the second the dialectic one. As for instance, in the former kind the question is whether this person has committed a murder; the proof is that he was found at the time covered with blood. But this is the oratorical method of employing the induction; since oratory is conversant about particulars, and does not concern itself about generals. For its object is not to ascertain abstract justice, but only particular justice. The other is the dialectic jkind, the general proposition having been established by particular ones. As for instance, the question is whether the soul is immortal, and whether the living consist of those who have once been dead; and this proposition Plato establishes in his book on the Soul, by a certain general proposition, that contraries arise out of contraries; and this identical general proposition is established by certain particular ones. As, for instance, that sleep follows on waking, and waking from sleeping, and the greater from the less, and reversely the less from the greater. And this kind of induction he used to employ for the establishment of his own opinions.

XXXIV. Anciently, in tragedy, it was only the chorus who did the whole work of the play; but subsequently, Thespis introduced one actor for the sake of giving the chorus some rest, and iEschylus added a second, and Sophocles a third, and so they made tragedy complete. So in the same manner, philosophical discourse was originally uniform, concerning itself solely about natural philosophy; then Socrates added to it a second character, the ethical: and Plato a third, the dialectic: and so he brought philosophy to perfection. XXXV. But Thrasybulus says that he published his dialogues as the dramatic poets published their tetralogies. For, they contended with four plays, (and at four festivals, the Dionysiac, the Lenaeau, the Panathenaean, and the Chytri), one of which was a satiric drama, and the whole four plays were called a tetralogy. Now, people say, the whole of his genuine dialogues amount to fifty-six; the treatise on the Republic being divided into ten books, (which Phavorinus, in the second book of his Universal History, says may be found almost entire in the Contradictions of Protagoras), and that on Laws into twelve. And there are nine tetralogies, if we consider the Republic as occupying the place of one book, and the Laws of another. He arranges, therefore, the first tetralogy of these dialogues which have a common subject, wishing to show what sort of life that of the philosopher may have been. And he uses two titles for each separate book, taking one from the name of the principal speaker, and the other from the subject.

This tetralogy then, which is the first, is commenced by the Euthyphron, or what is Holy; and that dialogue is a tentative one. The second is the Defence of Socrates, a moral one. The third is the Criton, or What is to be done, a moral one. The fourth is the Phdo, or the Dialogue on the Soul, a moral one.

The second tetralogy is that of which the first piece is the Cratylus, or the correctness of names, a logical one. The Meaetetus, or Knowledge, a tentative one-The Sophist, or a dialogue on the Existent, a logical one. The Statesman, or a dialogue of Monarchy, a logical one.

The first dialogue in the third tetralogy is the Parmenides, or a dialogue of Ideas, a logical one. The second is the Philelus, or on Pleasure, a moral one. The Banquet, or on the Good, a moral one. The Phaedrus, or on Love, a moral one.

The fourth tetralogy opens with the Alcibiades, or a treatise on the Nature of Man, a midwife-like work. The second Alcibiades, or on Prayer, a piece of the same character. The Hipparchus, or on the Love of Gain, a moral one. The Rival Lovers, or a treatise on Philosophy, a moral one.

The first dialogue in the fifth is the Theages, or another treatise on Philosophy, another midwife-like work. The Charmides, or on Temperance, a tentative essay. The Laches, or on Manly Courage, midwife-like. The Lysis, or a dissertation on Friendship, also midwife-like.

The sixth tetralogy commences with the Euthydemus, or the Disputatious Man, a distinctive dialogue. Then comes the Protagoras, or the Sophists, a demonstrative one. The Gorgias, or a dissertation on Rhetoric, another distinctive one. And the Meno, or on Virtue, a tentative dialogue.

The seventh begins with the two Hippias's. The first being a dissertation on the Beautiful, the second one on Falsehood, both distinctive. The third is the Ion, or a dissertation on the Iliad, a tentative one. The fourth is the Menexenus, or the Funeral Oration, a moral one.

The first dialogue in the eighth is the Clitophon, or the Exhortation, a moral piece. Then comes the Republic, or the treatise on Justice, a political one. The Timaeus, or a dissertation on Nature, a dialogue on Natural Philosophy. And the Critias, or Atlanticus, a moral one

The ninth begins with the Minos, or a treatise on Law, a political work. The Laws, or a dissertation on Legislation, another political work. The Epinomis, or the Nocturnal Conversation, or the Philosopher, a third political one.

XXXVI. And this last tetralogy is completed by thirteen epistles, all moral; to which is prefixed as a motto, *si irgaTTiiv*, just as Epicurus inscribed on his *su hayuv,* and Cleon on his *yeupn.* They are, one letter to Aristodemns, two to Arehytas, four to Dionysius, one to Hermeias, Erastus, and Coriscus, one to Leodamas, one to Dion, one to Perdiccas, and two to the friends of Dion.

XXXVII. And this is the way in which some people divide his works. But others, among whom is Aristophanes, the grammarian, arrange his dialogues in trilogies; and they make the first to consist of the Republic, the Timaeus and the Critias.

The second of the Sophist, the Statesman, the Cratylus. The third of the Laws, the Minos, the Epinomis. The fourth of the Theaetetus, the Euthypbro, the Defence of Socrates.

The fifth of the Crito, the Phaedo, the Epistles.

And the rest they arrange singly and independently, without any regular order. And some authors, as has been said already, place the Republic at the head of his works: others begin with the Greater Alcibiades: others with the Theages; some with the Euthyphro, others with the Clitophon; some with the Timaeus, some with the Phsedrus, others again with the Theaetetus. Many, make the Defence of Socrates the first piece.

There are some dialogues attributed to him which are confessedly spurious. The Midon, or the Horse-breeder; the Eryxias, or Erasistratus; the Alcyon; the Acephali, or Sisyphi; the Axiochus; the Phaeacians; the Demodorus; The Chilidon; the Seventh; the Epimenides. Of which the Alcyon is believed to be the work of a man named Leon; as Phavorinus tells us in the seventh book of his Commentaries.

XXXVIII. But he employs a great variety of terms in order to render his philosophical system unintelligible to the ignorant. In his phraseology he considers wisdom as the knowledge of things which can be understood by the intellect, and which have a real existence: which has the Gods for its object, and the soul as unconnected with the body. He also, with a peculiarity of expression, calls wisdom also philosophy, which he explains as a desire for divine wisdom. But wisdom and experience are also used by him in their common acceptation; as, for instance, when he calls an artisan wise *(eopbg).* He also uses the same words in different senses at different times. Accordingly he uses *paZXog* in the sense of *airXovg,. simple,* in which meaning also the word occurs in Euripides, in the Licymonius, where the poet speaks of Hercules in the following terms:—
Mean looking (0aCXof), rude, virtuous in great affairs,
Measuring all wisdom by its last results,
A hero unrefined in speech.

But Plato uses the word sometimes even for what is beautiful; and sometimes for small and insignificant; and very often he uses different words to express the same idea. Accordingly, besides the word *idea,* for a class, he uses also *ildog,* and *yevoj.*and *iragaduyi±a,* and *arj,* and*a/Wov.* Sometimes he uses opposite expressions for the same thing; accordingly, he says that it is an object of sensation that exists, while at other times he says it is that which does not exist; speaking of it as existing because of its origin, and as non-existent with reference to its continual changes. Then again, he defines his *id'sa* as something which is neither moving nor stationary, at one time calling the same thing, at another time one thing, at a third time many things, And he is in the habit of doing this in many instances.

And the explanation of his arguments is three-fold. For first of all, it is necessary to explain what each thing that is said is; secondly, on what account it is said, whether because of its bearing on the principal point, or figuratively, and whether it is said for the purpose of establishing an opinion of his own, or of refuting the arguments brought forward by the other party to the conversation; and thirdly, whether it has been said truly.

XXXIX. But since there are some particular marks put in his books, we must also say something about them, x indicates peculiar expressions and figures of speech, and generally any peculiarities of Plato's style. When doubled it points to the doctrines and peculiar opinions of Plato;-Xwhen dotted all round, points to some select bits of beautiful writing. When doubled and dotted it indicates corrections of some passages. A dotted obelus indicates hasty disapprovals. An inverted sigma dotted all round points out passages which may be taken in a double sense, and transpositions of words. The Ceraunium indicates a connection of philosophical ideas. An asterisk points out an agreement in doctrine. And an obelus marks the rejection of the expression or of the passage. These then are the marginal marks which occur, and the writings of which Plato was the author:—which, as Antigonus the Carystian says, in his treatise on Zeno, when they had been but lately published, brought in some gain to the possessors, if any one else was desirous of reading them. XL. These now were his chief opinions. He affirmed that the soul was immortal and clothed in many bodies successively, and that its first principle was number, and that the first principle of the body was geometry. And he defined it as an abstract idea of spirit diffused in every direction. He said also, that it was self-moving and threefold. For that that part of it which was capable of reasoning was situated in the head, that that portion which was affected by passion was seated around the heart, and that which was appetitive was placed around the navel and the liver. And that it is placed in the middle of the body, and embraces it at the same time in all its parts, and that it consists of elements; and that when it is divided according to harmonic intervals it forms two connected circles; of which the inner circle is divided into six portions, and makes in all seven circles; and that this is placed on the left hand of the diameter, and situated in the interior. But the other is on the right hand of the same line; on which account, and because it is one only, it is the superior of the two. For the other is divided internally; and this too, is the circle of that which is always the same; the other, the circle of that which is changeable and different. And the one he says is the motion of the soul, but the other is the motion of the universe and of the planets.

On the other side, the division of the circles from the centre to the extremities, being harmoniously appropriated to the essence of the soul, the one knows existing things and establishes harmony between them, because it is itself composed of harmonious elements. The circle of what is changeable, engenders opinion by its regular movements; but the circle of that which is always the same produces knowledge.

XLI. Plato lays down two primary causes or principles of all things, God and matter, which he also calls mind, This figure wa8 like a barbed arrow, according to Zevort. and the cause. And he defines matter as something without shape and without limitation, and says that from it all concretions arise. He affirms also that as it was moving about at random, it was brought by God into one settled place, as God thought order better than disorder; and that this nature is divided into four elements, fire, water, air, and earth, of which the world itself and everything in it was made. But he says that the earth is the only thing that is unchangeable, as he considers the cause to be the difference of the figures of which it is composed; for he says that the figures of the others are homogeneous; for that they are all composed equally of scalene triangles. The figure of the earth, however, is peculiar to itself; for the element of fire is a pyramid; of air, an octagon; of water, aneicosagon; and of the earth, a cube; owing to which these things cannot be changed into earth, nor earth into them. He teaches also that these elements are not separated so as to occupy each a peculiar and distinct place; for the spherical motion collects and compresses all the small things towards the centre, and the small things separate the great ones, on which account the species, as they change, do also change their positions. Moreover he asserts that the world is one, and has been produced, since it has been made by God, in such a manner as to be an object of sensation. And he considers it endowed with life, because that which is so endowed, is superior to that which is not, and it must be the production of the most excellent producer. It is also one, and illimitable; because the model after which it was made was one; and it is spherical, because its creator was of that form; for it also contains all other animals, and God who made it comprises all forms. And it is smooth, and has no instruments whatever all round it, because it has no need of any. But the whole world "remains imperishable, because it cannot be resolved into God; and God is the cause of universal production, because it is the nature of the good to be productive of good; and the best is the cause of the production of the heaven; for the best of all productions can have no other cause than the best: of all intelligible existences. And since God is of that character, and since heaven resembles the best, inasmuch as it is at least the most beautiful of all things, it cannot be like anything else that is produced, except God.

He also teaches that the world consists of fire, water, air, and earth; of fire, in order that it may be visible; of earth, in order that it may be firm; of water and air, that it may not be destitute of proportion; for two middle terms are indispensable to keep the solid bodies in due proportion to one another, and to realize the unity of the whole. In short, the world is formed of all the elements together, in order that it may be perfect and imperishable.

Again, time is the image of eternity; eternity subsists for ever; but the motion of the heaven is time; for day, and night, and the months, and all such divisions, are parts of time, on which account there could be no such thing as time apart from the nature of the world; for time existed contemporaneously and'simultaneously with the world. And it was with reference to time that the sun, and the moon, and the planets were made; and it was in order that the number of the seasons might be manifest, and that the animals might partake of number, that God kindled the light of the sun; and that the moon was above the circle of the earth, and that the sun was next to it, and in the still higher circles were the planets. And that the universe was animated, because it was altogether bound up in animated motion, and that the race of all other animals was produced in order that the world might be made perfect, and resembling an animal such as could be comprehended by intellect. Since then God had life, the heaven also must have life; and the Gods are to a great extent composed of fire. And there are three other races of animals, those which fly in the air; those which lives in the water; those which walk in the earth. The oldest of all the deities in heaven is the Earth; she was formed in order to be the dispenser of night and day; and as she is placed in the centre, she is constantly in motion around the centre.

And since there are two efficient causes, some things must, he says, be affirmed to exist in consequence of intellect, and some from some necessary cause. Now necessary causes are the air, fire, earth, and water, these not being real elements, but rather receptacles; and they too are formed of triangles in combination, and are resolvable into triangles; and their elements are the scalene triangle and the isoceles. These two before mentioned elements are the principles and causes of things, of which the models are God and matter, which last must necessarily be destitute of form, as is the case of other receptacles. And that the cause of these things was a necessary cause, which, receiving the ideas, produced the suhstances," and was moved by the dissimilarity of its own power, and again by its motion compelled those things which were moved by it to move other things in their turn.

But all these things were formerly moved without any reason or order; but after they began to form the world by their combination, they then received symmetry and regularity from God, according to the principles applicable to them; for the efficient causes, even before the creation of the heaven, were two in number. There was also a third, namely production; but these were not very evident, but rather traces than actual things, and quite devoid of regularity. But after the world was made, then they too assumed a regular form and arrangement; but the heaven was made of all existing bodies. And Plato considers that God is incorporeal just as the soul is, and that it is owing to that that he is not affected by any destruction or external circumstances. And ideas, as we have said before, he defines as certain causes and principles, owing to which it is that such and such things are by nature what they are.

XLII. On the subject of good and evil, these were his sentiments: that the end was to become like God; and that virtue was sufficient of herself for happiness, but nevertheless required the advantages of the body as instruments to work with; such as health, strength, the integrity of the senses, and things of that kind; and also external advantages, such as riches, and noble birth, and glory. Still that the wise man would be not the less happy, even if destitute of these auxiliary circumstances; for he would enjoy the constitution of his country, and would marry, and would not transgress the established laws, and that he would legislate for his country, as well as he could under existing circumstances, unless he saw affairs in an unmanageable condition, in consequence of the excessive factiousness of the people. He thinks too that the Gods superintend all the affairs of men, and that there are such beings as daemons. And he was the first person who defined the notion of the honourable, as that which borders on the praiseworthy, and the logical, and the useful, and the becoming, and the expedient, all which things are combined with that which is suitable to, and in accordance with, nature. XLIII. He also discussed in his dialogues the correctness of terms, so that he was the first person who reduced the science of giving correct answers, and putting correct questions to a system, which he himself used to satiety. XLIV. In his dialogues he used to speak of justice as a kind of law of God, as being of influence sufficient to excite men to act justly, in order to avoid suffering punishment as malefactors after death. Owing to which he appeared to some people rather fond of mythical stories, as he mingled stories of this kind with his writings, in order by the uncertainty of all the circumstances that affect men after their death, to induce them to abstain from evil actions. And these were his opinions. XLV. He used too, says Aristotle, to divide things in this manner:—Of good, some have their place in the mind, some in the body, and some are wholly external. As, for instance, justice, and prudence, and manly courage, and temperance, and qualities of that sort exist in the soul. Beauty, and a good constitution, and health, and strength exist in the body. But friends, and the prosperity of one's country, and wealth, are external goods. There are then three species of goods, some in the soul, some in the body, and some external to either. XLVI. There are also three species of friendship. For one kind is natural, another that which arises from companionship; and the third is that which is produced by ties of hospitality. We call that natural friendship which parents feel towards their offspring, and relations towards one another; and this is partaken of by other animals besides men. We call that the friendship of companionship which arises from a habit of association, and which has no reference to ties of blood, such as the friendship of Pylades for Orestes. That which arises from ties of hospitality is one which owes its origin to agree ments, and which is carried on by means of letters between strangers. There is, therefore, natural friendship, and friendship between companions, and between strangers. Some also add a fourth kind, namely, the friendship of love. XLVII. Of political constitutions there are five species. There is one kind which is democratical, a second which is aristocratical, a third is oligarchical, a fourth monarchical, and the fifth is tyrannical. Now, the democratical form of constitution exists in those cities in which the multitude has the chief power, and elects magistrates, and passes laws at its own pleasure. But an aristocracy is that form in which neither the rich, nor the poor, nor the most illustrious men of the city rule, but the most nobly born have the chief sway. And oligarchy is that constitution in which the magistracies are distributed according to some sort of rating: for the rich are fewer in number than the poor. The monarchical constitution is either dependent on law or on family. That in Carthage depends on law; that in Lacaedemon and Macedonia on, family; for they select their sovereign out of some particular family. But a tyranny is that kind of government in which the people are either cajoled or constrained into being governed by a single individual. Forms of government then, are divided into democracy, aristocracy, oligarchy, monarchy, and tyranny. XLVIII. Again, of justice there are three species. For there is one kind which is conversant with the gods; a second which has reference to men; and a third, which concerns the dead. For they who sacrifice according to the laws, and who pay due respect to the temples, are manifestly pious to the gods. And those who repay what has been lent to them, and restore ivhat has been deposited with them, act justly as to men. And those who pay due respect to the tombs, clearly are pious towards the dead. There is, therefore, one justice towards the Gods, a second towards men, and a third towards the dead. XLIX. In the same way, there are also three species of knowledge. There is one kind which is practical, a second which is productive, a third which is theoretical. For the science of building houses or ships, is production. For one can see the work which is produced by it. Political science, and the science of playing the flute, or the harp, or such things as that, is practical; for one cannot see any visible result which has been produced by them, and yet they are doing something. For one man plays the flute or plays the harp, and another occupies himself with state affairs. Again, geometrical, and harmonic, and astronomical science are all theoretical, for they do nothing, and produce nothing. But the geometrician theorizes as to what relation lines bear to one another; and the harmonist speculates about sounds, and the astronomer about stars and about the world. Accordingly, of sciences some are theoretical, others productive, and a third species is practical.

L. Of medical science there are five species: one, pharmaceutical; a second, manual; a third, conversant about the regulation of the manner of life, and the diet; a fourth, the business of which is to detect diseases; and the fifth is remedial. The pharmaceutical relieves infirmities by means of medicines; the manual heals men by cutting and cauterizing; the one which attends to the diet, gets rid of diseases by altering and regulating the diet; the fourth produces its effects by a thorough comprehension of the nature of the disease; and the last relieves men from suffering by bringing prompt assistance at the moment. Medical science, then, is divided into the pharmaceutical, the manual, the dietetic, the diagnostic, and the remedial.

LI. Of law there are two divisions. For there is a written and an unwritten law. The one by which we regulate our constitutions in our cities, is the written law; that which arises from custom, is the unwritten law. As, for instance, for a man to come naked into the market place, or to wear woman's clothes, are actions which are not prohibited by any law, and yet we never do them because they are forbidden by the unwritten law. Law, therefore, is divided into the written and the unwritten law. LII. Discourse is divided into five heads; one of which heads is that which statesmen employ when they speak in the public assemblies; and this is called political. Another division is that which orators use in their written harangues, and bring forward for the sake of display in panegyrics or reproaches, or impeachments. And such a description of discourse as this is the rhetorical. A third class is that which private individuals use when conversing with one another. This is called private discourse. Another kind is that which is employed when men converse by means of putting short questions and giving brief answers to those who question them. This is called the dialectic kind of discourse. The fifth division is that which artists adopt when conversing on their own particular art, and this is called professional discourse. Thus discourse, then, is divided into political, rhetorical, private, dialectic, and professional. LIII. Music again is divided into three species. For there is the music of the mouth alone, such as song; secondly, there is the music which is performed by the hands and mouth together, such as singing to the harp; thirdly, there is that which is executed by the hands alone, such as harp playing. Music, therefore, is divided into music of the mouth, music of the mouth and hands, and music of the hands. LTV. Nobleness of birth is divided into four species; the first is when one's ancestors are noble, and valiant, and just; in which case they say that their posterity are nobly born. The second kind is when one's ancestors have been princes and rulers of nations, and their posterity also we call noble. Another kind is when one's ancestors have been distinguished for personal renown, such, for instance, as is gained by generalship or by victory at the games. For their offspring also we address as nobly born. And the last kind is when a man is himself noble in his spirit, and magnanimous. For that man also we call noble, and this is the last kind of nobility. There is, therefore, nobility arising from virtuous ancestors, from royal ancestors, from illustrious ancestors, and from one's own excellent qualities. LV. Beauty also is divided into three kinds. For there is one kind which is praiseworthy, as that of a beautiful face. Another which is useful, as an instrument or a house, and things of that kind which are beautiful, with reference to our use of them. There is also a beauty with reference to laws, and habits, and things of that kind, which is likewise beautiful, because of its utility. So that beauty again is looked at in three ways, with reference to its praise, its utility, and to our use of it LVI. The soul is divided into three parts; for one part of it is capable of reason, another is influenced by appetite, the third part is liable to passion. Of these the reasoning part is the cause of deliberating, and reasoning, and understanding, and everything of that kind. The appetite part is that portion of the soul which is the cause of desiring to eat, and to embrace, and things of that kind. The passionate part is the cause of men feeling confidence and delight, and grief and anger. The soul therefore is divided into the reasoning part, the appetitive part, and the passionate part. LVII. Of perfect virtue there are four species. One is prudence, one is justice, the third is manly gallantry, and the fourth is temperance. Of these, prudence is the cause of a man acting rightly in affairs; justice is the cause of his acting justly in partnerships and bargains; manly gallantry is the cause of a man's not being alarmed amid dangers and formidable circum-

stances, but standing firm; and temperance is the cause of his subduing his appetites, and being enslaved by no pleasure, but living decorously. So that virtue is divided into prudence, justice, manly gallantry, and temperance. LVIII. Rule is divided into five parts. One is rule according to law; another is rule according to nature; a third kind is rule according to custom; a fourth division is rule with reference to family; the fifth is rule by force. Now when the rulers in cities are elected by the citizens, then they rule according to law; those who rule according to nature are the males, not only among men, but also among all other animals; for everywhere we shall find it as a general rule that the male rules the female; the rule of him who rules according to custom is such as this, when schoolmasters rule their pupils, and teachers their disciples. Rule according to family is that which prevails in places like Laceds;mon, where hereditary sovereigns reign. For the kingdom there belongs to a certain family; and in Macedonia they rule on the same principle. For there, too, the kingdom depends on family. But those who rule by force, only cajoling the citizens, rule in spite of them; and such a sway is called rule by force. So that there is rule by law, and by nature, and by custom, and by family, and by force. LIX. Of rhetoric he speaks of six species. For when orators exhort the people to make war upon or to form alliances against any one, this species of oratory is called exhortation. When they persuade the people not to make war, or to form alliances, but to keep quiet, this kind of rhetoric is called dissuasion. The third species of rhetoric, is when any one says that he has been injured by some one else, and impeaches that person as guilty of many crimes; for this species is called accusation. The fourth kind of rhetoric is called defence, when a man shows that he has done no wrong, and that he is not guilty of anything out of the way. Such a kind of speech they call a defence. The fifth species of rhetoric, is when any one speaks well of another, and shows him to be virtuous and honourable; and this kind is called encomium. The sixth species, is when any one shows that another person
L is worthless; and this kind is called blame. So that rhetoric is divided into encomium and blame, exhortation and dissuasion, accusation and defence.

Speaking correctly is divided under four heads. One, the saying what is right; one, the saying as much as is right; thirdly, the saying it to the proper people; and fourthly, the saying it at the proper time. Now as to the saying what is right, that is the saying what will be advantageous both to the speaker and to the hearer. The saying as much as is right, is saying neither more nor less than what is sufficient. The saying it to the proper people, is supposing one is speaking to one's elders who are mistaken in any point, the using expressions proper to be addressed to those older than one's self; or, on the other hand, if one is addressing those younger, then the using language such as is suitable to young people. The saying it at the proper time, is speaking neither too soon nor too late; for if one does, one will err and speak improperly. LX. Beneficence is divided under four heads. For it may be exerted either in money, or by personal exertion, or by knowledge, or by words. In money when any one assists those who are in want, so as to put them at ease with respect to money. And men benefit one another by personal exertion when they come upon those who are being beaten and assist them. Again, those who instruct, or heal, or who teach any good thing, benefit others by their knowledge; and when one person comes down to the court of justice as an advocate for another, and delivers some speech full of sense and good feeling in his behalf, that man assists his friend by words. So that there is one beneficence which is displayed in money, another in personal exertion, a third by means of knowledge, and the fourth kind by words. LXI. Again, Plato divides the end of all affairs into four species. An affair has one end in accordance with law, when a decree is passed, and when the law establishes it; it has an end in accordance with nature, when it is such a thing as a day, or a year, or the seasons. It has an end according to art, when it is architecture for instance, for a man builds a house; or when it is ship-building, for it makes a ship. And affairs also come to an end by chance, when they turn out differently from what any one expected. So that an end of an affair is regulated either by law, or by nature, or by art, or by chance. LXII. Power again is divided into four species. There is one power which we possess by our ability to reason and form conceptions by means of our intellect. There is another power which we owe to the body, such as the power of walking, or giving, or taking, and such like. There is a third which we possess through the multitude of soldiers or riches, on which account a king is said to have great power. And the fourth division of power consists in the being well or ill treated, and treating others well or ill; as, for instance, we may be sick, or we may be taught, or we may be in vigorous health, and many more cases of that sort. So that one kind of power dwells in the intellect, another in the body, another in an army and riches, and another in our capacity as agents or patients. LXIII. Of philanthropy there are three sorts. One which is displayed in addressing people, when some persons address every one whom they meet, and give them their right hand, and greet them heartily; another species is when one is disposed to assist every one who is unfortunate. The last kind is that sort of philanthropy which makes men pleasant boon companions. So that there is one kind of philanthropy displayed in addressing people, another in benefiting them, and a third in feasting and making merry with them. LXIV. Happiness is divided into five parts. For one part of it is wisdom in counsel; another is a healthy condition of the sensations and general health of body; a third is good fortune in one's affairs; a fourth kind is good reputation among men; a fifth is abundance of riches and of all those things which are useful in life. Now wisdom in counsel arises from good instruction, and from a person's having experience of many things. A healthy condition of the sensations depends on the limbs of the body; as, for instance, when one sees with one's eyes, and hears with one's ears, and smells with one's nose, and feels with one's body, just what one ought to see, and hear, and smell, and feel. Such a condition as this is a healthy condition. And good fortune is when a man does rightly and successfully what a good and energetic man ought to do. And good reputation is when a man is well spoken of. And abundance of riches is when a man has such a sufficiency of everything which relates to the uses of life, that he is able to benefit his friends, and to discharge all public obligations in a splendid and liberal manner. And the man who has all these different parts of happiness, is a perfectly happy man. So that happiness is made up of wisdom in counsel, a good condition of the sensations and health of body, good fortune, good reputation, and riches. LXV. The arts are divided into three kinds. The first, the second, and the third. The first are those of working mines and cutting wood, for these are preparatory arts. The second are such as working metals and carpentry, for they are alterative arts. For working in metals makes arms out of iron; and carpentry makes flutes and lyres out of wood. The third is the art which makes use of instruments; such as horsemanship, which uses bridles; the military art, which uses arms; music, which uses fluteg and lyres. So that there are three species of art; one of which is the first, another the second, and another the third. LXVI. Good is divided into four kinds. One of which we mean when we speak of a man endowed with private virtue, as good; another kind is that which we indicate, when we call virtue and justice, good. A third kind is that which we attribute to suitable food, and exercise, and medicine. The fourth good, is that which we mean, when we speak of good flute playing, good acting, and things of that sort. There are therefore four kinds of good. One the having virtue; another, virtue itself; a third, useful food and exercise; and fourthly, we call skill in flute playing and acting, good. LXVII. Of things existing, some are bad, some good, and some neither one thing nor the other. Of these, we call those things bad, which are invariably capable of doing injury, such as intemperance, folly, injustice, and things of that sort. And the opposites to these qualities are good. But those things, which may at times be beneficial, and at times injurious, such as walking, sitting down, and eating; or which have absolutely no power in any case to benefit or injure any one; these are neither bad nor good. Of things existing then, there are some bad, and some good, and some of a neutral character, neither bad nor good. LXVIII. A good state of affairs with reference to the laws, is divided under three heads. One when the laws are good, for that is a good state of affairs; so too is it, when the citizens abide by the existing laws; and the third case is, when although there are no positive laws, still men are good citizens in deference to custom and to established institutions; and this is also called a good state of affairs. So that of these three heads, one depends on the laws being good, another on obedience to existing laws, and the third on men yielding to good customs and institutions.

So again, lawlessness is divided into three heads. One of which is, when the laws are bad, both as concerns strangers, and the citizens; another, when the citizens do not obey the laws that are established; and the third is when there is actually no law at all. So that one kind of lawlessness arises from bad laws, another from disobedience to existing laws, and the third from the absence of laws.

LXIX. Contraries are of three sorts; for instance, we say that good is contrary to evil, as justice to injustice, wisdom to folly, and so on. Again, some evils are contrary to others, as extravagance is to stinginess, and the being tortured with justice to the being tortured with injustice. And such evils as these are the contraries of other evils. Again, the heavy is contrary to the light, the swift to the slow, the black to the white; so that some things which are of a neutral character, neither good nor evil, are contrary to other things of a neutral character. Of contraries then, there are some which are so, as what is good is contrary to what is evil; others, as one evil is contrary to another; and others again, as neutral things are contrary to other things of a neutral character. LXX. Of good things there are three kinds; for there are some which can be possessed; others, which can be shared; others, which one realizes in one's self. Those which can be possessed, are those which it is possible for a person to have, such as justice, or good health; those can be shared, which it is not possible for a person to have entirely to himself, but which he may participate in; as for instance, a person cannot be the sole possessor of abstract good, but he may participate in it. Those again a person realizes in himself, when they are such, that he cannot possess them himself, or share them with others, and yet they ought to exist; as for instance, it is good to be virtuous and just, but yet a man does not possess the being virtuous, or participate in it; but the being virtuous and just ought to exist in him. Of good things, therefore, there are those which are possessed, those which are shared, and those which ought to exist in a man. LXXI. In the same manner, good counsel is divisible into three kinds. For there is one kind which is derived from past time, another from the future, another from the present. That which is derived from past time is made up of instances, as for instance what the Lacedaemonians suffered by trusting to such and such people. That which relates to the present,is when what is wanted, is to show that the fortifications are weak, the men cowardly, or the provisions scanty. That which concerns, the future, is when the speaker urges that no injury ought to be offered to ambassadors, in order that Greece may not get an evil reputation; and supports his argument by instances. So that good counsel has reference, firstly to what is past, secondly to what is present, and thirdly to the future. LXXII. Voice is divided into two parts, one of which is animated, and the other inanimate. That is animated, which proceeds from living animals, while sounds and echoes are inanimate.

Again, animated voice may be divided into that which can be indicated by letters, and that which cannot; that which can be so indicated being the voice of men, and that which cannot being the voice of animals; so that one kind of voice is animated, the other inanimate.

LXXIII. Of existing things, some are divisible and some indivisible. Again, those which are divisible, consist either of similar or of dissimilar parts. Those which are indivisible are such as have no separate parts, and are not formed by any combination, such as unity, a point, or a sound. But those are divisible which are formed by some combination; as, for instance, syllables, and symphonies, and animals, and water, and gold. These too consist of similar parts, which are made up of particles resembling one another, and of which the whole does not differ from any part, except in number. As for instance, water and gold, and everything which is fusible, and so on. And these consist of dissimilar parts, which are made up of various things not resembling one another; as for instance, a house, and things of that sort; so that of existing things, some are divisible and others indivisible. And of those which are divisible, some consist of similar and others of dissimilar parts. LXXIV. Again, of existing things, some are spoken of as having an independent, and some only a relative existence. Those which are spoken of as having an independent existence, are those which require nothing else to be added to them, when we are explaining their nature; as man, a horse, and the other animals; for these have no need of any additional explanation. But those things are said to have a relative existence which do require some additional explanation. As for instance, that which is greater than something else, or less, or swifter, or more beautiful, and so on. For that which is greater, is greater than something which is less; and that which is swifter, is swifter than something else. So that, of existing things, some are spoken of as independently, and others relatively. And thus he divided them at first, according to Aristotle. LXXV. There was also another man of the name of Plato, a philosopher of Rhodes, a disciple of Panaetius, as Seleucus, the grammarian says in the first book of his treatise on Philosophy; and another was a Peripatetic, a pupil of Aristotle; and there was a third, a pupil of Praxiphanes; and there was besides all these, the poet of the Old Comedy.

152 BOOK IV. LIFE OF SPEUSIPPUS.

I. The long account which I have given of Plato was compiled to the best of my power, and in it I collected with great zeal and industry all that was reported of the man.

II. And he was succeeded by Speusippus, the son of Eurymedon, and a citizen of Athens, of the Myrrhinusian burgh, and he was the son of Plato's sister Potone. III. He presided over his school for eight years, beginning lo do so in the hundred and eighth olympiad. And he set up images of the Graces in the temple of the Muses, which had been built in the Academy by Plato. IV. And he always adhered to the doctrines which had been adopted by Plato, though he was not of the same disposition as he. For he was a passionate man, and a slave to pleasure. Accordingly, they say that he once in a rage threw a puppy into a well; and that for the sake of amusement, he went all the way to Macedonia to the marriage of Cassander.

V. The female pupils of Plato, Lasthenea of Mantinea, and Axiothea of Phlius, are said to have become disciples of Speusippus also. And Dionysius, writing to him in a petulant manner, says, " And one may learn philosophy too from your female disciple from Arcadia; moreover, Plato used to take his pupils without exacting any fee from them; but you collect tribute from yours, whether willing or unwilling.''

VI. He was the first man, as Diodorus relates in the first book of his Commentaries, who investigated in his school what was common to the several sciences; and who endeavoured, as far as possible, to maintain their connection with each other. He was also the first who published those things which Isocrates called secrets, as Caeneus tells us. And the first too who found out how to make light baskets of bundles of twigs.

VII. But he became afflicted with paralysis, aud sent to
Xenocrates inviting him to come to him, and to become his successor in his school.

VIII. And they say that once, when he was being borne in a carriage into the Academy, he met Diogenes, and said, " Hail;" and Diogenes replied, " I will not say hail to you, who, though in such a state as you are, endure to live." IX. And at last in despair he put an end to his life, being a man of a great age. And we have written this epigram on him:—

Had I not known Speusippua thus had died,

No one would have persuaded me that he

Was e'er akin to Plato; who would never

Have died desponding for so slight a grief.

But Plutarch, in his Life of Lysander, and again in his Life of Sylla, says that he was kept in a state of constant inflammation by lice. For he was of a weak habit of body, as Timotheus relates in his treatise on Lives.

X. Speusippus said to a rich man who was in love with an ugly woman, " What do you want with her? I will find you a much prettier woman for ten talents." XI. He left behind him a great number of commentaries, and many dialogues; among which was one on Aristippus; I one on Eiches; one on Pleasure; one on Justice; one on Philosophy; one on Friendship; one on the Gods; one called the Philosopher; one addressed to Cephalus; one called Cephalus; one called Clinomachus, or Lysias; one called the Citizen; one on the Soul; one addressed to Gryllus; one called Aristippus; one called the Test of Art. There were also Commentaries by way of dialogues; one on Art; and ten about those things which are alike in their treatment. There are also books of divisions.and arguments directed to similar things; Essays on the Genera and Species of Examples; an Essay addressed to Amartynus; a Panegyric on Plato; Letters to Dion, and Dionysius, and Philip; an Essay on Legislation. There is also, the Mathematician; the Mandrobulus; the Lysias; Definitions; and a series of Commentaries. There are in all, forty-three thousand four hundred and seventy-five lines.

Simonides dedicated to him the Histories, in which he had related the actions of Dion and Bion. And in the second book of his Commentaries, Pharorinus states that Aristotle purchased his books for three talents.

XII. There was also another person of the name of Speusippus, a physician of the school of Herophilus, a native of Alexandria. LIFE OF XENOCRATES.

I. Xenocrates was the son of Agathenor, and a native of I Chalcedon. From his early youth he was a pupil of Plato, and also accompanied him in his voyages to Sicily.

II. He was by nature of a lazy disposition, so that they say that Plato said once, when comparing him to Aristotle,— " The one requires the spur, and the other the bridle." And on another occasion, he said, " What a horse and what an ass am I dressing opposite to one another!" III. In other respects Xenocrates was always of a solemn and grave character, so that Plato was continually saying to him,—" Xenocrates, sacrifice to the Graces." And he spent the greater part of his time in the Academy, and whenever he was about to go into the city, they say all the turbulent and quarrelsome rabble in the city used to make way for him to pass by. And once, Phryne the courtesan wished to try him and pretending that she was pursued by some people, she fled and took refuge in his house; and he admitted her indeed, because of what was due to humanity; and as there was but one bed in the room, he, at her entreaty, allowed her to share it with him; but at last, in spite of all her entreaties, she got up and went away, without having been able to succeed in her purpose; and told those who asked her, that she had quitted a statue and not a man. But some say that the real story is, that his pupils put Lais into his bed, and that he was so continent, that he submitted to some severe operations of excision and cautery. Herophilus was one of the most celebrated physicians of antiquity, who founded the Medical School at Alexandria, in the time of the first Ptolemy. IV. And he was a very trustworthy man; so that, though it was not lawful for men to give evidence except on oath, the Athenians made an exception in his favour alone.

V. He was also a man of the most contented disposition; accordingly they say that when Alexander sent him a large sum of money, he took three thousand Attic drachmas, and sent back the rest, saying, that Alexander wanted most, as he had the greatest number of mouths to feed. And when some was sent him by Antipater, he would not accept any of it, as Myornianus tells us in his Similitudes. And once, when he gained a golden crown, in a contest as to who could drink most, which was offered in the yearly festival of the Choes by Dionysius, he went out and placed the crown at the feet of the statue of Mercury, which was at the gate, where he was also accustomed to deposit his garlands of flowers. It is said also, that he was once sent with some colleagues as an ambassador to Philip; and that they were won over by gifts, and went to his banquets and conversed with Philip; but that he would do none of these things, nor could Philip propitiate him by these means; on which account, when the other ambassadors arrived in Athens, they said that Xenocrates had gone with them to no purpose; and the people were ready to punish him; but when they had learnt from him that they had now more need than ever to look to the welfare of their city, for that Philip had already bribed all their counsellors, but that he had been unable to win him over by any means, then they say that the people honoured him with redoubled honour. They add also, that Philip said afterwards, that Xenocrates was the only one of those who bad come to him who was incorruptible. And when he went as ambassador to Antipater on the subject of the Athenian captives at the time of the Samian war, and was invited by him to a banquet, he addressed him in the following lines:—

I answer, Goddess human, is thy breast
By justice sway'd, by tender pity prest?
Ill fits it me, whose friends are sunk to beasts,
To quaff thy bowls, or riot in thy feasts:
Me would'st thou please, for them thy cares employ,
And them to me restore, and me to joy?
Horn. Od. x. 387. Pope's Version, 450.

And Antipater, admiring the appropriateness of the quotation, immediately released them.

VI. On one occasion, when a sparrow was pursued by a hawk, and flew into his bosom, he caressed it, and let it go again, saying that we ought not to betray a suppliant. And being ridiculed by Bion, he said that he would not answer him, for that tragedy, when ridiculed by comedy, did not condescend to make a reply. To one who had never learnt music, or geometry, or astronomy, but who wished to become his disciple, he said, " Be gone, for you have not yet the handles of philosophy." But some say that he said, " Be gone, for I do not card wool here." And when Dionysius said to Plato that some one would cut off his head, he, being present, showed his own, and said, " Not before they have cut off mine." VII. They say too that once, when Antipater had come to Athens and saluted him, he would not make him any reply before he had finished quietly the discourse which he was delivering. VIII. Being exceedingly devoid of every kind of pride, he often used to meditate with himself several times a day; and always allotted one hour of each day, it is said, to silence. IX. And he left behind him a great number of writings, and books of recommendation, and verses, which are these,— six books on Natural Philosophy; six on Wisdom; one on Pdches, the Arcadian; one volume on the Indefinite; one on a Child; one on Temperance; one on the Useful; one on the Free; one on Death; one on the Voluntary; two on Friendship; one on Courtesy; two on Contraries; two on Happiness; one on

Writing; one on Memory; one on Falsehood; the Callicles one; two on Prudence; one on Œconomy; one on Temperance; one on the Power of Law; one on Political Constitutions; one on Piety; one to show that Virtue may be transmitted; one about the Existent; one on Fate; one on the ' Passions; one on Lives; one on Unanimity; two on Pupils; one on Justice; two on Virtue; one on Species; two on Pleasure; one on Life; one on Manly Courage; one on The One; one on Ideas; one on Art; two on the Gods; two on the Soul; one on Knowledge; one on the Statesman; one on Science; one on Philosophy; one on the School of Parmenides; one the Archidemus, or an essay on Justice; one on the Good; eight of those things which concern the Intellect; ten essays in solution of the difficulties which occur respecting Orations; six books on the study of Natural Philosophy; the Principal, one; one treatise on Genus and Species; one on the doctrines of the Pythagoreans; two books of Solutions; seven of Divisions; several volumes of Propositions; several also about the method of conducting Discussions. Besides all this, there are one set of fifteen volumes, and another of sixteen, on the subject of those studies which relate to Speaking; nine more which treat of Ratiocination; six books on Mathematics; two more books on subjects connected with the Intellect; five books on Geometry; one book of Reminiscences; one of Contraries; one on Arithmetic; one on the Contemplation of Numbers; one on Intervals; six on Astronomy; four of elementary suggestions to Alexander, on the subject of Royal Power; one addressed to Arybas; one addressed to Hephaestion; two on Geometry; seven books of Verses.

X. But the Athenians, though he was such a great man, once sold him, because he was unable to pay the tax to which the metics were liable. And Demetriu3 Phalereus purchased him, and so assisted both parties, Xenocrates by giving him his freedom, and the Athenians in respect of the tax upon metics. This circumstance is mentioned by Myronianus of Amastra, in the first book of his chapters of Historical Coincidences.

XI. He succeeded Spuesippus, and presided over the school for. twenty-five years, beginning at the archonship of Lysimachides, in the second year of the hundred and tenth olympiad. XII. And he died in consequence of stumbling by night against a dish, being more than eighty-two years of age. And in one of our epigrams we speak thus of him:—

He struck against a brazen pot, And cut his forehead deep,
And crying cruel is my lot,
In death he fell asleep.
So thus Xenocrates did fall,
The universal friend of all.

XIII. And there were five other people of the name of Xenocrates. One was an ancient tactician, a fellow citizen, and very near relation of the philosopher of whom we have been speaking; and there is extant an oration of his which is scribed, On Arsinoe, and which was written on the death of Arsinoe. A third was a philosopher who wrote some very indifferent elegiac poetry; and that is not strange, for when poets take to writing in prose, they succeed pretty well; but when prose writers try their hand at poetry, they fail; from which it is plain, that the one is a gift of nature, and the other a work of art. The fourth was a statuary; the fifth a writer of songs, as we are told by Aristoxen".

LIFE OF POLEMO.

I. Polemo was the son of Philostratus, an Athenian, of the burgh of iEa. And when he was young, he was so very intemperate and profligate, that he used always to carry money about with him, to procure the instant gratification of his passions; and he used also to hide money in the narrow alleys, for this purpose. And once there was found in the Academy a piece of three obols, hidden against one of the columns, which he had put there for some purpose like that which I have indicated; and on one occasion he arranged beforehand with some young men, and rushed, adorned with a garland, and drunk, into the school of Xenocrates. But he took no notice of him, and continued his discourse as he had begun it, and it was in praise of temperance; and the young man, hearing it, was gradually charmed, and became so industrious, that he surpassed all the rest of the disciples, and himself became the successor of Xenocrates, in his school beginning in the hundred and sixteenth olympiad.

II. And Antigonus, of Carystus, says in his Lives, that his father had been the chief man of the city, and had kept chariots for the Olympic games. III. He also asserts that Polemo was prosecuted by his wife, on the charge of ill-treatment, because he indulged in illicit pleasures, and despised her. IV. But that when he began to devote himself to philosophy, he adopted such a rigorous system of morals, that he for the future always continued the same in appearance, and never even changed his voice, on which account Crantor was charmed by him. Accordingly, on one occasion, when a dog was mad and had bitten his leg, he was the only person who did not turn pale; and once, when there was a great confusion in the city, he, having heard the cause, remained where he was without fleeing. In the theatres too he was quite immoveable; accordingly, when Nicostratus the poet, who was surnamed Clytaemnestra, was once reading something to him and Crates, the latter was excited to sympathy, he behaved as though he heard nothing. And altogether, he was such as Melanthius, the painter, describes in his treatise on Painting; for he says that some kind of obstinacy and harshness ought to exist in works of art as in morals.

And Polemo used to say that a man ought to exercise himself in action, and not in dialectic speculations, as if one had drunk in and dwelt upon a harmonious kind of system of art, so as to be admired for one's shrewdness, in putting questions; but to be inconsistent with one's self in character. He was, then, a well-bred and high-spirited man, avoiding what Aristophanes says of Euripides, speeches of vinegar and assafcetida, such as he says himself:—

Are base delights compared with better things?

V. And he did not use to lecture on

the propositions before him while sitting down; but he would walk about, it is said, and so discuss them. And be was much honoured in the city because of his noble sentiments; and after he had been walking about, he would rest in his garden; and his pupils erected little cabins near it, and dwelt near his school and corridor.

VI. And as it seems, Polemo imitated Xenocrates in everything; and Aristippus, in the fourth book of his treatise on Ancient Luxury, says that Xenocrates loved him; at all events, Polemo used to be always speaking of him, and praising his guileless nature, and his rigorous virtues, and his chaste severity, like that of a Doric building. VII. He was/also very fond of Sophocles, and especially of those passages where, according to one of the comic poets, he seemed to have had a Molossian hound for his colleague in composing his poems; and when there was, to use the expression of Phrynichus:—

No sweet or washy liquor, but purest Pramnian wine.

And he used to say that Homer was an epic Sophocles, and Sophocles a tragic Homer.

VIII. And he died when he was very old, of decline, having left behind bim a great number of writings. And there is this epigram of ours upon him:—

Do you not hear, we've buried Polemo,
Whom sickness, worst affliction of mankind
Attacked, and bore off to the shades below;
Yet Polemo lies not here, but Polemo's body,
And that he did himself place here on earth,
Prepared in soul to mount up to the skies.

LIFE OF CRATES.

I. Crates was the son of Antigenes, and of the Thriasian burgh, and a pupil and attached friend of Polemo. He was also his successor as president of his school.

II. And they benefited one another so much, that not only did they delight while alive in the same pursuits, but almost to their latest breath did they resemble one another, and even after they were both dead they shared the same tomb. In reference to which circumstance Antagoras has written an epigram on the pair, in which he expresses himself thus:— -Stranger, who passest by, relate that here The God-like Crates lies, and Polemo;

Two men of kindred nobleness of mind;
Out of whose holy mouths pure wisdom flowed,
And they with upright lives did well display,
The strength of all their principles and teaching.

And they say too that it was in reference to this that Arcesilaus, when he came over to them from Theophrastus, said that they were some gods, or else a remnant of the golden race; for they were not very fond of courting the people, but had a disposition in accordance with the saying of Dionysodorus the flute player, who is reported to have said, with great exultation and pride, that no one had ever heard his music in a trireme or at a fountain as they had heard Ismenius.

III. Antigonus relates that he used to be a messmate of Crantor, and that these philosophers and Arcesilaus lived together; and that Arcesilaus lived in Crantor's house, but that Polemo and Crates lived in the house of one of the citizens, named Lysicles; and he says that Crates was, as I have already mentioned, greatly attached to Polemo, and so was Arcesilaus to Crantor. IV. But when Crates died, as Apollodorus relates in the third book of his Chronicles, he left behind him compositions, some on philosophical subjects and some on comedy, and some which were speeches addressed to assemblies of the people, or delivered on the occasion of embassies.

V. He also left behind him some eminent disciples, among whom were Arcesilaus, about whom we shall speak presently, for he too was a pupil of his, and Bion of the Borysthenes, who was afterwards called a Theodorean, from the sect which he espoused, and we shall speak of him immediately after Arcesilaus.

VI. But there were ten people of the name of Crates. The first was a poet of the old comedy; the second was an orator of Tralles, a pupil of Isocrates; the third was an engineer who served under Alexander; the fourth a Cynic, whom we shall mention hereafter; the fifth a Peripatetic philosopher; the sixth the Academic philosopher, of whom we are speaking; the seventh a grammarian of Malos; the eighth a writer in geometry; the ninth an epigrammatic poet; the tenth was an Academic philosopher, a native of Tarsus. LIFE OF CRANTOR.

I. Cbantor, a native of Soli, being admired very greatly in his own country, came to Athens and became a pupil of Xenocrates at the same time with Polemo.

II. And he left behind him memorials, in the shape of writings, to the number of 30,000 lines, some of which, however, are by some writers attributed to Arcesilaus. III. They say of him that when he was asked what it was that he was so charmed with in Polemo, he replied, " That he had never heard him speak in too high or too low a key." IV. When he was ill he retired to the temple of iEsculapius, and there walked about, and people came to him from air quarters, thinkng that he had gone thither, not on account of

M any disease, but because he wished to establish a school there.

V. And among those who came to him was Arcesilaus, wishing to be recommended by him to Polemo, although he was much attached to him, as we shall mention in the life of Arcesilaus. But when he got well he became a pupil of Polemo, and was excessively admired on that account. It is said,"also, that he left his property to Arcesilaus, to the amount of twelve talents; and *that,* being asked by him where he would like to be buried, he said:—

It is a happy fate to lie entombed
In the recesses of a well-loVd land.

VI. It is said also that he wrote poems, and that he sealed them up in the temple of Minerva, in his own country; and Meaetetus the poet wrote thus about him:—

Crantor pleased men; hut greater

pleasure still
He to the Muses gave, ere he aged grew.
Earth, tenderly embrace the holy man,
And let him lie in quiet undisturb'd.

And of all writers, Crantor admired Homer and Euripides most; saying that the hardest thing possible was to write tragically and in a manner to excite sympathy, without departing from nature; and he used to quote this line out of the Bellerophon:—'.

Alas! why should I say alas! for we
Have only borne the usual fate of man.

The following verses of Antagoras the poet are also attributed to Crantor: the subject is love, and they run thus:—

My mind is much perplexed; for what, 0 Love,
Dare I pronounce your origin? May I
Call you chiefest of the immortal Gods,
Of all the children whom dark Erebus
And Royal Night bore on the billowy waves
Of widest Ocean? Or shall I bid you hail,
As son of proudest Venus? or of Earth?
Or of the untamed winds? so fierce you rove,
Bringing mankind sad cares, yet not unmixed
With happy good, so two-fold is your nature.

And he was very ingenious at devising new words and expressions; accordingly, he said that one tragedian had an unnewn *(aireXixrirog)* voice, all over bark; and he said that the verses of a certain poet were full of moths; and that the propositions of Theophrastus had been written on an oyster shell. But the work of his which is most admired is his book on Mourning.

VII. And he died before Polemo and Crates, having been attacked by the dropsy; and we have written this epigram on him:—

The worst of sicknesses has overwhelmed you,
O Crantor, and you thus did quit the earth,
Descending to the dark abyss of Hell.
Now you are happy there; but all the while
The sad Academy, and your native land
Of Soli mourn, bereaved of your eloquence.

LIFE OF AECESILAUS.

I. Arcesilaus was the son of Seuthes or Scythes, as Apollodorus states in the third book of his Chronicles, and a native of Pitane in iEolia. II. He was the original founder of the Middle Academy, and i the first man who professed to suspend the declaration of his judgment, because of the contrarieties of the reasons alleged on either side. He was likewise the first who attempted to argue on both sides of a question, and who also made the method of discussion, which had been handed down by Plato, by means of question and answer, more contentious than before. III. He met with Crantor in the following manner. He) was one of four brothers, two by the same father and two by. the same mother. Of those who were by the same mother the eldest was Pylades, and of those by the same father the eldest was Maereas, who was his guardian; and at first he was a pupil of Autolycus the mathematician, who happened to be a fellow citizen of his before he went to Athens; and with Autolycus he travelled as far as Sardis. After that he became a pupil of Xanthus the musician, and after that attended the lectures of Theophrastus, and subsequently came over to the Academy to Crantor. For Maereas his brother, whom I have mentioned t before, urged him to apply himself to rhetoric; but he himself had a preference for philosophy, and when he became much attached to him Crantor asked him, quoting a line out of the Andromeda of Euripides:— 0 virgin, if I save you, will you thank me?
And he replied by quoting the next line to it: — 0 take me to you, stranger, as your slave,
Or wife, or what you please.

And ever after that they became very intimate, so that they say Theophrastus was much annoyed, and said, " That a most ingenious and well-disposed young man had deserted his school." IV. For he was not only very impressive in his discourse, and displayed a great deal of learning in it, but he also tried his hand at poetry, and there is extant an epigram which is attributed to him, addressed to Attalus, which is as follows:—

Pergamus is not famed for arms alone, But often hears its praise resound
For its fine horses, at the holy Pisa.
Yet, if a mortal may declare,
Its fate as hidden in the breast of Jove,
It will be famous for its woes.

There is another addressed to Menodorus the son of Eudamus, who was attached to one of his fellow pupils:—

Phrygia is a distant land, and so
Is saered Thyatira, and Cadanade,
Your country Menodorus. But from all,
As the unvaried song of bards relates,
An equal road does lie to Acheron,
That dark unmentioned river; so you lie
Here far from home; and here Eudamus raises'
This tomb above your bones, for he did love you,
Though you were poor, with an undying love.

But he admired Homer above all poets, and always used to read a portion of his works before going to sleep; and in the morning he would say that he was going to the object of his love, when he was going to read him. He said, too, that Pindar was a wonderful man for filling the voice, and pouring forth an abundant variety of words and expressions. He also, when he was a young man, wrote a criticism on Ion.

V. And he was a pupil likewise of Hipponicus, the geometrican, whom he used to ridicule on pther points as being lazy and gaping; but he admitted that in his own profession he was clear sighted enough, and said that geometry had flown into his mouth while he was yawning. And when he went out of his mind, he took him to his own house, and took care ol him till he recovered his senses.

VI. And when Crates died, he succeeded him in the presidency of his schools, a man of the name of Socrates willingly yielding to him. VII. And as he suspended his judgment on every point, he j never, as it is said, wrote one single book. But others say that he was once

detected correcting some passages in a work of his; and some assert that he published it, while others deny it, and affirm that he threw it into the fire. VIII. He seems to have been a great admirer of Plato, and he possessed all his writings. He also, according to somejf authorities, had a very high opinion of Pyrrho. IX. He also studied dialectics, and the discussions of the Eretrian school; on which account Ariston said of him:—
First Plato comes, and Pyrrho last,
And in the middle Diodorus.

And Timon speaks thus of him:—
For having on this side the heavy load
Of Menedemus plac'd beneath his breast,
He'll to stout Pyrrho run, or Diodorus.

And presently afterwards he represents him as saying:—
I'll swim to Pyrrho, or that crooked sophist
Called Diodorus.

X. He was exceedingly fond of employing axioms, very concise in his diction, and when speaking he laid an emphasis on each separate word..

XI. He was also very fond of attacking others, and very; free spoken, on which account Timon in another passage speaks of him thus:—
You'll not escape all notice while you thus
Attack the young man with your biting sarcasm.

Once, when a young man was arguing against him with more boldness than usual, he said, " Will no one stop his mouth with the knout?" And to a man who lay under the general imputation of low debauchery, and who argued with him that one thing was not greater than another, he asked him whether a cup holding two pints was not larger than one which held only one. There was a certain Chian named Hemon, exceedingly ugly, but who fancied himself good looking, and always went about in fine clothes; this man asked him one day, " If he thought that a wise man could feel attachment to him; " " Why should he not," said he, " when they love even those who are less handsome than you, and not so well-dressed either?" and when the man, though one of the vilest characters possible, said to Arcesilaus as if he were addressing a very rigid man:— 0, noble man, may I a question put,
Or must I hold my tongue?

Arcesilaus replied:—
O wretched woman, why do you thus roughen
Your voice, not speaking in your usual manner?

And once, when he was plagued by a chattering fellow of low extraction, he said:—
The sons of slaves are always talking vilely.t

Another time, when a talkative man was giving utterance to a great deal of nonsense, he said, that " He had not had a nurse who was severe enough." And to some people he never gave any answer at all. On one occasion a usurer, who made pretence to some learning, said in his hearing that he did not know something or other, on which he rejoined:—
For often times the passing winds do fill
The female bird, except when big with young. J Perhaps there is a pun here; atrrpayaXog means not only a knout composed of small bones strung together, but also a die.

t This is a quotation from some lost play of Euripides, slightly altered, the line, as printed in the Variorum Edition, vol. vii, Mc. Trag. cxxx. is— aKoXaara ir &vra yiverai, SovXotv reicva. X There is a pun here which is untranslateable. The Greek is Ttxj/v orav Tokog 7ropy, meaning usury, and also,offspring or delivery.,

And the lines come out of the Enomaus of Sophocles. He once reminded a certain dialectician, a pupil of Alexitnes, who was unable to explain correctly some saying of his master, of what had been done by Philoxenus to some brickmakers. For when they were singing some of his songs very badly he came upon them, and trampled their bricks under foot, saying, " As you spoil my works so will I spoil yours." XII. And he used to be very indignant with those who neglected proper opportunities of applying themselves to learning; and he had a peculiar habit, while conversing, of using the expression, " I think," and " So and so," naming the person, " will not agree to this." And this was imitated by several of his pupils, who copied also his style of expression and everything about him. He was a man very ready at inventing new words, and very quick at meeting objections, and at bringing round the conversation to the subject before him, and at adapting it to every occasion, and he was the most convincing! speaker that could be found, on which account numbers of people flocked to his school, in spite of being somewhat alarmed at his severity, which however they bore with complacency, for he was a very kind man, and one who inspired his hearers with abundant hope, and in his manner of life he was very affable and liberal, always ready to do any one a service without any parade, and shrinking from any expression of gratitude on the part of those whom he had obliged. Accordingly once, when he had gone to visit Ctesibius who was ill, seeing him in great distress from want, he secretly slipped his purse under his pillow; and when Ctesibius found it, " This," said he, " is the amusement of Arcesilaus." And at another time he sent him a thousand drachmas. He it was also who introduced Archias the Arcadian to Eumenes, and who procured lnm many favours from him.

XIII. And being a very liberal man and utterly regardless of money, he made the most splendid display of silver plate, and in his exhibition of gold plate he vied with that of Archecrates and Callecrates; and he was constantly assisting and contributing to the wants of others with money: and once, when some one had borrowed from him some articles of silver plate to help him entertain his friends, and did not offer to return them, he never asked for them back or reclaimed them; but some say that he lent them with the purpose that they should be kept, and that when the man returned them, he made him a present of them as he was a poor man. He had also property in Pitana, the revenues from which were transmitted to him by his brother

Pylades. XIV. Moreover, Eumenes, the son of Philetaerus, supplied him with many things, on which account he was the only king to whom he addressed any of his discourses. And when many philosophers paid court to Antigonus and went out to meet him when he arrived, he himself kept quiet, not wishing to make his acquaintance. But he was a great friend of Hierocles, the governor of the harbours of Munychia and the Piraeus; and at festivals he always paid him a visit. And when he constantly endeavoured to persuade him to pay his respects to Antigonus, he would not; but though he accompanied him as far as his gates, he turned back himself. And after the sea-fight of Antigonus, when many people went to him and wrote him letters to comfort him for his defeat, he neither went nor wrote; but still in the service of his country, he went to Demetrias as ambassador to Antigonus, and succeeded in the object of his mission. XV. And he spent all his time in the Academy, and avoided meddling with public affairs, but at times he would spend some days in the Piraeus of Athens, discoursing on philosophical subjects, from his friendship for Hierocles, which conduct of his gave rise to unfavourable reports being raised against him by some people. XVI. Being a man of very expensive habits, for he was in this respect a sort of second Aristippus, he often went to dine with his friends. He also lived openly with Theodote and. Philaete, two courtesans of Elis; and to those who reproached him for this conduct, he used to quote the opinions of Aristippus. He was also very fond of the society of young men, and of a very affectionate disposition, on which account Aristi, the Chian, a Stoic philosopher, used to accuse him of being a corrupter of the youth of the city, and a profligate man. He is said also to have been greatly attached to Demetrius, who sailed to Cyrene, and to Cleochares of Mydea, of whom he said to his messmates, that he wished to open the door to him, but that he prevented him. XVII. Demochares the son of Laches, and Pythocles the son of Bugelus, were also among his friends, and he said that he humoured them in all their wishes because of his great patience. And, on this account, those people to whom I have before alluded, used to attack him and ridicule him as a popularity hunter and vain-glorious man. And they set upon him very violently at an entertainment given by Hieronymus, the Peripatetic, when he invited his friends on the birthday of Alcymeus, the son of Antigonus, on which occasion Antigonus sent him a large sum of money to promote the conviviality. On this occasion, as he avoided all discussion during the continuance of the banquet, when Aridelus proposed to him a question which required some deliberation, and entreated him to discourse upon it, it is said that he replied, " But this is more especially the business of philosophy, to know the proper time for everything." With reference to the charge that was brought against him of being a popularity hunter, Timon speaks, among other matters, mentioning it in the following manner:—

He spoke and glided quick among the crowd,

They gazed on him as finches who behold

An owl among them. You then please the people!

Alas, poor fool, 'tis no great matter that;

Why give yourself such airs for such a trifle?

XVIII. However, in all other respects he was so free from vanity, that he used to advise his pupils to become the disciples of other men; and once, when a young man from Chios was not satisfied with his school, but preferred that of Hieronymus, whom I have mentioned before, he himself took him and introduced him to that philosopher, recommending him to preserve his regularity of conduct. And there is a very witty saying of his recorded. For when some one asked him once, why people left other schools to go to the Epicureans, but no one left the Epicureans to join other sects, he replied, " People sometimes make eunuchs of men, but no one can ever make a man out of an eunuch." XIX. At last, when he was near his end, he left all his property to his brother Pylades, because he, without the knowledge of Maereas, had taken him to Chios and had brought him from thence to Athens. He never married a wife, and never had any children. He made three copies of his will, and deposited one in Eretria with Amphicritus, and one at Athens with some of his friends, and the third he sent to his own home to Thaumasias, one of his relations, entreating him to keep it. And he also wrote him the following letter:— ARCESILAUS TO THAUMASIAS.

" I have given Diogenes a copy of my will to convey to you. For, because I am frequently unwell and have got very infirm, I have thought it right to make a will, that, if anything should happen to me I might not depart with the feehngs of having done you any injury, who have been so constantly affectionate to me. And as you have been at all times the most faithful to me of all my friends, I entreat you to preserve this for me out of regard for my old age and your regard for me. Take care then to behave justly towards me, remembering how much I entrust to your integrity, so that I may appear to have managed my affairs well, as far as depends on you; and there is another copy of this will at Athens, in the care of some of my friends, arid another at Eretria, in the hands of Amphicritus." XX. He died, as Hermippus relates, after having drunk au excessive quantity of wine, and then became delirious, when he was seventy-five years old; and he was more beloved by the Athenians than any one else had ever been. And we have written the following epigram on him:—

O wise Arcesilaus, why didst thou drink

So vast a quantity of unmixed wine,

As to lose all your senses, and then die?

1 pity you not so much for your death,

As for the insult that you thus did offer

The Muses, by your sad excess in wine.

XXI. There were also three other persons of the name of Arcesilaus; one a poet of the old Comedy; another an elegiac poet; the third a sculptor, on whom Simonides wrote the following epi-

gram:—
This is a statue of chaste Dian's self
The price two hundred Parian drachmas fine,
Stamp'd with the image of the wanton goat.
It is the work of wise Arcesilaus,
The son of Aristodicus: a man,
Whose hands Minerva guided in his art.

The philosopher of whom we have been speaking flourished, as Apollodorus tells us in his Chronicles, about the hundred and twentieth olympiad.

LIFE OF BION.

I. Bion was a native of the country around the Borysthenes; but as to who his parents were, and to what circumstances it was owing that he applied himself to the study of philosophy, we know no more than what he himself told Antigonus. For when Antigonus asked him:—

What art thou, say! from whence, from whom you came,
Who are your parents / tell thy race, thy name;

He, knowing that he had been misrepresented to the king, said to him, " My father was a freedman, who used to wipe his mouth with his sleeve," (by which he meant that he used to sell salt fish). " As to his race, he was a native of the district of the Borysthenes; having no countenance, but only a brand in his face, a token of the bitter cruelty of his master. My mother was such a woman as a man of that condition might marry, taken out of a brothel. Then, my father being in arrears to the tax-gatherers, was sold with all his family, and with me among them; and as I was young and good looking, a certain orator purchased me, and when he died he left me everything. And I, having burnt all his books, and torn up all his papers, came to Athens and applied myself to the study of Philosophy:—

Such was my father, and from him I came,
The honoured author of my birth and name.t

This is all that I can tell you of myself: so that Persaeus and Philonides may give up telling these stories about me: and you may judge of me on my own merits." Horn. Od. x. 335. Pope's Version, 387.

t Horn. IL vi. 211. Pope's Version, 254.

II. And Bion was truly a man of great versatility, and a.very subtle philosopher, and a man who gave all who chose great opportunities of practising philosophy. In some respects he was of a gentle disposition, and very much inclined to indulge in vanity.

III. And he left behind him many memorials of himself in the way of writings, and also many apophthegms full of useful sentiments. As for instance, once when he was reproved for having failed to charm a young man, he replied, " You cannot possibly draw up cheese with a hook before it has got hard." On another occasion he was asked who was the most miserable of men, and replied, " He who has set his heart on the greatest prosperity." When he was asked whether it was advisable to marry (for this answer also is attributed to him), he replied, " If you marry an ugly woman you will have a punishment *(iroivri)*, and if a handsome woman you will have one who is common" (xo/vij). He called old age a port to shelter one from misfortune; and accordingly, he said that every one fled to it. He said that glory was the mother of years; that beauty was a good which concerned others rather than one's self; that riches were the sinews of business. To a man who had squandered his estate he said, " The earth swallowed up Amphiaraus, but you have swallowed up the earth." Another saying of his was that it was a great evil not to be able to bear evil. And he condemned those who burnt the dead as though they felt nothing, and then mocked them as though they did feel. And he was always saying that it was better to put one's own beauty at the disposal of another, than to covet the beauty of others; for that one who did so was injuring both his body and his soul. And he used to blame Socrates saying, that if he derived no advantage from Alcibiades he was foolish, and if he never derived any advantage from him he then deserved no credit. He used to say that the way to the shades below was easy; and accordingly, that people went there with their eyes shut. He used to blame Alcibiades, saying that while he was a boy he seduced husbands from their wives, and when he had become a young man he seduced the wives from their husbands. While most of the Athenians at Rhodes practised rhetoric, he himself used to give lectures on philosophical subjects; and to one who blamed him for this he said, " I have bought wheat, and I sell barley."

It was a saying of his that the inhabitants of the shades below would be more punished if they carried water in buckets that were whole, than in such as were bored. To a chattering fellow who was soliciting him for aid, he said, " I will do what is sufficient for you, if you will send deputies to me, and forbear to come yourself." Once when he was at sea in the company of some wicked men, he fell into the hands of pirates; and when the rest said, " We are undone, if we are known." " But I," said he, "am undone if we are not known. " He used to say that self-conceit was the enemy of progress. Of a rich man who was mean and niggardly, he said, " That man does not possess his estate, but his estate possesses him." He used to say that stingy men took care of their property as if it was their own, but derived no advantage from it as if it belonged to other people. Another of his sayings was, that young men ought to display courage, but that old men ought to be distinguished for prudence. And that prudence was as much superior to the other virtues as sight was to the other senses. And that it was not right to speak of old age, at which every one is desirous to arrive. To an envious man who was looking gloomy, he said, " I know not whether it is because some misfortune has happened to you, or some good fortune to some one else." One thing that he used to say was, that a mean extraction was a bad companion to freedom of speech. For:—

It does enslave a man, however bold
His speech may be.

And another was that we ought to keep our friends, whatever sort of people they may be, so that we may not seem to have been intimate with wicked men, or to have abandoned good men.

IV. Very early in his career he abandoned the school of the Academy, and at the same time became a disciple of Crates. Then he passed over to the sect of the Cynics, taking their coarse cloak and wallet. For what else could ever have changed his nature into one of such apathy? After that he adopted the Theodorean principles, having become a disciple of Theodorus the Atheist, who was used to employ every kind of reasoning in support of his system of philosophy. After This is a quotation from the Hippolytus of Euripides, v. 424. leaving him, he became a pupil of Theophrastus, the Peripa tetic.

V. He was very fond of theatrical entertainments, and very skilful in distracting his hearers by exciting a laugh, giving things disparaging names. And because he used to avail himself of every species of reasoning, they relate that Eretosthenes said that Bion was the first person who had clothed philosophy in a flowery robe.

VI. He was also very ingenious in parodying passages, and adapting them to circumstances as they arose. As for instance, I may cite the following:—
Tender Archytas, born of tuneful lyre,
Whom thoughts of happy vanity inspire;
Most skilled of mortals in appeasing ire.
And he jested on every part of music and geometry.

VII. He was a man of very expensive habits, and on this account he used to go from city to city, and at times he would contrive the most amazing devices. VIII. Accordingly, in Ehodes, he persuaded the sailors to put on the habiliments of philosophical students and follow him about; and then he made himself conspicuous by entering the gymnasium with this train of followers. IX. He was accustomed also to adopt young men as his sons, in order to derive assistance from them in his pleasures, and to be protected by their affection for him. But he was a very selfish man, and very fond of quoting the saying, " The property of friends is common;" owing to which it is that no one is spoken of as a disciple of his, though so many men I doubt if the wit of these parodies will be appreciated by the modern reader. The lines of Homer, which they are intended to parody, are:—
"Q *fiinap* ArpeKi;, *fioiptytvlc, 6Xl3io-latutiv.—ll.* 3, 182.
r/i av n»jXttij, iravTutv kKirayXoraT' avSpuiv.—ll. v. 146.

The first of which is translated by Pope:—
Oh, blest Atrides, born of prosperous fate,
Successful monarch of a mighty state!
The Greek parody in the text is:—
'Q 7TS7TOV 'Apx"""", *tyaWtfyevig*, 6X/3ioruSe
Tje ijrarijs *ifiSo iravriov ijiirupoTaT dvSpSv.*

attended his school. And he made some very shameless; accordingly, Betion, one of his intimate acquaintances, is reported to have said once to Menedemus, " So Menedemus constantly spends the evening with Bion, aud I see no harm in it." He used also to talk with great impiety to those who conversed with him, having derived his opinions on this subject from Theodorus.

X. And when at a later period he became afflicted with disease, as the people of Chalcis said, for he died there, he was persuaded to wear amulets and charms, and to show his repentance for the insults that he had offered to the Gods.

But he suffered fearfully for want of proper people to attend. him, until Antigonus sent him two servants. And he followed him in a litter, as Pharorinus relates in his Universal History.

And the circumstances of his death we have ourselves spoken of in the following lines:—
We hear that Bion the Borysthenite,
Whom the ferocious Scythian land brought forth,
Used to deny that there were Gods at all.
Now, if he'd persevered in this opinion,
One would have said he speaks just as he thinks;
Though certainly his thoughts are quite mistaken.
But when a lengthened sickness overtook him,
And he began to fear lest he should die;
This man who heretofore denied the Gods,
And would not even look upon a temple,
And mocked all those who e'er approached the Gods
With prayer or sacrifice; who ne'er, not even
For his own hearth, and home, and household table,
Regaled the Gods with savoury fat and incense,
Who never once said, " I have sinned, but spare me."
Then did this atheist shrink, and give his neck
To an old woman to hang charms upon,
And bound his arms with magic amulets,
With laurel branches blocked his doors and windows,
Beady to do and venture anything
Bather than die. Fool that he was, who thought
To win the Gods to come into existence,
Whenever he might think he wanted them.
So wise too late, when now mere dust and ashes,
He put his hand forth, Hail, great Pluto, Hail!

XI. There were ten people of the name of Bion. First of all, the one who flourished at the same time with Pherecydes of Syros, and who has left two books behind him, which are still extant; he was a native of Proconnesas. The second was a Syracusan, the author of a system of rhetoric. The third was the man of whom we have been speaking. The fourth was a pupil of Democritus, and a mathematician, a native of Abdera, who wrote in both the Attic and Ionic dialect. He was the person who first asserted that fthere were countries where there was night for six months, and day for six months. The fifth was a native of Soli; who wrote a history of Ethiopia. The sixth was a rhetorician, who has left behind him nine books, inscribed with the names of the Muses, which are still extant. The eighth was a Milesian statuary, who is mentioned by Polemo. The ninth was a tragic poet of the number of those who are called Tarsicans. The tenth was a statuary, a native of Clazomenae or Chios, who is mentioned by Hipponax.

LIFE OF LACYDES.

I. Lacydes, the sen of Alexander, was a native of Cyrene. He it is who was the founder of the New Academy, having succeeded Arcesilaus: and he was a man of great gravity of character and demeanour, and one who had many imitators.

II. He was industrious from his very childhood, and poor, but very pleasing and sociable in his manners. III. They say that he had a pleasant way of managing his house-keeping affairs. For when he had taken anything out of his store-chest, he would seal it up again, and throw in his seal through the hole, so that it should be impossible for anything of what he had laid up there to be stolen from him, or carried off. But his servants learning this contrivance of his, broke the seal, and carried off as much as they pleased, and then they put the ring back through the hole in the same manner as before; and though they did this repeatedly, they were never detected. IV. Lacydes now used to hold his school in the Academy in the garden which had been laid out by Attalus the king, and it was called the Lacydeum, after him. And he was the only-man, who, while alive, resigned his school to a successor: but he resigned this to Telicles and Evander, of Phocis; and Hegesinus, of Pergamus, succeeded Evander; and he himself was in his turn succeeded by Carneades.

V. There is a witty saying, which is attributed to Lacydes. For they say that when Attalus sent for him, he answered that statues ought to be seen at a distance. On another occasion, as it is reported, he was studying geometry very late in life, and some said to him, " Is it then a time for you to be learning now?" " If it is not," he replied, " when will it be?" VI. And he died in the fourth year of the hundred and thirty-fourth Olympiad, when he had presided over his school twenty-six years. And his death was caused by paralysis, which was brought on by drinking. And we ourselves have.jested upon him in the following language.

'Tis an odd story that I heard of you—
Lacydes, that you went with hasty steps,
Spurred on by Bacchus, to the shades below.
How then, if this be true, can it be said,
That Bacchus e'er trips up his votaries' feet
'Tis a *mistake his being* named Lyjus.

LIFE OF CARNEADES.

I. Carneades was the son of Epicomus, or Philocomus, as Alexander states in his Successions; and a native of Cyrene.

II. He read all the books of the Stoics with great care,.» and especially those of Chrysippus; and then he wrote replies to them, but did it at the same time with such modesty that he used to say, " If Chrysippus had not lived, I should never have existed." III. He was a man of as great industry as ever existed; not, however, very much devoted to the investigation of subjects of natural philosophy, but more fond of the discussion of ethical i topics, on which account he used to let his hair and his nails grow, from his entire devotion of all his time to philosophical From Xuw, *solvo,* to relax or weaken the limbs.
N
discussion. And he was so eminent as a philosopher, thst the orators would quit their own schools and come and listen to his lectures. IV. He was also a man of a very powerful voice, so that the president of the Gymnasium sent to him once, to desire he would not shout so loudly. And he replied, " Give me then, measure for my voice." And the gymnasiarch again rejoined with great wit, for he said, "You have a measure in your pupils."

V. He was a very vehement speaker, and one difficult to contend with in the investigation of a point. And he used to decline all invitations to entertainments, for the reasons I have already mentioned.

VI. On one occasion, when Mentor, the Bithynian, one of his pupib, came to him to attend his school, observing that he was trying to seduce his mistress (as Phavoriuus relates in his Universal History), while he was in the middle of his lecture, he made the following parody in allusion to him:—

A weak old man comes hither, like in voice,
And gait, and figure, to the prudent Mentor.
I order him to be expelled this school.

And Mentor rising up, replied:—
Thus did they speak, and straight the others rose.

VII. He appears to have been beset with fears of death; as he was continually saying, " Nature, who has put this frame together, will also dissolve it." And learning that Antipater had died after having taken poison, he felt a desire to imitate the boldness of his departure, and said, " Give me some too." And when they asked "What?'' "Some mead," said he. And it is said that an eclipse of the moon happened when he died, the most beautiful of all the stars, next to the sun, indicating (as any one might say) its sympathy with the philosopher. And Apollodorus, in his Chronicles, says that he died in the fourth year of the hundred and sixty-second olympiad, being eighty-five years old. VIII. There are some letters extant addressed by him to Ariarathes, the king of the Cappadocians. All the other writings which are attributed to him were written by his disciples, for he himself left nothing behind him. And I have written on him the following lines in logoaedical Archebulian metre.

Why now, 0 Muse, do you wish me Carneades to confute?
He was an ignoramus, as he did not understand
Why he should stand in fear of death: so once, when he'd a cough,
The worst of all diseases that affect the human frame,
He cared not for a remedy; but when the news did reach him,
That brave Antipater had ta'en some poison, and so died,
" Give me, said he, some stuff to drink."

" Some what P—" Some luscious mead. "

Moreover, he'd this saying at all times upon his lips:
" Nature did-make me, and she does together keep me still;
But soon the time will come when she will pull me all to pieces."
But still at last he yielded up the ghost: though long ago
He might have died, and so escaped the evils that befell him.

IX. It is said that at night he was not aware when lights were brought in; and that once he ordered his servant to light the candles, and when he had brought them in and told him, " I have brought them;" "Well then," said he, "read by the light of them."

X. He had a great many other disciples; but the most eminent of them was Clitomachus, whom we must mention presently.

XI. There was also another man of the name of Carneades, a very indifferent elegiac poet. LIFE OF CLITOMACHUS.

I. Clitomachus was a Carthaginian. He was called Asdrubal, and used to lecture on philosophy in his own country in his native language.

II. But when he came to Atjiens, at the age of forty years, he became a pupil of Carneades; and, as he was pleased with his industry, he caused him to be instructed in literature, and himself educated the man carefully. And he carried his diligence to such a degree, that he composed more than four hundred books. III. And he succeeded Carneades in his schools; and he illustrated his principles a great deal by his writings: as he himself had studied the doctrines of their sects, the Academic, the Peripatetic, and the Stoic. Timon attacks the whole school of Academics, as a body, in these lines:—

Nor the unprofitable chattering
Of all the Academics.

But now that we have gone through the philosophers of Plato's school, let us go to the Peripatetics, who also derived their doctrines from Plato; and the founder of their sect was Aristotle.

BOOK V. LIFE OF ARISTOTLE.

I. Aristotle was the son of Nicomachus and Phaestias, a citizen of Stagira; and Nicomachus was descended from Nicomachus, the son of Machaon, the son of Esculapius, as Hermippus tells us in his treatise on Aristotle; and he lived with Amyntas, the king of the Macedonians, as both a physician and a friend.

II. He was the most eminent of all the pupils of Plato; he had a lisping voice, as is asserted by Timotheus the Athenian, in his work on Lives. He had also very thin legs, they say, and small eyes; but he used to indulge in very conspicuous dress, and rings, and used to dress his hair carefully. III. He had also a son named Nicomachus, by Herpyllis his concubine, as we are told by Timotheus.

IV. He seceded from Plato while he was still alive; so that they tell a story that he said, " Aristotle has kicked us off just as chickens do their mother after they have been hatched." But Hermippus says in his Lives, that while he was absent on an embassy to Philip, on behalf of the Athenians, Xenocrates became the president of the school in the Academy; and that when he returned and saw the school under the presidency of some one else, he selected a promenade in the 'Lyceum, in which he used to walk up and down with his disciples, discussing subjects of philosophy till the time for anointing themselves came; on which account he was called a Peripatetic. But others say that he got this name because once when Alexander was walking about after recovering from a sickness, he accompanied him and kept conversing with him. But when his pupils became numerous, he then gave them seats, saying: — It would be shame for me to hold my peace,

And for Isocratea to keep on talking.
From *irtpmariu),* "to walk about."

And he used to accustom his disciples to discuss any question which might be proposed, training them just as an orator might.

V. After that he went to Hermias the Eunuch, the tyrant of Atarneus, who, as it is said, allowed him all kinds of liberties; and some say that he formed a matrimonial connection with him, giving him either his daughter or his niece in marriage, as is recorded by Demetrius of Magnesia, in his essay on Poets and Prose-writers of the same name. And the same authority says that Hermias had been the slave of Eubulus, and a Bithynian by descent, and that he slew his master. But Aristippus, in the first book of his treatise on Ancient Luxury, says that Aristotle was enamoured of the concubine of Hermias, and that, as Hermias gave his consent, he married her; and was so overjoyed that he sacrificed to her, as the Athenians do to the' Eleusinian Ceres. And he wrote a hymn to Hermias, which is given at length below.

VI. After that he lived in Macedonia, at the court of Philip, and was entrusted by him with his son Alexander as a pupil; and he entreated him to restore his native city which had been destroyed by Philip, and had his request granted; and he also made laws for the citizens. And also he used to make laws in his schools, doing this in imitation of Xenocrates, so that he appointed a president every ten days. And when he thought that he had spent time enough with Alexander, he departed for Athens, having recommended to him his relation Oallisthenes, a native of Olynthus; but as he spoke too freely to the king, and would not take Aristotle's advice, he reproached him and said:—

Alas! my child, in life's primeval bloom,
Such hasty words will bring thee to thy doom.

And his prophecy was fulfilled, for as he was believed by Hermolaus to have been privy to the plot against Alexander, he was shut up in an iron cage, covered with lice, and untended; and at last he was given to a lion, and so died, VII. Aristotle then having come to Athens, and having presided over his school there for thirteen years, retired secretly to Chalcis, as Eurymedon, the hierophant had impeached him on an indictment for impiety, though Pharorinus, B. 18, 95.

in his Universal History, says that his prosecutor was Demophelus, on the ground of having written the hymn to the beforementioued Herruias, and also the following epigram which was engraven on his statue at Delphi:—

The tyrant of the Persian archer race,
Broke through the laws of God to slay this man;
Not by the manly spear in open fight,
But by the treachery of a faithless friend.

And after that he died of taking a draught of aconite, as Eumelus says in the fifth book of his Histories, at the age of seventy years. And the same author says that he was thirty years old when he first became acquainted with Plato. But this is a mistake of his, for he did only live in reality sixtythree years, and he was seventeen years old when he first attached himself to Plato. And the hymn in honour of Hermias is as follows:— O Virtue, won by earnest strife,
And holding out the noblest prize
That ever gilded earthly life,
Or drew it on to seek the skies;
For thee what son of Greece would not Deem it an enviable lot,
To live the life, to die the death,
That fears no weary hour, shrinks from no fiery breath!
Such fruit hast thou of heavenly bloom, A lure more rich than golden heap,
More tempting than the joys of home,
More bland than spell of soft-eyed sleep.
For thee Alcides, son of Jove,
And the twin boys of Leda strove,
With patient toil and sinewy might,
Thy glorious prize to grasp, to reach thy lofty height.
Achilles, Ajax, for thy love Descended to the realms of night;
Atarneus' King thy vision drove,
To quit for aye the glad sun-light,
Therefore, to memory's daughters dear,
His deathless name, his pure career,
Live shrined in song, and link'd with awe,
The awe of Xenian Jove, and faithful friendship's law.
This very spirited version I owe to the kindness of my brother, t!ie Kev. J. E. Yonge, of Eton College.

There is also an epigram of ours upon him, which runs thus:— '
Eurymedon, the faithful minister
Of the mysterious Eleusinian Queen,
Was onee about t' impeach the Stagirite
Of impious guilt. But he escaped his hands
By mighty draught of friendly aconite,
And thus defeated all Mb wicked arts.

Pharorinus, in his Universal History, says that Aristotle was the first person who ever composed a speech to be delivered in his own defence in a court of justice, and that he did so on the occasion of this prosecution, and said that at Athens:—

Pears upon pear-trees grow; on fig-trees, figs.

Apollodorus, in his Chronicles, says that he was born in the first year of the ninety-ninth olympiad, and that he attached himself to Plato, and remained with him for twenty years, having been seventeen years of age when he originally joined him. And he went to Mitylene in the archonship of Eubulus, in the fourth year of the hundred and eighth olympiad. But as Plato haddied in the first year of this same olympiad, in_ the archonship of Theophilus, he departed for the court of Hermias, and remained there three years. And in the archonship of Pythodotus he went to the court of Philip, in the second year of the hundred and ninth olympiad, when Alexander was fifteen years old; and he came to Athens in the second year of the hundred and eleventh olympiad, and presided over his school in the Lyceum for thirteen years: after that he departed to Chalcis, in the third year of the hundred and fourteenth olympiad, and died, at about the age of sixty-three years, of disease, the same year that Demosthenes died in Calumia, in the archonship of Philocles.

VIII. It is said also that he was offended with the king, because of the result of the conspiracy of Calisthenes against Alexander; and that the king, for the sake of annoying him, promoted Anaximenes to honour, and sent presents to Xenocrates. And Theocritus, of Chios, wrote an epigram upon him to ridicule him, in the following terms, as it is quoted by Ambryon in his account of Theocritus:—

The empty-headed Aristotle rais'd
This empty tomb to Hermias the Eunuch,
The ancient slave of the ill-us'd Eubulus.
Who, for his monstrous appetite, preferred
The Bosphorus to Academia's groves.

And Timon attacked him too, saying of him:—

Nor the sad chattering of the empty Aristotle.

Such was the life of the philosopher.

IX. We have also met with his will, which is couched in the following terms:—" May things turn out well; but if any thing happens to hrm, in that case Aristotle has made the following disposition of his affairs. That Antipater shall be the general and universal executor. And until Nicanor marries my daughter, I appoint Aristomedes, Timarehus, Hipparchus. Dioteles, and Theophrastus, if he will consent and accept the charge, to be the guardians of my children and of Herpyllis, and the trustees of all the property I leave behind me; and I desire them, when my daughter is old enough, to give her in marriage to Nicanor; but if any thing should happen to the girl, which may God forbid, either before or after she is married, but before she has any children, then 1 will that Nicanor shall have the absolute disposal of my son, and of all other things, in the full confidence that he will arrange them in a manner worthy of me and of himself. Let him also be the guardian of my daughter and son Nicomachus, to act as he pleases with respect to them, as if he were their father or brother. But if anything should happen to Nicanor, which may God forbid, either before he receives my daughter in marriage, or after he is married to her, or before he has any children by her, then any arrangements which he may make by will shall stand. But, if Theophrastus, in this case, should choose to take my daughter in marriage, then he is to stand exactly in the same position as Nicanor. And if not, then I will, that my trustees, consulting with Antipater concerning both the boy and girl, shall arrange everything respecting them as they shall think fit; and that my trustees and Nicanor, remembering both me and Herpyllis, and how well she has behaved to me, shall take care, if she be inclined to take a husband, that one be found for her who shall not be unworthy of us; and shall give her, in addition to all that has been already given her, a talent of silver, and three maidservants if she please to accept them, and the handmaid whom she has now, and the boy Pyrrhaeus. And if she likes to dwell at Chalcis, she shall have the house which joins the garden; but if she likes to dwell in Stagira, then she shall have my father's house. And whichever of these houses she elects to take, £ will that my executors do furnish it with all necessary furniture, in such manner as shall seem to them and to Herpyllis to be sufficient. And let Nicanor be the guardian of the child Myrmex, so that he shall be conducted to his friends in a manner worthy of us, with all his property which I received. I also will that Aubracis shall have her liberty, and that there shall be given to her when her daughter is married, five hundred drachmas, and the handmaid whom she now has. And I will that there be given to Thales, besides the handmaiden whom she now has, who was bought for her, a thousand drachmas and another handmaid. And to Timon, in addition to the money that has been given to him before for another boy, an additional slave, or a sum of money which shall be equivalent. I also will that Tychon shall have his liberty when his daughter is married, and Philon, and Glympius, and his son. Moreover, of those boys who wait upon me, I will that none shall be sold, but my executors may use them, and when they are grown up then they shall emancipate them if they deserve it. I desire too, that my executors will take under their care the statues which it has been entrusted to Gryllion to make, that when they are made they may be erected in their proper places; and so too shall the statues of Nicanor, and of Proxenus, which I was intending to give him a commission for, and also that of the mother of Nicanor. I wish them also to erect in its proper place the statue of Arimnestus which is already made, that it may be a memorial of her, since she has died childless. I wish them also to dedicate a statue of my mother to Ceres at Nemea, or whereever else they think fit. And wherever they bury me, there I desire that they shall also place the bones of Pythias, having taken them up from the place where they now lie, as she herself enjoined. And I desire that Nicanor, as he has been preserved, will perform the vow which I made on his behalf, and dedicate some figures of animals in stone, four cubits high, to Jupiter the saviour, and Minerva the saviour, in Stagira." These are the provisions of his will.

X. And it is said that a great many dishes were found in his house; and that Lycon stated that he used to bathe in a bath of warm oil, and afterwards to sell the oil. But some say that he used to place a leather bag of warm oil on his stomach. And whenever he went to bed, he used to take a brazen ball in his hand, having arranged a brazen dish below it; so that, when the ball fell into the dish, he might be awakened by the noise.

XI. The following admirable apophthegms are attributed to him.

He was once asked, what those who tell lies gain by it; " They gain this," said he, " that when they speak truth they are not believed."

On one occasion he was blamed for giving alms to a worthless man, and he replied, " I did not pity the man, but his condition."

He was accustomed continually to say to his friends and pupils wherever he happened to be, " That sight receives the light from the air which surrounds it, and in like manner the soul receives the light from the science."

Very often, when he was inveighing against the Athenians, he would say that they had invented both wheat and laws, but that they used only the wheat and neglected the laws.

It was a saying of his that the roots of education were bitter, but the fruit sweet.

Once he was asked what grew old most speedily, and he replied, " Gratitude."

On another occasion the question was put to him, what hope is? and his answer was, " The dream of a waking man."

Diogenes once offered him a dry fig, and as he conjectured that if he did not take it the cynic had a witticism ready prepared, he accepted it, and then said that Diogenes had lost his joke and his fig too; and another time when he took one from him as he offered it, he held it up as a child does, and said, " O great Diogenes; " and then he gave it to him back again.

He used to say that there were three things necessary to education; natural qualifications, instruction, and practice.

Having heard that he was abused by some one, he said, " He may beat me too, if he likes, in my absence."

He used to say that beauty is the best of all recommendations, but others say that it was Diogenes who gave this description of it; and that Aristotle called beauty, " The gift of a fair appearance;" that Socrates called it " A short-lived tyranny; " Plato, " The privilege of nature; " Theophrastus, " A silent deceit;" Theocritus, " An ivory mischief; " Carneades, " A sovereignty which stood in need of no guards."

On one occasion he was asked how much educated men were superior to those uneducated; " As much," said he, " as the living are to the dead."

It was a saying of his that education was an ornament in prosperity, and a refuge in adversity. And that those parents who gave their children a good education deserved more honour than those who merely beget them: for that the latter only enabled their children to live, but the former gave them the power of living well.

When a man boasted in his presence that he was a native of an illustrious city, he said, " That is not what one ought to look at, but whether one is worthy of a great city."

He was once asked what a friend is; and is answer was, " One soul abiding in two bodies."

It was a saying of his that some men were as stingy as if they expected to live for ever, and some as extravagant as if they expected to die immediately.

When he was asked why people like

to spend a great deal of their time with jhandsome people, "That," said he, " is a question fit for a blind man to ask."

The question was once put to him, what he had gained by philosophy; and the answer he made was this, " That I do without being commanded, what others do from fear of the laws."

He was once asked what his disciples ought to do to get on; and he replied, " Press on upon those who are in front of them, and not wait for those who are behind to catch them.''

A chattering fellow, who had been abusing him, said to him, " Have not I been jeering you properly? " Not that I know of," said he, " for I have not been listening to you."

A man on one occasion reproached him for having given a contribution to one who was not a good man (for the story which I have mentioned before is also quoted in this way), and his answer was, " I gave not to the man, but to humanity."

The question was once put to him, how we ought to behave to our friends; and the answer he gave was, " As we should wish our friends to behave to us. "

He used to define justice as " A virtue of the soul distributive of what each person deserved."

Another of his sayings was, that education was the best viaticum for old age.

Pharorinus, in the second book of his Commentaries, says that he was constantly repeating, " The man who has friends has no friend." And this sentiment is to be found also in the seventh book of the Ethics.

These apophthegms then are attributed to him.

XII. He also wrote a great number of works; and I have thought it worth while to give a list of them, on account of the eminence of their author in every branch of philosophy. Four books on Justice; three books on Poets; three books on Philosophy; two books of The Statesman; one on Rhetoric, called also the Gryllus; the Nerinthus, one; the Sophist, one; the Menexenus, one; the Erotic, one; the Banquet, one; on Riches, one; the Exhortation, one; on the Soul, one; on Prayer, one; on Nobility of Birth, one; on Pleasure, one; the Alexander, or an Essay on Colonists, one; on Sovereignty, one; on Education, one; on the Good, three; three books on things in the Laws of Plato; two on Political Constitutions; on Economy, one; on Friendship, one; on Suffering, or having Suffered, one; on Sciences, one; on Discussions, two; Solutions of Disputed Points, two; Sophistical Divisions, four; on Contraries, one; on Species and Genera, one; on Property, one; Epicheirematic, or Argumentative Commentaries, three; Propositions relating to Virtue, three; Objections, one; one book on things which are spoken of in various ways, or a Preliminary Essay; one on the Passion of Anger; five on Ethics; three on Elements; one on Science; one on Beginning;' "seventeen on Divisions; on Divisible Things, one; two books of Questions and Answers; two on Motion; one book of Propositions; four of Contentious Propositions; one of Syllogisms; eight of the First Analytics; two of the second greater Analytics; one on Problems; eight on Method; one on the Better; one on the Idea; Definitions serving as a preamble to the Topics, seven; two books more of Syllogisms; one of Syllogisms and Definitions; one on what is Eligible, and on what is Suitable; the Preface to the Topics, one; Topics relating to the Definitions, two; one on the Passions; one on Divisions; one on Mathematics; thirteen books of Definitions; two of Epicheiremata, or Arguments; one on Pleasure; one of Propositions; on the Voluntary, one; on the Honourable, one; of Epicheirematic or Argumentative Propositions, twenty-five books; of Amatory Propositions, four; of Propositions relating to Friendship, two; of Propositions relating to the Soul, one; on Politics, two; Political Lectures, such as that of Theophrastus, eight; on Just Actions, two; two books entitled, A Collection of Arts; two on the Art of Rhetoric; one on Art; two on other Art; one on Method; one, the Introduction to the Art of Theodectes; two books, being a treatise on the Art of Poetry; one book of Rhetorical Enthymemes on Magnitude; one of Divisions of Enthymemes; on Style, two; on Advice, one; on Collection, two; on Nature, three; on Natural Philosophy, one; on the Philosophy of Archytas, three; on the Philosophy of Speusippus and Xenocrates, one; on things taken from the doctrines of Timaeus and the school of Archytas, one; on Doctrines of Melissus, one; on Doctrines of Alcmaeon, one; on the Pythagoreans, one; on the Precepts of Gorgias, one; on the Precepts of Xenophanes, one; on the Precepts of Zeno, one; on the Pythagoreans, one; on Animals, nine; on Anatomy, eight; one book, a Selection of Anatomical Questions; one on Compound Animals; one on Mythological Animals; one on Impotence; one on Plants; one on Physiognomy; two on Medicine; one on the Unit; one on Signs of Storms; one on Astronomy; one on Optics; one on Motion; one on Music; one on Memory '; six on Doubts connected with Homer; one on Poetry; thirty-eight of Natural Philosophy in reference to the First Elements; two of Problems Resolved; two of Encyclica, or General Knowledge; one on Mechanics; two consisting of Problems derived from the writings of Democritus; one on Stone; one book of Comparisons; twelve books of Miscellanies; fourteen books of things explained according to their Genus; one on Rights; one book, the Conquerors at the Olympic Games; one, the Conquerors at the Pythian Games in the Art of Music; one,) the Pythian; one, a List of the Victors in the Pythian Games; one, the Victories gained at the Olympic Games; one on Tragedies; one, a List of Plays; one book of Proverbs; one on the Laws of Recommendations; four books of Laws; one of Categories; one on Interpretation; a book containing an account of the Constitutions of a hundred and fifty-eight cities, and also some individual democratic, oligarchic, aristocratic, and tyrannical Constitutions; Letters to Philip: Letters of the Selymbrians; four Letters to Alexander; nine to Antipater; one to Mentor; one to Ariston; one to Olympias; one to Hephaestion; one to Themistagoras; one to Philoxenus; one to Democritus; one

book of Poems, beginning:—
Hail! holy, sacred, distant-shooting God.

A book of Elegies which begins:—
Daughter of all-accomplish'd mother.

The whole consisting of four hundred and forty-five thousand two hundred and seventy lines.

XIII. These then are the books which were written by hjm. And in them he expresses the following opinions:—that there is in philosophy a two-fold division; one practical, and the other theoretical. Again, the practical is divided into ethical and political, under which last head are comprised considerations affecting not only the state, but also the management, of a single house. The theoretical part, too, is subdivided into physics and logic; the latter forming not a single division, turning on one special point, but being rather an instrument for every art brought to a high degree of accuracy. And he has laid down two separate objects as what it is conversant about, the persuasive and the true. And he has used two means with reference to each end; dialectics and rhetoric, with reference to persuasion; analytical examination and philosophy, with reference to truth; omitting nothing which can bear upon discovery, or judgment, or use. Accordingly, with reference to discovery, he has furnished us with topics and works on method, which form a complete armoury of propositions, from which it is easy to provide one's-self with an abundance of probable arguments for every kind of question. nd with reference to judgment, he has given us the former and posterior analytics; and by means of the former analytics, we may arrive at a critical examination of principles; by means of the posterior, we may examine the conclusions which are deduced from them. With reference to the use or application of his rules, he has given us works on discussion, on question, on disputation, on sophistical refutation, on syllogism, and on things of that sort.

He has also furnished us with a double criterion of truth. One, on the perception of those effects, which are according to imagination; the other, the intelligence of those things which are ethical, and which concern politics, and economy, and laws. The chief.good he has defined to be the exercise of virtue in a perfect life. He used also to say, that happiness was a thing made up of three kinds of goods. First of all, the goods of the soul, which he also calls the principal goods in respect of their power; secondly, the goods of the body, such as health, strength, beauty, and things of that sort; thirdly, external goods, such as wealth, nobility of birth, glory, and things like those. And he taught that virtue was not sufficient of itself to confer happiness; for that it had need besides of the goods of the body, and of the extenial goods, for that a wise man would be miserable if he were surrounded by distress, and poverty, and circumstances of that kind. But, on the other hand, he said, that vice was sufficient of itself to cause unhappiness, even if the goods of the body and the external goods were present in the greatest possible degree. He also asserted that the virtues did not reciprocally follow one another, for that it was possible for a prudent, and just, and impartial man, to be incontinent and intemperate; and he said, that the wise man was not destitute of passions, but endowed with moderate passions.

He also used to define friendship as an equality of mutual benevolence. And he divided it into the friendship of kindred, and of love, and of those connected by ties of hospitality. And he said, that love was divided into sensual and philosophical love. And that the wise man would feel the influence of love, and would occupy himself in affairs of state, and would marry a wife, and would live with a king. And as there were three kinds of life, the speculative, the practical, and the voluptuous, he preferred the speculative. He also considered the acquisition of general knowledge serviceable to, the acquisition of virtue. As a natural philosopher, he was the most ingenious man that ever lived in tracing effects back to their causes, so that he could explain the principles of the most trifling circumstances; on which account he wrote a great many books of commentaries on physical questions.

He used to teach that God was incorporeal, as Plato also asserted, and that his providence extends over all the heavenly bodies; also, that he is incapable of motion. And that he governs all things upon earth with reference to their sympathy with the heavenly bodies. Another of his doctrines was, that besides the four elements there is one other, making the fifth, of which all the heavenly bodies are composed; and that this one possesses a motion peculiar to itself, for it is a circular one. That the soul is incorporeal, being the first *hriXiytia*; for it is the *svriXiyiia* of a physical and organic body, having an existence in consequence of a capacity for existence. And this is, according to him, of a twofold nature. By the word *iMTtXiyeia,* he means something which has an incoporeal species, either in capacity, as a figure of Mercury in wax, which has a capacity for assuming any shape; or a statue in brass; and so the perfection of the Mercury or of the statue is called *ivriXiyjia.* with reference to its habit. But when he speaks of the *hrtlAyriia* of a natural body, he does so because, of bodies some are wrought by the hands, as for instance, those which are made by artists, for instance, a tower, or a ship; and some exist by nature, as the bodies of plants and animals. He has also used the term with reference to an organic body, that is to say, with reference to something that is made, as the faculty of sight for seeing, or the faculty of hearing for the purpose of hearing. The capacity of having life must exist in the thing itself. But the capacity is twofold, either in habit or in operation. In operation, as a man, when awake, is said to have a soul; in habit, as the same is said of a man when asleep. That, therefore, he may come under his definition, he has added the word capacity.

He has also given other definitions on a great many subjects, which it would be tedious to enumerate here. For he was in every thing a man of the greatest industry and ingenuity, as is plain from all his works which I have lately given a list of; which are in number nearly four hundred, the genuineness of which is undoubted. There are, also, a great " *IvriX'it 1a,* the actuality of a thing, as opposed to simple capability or potentiality *(Pvvafiic)*; a philosophic word invented by Aristotle.—.... quite distinct from *IvliKixua,* though Cicero (Tusc. i. 10,) confounded them."—*L. & S. m voc. 0* many other works attributed to him, and a number of apophthegms which he never committed to paper.

XIV. There were eight persons of the name of Aristotle. First of all, the philosopher of whom we have been speaking; the second was an Athenian statesman, some of whose forensic orations, of great elegance, are still extant; the third was a man who wrote a treatise on the Iliad; the fourth, a Siciliot orator, who wrote a reply to the Pttnegyric of Isocrates; the fifth was the man who was surnamed Myth, a friend of Eschines, the pupil of Socrates; the sixth was a Cyrenean, who wrote a treatise on Poetry; the seventh was a schoolmaster, who is mentioned by Aristoxenus in his Life of Plato; the eighth, was an obscure grammarian, to whom a treatise on Pleonasm is attributed. XV. And the Stagirite had many friends, the most eminent of whom was Theophrastus, whom we must proceed to speak of.

LIFE OF THEOPHRASTUS.

I. Theophrastus was a native of Eresus, the son of Melantas, a fuller, as we are told by Athenodorus in the eighth book of his Philosophical Conversations. II. He was originally a pupil of Leucippus, his fellow citizen, in his own country; and subsequently, after having attended the lectures of Plato, he went over to Aristotle. And when he withdrew to Chalcis, he succeeded him as president) of his school, in the hundred and fourteenth olympiad.

III. It is also said that a slave of his, by name Pomphylus, was a philosopher, as we are told by Myronianus of Amastra, in the first book of Similar Historical Chapters. IV. Theophrastus was a man of great acuteness and in-" dustry, and, as Pamphila asserts in the thirty-second book of his Commentaries, he was the tutor of Menandar, the'comic poet. He was also a most benevolent man, and very affable.'

V. Accordingly, Cassander received him as a friend; and Ptolemy sent to invite him to his court. And he was thought

' so very highly of at Athens, that when Agonides ventured to impeach him on a charge of impiety, he was very nearly fined for his hardihood. And there thronged to his school a crowd of disciples to the number of two thousand. In his letter to Phanias, the Peripatetic, among other subjects he speaks of the court of justice in the following terms: " It is not only out of the question to find an assembly (sranjyug/s), but it is not easy to find even a company *(evn &giov)* such as one would like; but yet recitations produce corrections of the judgment. And my age does not allow me to put off everything and to feel indifference on such a subject." In this letter he speaks of himself as one who devotes his whole leisure to learning.

And though he was of this disposition, he nevertheless went away for a short time, both he and all the rest of the philosophers, in consequence of Sophocles, the son of Amphiclides, having brought forward and carried a law that no one of the philosophers should preside over a school unless the council and the people had passed a resolution to sanction their doing so, if they did, death was to be the penalty. But they returned again the next year, when Philion had impeached Sophocles for illegal conduct; when the Athenians abrogated his law, and fined Sophocles five talents, and voted that the philosophers should have leave to return, that Theophrastus might return and preside over his school as before.

VI. His name had originally been Tyrtanius, but Aristotle changed it to Theophrastus, from the divine character of his eloquence. VII. He is said also to have been very much attached to Aristotle's son, Nicomachus, although he was his master; at least, this is stated by Aristippus in the fourth book of his treatise on the Ancient Luxury. VIII. It is also related that Aristotle used the same expression about him and Callisthenes, which Plato, as I have previously mentioned, employed about Xenocrates and Aristotle himself. For he is reported to have said, since Theophrastus was a man of extraordinary acuteness, who could both comprehend and explain everything, and as the other was somewhat slow in his natural character, that Theophrastus required a bridle, and Callisthenes a spur. IX. It is said, too, that he had a garden of his own after From fltioc divine, and *jpdai£* diction. the death of Aristotle, by the assistance of Demetrius Phalerius, who was an intimate friend of his.

X. The following very practical apophthegms of his are quoted. He used to say that it was better to trust to a horse without a bridle than to a discourse without arrangement. And once, when a man preserved a strict silence during the whole of a banquet, he said to him, " If you are an ignorant man, you are acting wisely; but if you have had any education, you are behaving like a fool." And a very favourite expression of his was, that time was the most valuable thing that a man could spend.

XI. He died when he was of a great age, having lived eighty-five years, when he had only rested from his labours a short time. And we have composed the following epigram on him:—

The proverb then is not completely false,
That wisdom's bow unbent is quickly broken;
While Theophrastus laboured, he kept sound,
When he relaxed, he lost his strength and died.

They say that on one occasion, when dying, he was asked by his disciples whether he had any charge to give them; and he replied, that he had none but that they should " remember that life holds out many pleasing deceits to us by the vanity of glory; for that when we are beginning to live, then we are dying. There is, therefore, nothing more profitless than ambition. But may you all be fortunate, and either abandon philosophy (for it is a great labour), or else cling to it diligently, for then the credit of it is great; but the vanities of life exceed the advantage of it. However, it is not requisite for me now to advise you what you should do; but do you yourselves consider what line of conduct to adopt." And when he had said this, as report goes, he expired. And the Athenians accompanied him to the grave, on foot, with the whole population of the city, as it is related, honouring the man greatly.

XII. But Pharorinus says, that when be was very old he used to go about in a litter; and that Hermippus states this, quoting Arcesilaus, the Pitanaean, and the account which he sent to Lacydes of Cyrene. XIII. He also left behind him a very great number of works, of which I have thought it proper to give a list on account of their being full of every sort of excellence. They are as follows:—

Three books of the First Analytics; seven of the Second Analytics; one book of the Analysis of Syllogisms; one book, an Epitome of Analytics; two books, Topics for referring things to First Principles; one book, an Examination of Speculative Questions about Discussions; one on Sensations; one addressed to Anaxagoras; one on the Doctrines of Anaxagoras; one on the Doctrines of Anaximenes; one on the Doctrines of Archelaus; one on Salt, Nitre, and Alum; two on Petrifactions; one on Indivisible Lines; two on Hearing; one on Words; one on the Differences between Virtues; one on Kingly Power; one on the Education of a King; three on Lives; one on Old Age; one on the Astronomical System of Democritus; one on Meteorology; one on Images or Phantoms; one on Juices, Complexions, and Flesh; one on the Description of the World; one on Men; one, a Collection of the Sayings of Diogenes; three books of Definitions; one treatise on Love; another treatise on Love; one book on Happiness; two books on Species; on Epilepsy, one; on Enthusiasm, one; on Empedocles, one; eighteen books of Epicheiremes; three books of Objections; one book on the Voluntary; two books, being an Abridgment of Plato's Polity; one on the Difference of the Voices of Similar Animals; one on Sudden Appearances; one on Animals which Bite or Sting; one on such Animals as are said to be Jealous; one on those which live on Dry Land; one on those which Change their Colour; one on those which live in Holes; seven on Animals in General; one on Pleasure according to the Definition of Aristotle; seventy-four books of Propositions; one treatise on Hot and Cold; one essay on Giddiness and Vertigo and Sudden Dimness of Sight; one on Perspiration; one on Affirmation and Denial; the Callisthenes, or an essay on Mourning, one; on Labours, one; on Motion, three; on Stones, one; on Pestilences, one; on Fainting Fits, one; the Megaric Philosopher, one; on Melancholy, one; on Mines, two; on Honey, one; a collection of the Doctrines of Metrodorus, one; two books on those Philosophers who have treated of Meteorology; on Drunkenness, one; twenty-four books of Laws, in alphabetical order; ten books, being an Abridgment of Laws; one on Definitions; one on Smells; one on Wine and Oil; eighteen books of Primary Propositions; three books on Lawgivers; six books of Political Disquisitions: a treatise on Politicals, with reference to occasions as they arise, four books; four books of Political Customs; on the best Constitution, one; five books of a Collection of Problems; on Proverbs, one; on Concretion and Liquefaction, one; on Fire, two; on Spirits, one; on Paralysis, one; on Suffocation, one; on Aberration of Intellect, one; on the Passions, one; on Signs, one; two books of Sophisms; one on the Solution of Syllogisms; two books of Topics; two on Punishment; one on Hair; one on Tyranny; three on Water; one on Sleep and Dreams; three on Friendship; two on Liberality; three on Nature; eighteen on Question s of Natural Philosophy; two books, being an Abridgment of Natural Philosophy; eight more books on Natural Philosophy; one treatise addressed to Natural Philosophers; two books on the History of Plants; eight books on the Causes of Plants; five on Juices; one on Mistaken Pleasures; one, Investigation of a proposition concerning the Soul; one on Unskilfully Adduced Proofs; one on Simple Doubts; one on Harmonics; one on Virtue; one entitled Occasions or Contradictions; one on Denial; one on Opinion; one on the Ridiculous; two called Soirees; two books of Divisions; one on Differences; one on Acts of Injustice; one on Calumny; one on Praise: one on Skill; three books of Epistles; one on Self-produced Animals; one on Selection; one entitled the Praises of the Gods; one on Festivals; one on Good Fortune; one on Enthymemes; one on Inventions; one on Moral Schools; one book of Moral Characters; one treatise on Tumult; one on History: one on the Judgment Concerning Syllogisms; one on Flattery; one on the Sea; one essay, addressed to Cassander, Concerning Kingly Power; one on Comedy; one on Meteors; one on Style; one book called a Collection of Sayings; one book of Solutions; three books on Music; one on Metres; the Megades, one; on Laws, one; on Violations of Law, one; a collection of the Sayings and Doctrines of Xenocrates, one; one book of Conversations; on an Oath, one; one of Ora— torical Precepts; one on Riches; one on Poetry; one beins; ' a collection of Political, Ethical, Physical, and amatory

Problems; one book of Proverbs; one book, being a Collection of General Problems; one on Problems in Natural Philosophy; one on Example; one on Proposition and Expose sition; a second treatise on Poetry; one on the Wise Men; one on Counsel; one on Solecisms; one on Rhetorical Art, _ a collection of sixty-one figures of Oratorical Art; one book on Hypocrisy; six books of a Commentary of Aristotle or Theophrastus; sixteen books of Opinions on Natural Philosophy; one book, being an Abridgment of Opinions on Natural Philosophy; one on Gratitude; one called Moral Characters; one on Truth and Falsehood; six on the History of Divine Things; three on the Gods; four on the History of Geometry; six books, being an Abridgment of the work of Aristotle on Animals; two books of Epicheiremes; three books of Propositions; two on Kingly Power; one on Causes; one on Democritus; one on Calumny; one on Generation; one on the Intellect and Moral Character of Animals; two on Motion; four on Sight; two on Definitions; one on being given in Marriage; one on the Greater and the Less; one on Music; one on Divine Happiness; one addressed to the Philosophers of the Academy; one Exhortatory Treatise; one discussing how a City may be best Governed; one called Commentaries; one on the Crater of Mount Etna in Sicily; one on Admitted Facts; one on Problems in Natural Natural History; one, What are the Different Manners of Acquiring Knowledge; three on Telling Lies; one book, which is a preface to the Topics; one addressed to iEschylus; six books of a History of Astronomy; one book of the History of Arithmetic relating to Increasing Numbers; one called the Acicharus; one on Judicial Discourses; one on Calumny; one volume of Letters to Astyceron, Phanias, and Nicanor; one book on Piety; one called the Evias; one on Circumstances; one volume entitled Familiar Conversations; one on the Education of Children; another on the same subject, discussed in a different manner; one on Education, called also, a treatise on Virtue, or on Temperance; one book of Exhortations; one on Numbers; one consisting of Definitions referring to the Enunciation of Syllogisms: one on Heaven; two on Politics; two on Nature, on j, Fruits, and on Animals. And these works contain in all two hundred and thirty-two thousand nine hundred and eight lines. These, then, are the books which Theophrastus composed.

XIV. I have also found his will, which is drawn up in the following terms:—

May things turn out well, but if anything should happen to me, I make the following disposition of my property. I give everything that I have in my house to Melantes and Pancreon, the sons of Leon. And those things which have been given to me by Hipparchus, I wish to be disposed of in the following manner:—First of all, I wish everything about the Museum and the statue of the goddesses to be made perfect, and to be adorned in a still more beautiful manner than at present, wherein there is room for improvement. Then I desire the statue of Aristotle to be placed in the temple, and all the other offerings which were in the temple before. Then I desire the colonnade which used to be near the Museum to be rebuilt in a manner not inferior to the previous one. I also enjoin my executors to put up the tablets on which the maps of the earth are drawn, in the lower colonnade, and to take care that an altar is finished in such a manner that nothing may be wanting to its perfectness or its beauty. I also direct a statue of Kicomachus, of equal size, to be erected at the same time; and the price for making the statue has been already paid to Praxiteles; and he is to contribute what is wanting for the expense. And I desire that it shall be placed wherever it shall seem best to those who have the charge of providing for the execution of the other injunctions contained in this will. And these are my orders respecting the temple and the offerings. The estate which I have at Stagira, I give to Callinus, and all my books I bequeath to Neleus. My garden, and my promenade, and my houses which join the garden, I give all of them to any of the friends whose names I set down below, who choose to hold a school in them and to devote themselves to the study of philosophy, since it is not possible for any one to be always travelling, but I give them on condition that they are not to alienate them, and that no one is to claim them as his own private property; but they are to use them in common as if they were sacred ground, sharing them with one another in a kindred and friendly spirit, as is reasonable and just. And those who are to have this joint property in them are Hipparchus, Neleus, Strato, Callenus, Demotimus, Demaratus, Callisthenes, Melantes, Pan This was a temple of the Muses which he had built for a school. creon, and Nicippus. And Aristotle, the son of Metrodorus and Pythias, shall also be entitled to a share in this property, if he likes to join these men in the study of philosophy. And I beg the older men to pay great attention to his education that he may be led on to philosophy as much as possible. I also desire my executors to bury me in whatever part of the garden shall appear most suitable, incurring no superfluous expense about my funeral or monument. And, as has been said before, after the proper honours have been paid to me, and after provision has been made for the execution of my will as far as relates to the temple, and the monument, and the garden, and the promenade, then I enjoin that Pamphylus, who dwells in the garden, shall keep it and everything else in the same condition as it has been in hitherto. And those who are in possession of these things are to take care of his interests. I further bequeath to Pamphylus and Threptes, who have been some time emancipated, and who have been of great service to me, besides all that they have previously received from me, and all that they may have earned for themselves, and all that I have provided for being given them by Hipparchus, two thousand drachmas, and I enjoin that they should have them in firm and secure possession, as I have often said to them, and to Melantes and Pancreon, and they have agreed to provide for this my will taking effect. I also give them the little handmaid Somatale; and of my slaves, I ratify the emancipation of Molon, and Cimon, and Parmenon which I have already given them. And I hereby give their liberty to Manes and Callias, who have remained four years in the garden, and have worked in it, and have conducted themselves in an unimpeachable manner. And I direct that my executors shall give Pamphylus as much of my household furniture as may seem to them to be proper, and shall sell the rest. And I give Carion to Demotimus, and Donar to Neleus. I order Eulius to be sold, and I request Hipparchus to give Callinus three thousand drachmas. And if I had not seen the great service that Hipparchus has been to me in former times, and the embarrassed state of his affairs at present, I should have associated Melantes and Pancreon with him in these gifts. But as I see that it would not be easy for them to arrange to manage the property together, I have thought it likely to be more advantageous for them to receive a fixed sum from Hipparchus. Therefore, let Hipparchus pay to Melantes and to Pancreon a talent a-piece; and let him also pay to my executors the money necessary for the expenses which I have here set down in my will, as it shall require to be expended. And when he has done this, then I will that he shall be discharged of all debts due from him to me or to my estate. And if any profit shall accrue to him in Chalcis, from property belonging to me, it shall be all his own. My executors, for all the duties provided for in this will, shall be Hipparchus, Neleus, Strato, Callinus, Demotimus, Callisthenes, and Ctesarchus. And this my will is copied out, and all the copies are sealed with the seal-ring of me, Theophrastus; one copy is in the hands of Hegesias the son of Hipparchus; the witnesses thereto are Callippus of Pallene, Philomelus of Euonymus, Lysander of Hybas, and Philion of Alopece. Another copy is deposited with Olympiodorus, and the witnesses are the same. A third copy is under the care of Adimantus, and it was conveyed to him by Androsthenes, his son. The witnesses to that copy are Arimnestus the son of Cleobulus, Lysistratus of Thrasos, the son of Phidon; Strato of Lampsacus, the son of Arcesilaus; Thesippus of Cerami, the son of Thesippus; Dioscorides of the banks of the Cephisus, the son of Dionysius.— This was his will. XV. Some writers have stated that Erasistratus, the physician, was a pupil of his; and it is very likely. LIFE OF STRATO.

I. Theophrastus was succeedod in the presidency of his school by Strato of Lampsacus, the son of Arcesilaus, of whom he had made mention in his will.
II. He was a man of great eminence, surnamed the Natural Philosopher, from his surpassing all men in the dilligence with which he applied himself to the investigation of matters of that nature. i
III. He was also the preceptor of Ptolemy Philadelphus, and received from him, as it is said, eighty talents; and he began to preside over the school, as Apollodorus tells us in his Chronicles, in the hundred and twenty-third olympiad, and continued in that post for eighteen years. IV. There are extant three books of his on Kingly Power; three on Justice; three on the Gods; three on Beginnings; and one on each of the subjects of Happiness, Philosophy, Manly Courage, the Vacuum, Heaven, Spirit, Human Nature, the Generation of Animals, Mixtures, Sleep, Dreams, Sight, Perception, Pleasure, Colours, Diseases, Judgments, Powers, Metallic Works, Hunger, and Dimness of Sight, Lightness and Heaviness, Enthusiasm, Pain, Nourishment and Growth, Animals whose Existence is Doubted, Fabulous Animals, Causes, a Solution of Doubts, a preface to Topics; there are, also, treatises on Contingencies, on the Definition, on the More and Less, on Injustice, on Former and Later, on the Prior Genus, on Property, on the Future. There are, also, two books called the Examination of Inventions; the Genuineness of the Commentaries attributed to him, is doubted. There is a volume of Epistles, which begins thus: " Strato wishes Arsinoe prosperity."

V. They say that he became so thin and weak, that he died without its being perceived. And there is an epigram of ours upon him in the following terms:—

The man was thin, believe me, from the use
Of frequent unguents; Strato was his name,
A citizen of Lampsaeus; he struggled long
With fell disease, and died at last unnoticed.

VI. There were eight people of the name of Strato. The first was a pupil of Isocrates; the second was the man of whom we have been speaking; the third was a physician, a pupil of Erasistratus, or, as some assert, a foster-child of his; the fourth was an historian, who wrote a history of the Achievements of Philip and Perses in their wars against the

Komans The sixth was an epigrammatic poet; the seventh was an ancient physician, as Aristotle tells us; the eighth was a Peripatetic philosopher, who lived in Alexandria.
VII. But the will, too, of this natural philosopher is extant, and it is couched in the following language:—" If anything happens to me, I make this disposition of my property. I leave all my property in my house to Lampyrion and Arcesilaus; and with the money which I have at Athens, in the first place, let my executors provide for my funeral and for all other customary expenses; without doing anything extravagant, or, on the other hand, anything mean. And the following shall be my executors, according to this my will: Olympichus, Aristides, Inuesigenes, Hippocrates, Epicrates, Gorgylus, Diocles, Lycon, and Athanes, And my school I leave to Lycon, since of the others some are too old, and others too busy. And the rest will do well, if they ratify this arrangement of mine. I also bequeath to him all my books, except such as we have written ourselves; and all my furniture in the dining-room, and the couches, and the drinking cups. And let my executors give Epicrates five hundred drachmas, and one of my slaves, according to the choice made by Arcesilaus. And first of all, let Lampyrion and Arcesilaus cancel the engagements which Daippus has entered into for Iraeus. And let him be acquitted of all obligation to Lampyrion or the heirs of Lampyrion; and let him also be discharged from any bond or note of hand he may have given. And let my executors give him five hundred drachmas of silver, and one of my slaves, whichever Arcesilaus may approve, in order that, as he has done me great service, and co-operated with me in many things, he may have a competency, and be enabled to live decently. And I give their freedom to Diophantus, and Diocles, and Abus. Simias I give to Arcesilaus. I also give his freedom to Dromo. And when Arcesilaus arrives, let Iraeus calculate with Olympicus and Epicrates, and the rest of my executors, the amount that has been expended on my funeral and on other customary expenses. And let the money that remains, be paid over to Arcesilaus by Olympichus, who shall give him no trouble, as to the time or manner of payment. And Arcesilaus shall discharge the engagements which Strato has entered into with Olympichus and Ausinias, which are preserved in writing in the care of Philoreatos, the son of Tisamenus. And with respect to my monument, let them

do whatever seems good to Arcesilaus, and Olympichus, and Lycon.

This is his will, which is still extant, as Aristo, the Chian, has collected and published it.

VIII. And this Strato was a man, as has been shown above, of deservedly great popularity; having devoted himself to the study of every kind of philosophy, and especially of that branch of it called natural philosophy, which is one of the most ancient and important branches of the whole.

LIFE OF LYCON.

I. He was succeeded by Lycon, a native of the Troas, the son of Astyanax, a man of great eloquence, and of especial ability in the education of youth. For he used to say that it was fit for boys to be harnessed with modesty and rivalry, as much as for horses to be equipped with a spur and a bridle. And his eloquence and energy in speaking is apparent, from this instance. For he speaks of a virgin who was poor in the following manner:—" A damsel, who, for want of a dowry, goes beyond the seasonable age, is a heavy burden to her father; " on which acccount they say that Antigonus said with reference to him, that the sweetness and beauty of an apple could not be transferred to anything else, but that one might see, in the case of this man, all these excellencies, in as great perfection as on a tree; and he said this, because he was a surpassingly sweet speaker. On which account, some people prefixed a r to his name. But as a writer, he was very unequal to his reputation. And he used to jest in a careless way, upon those who repented that they had not learnt when they had the opportunity, and who now wished that they had done so, saying, said that they were accusing themselves, showing by a prayer which could not possibly be accomplished, their misplaced repentance for their idleness. He used also to say, that those who deliberated without coming to a right conclusion, erred in their calculations, like men who investigate a correct nature by an incorrect standard, or who look at a face in disturbed water, or a distorted mirror. Another of his saying was, that many men go in pursuit of the crown to be won in the forum, but few or none seek to attain the one to be gained at the Olympic games.

II. And as he in many instances gave much advice to the Athenians, he was of exceedingly great service to them. So as to make it appear connected with $\gamma X\nu K\nu\varsigma$, sweet. III. He was also a person of great neatness in his dress, wearing garments of an unsurpassable delicacy, as we are told by Hermippus. He was at the same time exceedingly devoted to the exercises of the Gymnasium, and a man who was always in excellent condition as to his body, displaying every quality of an athlete (though Antigonus of Carystus, pretends that he was bruised about the ears and dirty); and in his own country he is said to have wrestled and played at ball at the Iliaean games. IV. And he was exceedingly beloved by Eumenes and Attalus, who made him great presents; and Antigonus also tried to seduce him to his court, but was disappointed. And he was so great an enemy to Hieronymus the Peripatetic, that he was the only person who would not go to see him on the anniversary festival which he used to celebrate, and which we have mentioned in our life of Arcesilaus.

V. And he presided over his school forty-four years, as Strato had left it to him in his will, in the hundred and twenty-seventh olympiad.

VI. He was also a pupil of Panthoides, the dialectician. VII. He died when he was seventy-four years of age, having been a great sufferer with the gout, and there is an epigram of ours upon him:—

Nor shall wise Lycon be forgotton, who
Died of the gout, and much I wonder at it.
For he who ne'er before could walk alone,
Went the long road to hell in a single night.

VIII. There were several people of the name of Lycon. The first' was a Pythagorean; the second was this man of whom we are speaking; the third was an epic poet; the fourth was an epigrammatic poet.

IX. I have fallen in with the following will of this philosopher. " I make the following disposition of my property; if I am unable to withstand this disease:—All the property in my house I leave to my brothers Astyanax and Lycon; and I think that they ought to pay all that I owe at Athens, and that I may have borrowed from any one, and also all the expenses that may be incurred for my funeral, and for other customary solemnities. And all that I have in in the city, or in iEgina, I give to Lycon because he bears the same name that I do, and because he has spent the greater part of his life with me, showing me the greatest affection, as it was fitting that he should do, since he was in the place of a son to me. And I leave my garden walk to those of my friends who like to use it; to Bulon, and Callinus, and Ariston, and Amplicon, and Lycon, and Python, and Aristomachus, and Heracleus, and Lycomedes, and Lycon my nephew. And I desire that they will elect as president him whom they think most likely to remain attached to the pursuit of philosophy, and most capable of holding the school together. And I entreat the rest of my friends to acquiesce in their election, for my sake and that of the place. And I desire that Bulon, and Callinus, and the rest of my friends will manage my funeral and the burning of my body, so that my obsequies may not be either mean or extravagant. And the property which I have in./Egina shall be divided by Lycon after my decease among the young men there, for the purpose of anointing themselves, in order that the memory of me and of him who honoured me, and who showed his affection by useful presents, may be long preserved. And let him erect a statue of me; and as for the place for it, I desire that Diophantus and Heraclides the son of Demetrius, shall select that, and take care that it be suitable for the proposed erection. With the property that I have in the city let Lycon pay all the people of whom I have borrowed anything since his departure; and let Bulon and Callinus join him in this, and also in discharging all the expenses incurred for my funeral, and for all other customary solemnities, and let him deduct the amount from the funds which I have left in my house, and bequeathed to them both in common. Let him also pay the physicians, Pasithemis and Medias, men who, for their attention to me and for their skill, are very deserving of still greater honour. And I give to the son of Callinus my pair of Thericlean cups; and to his wife I give my pair of Ehodian cups, and my smooth carpet, and my double carpet, and my curtains, and the two best pillows of all that I leave behind me; so that as far as the compliment goes, I may be seen not to have forgotten them. And with respect to those who have been my servants, I make the following disposition: —To Demetrius who has long been freed, I remit the price of his freedom, and I further give five minae, and a cloak, and a tunic, that as he has a great deal of trouble about me, he may pass the rest of his life comfortably. To Criton, the Chalcedonian, I also remit the price of his freedom, and I further give him four minae. Micras I hereby present with his freedom; and I desire Lycon to maintain him, and instruct him for six years from the present time. I also give his freedom to Chares, and desire Lycon to maintain him. And I further give him two minae, and all my books that are published; but those which are not published, I give to Callinus, that he may publish them with due care. I also give to Syrus, whom I have already emancipated, four minae, and Menedora; and if he owes me anything I acquit him of the debt. And I give to Hilaras four minae, and a double carpet, and two pillows, and a curtain, and any couch which he chooses to select. I also hereby emancipate the mother of Micras, and Noemon, and Dion, and Theon, and Euphranor, and Hermeas; and I desire that Agathon shall have his freedom when he has served two years longer; and that Ophelion, and Poseideon, my litter-bearers, shall have theirs when they have waited four years more. I also give to Demetrius, and Criton, and Syrus, a couch a piece, and coverlets from those which I leave behind me, according to the selection which Lycon is hereby authorised to make. And these are to be their rewards for having performed the duties to which they were appointed well. Concerning my burial, let Lycon do as he pleases, and bury me here or at home, just as he likes; for 1 am sure that he has the same regard for propriety that I myself have. And I give all the things herein mentioned, in the confidence that he will arrange everything properly. The witnesses to this my will are Callinus of Hermione, Ariston of Ceos, and Euphronius of Paeania."

As he then was thoroughly wise in everything relating to education, and every branch of philosophy, he was no less prudent and careful in the framing of his will. So that in this respect to he deserves to be admired and imitated.

LIFE OF DEMETRIUS.

I. Demetrius was a native of Phalerus, and the son of Phanostratus. He was a pupil of Theophrastus.

II. And as a leader of the people at Athens he governed the city for ten years, and was honoured with three hundred and sixty brazen statues, the greater part of which were equestrian: and some were placed in carriages or in pairhorse chariots, and the entire number were finished within three hundred days, so great was the zeal with which they were worked at. And Demetrius, the Magnesian, in his treatise on People of the same Name, says that he began to be the leader of the commonwealth, when Harpalus arrived in Athens, having fled from Alexander. And he governed his country for a long time in a most admirable manner. For he aggrandised the city by increased revenues and by new buildings, although he was a person of no distinction by birth. III. Though Pharorinus, in the first book of his Commentaries, asserts that he was of the family of Conon. IV. He lived with a citizen of noble birth, named Lamia, as his mistress, as the same author tells us in his first book.

V. Again, in his second book he tells us that Demetrius was the slave of the debaucheries of Cleon.

VI. Didymus, in his Banquets, says that he was called £ag/ro/3X£pagos, or Beautiful Eyed, and Lampeto, by some courtesan. VII. It is said that he lost his eye-sight in Alexandria, and recovered it again by the favour of Serapis; on which account he composed the paeans which are sung and spoken of as his composition to this day. VIII. He was held in the greatest honour among the Athenians, but nevertheless, he found his fame darkened by envy, which attacks every thing; for he was impeached by some one on a capital charge, and as he did not appear, he was con demned. His accusers, however, did not become masters of his person, but expended their venom on the brass, tearing down his statues and selling some and throwing others into the sea, and some they cut up into chamber-pots. For even this is stated. And one statue alone of him is preserved p which is in the Acropolis. But Pharorinus in his Universal History, says that the Athenians treated Demetrius in this manner at the command of the king; aud they also impeached him as guilty of illegality in his administration, as Pharorinus says. But Hermippus says, that after the death of Cassander, he feared the enmity of Antigonus, and on that account fled to Ptolemy Soter; and that he remained at his court for a long time, and, among other pieces of advice, counselled the king to make over the kingdom to his sons by Eurydice. And as he would not agree to this measure, but gave the crown to his son by Berenice, this latter, after the death of his father, commanded Demetrius to be kept in prison until he should come to some determination about him. And there he remained in great despondency; and while asleep on one occasion, he was bitten by an asp in the hand, and so he died. And he is buried in the district of Busiris, near Diospolis, and we have written the following epigram on him:—

An asp, whose tooth of venom dire was full, Did kill the wise Demetrius.
The serpent beamed not light from out his eyes,-

But dark and lurid hell.

But Heraclides, in his Epitome of the Successions of Sotion, says that Ptolemy wished to transmit the kingdom to Philadelphia, and that Demetrius dissuaded him from doing so by the argument, " If you give it to another, you will not have it yourself." And when

Menander, the comic poet, had an information laid against him at Athens (for this is a statement which I have heard), he was very nearly convicted, for no other reason but that he was a friend of Demetrius. He was, however, successfully defended by Telesphorus, the sonin-law of Demetrius.

IX. In the multitude of his writings and the number of lines which they amount to, he exceeded nearly all the Peripatetics of his day, being a man of great learning and experience on every subject. And some of his writings are historical, some political, some on poets, some rhetorical, some also are speeches delivered in public assemblies or on embassies; there are also collections of Esop's Fables, and many other books. There are five volumes on the Legislation of Athens; two on Citizens of Athens; two on the Managemeut of the People; two on Political Science; one on Laws; two on Rhetoric; two on Military Affairs; two on the Iliad; four on the Odyssey; one called the Ptolemy; one on Love; the Phaedondas, one; the Maedon, one; the Cleon, one; the Socrates, one; the Artaxerxes, one; the Homeric, one; the Aristides, one; the Aristomachus, one; the Exhortatory, one; one on the Constitution; one on his Ten Years' Government; one on the Ionians; one on Ambassadors; one on Good Faith; one on Gratitude; one on Futurity; one on Greatness of Soul; one on Marriage; one on Opinion; one on Peace; one on Laws; one on Studies; one on Opportunity; the Dionysius, one; the Chalcidean, one; the Maxims of the Athenians, ODe; on Antiphones, one; a Historic Preface, one; one Volume of Letters; one called an Assembly on Oath; one on Old Age; one on Justice; one volume of iEsop's Fables; one of Apophthegms. His style is philosophical, combined with the energy and impressiveness of an orator.

X, When he was told that the Athenians had thrown down his statues, he said, " But they have not thrown down my virtues, on account of which they erected them." He used to say that the eyebrows were not an insignificant part of a man, for that they were able to overshadow the whole life. Another of his sayings was that it was not Plutus alone who was blind, but Fortune also, who acted as his guide. Another, that reason had as much influence on government, as steel had in war. On one occasion, when he saw a debauched young man, he said, " There is a square Mercury with a long robe, a belly, and a beard." It was a favourite saying of his, that in the case of men elated with pride one ought to cut something off their height, and leave them their spirit. Another of his apophthegms was, that at home young men ought to show respect to their parents, and in the streets to every one whom they met, and in solitary places to themselves. Another, that friends ought to come to others in good fortune only when invited, but to those in distress of their own accord.

These are the chief sayings attributed to him.

XI. There were twenty persons of the name of Demetrius, of sufficient consideration to be entitled to mention. First, a Chalcedonian, an orator, older than Thrasymachus; the second, this person of whom we are speaking; the third was a Byzantine, a Peripatetic philosopher; the fourth was a man surnamed Graphicus, a very eloquent lecturer, and also a painter; the fifth was a native of Aspendus, a disciple of Apollonius, of Soli; the sixth was a native of Colatia, who wrote twenty books about Asia and Europe; the seventh was a Byzantine, who wrote an account of the crossing of the Gauls from Europe into Asia, in thirteen books, and the History of Antiochus and Ptolemy, and their Administration of the Affairs of Africa, in eight more; the eighth was a Sophist who lived in Alexandria, and who wrote a treatise on Rhetorical Art; the ninth was a native of Adramyttium, a grammarian, who was nick-named Ixion, in allusion to some crime he had committed against Juno; the tenth was a Cyrenean, a grammarian, who was surnamed Stamnus, a very distinguished man; the eleventh was a Scepsian, a rich man of noble birth, and of great eminence for learning. He it was who advanced the fortunes of Metrodorus his fellow citizen; the twelfth was a grammarian of Euthyne, who was made a citizen of Lemnos; the thirteenth was a Bythinian, a son of Diphilus the Stoic, and a disciple of Pamotus of Rhodes; the fourteenth was an orator of Smyrna. All of these were prose writers.

The following were poets: —The first a poet of the Old Comedy. The second an Epic poet, who has left nothing behind him that has come down to us, except these lines which he wrote against some envious people:— -They disregard a man while still alive,

Whom, when he's dead, they honour; cities proud, . And powerful nations, have with contest fierce,
Fought o'er a tomb and unsubstantial shade.

The third was a native of Tarsus; a writer of Satires. The fourth was a composer of Iambics, a bitter man. The fifth was a statuary, who is mentioned by Polemo. The sixth was a native of Erythrae, a man who wrote on various subjects, and who composed volumes of histories and relations.

rrrafivog, means an earthenware jar for wine. t The foregoing account hardly does justice to Demetrius, who was a man of real ability, and of a very different class to the generality of those whom the ancients dignified with the title of philosophers. He was called Phalereus, to distinguish him from his contemporary Demetrius Poliorcetes. His administration of the affairs of Athens was so successful, that Cicero gives him the praise of having re-established the sinking and almost prostrate power of the republic. LIFE OF HERACLIDES.

I. Heraclides was the son of Euthyphron, and was born at Heraclea, in Pontus; he was also a wealthy man.

II. After he came to Athens, he was at first a disciple of Speusippus, but he also attended the schools of the Pythagorean philosophers, and he adopted the principles of Plato; last of all he became a pupil of Aristotle, as we are told by Sotion in his book entitled the Successions. III. He used to wear delicate garments, and was a man of great size, so that he was nicknamed by the Athenians Pompicus instead of

Ponticus. But he was of quiet manners and noble aspect. IV. There are several books extant by him, which are exceedingly good and admirable. They are in the form of dialogue; some being Ethical dialogues; three ou the subject of Justice; one on Temperance; five on Piety; one on Manly Courage; one, and a second which is distinct from it, on Virtue; one on Happiness; one on Supremacy; one on Laws and questions connected with them; one on Names; one called Covenants; one called The Unwilling Lover; and the Clinias. (Cio. de Rep. ii. 1.) As an orator, he is spoken of by the same great authority with the highest admiration. Cicero calls him " a subtle disputer, not vehement, but very sweet, as a pupil of Theophrastus might be expected to be." (de Off. i. 3). In another place he praises him as possessed of great learning, and as one who " rather delighted than inflamed the Athenians." (de Clav. Orat. § 37.) And says, " that he was the first person who endeavoured to soften eloquence, and who made it tender and gentle; preferring to appear sweet, as indeed he was, rather than vehement." (Ibid § 38.) In another place he says, " Demetrius Phalereus the most polished of all those orators" (he has been mentioning Demosthenes, Hyperides, Lycurgus, Eschines, and Dinarchus) " in my opinion." (de Orat. ii. 23.) And he praises him for not confining his learning to the schools, but for bringing it into daily use, and employing it as one of his ordinary weapons, (de Leg. iii. 14.) And asks who can be found besides him who excelled in both ways, so as to be pre-eminent at the same time as a scholar, and a governor of a state. (Ibid.) He mentions his death in the oration. for Rabirius Postumus, § 9. He appears to have died about B.C. 282. From *irofiiri),* a procession.

Of the physical dialogues, one is on the Mind; one on the Soul; one on the Soul, and Nature and Appearances; one addressed to Democritus; one on the Heavenly Bodies; one on the State of Things in the Shades below; two on Lives; one on the Causes of Diseases; one on the Good; one on the doctrines of Zeno; one on the Doctrines of Metron.

Of his grammatical dialogues, there are two on the Age of Homer and Hesiod; two on Archilochus and Homer.

There are some on Music too; three on Euripides and Sophocles, and two on Music. There are also two volumes, Solutions of Questions concerning Homer; one on Speculations; one, the Three Tragedians; one volume of Characters; one dialogue on Poetry and the Poets; one on Conjecture; one on Foresight; four, being Explanations of Heraclitus; one, Explanations with reference to Democritus; two books of Solutions of Disputed Points; one, the Axiom; one on Species; one book of Solutions; one of Suppositions; one addressed to Dionysius.

Of rhetorical works, there is the dialogue on the being an Orator, or the Protagoras.

Of historical dialogues, there are some on the Pythagoreans, and on Inventions. Of these, some he has drawn up after the manner of Comic writers; as, for instance, the one about Pleasure, and that about Temperance. And some in the style of the Tragedians, as, for instance, the dialogues on the State of Things in the Shades below; and one on Piety, and that on Supremacy. And his style is a conversational and moderate one, suited to the characters of philosophers and men occupied in the military or political affairs conversing together. Some of his works also are on Geometry, and on Dialectics; and in all of them he displays a very varied and elevated style; and he has great powers of persuasion.

V. He appears to have delivered his country when it was under the yoke of tyrants, by slaying the monarch, as Demetrius of Magnesia tells us, in his treatise on People of the Same Name.

VI. And he gives the following account of him. That he brought up a young serpent, and kept it till it grew large; and that when he was at the point of death, he desired one of his faithful friends to hide his body, and to place the serpent in his bed, that he might appear to have migrated to the Gods. And all this was done; and while the citizens were all attending his funeral and extolling his character, the serpent hearing the noise, crept out of his clothes and threw the multitude into confusion. And afterwards everything was revealed, and Heraclides was seen, not as he hoped to have been, but as he really was. And we have written an epigram on him which runs thus:—

You wish'd, 0 Heraclidef, when you died,

To leave a strange belief among mankind,

That you, when dead, a serpent had become.

But all your calculations were deceived,

For this your serpent was indeed a beast,

And you were thus discovered and pronounced another.

And Hippobotus gives the same account But Hermippus says that once, when a famine oppressed the land, the people of Heraclea consulted the Pythian oracle for the way to get rid of it; and that Heraclides corrupted the ambassadors who were sent to consult the oracle, and also the priestess, with bribes; and that she answered that they would obtain a deliverance from their distresses, if Heraclides, the son of Euthyphron, was presented by them with a golden crown, and if when he was dead they paid him honours as a hero. Accordingly, this answer was brought back from the oracle to Heraclea, but they who brought it got no advantage from it; for as soon as Heraclides had been crowned iu the theatre, he was seized with apoplexy, and the ambassadors who had been sent to consult the oracle were stoned, and so put to death; and at the very same moment the Pythian priestess was going down to the inner shrine, and while standing there was bitten by a serpent, and died immediately. This then is the account given of his death.

VII. And Aristoxenus the musician says, that he composed tragedies, and inscribed them with the name of Thespis. And Chamaeleon says, that he stole essays from him on the subject of Homer and Hesiod, and published them as his own. And Aretodorus the Epicurean reproaches him, and contradicts all the arguments which he advanced in his treatise on Justice. Moreover, Dionysius. called the Deserter, or as some say Spentharus, wrote a tragedy called Parthenopaeus, and forged the name of Sophocles to it. And Heraclides was so much deceived that he took some passages out of one of his works, and cited them as the words of Sophocles; and Dionysius, when he perceived it, gave him notice of the real truth; and as he would not believe it, and denied it, he sent him word to examine the first letters of the first verses of the book, and they formed the name of Panculus, who was a friend of Dionysius. And as Heraclides still refused to believe it, and said that it was possible that such a thing might happen by chance, Dionysius sent him back word once more, " You will find this passage too:—

" An aged monkey is not easily caught; He's caught indeed, but only after a time."

And he added, " Heraclides knows nothing of letters, and has no shame." VIII. And there were fourteen persons of the name of Heraclides. First, this man of whom we are speaking; the second was a fellow citizen of his, who composed songs for Pyrrhic dances, and other trifles; the third was a native of Cumae, who wrote a history of the Persian war in five books; the fourth was also a citizen of Cumae, who was an orator, and wrote a treatise on his art; the fifth was a native of Calatia or Alexandria, who wrote a Succession in six books, and a treatise on Ships, from which he was called Lembos; the sixth was an Alexandrian, who wrote an account of the peculiar habits of the Persians; the seventh was a dialectician of Bargyleia, who wrote against Epicurus; the eighth was a physician, a pupil of Nisius; the ninth was a physician of Tarentum, a man of great skill; the tenth was a poet, who wrote Precepts; the eleventh was a sculptor of Phocaea: the twelfth was an Epigrammatic poet of considerable beauty; the thirteenth was a Magnesian, who wrote a history of the reign of Mithridates; the fourteenth was an astronomer, who wrote a treatise on Astronomy.

BOOK VI. LIFE OF ANTISTHENES.

I. Antisthenes was an Athenian, the son of Antisthenes. And he was said not to be a legitimate Athenian; in reference to which he said to some one who was reproaching him with the circumstance, " The mother of the Gods too is a Phrygian;" for he was thought to have had a Thracian mother. On which account, as he had borne himself bravely in the battle of Tanagra, he gave occasion to Socrates to say that the son of two Athenians could not have been so brave. And he himself, when disparaging the Athenians who gave themselves great airs as having been born out of the earth itself, said that they were not more noble as far as that went than snails and locusts.

II. Originally he was a pupil of Gorgias the rhetorician; owing to which circumstance he employs the rhetorical style . of language in his Dialogues, especially in his Truth and in —. his Exhortations. And Hermippus says, that he had originally intended in his address at the assembly, on account of the Isthmian games, to attack and also to praise the Athenians, and Thebans, and Lacedaemonians; but that he afterwards abandoned the design, when he saw that there were a great many spectators come from those cities. Afterwards, he attached himself to Socrates, and made such progress in philosophy while with him, that he advised all his own pupils to become his fellow pupils in the school of Socrates. And as he lived in the Piraeus, he went up forty furlongs to the city every day, in order to hear Socrates, from whom he learnt the art of enduring, and of being indifferent to external circumstances, and so became the original founder of the Cynic school. III. And he used to argue that labour was a good thing, by adducing the examples of the great Hercules, and of Cyrus, one of which he derived from the Greeks and the other from the barbarians. IV. He was also the first person who ever gave a definition of discourse, saying, " Discourse is that which shows what anything is or was." And he used continually to say, " I would rather go mad than feel pleasure." And, " One ought to attach one's self to such women as will thank one for it." He said once to a youth from Pontus, who was on the point of coming to him to be his pupil, and was asking him what things he wanted, " You want a new book, and a new pen, and a new tablet;"—meaning a new mind. Aud to a person who asked him from what country he had better marry a wife, he said, " If you marry a handsome woman, she will be common; if an ugly woman, she will he a punishment to you." He was told once that Plato spoke ill of him, and he replied. " It is a royal privilege to do well, and to be evil spoken of." When he was being initiated into the mysteries of Orpheus, and the priest said that those who were initiated enjoyed many good things in the shades below, " Why, then," said he " do not you die?" Being once reproached as not being the son of two free citizens, he said, " And I am not the son of two people skilled in wrestling; nevertheless, I am a skilful wrestler." On one occasion he was asked why he had but few disciples, and said, " Because I drove them away with a silver rod." When he was asked why he reproved his pupils with bitter language, he said, " Physicians too use severe remedies for their patients." Once he saw an adulterer run ning away, and said, " 0 unhappy man! how much danger could you have avoided for one obol!" He used to say, as Hecaton tells us in his Apophthegms, " That it was better to fall among crows,f than among flatterers; for that they only devour the dead, but the others devour the living." When he was asked what was the most happy event that could take place in human life, he said, " To die while prosperous."

On one occasion one of his friends was lamenting to him that he had lost his memoranda, and he said to him, " You ought to have written them on your mind, and not on paper." A favourite saying of his was, " That envious people were devoured by their own disposition, just as iron is by rust." Another was, " That those who wish to be immortal ought to live piously and justly." He used to say too, " That cities There ia a play on the similarity of the two sounds, (cotvi), common, and *iroivt,* punishment.

† The Greek is, tc *Kopacag,* which was a proverb for utter destruction. were ruined when they were unable to distinguish worthless citizens from virtuous ones." On one occasion he was being praised by some wicked men, and said, " I am sadly afraid that I must have done some wicked thing." One of his favourite sayings was, " That the fellow-*i* ship of brothers of one mind was stronger than any fortified city." He used to say, " That those things were the best for a man to take on a journey, which would float with him if he were shipwrecked. " He was once reproached for being intimate with wicked men, and said, " Physicians also live with, those who are sick; and yet they do not catch fevers." He used to say, " that it was an absurd thing to clean a cornfield of tares, and in war to get rid of bad soldiers, and yet not to rid one's self in a city of the wicked citizens." When he was asked what advantage he had ever derived from philosophy, he replied, " The advantage of being able to converse with myself." At a drinking party, a man once said to him, " Give us a song," and he replied, " Do you'play us a tune on the flute." When Diogenes asked him for a tunic, he bade him fold his cloak. He was asked on one occasion what learning was the most necessary, and he replied, " To unlearn one's bad habits." And he used to exhort those who found themselves ill spoken of, to endure it more than they would any one's throwing stones at them. He used to laugh at Plato as conceited; accordingly, once when there was a fine procession, seeing a horse neighing, he said to Plato, " I think you too would be a yerv_fnsky horse:" and he said this all the more, because Plato keptTcontinually praising the horse. At another time, he had gone to see him when he was ill. and when he saw there a dish in which Plato had been sick, he said, " I see your bile there, but I do not see your conceit." He used to advise the Athenians to pass a vote that asses j were horses; and, as they thought that irrational, he said,. " Why, those whom you make generals have never learnt to be really generals, they have only been voted such."

A man said to him one day, " Many people praise you." " Why, what evil," said he, " have I done?" When he turned the rent in his cloak outside, Socrates seeing it, said to him, " I see your vanity through the hole in your cloak." On another occasion, the question was put to him by some one, as Phanias relates, iu his treatise on the Philosphers of the Socratic school, what a man could do to show himself an honourable and a virtuous man; and he replied, " If you attend to those who understand the subject, and learn from them that you ought to shun the bad habits which you have. " Some one was praising luxury in his hearing, and he said, " May the children of my enemies be luxurious." Seeing a young man place himself in a carefully studied attitude before a modeller, he said, "Tell me, if the brass could speak, on what would it pride itself?" And when the young man replied, " On its beauty." " Are you not then," said he, " ashamed to rejoice in the same thing as an inanimate piece of brass?" A young man from Pontus once promised to recollect him, if a vessel of salt fish arrived; and so he took him with him, and also an empty bag, and went to a woman who sold meal, and filled his sack and went away; and when the woman asked him to pay for it, he said, "The young man will pay you, when the vessel of salt fish comes home."

He it was who appears to have been the cause of Anytus's banishment, and of Meletus's death. For having met with some young men of Pontus, who had come to Athens, on account of the reputation of Socrates, he took them to Anytus, telling them, that in moral philosophy he was wiser than Socrates; and they who stood by were indignant at this, and drove him away. And whenever he saw a woman beautifully adorned, he would go off to her house, and desire her husband to bring forth his horse and his arms; and then if he had such things, he would give him leave to indulge in luxury, for that he had the means of defending himself; but if he had them not, then he would bid him strip his wife of her ornaments. I V. And the doctrines he adopted were these. He used to; insist that virtue was a thing which might be taught; also.

; I that the nobly born and virtuously disposed, were the same J people; for that virtue was of itself sufficient for happiness.; and was in need of nothing, except the strength of Socrates. I He also looked upon virtue as a species of work, not wanting -J many arguments, or much instruction; and he taught that the wise man was sufficient for himself; for that everything that belonged to any one else belonged to him. He considered obscurity of fame a good thing, and equally good with labour. And he used to say that the wise man would regulate his conduct as a citizen, not according to the established laws of the state, but according to the law of virtue. And that he would marry for the sake of having children, selecting' the most beautiful woman for his wife. And that he would love her; for that the wise man alone knew what object deserved love.

Diocles also attributes the following apophthegms to him. To the wise man, nothing is strange and nothing remote. The virtuous man is worthy to be loved. Good men are friends. It is right to make the brave and just one's allies. Virtue is a weapon of which a man cannot be deprived. It is better to fight with a few good men against all the wicked, than with many wicked men against a few good men. One should attend to one's enemies, for they are the first persons to detect one's errors. One should consider a just man as of more value than a relation. Virtue is the same in a man as in a woman. What is good is honourable, and what is bad is disgraceful. Think everything that is wicked, foreign. Prudence is the safest fortification; for it can neither fall to pieces nor be betrayed. One must prepare one's self a fortress in one's own impregnable thoughts.

VI. He used to lecture in the Gymnasium, called Cynosarges, not far from the gates; and some people say that it is from that place that the sect got the

name of Cynics. And he himself was called Haplocyon (downright dog). VII. He was the first person to set the fashion of doubling his cloak, as Diocles says, and he wore no other garment. And he used to carry a stick and a wallet; but Neanthes says that he was the first person who wore a cloak without folding it. But Sosicrates, in the third book of his Successions, says that Diodorus, of Aspendos, let his beard grow, and used to carry a stick and a wallet. VIII. He is the only one of all the pupils of Socrates, whom Theopompus praises and speaks of as clever, and able to persuade whomsoever he pleased by the sweetness of his conversation. And this is plain, both from his own writings, and from the Banquet of Xenophon. He appears to have been the founder of the more manly Stoic school; on which account Athenaeus, the epigrammatist, speaks thus of them:— 0 ye, who learned are in Stoic fables,
Ye who consign the wisest of all doctrines
To your most sacred books; you say that virtue
Is the sole good; for that alone can save
The life of man, and strongly fenced cities.
But if some fancy pleasure their best aim,
One of the Muses 'tis who has convinc'd them.

He was the original cause of the apathy of Diogenes, and the temperance of Crates, and the patience of Zeno, having himself, as it were, laid the foundations of the city which they afterwards built. And Xenophon says, that in his conversation and society, he was the most delightful of men, and in every respect the most temperate.

IX. There are ten volumes of his writings extant. The first volume is that in which there is the essay on Style, or on Figures of Speech; the Ajax, or speech of Ajax; the Defence, of Orestes or the treatise on Lawyers; the Isographe, or the Lysias and Isocrates; the reply to the work of Isocvates, entitled the Absence of Witnesses. The second volume is that in which we have the treatise on the Nature of Animals; on the Pro-creation of Children, or on Marriage, an essay of an amatory character; on the Sophists, an essay of,a physiognomical character; on Justice and Manly Virtue, being three essays of an hortatory character; two treatises on Theognis. The third volume contains a treatise on the Good; on Manly Courage; on Law, or Political Constitutions; on Law, or what is Honourable and Just; on Freedom and Slavery; on Good Faith; on a Guardian, or on Persuasion; on Victory, an economical essay. The fourth volume contains the Cyrus; the Greater Heracles, or a treatise on Strength. The fifth volume contains the Cyrus, or a treatise on Kingly Power; the Aspasia.

The sixth volume is that in which there is the treatise Truth; another (a disputatious one) concerning Arguing; the Sathon, or on Contradiction, in three parts; and an essay on Dialect. The seventh contains a treatise on Education, or Names, in five books; one on the Use of Names, or the Contentious Man; one on Questions and Answers; one on Opinion and Knowledge, in four books; one on Dying; one on Life and Death; one on those who are in the Shades below; one on Nature, in two books; two books of Questions in Natural Philosophy; one essay, called Opinions on the Contentious Man; one book of Problems, on the subject of Learning. The eighth volume is that in which we find a treatise on Music; one on Interpreters; one on Homer; one on Injustice and Impiety; one on Calchas; one on a Spy; one on Pleasure. The ninth book contains an essay on the Odyssey; one on the Magic Wand; the Minerva, or an essay on Telemachus; an essay on Helen and Penelope; one on Proteus; the Cyclops, being an essay on Ulysses; an essay on the Use of Wine, or on Drunkenness, or on the Cyclops; one on Circe; one on Amphiaraus; one on Ulysses and Penelope, and also on Ulysses' Dog. The tenth volume is occupied by the Heracles, or Medas; the Hercules, or an Essay on Prudence or Strength; the Lord or the Lover; the Lord or the Spies; the Menexenus, or an essay on Governing; the Alcibiades; the Archelaus, or an essay on Kingly Power.

These then are the names of his works. And Timon, rebuking him because of their great number, called him a universal chatterer.

X. He died of some disease; and while he was ill Diogenes came to visit him, and said to him, " Have you no need of a friend?" Once too he came to see him with a sword in his hand; and when Antisthenes said, " Who can deliver me from this suffering?" he, pointing to the sword, said, "This can;" But he rejoined, " I said from suffering, but not from life;" for he seemed to bear his disease the more calmly from his love of life. And there is an epigram on him written by ourselves, which runs thus:—

In life you were a bitter dog, Antisthenes,
Born to bite people's minds with sayings sharp,
Not with your actual teeth. Now you are slain
By fell consumption, passers by may say,
Why should he not, one wants a guide to Hell.

There were also three other people of the name of Antisthenes. One, a disciple of Heraclitus; the second, an Ephesian; the third, a historian of Ehodes. And since we have spoken of those who proceeded from the school of Aristippus and Phaedon, we may now go on to the Cynics and Stoics, who derived their origin from Antisthenes. And we will take them in the following order.

LIFE OF DIOGENES.

I. Diogenes was a native of Sinope, the son of Tresius, a money-changer. And Diocles says that he was forced to flee from his native city, as his father kept the public bank there, and had adulterated the coinage. But Eubulides, in his essay on Diogenes, says, that it was Diogenes himself who did this, and that he was banished with his father. And, indeed, he himself, in his Perdalus, says of himself that he had adulterated the public money. Others say that he was one of the curators, and was persuaded by the artisans employed, and that he went to Delphi, or else to the oracle at Delos, and there consulted Apollo as to whether he should do what people were trying to persuade him to do; and that, as the God gave him permission to do so, Diogenes, not comprehending that the God meant that he might change the political customs of his country if he could, adulterated the coinage; and being detected, was banished, as some people say, but as other accounts have it, took the alarm and fled away of his own accord. Some again, say that he adulterated the money which he had received from his father; and that his father was thrown into prison and died there; but that Diogenes escaped and went to Delphi, and asked, not whether he might tamper with the coinage, but what he could do to become very celebrated, and that in consequence he received the oracular answer which I have mentioned.

II. And when he came to Athens he attached himself to Antisthenes; but as he repelled him, because he admitted no one; he at last forced his way to him by his pertinacity. And once, when he raised his stick at him, he put his head under it, and said, " Strike, for you will not find any stick hard enough to drive me away as long as you continue to speak." And from this time forth he was one of his pupils; and being an exile, he naturally betook himself to a simple mode of life. III. And when, as Theophrastus tells us, in his Megaric Philosopher, he saw a mouse running about and not seeking The passage is not free from difficulty; but the thing which misled Diogenes appears to have been that Vo/hit/jot, the word here used, meant both " a coin, or coinage," and " a custom." for a bed, nor taking care to keep in the dark, nor looking for any of those things which appear enjoyable to such an animal, he found a remedy for his own poverty. He was, according to the account of some people, the first person who doubled up his cloak out of necessity, and who slept in it; and who carried a wallet, in which he kept his food; and who used whatever place was near for all soils of purposes, eating, and sleeping, and conversing in it. In reference to which habit he used to say, pointing to the Colonnade of Jupiter, and to the Public Magazine, " that the Athenians had built him places to live in." Being attacked with illness, he supported himself with a staff; and after that he carried it continually, not indeed in the city, but whenever he was walking in the roads, together with his wallet, as Olympiodorus, the chief man of the Athenians tells us; and Polymeter, the orator, and Lysanias, the son of Eschorion, tell the same story.

When he had written to some one to look out and get ready a small house for him, as he delayed to do it, he took a cask which he found in the Temple of Cybele, for his house, as he himself tells us in his letters. And during the summer he used to roll himself in the warm sand, but in winter he would embrace statues all covered with snow, practising himself, on every occasion, to endure anything. *U* IV. He was very violent in expressing his haughty disdain of others. He said that the *e‰oXii* (school) of Euclides was *‰oXri* (gall). And he used to call Plato's *diaTgifiri* (discussions) *xarargiBii* (disguise). It was also a saying of his that the Dionysian games were a great marvel to fools; and that the demagogues were the ministers of the multitude. He used likewise to say, " that when in the course of his life he beheld pilots, and physicians, and philosophers, he thought man the wisest of all animals; but when again he beheld interpreters of dreams, and soothsayers, and those who listened to them, and men puffed up with glory or riches, then he thought that there was not a more foolish animal than man." Another of his sayings was, " that he thought a man ought oftener to provide himself with a reason than with a halter." On oiio occasion, when he noticed Plato at a very costly entertainment tasting some olives, he said, " 0 you wise man! why, after having sailed to Sicily for the sake of such a feast, do you not now enjoy what you have before you?" And Plato replied,

Q

" By the Gods, Diogenes, while I was there I ate olives and all such things a great deal." Diogenes rejoined, " What then did you want to sail to Syracuse for? Did not Attica at that time produce any olives?" But Phavorinus, in his Universal History, tells this story of Aristippus. At another time he was eating dried figs, when Plato met him, and he said to him, " You may have a share of these;" and as he took some and ate them, he said, " I said that you might have a share of them, not that you might eat them all." On one occasion Plato had invited some friends who had come to him from Dionysius to a banquet, and Diogenes trampled on his carpets, and said, " Thus I trample on the empty pride of Plato and Plato made him answer, " How much arrogance are you displaying, 0 Diogenes! when you think that you are not arrogant at all." But, as others tell the story, Diogenes said, " Thus I trample on the pride of Plato;" and that Plato rejoined, " With quite as much pride yourself, 0 Diogenes." Sotion too, in his fourth book, states, that the Cynic made the following speech to Plato: Diogenes once asked him for some wine, and then for some dried figs; so he sent him an entire jar full; and Diogenes said to him, " Will you, if you are asked how many two and two make, answer twenty? In this way, you neither give with any reference to what you are asked for, nor do you answer with reference to the question put to you." He used also to ridicule him as an intenmnabletalker. When he was asked where in Greece he saw virtuous men; " Men," said he, " nowhere; but I see good boys in Lacedaamon." On one occasion, when no one came to listen to him while he was discoursing seriously, he began to whistle. And then when people flocked round him, he reproached them for coming with eagerness to folly, but being lazy and indifferent about good things. One of his frequent sayings was, " That men contended with one another in punching and kicking, but that no one showed any emulation in the pursuit of virtue." He used to express his astonishment at the grammarians for being desirous to learn everything about the misfortunes of Ulysses, and being ignorant of their own. He used also to say, " That the musicians fitted the strings to the lyre properly, but left all the habits of their soul ill-arranged." And, " That mathematicians kept their eyes fixed on the sun and moon, and overlooked what was under their feet." " That orators were anxious to speak justly, but not at all about acting so." Also, " That misers blamed money, but were preposterously fond of it." He often condemned those who praise the just for being superior to money, but who at the same time are eager themselves for great riches. He was also very indignant at seeing men sacrifice to the Gods to procure good health, and yet at the sacrifice eating in a manner injurious to health. He often expressed his surprise at slaves, who, seeing their masters eating in a gluttonous manner, still. do not themselves lay hands on any of the eatables. He would frequently praise those who were about to marry, and yet did not marry; or who were about to take a voyage, and yet did not take a voyage; or who were about to engage in affairs of state, and did not do so; and those who were about to rear children, yet did not rear any; and those who were preparing to take up their abode with princes, and yet did not take it up. One of his sayings was, " That one ought to hold out one's hand to a friend without closing the fingers."

Hermippus, in his Sale of Diogenes, says that he was taken prisoner and put up to be sold, and asked what he could do; and he answered, " Govern men." And so he bade the crier " give notice that if any one wants to purchase a master, there is one here for him." When he was ordered not to sit down; " It makes no difference," said he, " for fish are sold, be where they may." He used to say, that he wondered at men always ringing a dish or jar before buying it, but being content to judge of a man by his look alone. When Xeniades bought him, he said to him that he ought to obey him even though he was his slave; for that a physician or a pilot would find men to obey them even though they might be slaves.

V. And Eubulus says, in his essay entitled, The Sale of Diogenes, that he taught the children of Xeniades, after their other lessons, to ride, and shoot, and sling, and dart. And then in the Gymnasium he did not permit the trainer to exercise them after the fashion of athletes, but exercised them himself to just the degree sufficient to give them a good colour and good health. And the boys retained in their memory many sentences of poets and prose writers, and of Diogenes himself; and he used to give them a concise statement of everything in order to strengthen their memory; and at home he used to teach them to wait upon themselves, contenting themselves with plain food, and drinking water. And he accustomed them to cut their hair close, and to eschew ornament, and to go without tunics or shoes, and to keep silent, looking at nothing except themselves as they walked along. He used, also to take them out hunting; and they paid the greatest attention and respect to Diogenes himself, and spoke well of him to their parents.

VI. And the same author affirms, that he grew old in the household of Xeniades, and that when he died he was buried by his sons. And that while he was living with him, Xeniades once asked him how he should bury him; and he said, " On my face;" and when he was asked why, he said, " Because, in a little while, everything will be turned upside down. " And he said this because the Macedonians were already attaining power, and becoming a mighty people from having been very inconsiderable. Once, when a man had conducted him into a magnificent house, and had told him that he must not spit, after hawking a little, he spit in his face, saying that he could not find a worse place. But some tell this story of Aristippus. Once, he called out, " Holloa, men." And when some people gathered round him in consequence, he drove them away with his stick, saving, " I called men, and not dregs." This anecdote I have derived'from Hecaton, in the first book of his Apophthegms. They also relate that Alexander said that if he had not been Alexander, he should have liked to be Diogenes. He used to call *avaxrigoi* (cripples), not those who were dumb and blind, but those who had no wallet *(irqga)*. On one occasion he went half shaved into an entertainment of young men, as Metrocles tells us in his Apophthegms, and so was beaten by them. And afterwards he wrote the names of all those who had beaten him, on a white tablet, and went about with the tablet round his neck, so as to expose them to insult, as they were generally condemned and reproached for their conduct.

He used to say that he was the hound of those who were praised; but that none of those who praised them dared to go out hunting with him. A man once said to him, " I conquered men at the Pythian games:" on which he said, " I conquer men, but you only conquer slaves." When some people said to him, " You are an old man, and should rest for the remainder of your life " Why so?" replied he, " suppose I had run a long distance, ought I to stop when I was near the end, and not rather press on? " Once, when he was invited to a banquet, he said that he would not come: for that the day before no one had thanked him for coming. He used to go bare foot through the snow, and to do a number of other things which have been already mentioned. Once he attempted to eat raw meat, but he could not digest it. On one occasion he found Demosthenes, the orator, dining in an inn; and as he was slipping away, he said to him, " You will now be ever so much more in an inn." Once, when some strangers wished to see Demosthenes, he stretched out his middle finger, and said, " This is the great demagogue of the Athenian people." When some one had dropped a loaf, and was ashamed to pick it up again, he, wishing to give him a lesson, tied a cord round the neck of a bottle and dragged it all through the Ceramicus. He used to say, that he imitated the teachers of choruses, for that they spoke too loud, in order that the rest might catch the proper tone. Another of his sayings, was that most men were within a finger's breadth of being mad. If, then, any one were to walk along, stretching out his middle finger, he will seem to be mad; but if he puts out his fore finger, he will not be thought so. Another of his sayings was, that things of great value were often sold for nothing, and *vice versa*. Accordingly, that a statue would fetch three thousand drachmas, and a bushel of meal only two obols; and when Xeniades had bought him, he said to him, " Come, do what you are ordered to." And when he said—

" The streams of sacred rivers now Run backwards to their source I"

" Suppose," rejoined Diogenes, J you had been sick, and had bought a physician, could you refuse to be guided by him, and tell him—

" The streams of sacred rivers now Run backwards to their source *V*

Once a man came to him, and wished to study philosophy
This line is from Euripides, Medea, 411. as his pupil; and he gave him a saperda and made him follow him. And as he from shame threw it away and departed, he soon afterwards met him and, laughing, said to him, " A saperda has dissolved your friendship for me." Bnt Diocles tells this story in the following manner; that when some one said to him, " Give me a commission, Diogenes," he carried him off, and gave him a halfpenny worth of cheese to carry. And as he refused to carry it, " See," said Diogenes. " a halfpenny worth of cheese has broken off our friendship."

On one occasion he saw a child drinking out of its hands, and so he threw away the cup which belonged to his wallet, saying, " That child has beaten me in simplicity." He also threw away his spoon, after seeing a boy, when he had broken his vessel, take up his lentils with a crust of bread. And he used to argue thus,—" Everything belongs to the gods; and wise men are the friends of the gods. All things are in common among friends; therefore everything belongs to wise men." Once he saw a woman falling down before the Gods in an unbecoming attitude; he, wishing to cure her of her superstition, as Zoilus of Perga tells us, came up to her, and said, " Are you not afraid, O woman, to be in such an indecent attitude, when some God may be behind you, for every place is full of him?" He consecrated a man to Esculapius, who was to run up and beat all these who prostrated themselves with their faces to the ground; and he was in the habit of saying that the tragic curse had come upon him, for that he was—

Houseless and citiless, a piteous exile From his dear native land; a wandering beggar,

Scraping a pittance poor from day to day.

And another of his sayings was that he opposed confidence to fortune, nature to law, and reason to suffering. Once, while he was sitting in the sun in the Craneum, Alexander was standing by, and said to him, "Ask any favour you choose of me." And he replied, " Cease to shade me from the sun." On one occasion a man was reading some long passages, and when he came to the end of the book and showed that there was nothing more written, " Be of good cheer, my friends," exclaimed Diogenes, " I see land.'' A man once proved to The saperda was the coracinus (a kind of fish) when salted.
him syllogistically that he had horns, so he put his hand to his forehead and said, "I do not see them." And in a similar manner he replied to one who had been asserting that, there was no such thing as motion, by getting up and walking away. When a man was talking about the heavenly bodies and meteors, " Pray how many days," said he to him, " is it since you came down from heaven?"
A profligate eunuch had written on his house, " Let no evil thing enter in." " Where," said Diogenes, " is the master of the house going?'' After having anointed his feet with perfume, he said that the ointment from his head mounted up to heaven, and that from his feet up to his nose. When the Athenians entreated him to be initiated in the Eleusinian mysteries, and said that in the shades below the initiated had the best seats; " It will," he replied, " be an absurd thing if iEgesilaus and Epaminondas are to live in the mud, and some miserable wretches, who have been initiated, are to be in the islands of the blest." Some mice crept up to his table, and he said, " See, even Diogenes maintains his favourites." Once, when he was leaving the bath, and a man asked him whether many men were bathing, he said, " No;" but when a number of people came out, he confessed that there were a great many. When Plato called him a dog, he said, " Undoubtedly, for I have come back to those who sold me."

Plato defined man thus: " Man is a two-footed, featherless I animal," and was much praised for the definition; so Diogenes plucked a cock and brought it into his school, and I said, " This is Plato's man." On which account this addition) was made to the definition, " With broad flat nails." A man once asked him what was the proper time for supper, and he made answer, " If you are a rich man, whenever you please; and if you are a poor man, whenever you can." When he was at Megara he saw some sheep carefully covered over with skins, and the children running about naked; and so he said, " It is better at Megara to be a man's ram, than his son." A man once struck him with a beam, and then said, " Take care." " What," said he, " are you going to strike me again?" He used to say that the demagogues were the servants of the people; and garlands the blossoms of glory. Having lighted a candle in the day time, he said, " I am looking for a man." On one occasion he stood under a foun tain, and as the bystanders were pitying him, Plato, who was present, said to them, " If you wish really to show your pity for j him, come away;" intimating that he was only acting thus out of a desire for notoriety. Once, when a man had struck him. with his fist, he said," " 0 Hercules, what a strange thing that I should be walking about with a helmet on without knowing it!"

When Midias struck him with his fist and said, "There are three thousand drachmas for you;" the next day Diogenes took the cestus of a boxer and beat him soundly, and said, " There are three thousand drachmas for you." When Lysias, the drug-seller, asked him whether he thought that there were any Gods: " How," said he, " can I help thinking so, when I consider you to be hated by them? " but some attribute this reply to Theodorus. Once he saw a man purifying himself by washing, and said to him, " Oh, wretched man, do not you know that as you cannot wash away blunders in grammar by purification, so, too, you can no more efface the errors of a life in that same manner? "

He used to say that men were wrong for complaining of fortune; for that they ask of the Gods what appear to be good things, not what are really so. And to those who were alarmed at dreams he said, that they did not regard what they do while they are awake, but make a great fuss about what they fancy they see while they are asleep. Once, at the Olympic games, when the herald proclaimed, " Dioxippus is the conqueror of men;" he said, " He is the conqueror of slaves, I am the conqueror of men,"

He was greatly beloved by the Athenians; accordingly, when a youth had broken his cask they beat him, and gave Diogenes another. And Dionysius, the Stoic, says that after the battle of Chaeronea he was taken prisoner and brought to Philip; and being asked who he was, replied, " A spy, to spy upon your insatiability." And Philip marvelled at him and let him go. Once, when Alexander had sent a letter to Athens to Antipater, by the hands of a man named Athlias, he, being present, said, " Athlias from Athlius, by means of This is probably an allusion to a prosecution instituted by Demosthenes against Midias, which was afterwards compromised by Midias paying Demosthenes thirty minae, or three thousand drachmae. See Dem. Or. cont. Midias.

Athlias to Athlius When Perdiccas threatened that he would put him to death if he did not come to him, he replied, " That is nothing strange, for a scorpion or a tarantula could do as much: you had better threaten me that, if I kept away, you should be very happy." He used constantly to repeat with emphasis that an easy life had been given to man by the Gods, but that it had been overlaid by their seeking for honey, cheese-cakes, and unguents, and things of that sort. On which account he said to a man, who had his shoes put on by his servant, " You are not thoroughly happy, unless he also wipes your nose for you; and he will do this, if you are crippled in your hands." On one occasion, when he had seen the hieromnemones t leading off one of the stewards who had stolen a goblet, he said, " The great thieves are carrying off the little thief." At another time, seeing a young man throw ing stones at a cross, he said, "Well done, you will be sure to reach the mark." Once, too, some boys got round him and said, " We are taking care that you do not bite us;" but he said, " Be of good cheer, my boys, a dog does not eat beef." He saw a man giving himself airs because he was clad in a lion's skin, and said to him, " Do not go on disgracing the garb of nature." When people were speaking of the happiness of Calisthenes, and saying what splendid treatment he received from Alexander, he replied, " The man then is wretched, for he is forced to breakfast and dine whenever Alexander chooses." When he was in want of money, he said that he reclaimed it from his friends and did not beg for it.

On one occasion he was working with his hands in the market-place, and said, " I wish I could rub my stomach in the same way, and so avoid hunger." When he saw a young man going with some satraps to supper, he dragged him away and led him off to his relations, and bade them take care of him. He was once addressed by a youth beautifully adorned, who asked him some question; and he refused to give him any answer, till he satisfied him whether he was a man or a woman. And on one occasion, when a youth was playing the This is a pun upon the similarity of Athlias's name to the Greek adjective *a8ioc,* which signifies miserable.

t The *ieponvrifiovtg* were the sacred secretaries or recorders sent by each Amphictyonic state to the council along with their *irvXayopa£,* (the actual deputy or minister). *L. b S.* Gr. & Eng. Lex., *in voc.* coltabus in the bath, he said to him, " The better you do it, the worse you do it." Once at a banquet, some of the guests threw him bones, as if he had been a dog; so he, as he went away, put up his leg against them as if he had been a dog in reality. He used to call the orators, and all those who speak for fame rg/sa&wro/ (thrice men), instead of rfija0X/o/ (thrice miserable). He said that a rich but ignorant man, was like a sheep with a golden fleece. When he saw a notice on the house of a profligate man, " To be sold." " I knew," said he, " that you who are so incessantly drunk, would soon vomit up your owner." To a young man, who was complaining of the number of people who sought his acquaintance, he said, " Do not make such a parade of your vanity."

Having been in a very dirty bath, he said, " I wonder where the people, who bathe here, clean themselves." When all the company was blaming an indifferent harp-player, he alone praised him, and being asked why he did so, he said, " Because, though he is such as he is, he plays the harp and does not steal." He saluted a harp player who was always left alone by his hearers, with, " Good morning, cock;" and when the man asked him, "Why so?" he said, " Because you, when you sing, make every one get up." When a young man was one day making a display of himself, he, having filled the bosom of his robe with lupins, began to eat them; and when the multitude looked at him, he said, " that he marvelled at their leaving the young man to look at him." And when a man, who was very superstitious, said to him, " With one blow I will break your head;" " And I," he replied, " with one sneeze will make you tremble." When Hegesias entreated him to lend him one of his books, he said, " You are, a silly fellow, Hegesias, for you will not take painted figs, but real ones; and yet you overlook the genuine practice of virtue, and seek for what is merely written." A man once reproached him with his banishment, and his answer was, " You wretched man, that is what made me a philosopher." And when, on another occasion, some one said to him, " The people of Sinope condemned you to banishment," he replied, " And I condemned them to remain where they were." Once he saw a man who had been victor at the Olympic games, feeding *(vifiovra)* sheep, and he said to him, " You have soon come across my friend from the Olympic games, to the Neinean." When he was asked why athletes are insensible to pain, he Said, " Because they are built up of pork and beef."

He once asked for a statue; and being questioned as to his reason for doing so, he said, " I am practising disappointment," Once he was begging of some one (for he did this at first out of actual want), he said, " If you have given to any one else, give also to me; and if you have never given to any one, then begin with me." On one occasion, he was asked by the tyrant, " What sort of brass was the best for a statue?" and he replied, " That of which the statues of Harmodius and Aristogiton are made. " When he was asked how Dionysius treats his friends, he said, " Like bags; those which are full he hangs up, and those which are empty he throws away. " A man who was lately married put an inscription on his house, " Hercules Callinicus, the son of Jupiter, lives here; let no evil enter." And so Diogenes wrote in addition, "An alliance is made after the war is over." He used to say that covetousness was the metropolis of all evils. Seeing on one occasion a profligate man in an inn eating olives, he said, " If you had dined thus, you would not have supped thus." One of his apophthegms was, that good men were the images of the Gods; another, that love was the business of those who had nothing to do. When he was asked what was miserable in life, he answered, " An indigent old man." And when the question was put to him, what beast inflicts the worst bite, he said, " Of wild beasts the sycophant, and of tame animals the flatterer."

On one occasion he saw two Centaurs very badly painted; he said, " Which of the two is the wors?" He used to say that a speech, the object of which was solely to please, was a honeyed halter. He called the belly, the Charybdis of life. Having heard once that Didymon the adulterer, had been caught in the fact, he said, " He deserves to be hung by his name."t When the question was put to him, why gold is of a pale colour, he said, " Because it has so many people

plotting There is a pun here. Xf/pwv is the word used for worse. Chiron was also the most celebrated of the Centaurs, the tutor of Achilles.

t There is a pun intended here; as Diogenes proposed Didymus a fate somewhat similar to that of the beaver.

Cupiens evadere damno
Testiculorum.

against it." When he saw a woman in a litter, he said, " The cage is not suited to the animal." And seeing a runaway slave sitting on a well, he said, " My boy, take care you do not fall in." Another time, he saw a little boy who was a stealer of clothes from the baths, and said, " Are you going for unguents, (tic aXei/i/ianov), or for other garments (ei r aXX' 1/iaTiov). Seeing some women hanging on olive trees, he said, " I wish every tree bore similar fruit." At another time, he saw a clothes' stealer, and addressed him thus:—

What moves thee, say, when sleep has clos'd the sight,
To roam the silent fields in dead of night?
Art thou some wretch by hopes of plunder led,
Through heaps of carnage to despoil the dead.

When he was asked whether he had any girl or boy to wait on him, he said, " No." And as his questioner asked further, " If then you die, who will bury you?" He replied, "Whoever wants my house." Seeing a handsome youth sleeping without any protection, he nudged him, and said, " Wake up:—

Mix'd with the vulgar shall thy fate be found,
Pierc'd in the back, a vile dishonest wound.t

And he addressed a man who was buying delicacies at a great expense:—

Not long, my son, will you on earth remain,
If such your dealings. J

When Plato was discoursing about his " ideas," and using the nouns " tableness " and " cupness;" " I, O Plato!" interrupted Diogenes, " see a table and a cup, but I see no tableness or cupness. " Plato made answer, " That is natural enough, for you have eyes, by which a cup and a table are contemplated; but you have not intellect, by which tableness and cupness are seen."

On one occasion, he was asked by a certain person, " What sort of a man, 0 Diogenes, do you think Socrates?" and he This is taken from Homer, H. K. 387. Pope's Version, 455.

t This is also from Homer. II. 9. 95. Pope's Version, 120. X This is a parody on Homer, II?. 95, where the line ends oP dyopeutic—" if such is your language," which Diogenes here changes to of ayopaU'Cj if you buy such things. said, " A madman.'' Another time, the question was put to him, when a man ought to marry? and his reply was, " Young men ought not to marry yet, and old men never ought to marry at all." When asked what he would take to let a man give him a blow on the head?" he replied, "A helmet." Seeing a youth smartening himself up very carefully, he said to him, " If you are doing that for men, you are miserable; and if for women, you are profligate." Once he saw a youth blushing, and addressed him, " Courage, my boy, that is the complexion of virtue." Having once listened to two lawyers, he condemned them both; saying," That the one had stolen the thing in question, and that the other had not lost it." When asked what wine he liked to drink, he said, " That which belongs to another," A man said to him one day, " Many people laugh at you." " But I," he replied, " am not laughed down." When a man said to him, that it was a bad thing to live; " Not to live," said he, " but to live badly. " When some people were advising him to make search for a slave who had run away," he said, " It would be a very absurd thing for Manes to be able to live without Diogenes, but for Diogenes not to be able to live without Manes." When he was dining on olives, a cheese-cake was brought in, on which he threw the olive away, saying:—

Keep well aloof, 0 stranger, from all tyrants.

And presently he added:—

He drove the olive off (jiaariZtv i' iXaav).f

When he was asked what sort of a

dog he was, he replied, " When hungry, I am a dog of Melita; when satisfied, a Molossian; a sort which most of those who praise, do not like to take out hunting with them, because of the labour of keeping up with them; and in like manner, you cannot associate with me, from fear of the pain I give you." The question was put to him, whether wise men ate cheese-cakes, and he replied, " They eat everything, just as the rest of mankind." When asked why people give to beggars and not to philoso This is a line of the Phoenissse of Euripides, v. 40.

t The pun here is on the similarity of the noun *tXaav,* an olive, to the verb *lXaav,* to drive; the words *fidaTiKtv I' lXaav* are of frequent occurrence in Homer. phers, he said, " Because they think it possible that they themselves may become lame and blind, but they do not expect ever to turn out philosophers." He once begged of a covetous man, and as he was slow to give, he said, " Man, I am asking you for something to maintain me («/' *Tgopfiv* and not to bury me (s/'s *rapnv)."* When some one reproached him for having tampered with the coinage, he said, " There was a time when I was such a person as you are now; but there never was when you were such as I am now, and never will be." And to another person who reproached him on the same grounds, he said, " There were times when 1 did what I did not wish to, but that is not the case now." When he went to Myndus, he saw some very large gates, but the city was a small one, and so he said, " Oh men of Myndus, shut your gates, lest your city should steal out." On one occasion, he saw a man who had been detected stealing purple, and so he said:—
A purple death, and mighty fate o'ertook him

When Craterus entreated him to come and visit him, he said, " I would rather lick up salt at Athens, than enjoy a luxurious table with Craterus." On one occasion, he met Anaximenes, the orator, who was a fat man, and thus accosted him; " Pray give us, who are poor, some of your belly; for by so doing you will be relieved yourself, and you will assist us." And once, when he was discussing some point, Diogenes held up a piece of salt fish, and drew off the attention of his hearers; and as Anaximenes was indignant at this, he said, " See, one pennyworth of salt fish has put an end to the lecture of Anaximenes." Being once reproached for eating in the market-place, he made answer, " 1 did, for it was in the market-place that I was hungry." Some authors also attribute the following repartee to him. Plato saw him washing vegetables, and so, coming up to him, he quietly accosted him thus, " If you had paid court to Dionysius, you would not have been washing vegetables.'' " And," he replied, with equal quietness, " if you had washed vegetables, you would never have paid court to Dionysius." When a man said to him once, " Most people laugh at you; " " And very This line occurs, Horn. II. e. 83.

likely,' he replied, " the asses laugh at them; but they do not regard the asses, neither do I regard them." Once he saw a youth studying philosophy, and said to him, " Well done; inasmuch as you are leading those who admire your person to contemplate the beauty of your mind. "

A certain person was admiring the offerings in the temple at Samothrace, and he said to him, " They would have been much more numerous, if those who were lost had offered them instead of those who were saved;" but some attribute this speech to Diagoras the Thelian. Once he saw a handsome youth going to a banquet, and said to him, " You will come back worse *(xelgw);*" and when he the next day after the banquet said to him, " I have left the banquet, and was no worse for it;" he replied, " You were not Chiron, but Eurytion."f He was begging once of a very ill-tempered man, and as he said to him, " If you can persuade me, I will give you something;" he replied, " If I could persuade you, I would beg you to hang yourself." He was on one occasion returning from Lacedaemon to Athens; and when some one asked him, " Whither are you going, and whence do you come?" he said, " I am going from the men's apartments to the women's." Another time he was returning from the Olympic games, and when some one asked him whether there had been a great multitude there, he said, "A great multitude, but very few men." He used to say that debauched men resembled figs growing on a precipice; the fruit of which is not tasted by men, but devoured by crows and vultures. When Phryne had dedicated a golden statue of Venus at Delphi, he wrote upon it, " From the profligacy of the Greeks."

Once Alexander the Great came and stood by him, and said, " I am Alexander, the great king." " And I," said he, " am Diogenes the dog." And when he was asked to what actions of his it was owing that he was called a dog, he said, " Because I fawn upon those who give me anything, and bark at those who give me nothing, and bite the rogues." On one occasion he was gathering some of the fruit of a fig-tree, and The Samothraeian Gods were Gods of the sea, and it was customary for those who had been saved from shipwreck to make them an offering of some part of what they had saved; and of their hair, if they had saved nothing but their lives.

t Eurytion was another of the Centaurs, who was killed by Hercules. when the man who was guarding it told him a man hung himself on this tree the other day, " I, then," said he, " will now purify it." Once he saw a man who had been a conqueror at the Olympic games looking very often at a courtesan; " Look," said he, " at that warlike ram, who is taken prisoner by the first girl he meets. " One of his sayings was, that good-looking courtesans were like poisoned mead.

On one occasion he was eating his dinner in the marketplace, and the bystanders kept constantly calling out " Dog;" but he said, " It is you who are the dogs, who stand around me while I am at dinner." When two effeminate fellows were getting out of his way, he said, " Do not be afraid, a dog does not eat beetroot." Being once asked about a debauched boy, as to what country he came from, he said, " He is a Tegean." Seeing an unskilful wrestler professing to heal a man he said, " What are you about, are you in hopes now to overthrow those who formerly conquered you?" On one occasion he saw the son of a courtesan throwing a stone at a crowd, and said to him, " Take care, lest you hit your father." When a boy showed him a sword that he had received from one to whom he had done some discreditable service, he told him, " The sword is a good sword, but the handle is infamous." And when some people were praising a man who had given him something, he said to them, " And do not you praise me who was worthy to receive it?" He was asked by some one to give him back his cloak; but he replied, " If you gave it me, it is mine; and if you only lent it me, I am using it." A supposititious son (wo-j3oX//i5./£s) of somebody once said to him, that ' he had gold in his cloak; " No doubt," said he, " that is the very reason why I sleep with it under my head (iiiroiXr.fiivog)." When he was asked what advantage he had derived from philosophy, he replied, " If no other, at least this, that I am prepared for every kind of fortune." The question was put to him what countryman he was, and he replied, " A Citizen of This is a pun on the similarity of the sound, Tegea, to *riyog*, a f brothel.

t The Greek is *ipavov aiTovfitvog irpbg rbv kpavdpxiv tyv*,—*ipavog* was not only a subscription or contribution for the support of the poor, but also a club or society of subscribers to a common fund for any purpose, social, commercial, or charitable, or especially political... On the various tpavoi, v. Bockh, P. E. i 328. Att. Process, p. 540, s. 99. i. fc 5. *in voc. epaveg.* the world." Some men were sacrificing to the Gods to prevail on them to send them sons, and he said, "And do you not sacrifice to procure sons of a particular character?" Once he was asking the president of a society for a contribution, and said to him:—

" Spoil all the rest, but keep your hands from Hector."

He used to say that courtesans were the queens of kings; for that they asked them for whatever they chose. When the Athenians had voted that Alexander was Bacchus, he said to them, " Vote, too, that I am Serapis." When a man reproached him for going into unclean places, he said, " The sun too penetrates into privies, but is not polluted by them. " When supping in a temple, as some dirty loaves were set before him, he took them up and threw them away, saying that nothing dirty ought to come into a temple; and when some one said to him, " You philosophize without being possessed of any knowledge," he said, " If I only pretend to wisdom, that is philosophizing." A man once brought him a boy, and said that he was a very clever child, and one of an admirable disposition." " What, then," said Diogenes, " does he want of me? " He used to say, that those who utter virtuous sentiments but do not do them, are no better than harps, for that a harp has no hearing or feeling. Once he was going into a theatre while every one else was coming out of it; and when asked why he did so, " It is," said he, " what I have been doing all my life." Once when he saw a young man putting on effeminate airs, he said to him, " Are you not ashamed to have worse plans for yourself than nature had for you? for she has made you a man, but you are trying to force yourself to be a woman." When he saw an ignorant man tuning a psaltery, he said to him, " Are you not ashamed to be arranging proper sounds on a wooden instrument, and not arranging your soul to a proper life? " When a man said to him, " I am not calculated for philosophy," he said, "Why then do you live, if you have no desire to live properly? " To a man who treated his father with contempt, he said, "Are you not ashamed to despise him to whom you owe it that you have it in your power to give yourself airs at all? " Seeing a handsome young man chattering in an unseemly manner,

B he said, " Are you not ashamed to draw a sword cut of lead out of a scabbard of ivory?" Being once reproached for drinking in a vintner's shop, he said, " I have my hair cut, too, in a barber's. " At another time, he was attacked for having accepted a cloak from Antipater, but he replied:— " Befuse not thou to heed

The gifts which from the mighty Gods proceed."

A man once struck him with a broom, and said, '' Take'care;" so he struck him in return with his staff, and said, " Take care."

He once said to a man who was addressing anxious entreaties to a courtesan, " What can you wish to obtain, you wretched man, that you had not better be disappointed in? " Seeing a man reeking all over with unguents, he said to him, " Have a care, lest the fragrance of your head give a bad «dour to your life." One of his sayings was, that servants serve their masters, and that wicked men are the slaves of their appetites. Being asked why slaves were called *MgairoHa*, he replied, " Because they have the feet of men (rous *irodag Avdguv)*, and a soul such as you who are asking this question." He once asked a profligate fellow for a mina; and when he put the question to him, why he asked others for an obol, and him for a mina, he said, " Because I hope to get something from the others another time, but the Gods alone know whether I shall ever extract anything from you again." Once he was reproached for asking favours, while Plato never asked for any; and he said;—

" He asks as well as I do, hut he does it

Bending his head, that no one else may hear.

One day he saw an unskilful archer shooting; so he went and sat down by the target, saying, " Now I shall be out of harm's way." He used to say, that those who were in love were disappointed in regard of the pleasure they expected. When he was asked whether death was an evil, he replied, " How can that be an evil which we do not feel when it is present?'' When Alexander was once standing by him, and saying, " Do not you fear me?" He replied, " No; for what are you, a good or an evil? " And as he said that he was good, " Who, then," said Diogenes, " fears the good?" He used to say, that education was, for the young sobriety, for the old comfort, for the poor riches, and for the rich an ornament." When Didymus the adulterer was once trying to cure the eye of a young girl (xtjj), he said, " Take care, lest when you are curing the eye of the maiden, you do not hurt the pupil." A man once said to him, that his friends laid plots against him; " What then," said he, " are you to do, if you must look upon both your friends and enemies in the same light?"

On one occasion he was asked, what was the most excellent thing among men; and he said, "Freedom of speech. " He went once into a school, and saw many statues of the Muses, but very few pupils, and said, " Gods, and all my good schoolmasters, you have plenty of pupils." He was in the habit of doing everything in public, whether in respect of Venus or Ceres; and he used to put his conclusions in this way to people: '' If there is nothing absurd in dining, then it is not absurd to dine in the market-place. But it is not absurd to dine, therefore it is not absurd to dine in the market-place." And as he was continually doing manual work in public, he said one day, " Would that by rubbing my belly I could get rid of hunger." Other sayings also are attributed to him, which it would take a long time to enumerate, there is such a multiplicity of them.

He used to say, that there were two kinds of exercise: that, namely, of the mind and that of the body; and that the latter of these created in the mind such quick and agile phantasies at the time of its performance, as very much facile tated the practice of virtue; but that one was imperfect without the other, since the health and vigour necessary for the practice of what is good, depend equally on both mind and body. And he used to allege as proofs of this, and of the ease which practice imparts to acts of virtue, that people could see that in the case of mere common working trades, and other employments of that kind, the artisans arrived at no inconsiderable accuracy by constant practice; and that any one may see how much one flute player, or one wrestler, is superior to another, by his own continued practice. And that if these There is a pun here; icopjj meana both " a girl" and " the pupil of the eye." And Oeipw, " to destroy,"

is also especially used for " to seduce. " men transferred the same training to their minds they would not labour in a profitless or imperfect manner. He used to say also, that there was nothing whatever in life which could be brought to perfection without practice, and that that alone was able to overcome every obstacle; that, therefore, as we ought to repudiate all useless toils, and to apply ourselves to useful labours, and to live happily, we are only unhappy in consequence of most exceeding folly. For the very contempt of pleasure, if we only inure ourselves to it, is very pleasant; and just as they who are accustomed to live luxuriously, are brought very unwillingly to adopt the contrary system; so they who have been originally inured to that opposite system, feel a sort of pleasure in the contempt of pleasure.

This used to be the language which he held, and he used to show in practice, really altering men's habits, and deferring in all things rather to the principles of nature than to those of law; saying that he was adopting the same fashion of life as Hercules had, preferring nothing in the world to liberty; and saying that everything belonged to the wise, and advancing arguments such as I mentioned just above. For instance: every thing belongs to the Gods; and the Gods are friends to the wise; and all the property of friends is held in common; therefore everything belong to the wise. He also argued about the law, that without it there is no possibility of a constitution being maintained; for without a city there can be nothing orderly, but a city is an orderly thing; and without a city there can be no law; therefore law is order. And he played in the same manner with the topics of noble birth, and reputation, and all things of that kind, saying that they were all veils, as it were, for wickedness; and that that was the only proper constitution which consisted in order. Another of his doctrines was that all women ought to be possessed in common; and he said that marriage was a nullity, and that the proper way would be for every man to live with her whom he could persuade to agree with him. And on the same i principle

he said, that all people's sons ought to belong to every one in common; and there was nothing intolerable in the idea of taking anything out of a temple, or eating any animal whatever, and that there was no impiety in tasting even human flesh; as is plain from the habits of foreign nations; and he said that this principle might be correctly extended to every case and every people. For he said that in reality everything was a combination of all things. For that in bread there was meat, and in vegetables there was bread, and so there were some particles of all other bodies in everything, communicating by invisible passages and evaporating.

VII. And he explains this theory of his clearly in the Thyestes, if indeed the tragedies attributed to him are really his composition, and not rather the work of Philistus, of.2Cgina, his intimate friend, or of Pasiphon, the son of Lucian, who is stated by Phavorinus, in his Universal History, to have written them after Diogenes' death. VIII. Music and geometry, and astronomy, and all things of that kind, he neglected, as useless and unnecessary. But he was a man very happy in meeting arguments, as is plain from what we have already said. IX. And he bore being sold with a most magnanimous spirit. For as he was sailing to Egina, and was taken prisoner by some pirates, under the command of Scirpalus, he was carried off to Crete and sold; and when the Circe asked him what art he understood, he said, " That of governing men." And presently pointing out a Corinthian, very carefully dressed, (the same Xeniades whom we have mentioned before), he said, " Sell me to that man; for he wants a master. " Accordingly Xeniades bought him and carried him away to Corinth; and then he made him tutor of his sons, and committed to him the entire management of his house. And he behaved himself in every affair in such a manner, that Xeniades, when looking over his property, said, " A good genius has come into my house." And Cleomenes, in his book which is called the Schoolmaster, says, that he wished to ransom all his relations, but that Diogenes told him that they were all fools; for that lions did not become the slaves of those who kept them, but, on the contrary, those who maintained lions were their slaves. For that it was the part of a slave to fear, but that wild beasts were formidable to men.

X. And the man had the gift of persuasion in a wonderful degree; so that he could easily overcome any one by his arguments. Accordingly, it is said that an iEginetan of the name of Onesicritus, having two sons, sent to Athens one of them, whose name was Androsthenes, and that he, after having heard Diogenes lecture, remained there; and that after that, he sent the elder, Philiscus, who has been already mentioned, and that Philiscus was charmed in the same manner. And last of all, he came himself, and then he too remained, no less than his son, studying philosophy at the feet of Diogenes. So great a charm was there in the discourses of Diogenes. Another pupil of his was Phocion, who was surnamed the Good; and Stilpon, the Megarian, and a great many other men of eminence as statesmen.

XI. He is said to have died when he was nearly ninety years of age, but there are different accounts given of his death. For some say that he ate an ox's foot raw, and was in consequence seized with a bilious attack, of which he died; others, of whom Cercidas, a Megalopolitan or Cretan, is one, say that he died of holding his breath for several days; and Cercidas speaks thus of him in his Meliambics:—

He, that Sinopian who bore the stick,
Wore his cloak doubled, and in th' open air
Dined without washing, would not bear with life
A moment longer: but he shut his teeth,
And held his breath. He truly was the son
Of Jove, and a most heavenly-minded dog,
The wise Diogenes,

Others say that he, while intending to distribute a polypus to his dogs, was bitten by them through the tendon of his foot, and so died. But his own greatest friends, as Antisthenes tells us in his Successions, rather sanction the story of his having died from holding his breath. For he used to live in the Craneum, which was a Gymnasium at the gates of Corinth. And „ his friends came according to their custom, and found him with his head covered; and as they did not suppose that he was asleep, for he was not a man much subject to the influence of night or sleep, they drew away his cloak from his face, and found him no longer breathing; and they thought that he had done this on purpose, wishing to escape the remaining portion of his life.

On this there was a quarrel, as they say, between his friends, as to who should bury him, and they even came to blows; but when the elders and chief men of the city came there, they say that he was buried by them at the gate which leads to the Isthmus. And they placed over him a pillar, and on that a dog in Parian marble. And at a later period his fellow citizens honoured him with brazen statues, and put this inscription on them:—

E'en brass by lapse of time doth old become,
But there is no such time as shall efface,
Your lasting glory, wise Diogenes;
Since you alone did teach to men the art
Of a contented life: the surest path
To glory and a lasting happiness.

We ourselves have also written an epigram on him in the proceleusmatic metre.

A. Tell me, Diogenes, tell me true, I pray,
How did you die; what fate to Pluto bore you?
B. The savage bite of an envious dog did kill me.

Some, however, say that when he was dying, he ordered his friends to throw his corpse away without burying it, so that every beast might tear it, or else to throw it into a ditch, and sprinkle a little dust over it. And others say that his injunctions were, that he should be thrown into the Ilissus; that so he might be useful to his brethren. But Demetrius, in his treatise on Men of the Same Name, says that Diogenes died in Corinth the same day that Alexander died in Babylon. And he was already an old man, as early as the hundred and thirteenth olympiad.

XII. The following books are attributed to him. The. dialogues entitled the Cephalion; the Icthyas; the Jackdaw; the Leopard; the People of the Athenians; the Republic; one called Moral Art; one on Wealth; one on Love; the Theodorus; the Hypsias; the Aristarchus; one on Death; a volume of Letters; seven Tragedies, the Helen, the Thyestes, the Hercules, the Achilles, the Medea, the Chrysippus, and the CEdippus.

But Sosicrates, in the first book of his Successions, and Satyrus, in the fourth book of bis Lives, both assert that none of all these are the genuine composition of Diogenes. And Satyrus affirms that the tragedies are the work of Philiscus, the iEginetan, a friend of Diogenes. But Sotion, in his seventh book, says that these are the only genuine works of Diogenes: a dialogue on Virtue; another on the Good; another on Love; the Beggar; the Solmaeus; the Leopard; the Cassander; the Cephalion; and that the Aristarchus, the Sisyphus, the Ganymede, a volume of Apophthegms, and another of Letters, are all the work of Philiscus.

XIII. There were five persons of the name of Diogenes. The first a native of Apollonia, a natural philosopher; and the beginning of his treatise on Natural Philosophy is *as* follows: " It appears to me to be well for every one who commences any kind of philosophical treatise, to lay down some undeniable principle to start with." The second was a Sicymian, who wrote an account of Peloponnesus. The third was the man of whom we have been speaking. The fourth was a Stoic, a native of Seleucia, but usually called a Babylonian, from the proximity of Seleucia to Babylon. The fifth was a native of Tarsus, who wrote on the subject of some questions concerning poetry which he endeavours to solve. XIV. Athenodorus, in the eighth book of his Conversations, says, that the philosopher always had a shining appearance, from his habit of anointing himself. LIFE OF MONIMUS.

I. Monimus was a Syracusan, and a pupil of Diogenes, but also a slave of some Corinthian money-changer, as Sosicrates tells us. Xeniades, who bought Diogenes, used often to come to him, extolling the excellency of Diogenes both in actions and words, till he excited a great affection for the man in the mind of Monimus. For he immediately feigned madness, and threw about all the money and all the coins that were on the table, until his master discarded him, and then he straightway went to Diogenes and became his pupil. He also followed Crates the Cynic a good deal, and devoted himself to the same studies as he did; and the sight of this conduct of his made his master all the more think him mad.

II. And he was a very eminent man, so that even Menander, the comic poet, speaks of him; accordingly, in one of his plays, namely in the Hippocomus, he mentions him thus:—

There is a man, 0 Philo, named Monimus,
A wise man, though but little known, and one
Who bears a wallet at his back, and is not
Content with one but three. He never spoke
A single sentence, by great Jove I swear,
Like this one, " Know thyself," or any other
Of the oft-quoted proverbs: all such sayings
He scorned, as he did beg his way through dirt;
Teaching that all opinion is but vanity.

But he was a man of such gravity that he despised glory, and sought only for truth.

III. He wrote some jests mingled with serious treatises, and two essays on the Appetites, and an Exhortation. LIFE OF ONESICRITUS.

I. Osnesiceitus is called by some authors an iEginetan, but Demetrius the Magnesian affirms that he was a native of Astypalaea. He also was one of the most eminent of the disciples of Diogenes.

II. And he appears in some points to resemble Xenophon. For Xenophon joined in the expedition of Cyrus, and Onesicritus in that of Alexander; and Xenophon wrote the Cyropaedia, and Onesicritus wrote an account of the education of Alexander. Xenophon, too, wrote a Panegyric on Cyrus, and Onesicritus one on Alexander.' They were also both similar to one another in style, except that a copyist is naturally inferior to the original. III. Menander, too, who was surnamed Drymus, was a pupil of Diogenes, and a great admirer of Homer: and so was Hegesaeus of Sinope, who was nicknamed Clocus, and Philiscus the iEginetan, as we have said before. LIFE OF CRATES.

I. Crates was a Theban by birth, and the son of Ascondus. He also was one of the eminent disciples of the Cynic. But Hippobotus asserts that he was not a pupil of Diogenes, but of Bryson the Achsean.

II. There are the following sportive lines of his quoted:—

The waves surround vain Peres' fruitful soil,
And fertile acres crown the sea-born isle;
Land which no parasite e'er dares invade,
Or lewd seducer of a hapless maid;
It bears figs, bread, thyme, garlic's savoury charms,
Gifts which ne'er tempt men to detested Trms,
They'd rather fight for gold than glory's dreams.

There is also an account-book of his much spoken of, which is drawn up in such terms as these:—

Put down the cook for minas half a score,
Put down the doctor for a drachma more:
Five talents to the flatterer; some smoke
To the adviser, an obol and a cloak
For the philosopher; for the willing nymph,
A talent....

He was also nicknamed Door-opener, because he used to enter every house and give the inmates advice. These lines, too, are his:—

All this I learnt and pondered in my mind,
Drawing deep wisdom from the Muses kind,
But all the rest is vanity.

There is a line, too, which tells us that he gained from philosophy:—

A peck of lupins, and to care for nobody.

This, too, is attributed to him:—

Hunger checks love; and should it not, time does.
If both should fail you, then a halter choose.

III. He flourished about the hundred and thirteenth olympiad.

IV. Antisthenes, in his Successions, says that he, having once, in a certain tragedy, seen Telephus holding a date basket, and in a miserable plight in other respects, betook himself to the Cynic philosophy; and having turned his patrimony into money (for he was of illustrious extraction), he collected three hundred talents by that means, and divided them among the citizens. And after that he devoted himself to philosophy with such eagerness, that even Philemon the comic poet mentions him. Accordingly he says:—

And in the summer he'd a shaggy gown,
To inure himself to hardship: in the winter
He wore mere rags.

But Diocles says that it was Diogenes who persuaded him to discard all his estate and his flocks, and to throw his money into the sea; and he says further, that the house of Crates was destroyed by Alexander, and that of Hipparchia under Philip. And he would very frequently drive away with his staff those of his relations who came after him, and endeavoured to dissuade him from his design; and he remained immoveable.

V. Demetrius, the Magnesian, relates that he deposited his money with a banker, making an agreement with him, that if his sons turned out ordinary ignorant people, he was then to restore it to them; but if they became philosophers, then he was to divide it among the people, for that they, if they were philosophers, would have no need of anything. And Eratosthenes tells us that he had by Hipparchia, whom we shall mention hereafter, a son whose name was Pasicles, and that when he grew up, he took him to a brothel kept by a female slave, and told him that that was all the marriage that his father designed for him; but that marriages which resulted in adultery were themes for tragedians, and had exile and bloodshed for their prizes; and the marriages of those who lived with courtesans were subjects for the comic poets, and often produced madness as the result of debauchery and drunkenness.

VI. He had also a brother named Pasicles, a pupil of Euclides. VII. Phavorinus, in the second book of his Commentaries, relates a witty saying of his; for he says, that once, when he was begging a favour of the master of a gymnasium, on the behalf of some acquaintance, he touched his thighs; and as he expressed his indignation at this, he said, " Why, do they not belong to you as well as your knees?" He used to say that it was impossible to find a man who had never done wrong, in the same way as there was always some worthless seed in a pomegranate. On one occasion he provoked Nicodromus, the harp-player, and received a black eye from him; so he put a plaster on his forehead and wrote upon it, "Nicodromus did this." He used to abuse prostitutes designedly, for the purpose of practising himself in enduring reproaches. When Demetrius Phalereus sent him some loaves and wine, he attacked him for his present, saying, " I wish that the fountains bore loaves;" and it is notorious that he was a water drinker.

He was once reproved by the aediles of the Athenians, for wearing fine linen, and so he replied, " I will show you Theophrastus also clad in fine linen." And as they did not believe him, he took them to a barber's shop, and showed him to them as he was being shaved. At Thebes he was once scourged by the master of the Gymnasium, (though some say it was by Euthycrates, at Corinth), and dragged out by the feet; but he did not care, and quoted the line:—

I feel, 0 mighty chief, your matchless might,

Dragged, foot first, downward from th' ethereal height.

But Diocles says that it was hy Menedemus, of Eretria, that he was dragged in this manner, for that as he was a handsome man, and supposed to be very obsequious to Asclepiades, the Phliasian, Crates touched his thighs and said, " Is Asclepiades within?" And Menedemus was very much offended, and dragged him out, as has been already said; and then Crates quoted the above-cited line.

VIII. Zeno, the Cittiaean, in his Apophthegms, says, that he once sewed up a sheep's fleece in his cloak, without thinking of it; and he was a very ugly man, and one who excited laughter when he was taking exercise. And he used to say, when he put up his hands, " Courage, Crates, as far as your eyes and the rest of your body is concerned;— IX. " For you shall see those who now ridicule you, convulsed with disease, and envying your happiness, and accusing themselves of slothfulness." One of his sayings was, " That a man ought to study philosophy, up to the point of looking on generals and donkey-drivers in the same light." Another was, that those who live with flatterers, are as desolate as calves when in the company of wolves; for that neither the one nor the other are with those whom they ought to be, or their own kindred, but only with those who are plotting against them.

X. When he felt that he was dying, he made verses on himself, saying:— This is a parody on Homer. H. 591. Pope's Version, 760.

You're going, noble hunchback, you are going

To Pluto's realms, bent double by old age.

For he was humpbacked from age.

XI. When Alexander asked him whether he wished to see the restoration of his country, he said, " What would be the use of it? for perhaps some other Alexander would come at some future time and destroy it again.

" But poverty and dear obscurity,

Are what a prudent man should think his country;

For these e'en fortune can't deprive him of."

He also said that he was:—

A fellow countryman of wise Diogenes,

Whom even envy never had attacked.

Menander, in his Twin-sister, mentions him thus:—

For you will walk with me wrapped in your cloak,

As his wife used to with the Cynic Crates.

XII. He gave his daughter to his pupils, as he himself used to say:—

To have and keep on trial for a month.

LIFE OF METROCLES.

I. Meteocles was the brother of Hipparchia; and though he had formerly been a pupil of Theophrastus, he had profited so little by his instructions, that once, thinking that, while listening to a lecture on philosophy, he had disgraced himself by his inattention, he fell into despondency, and shut himself up in his house, intending to starve himself to death. Accordingly, when Crates heard of it, he came to him, having been sent for; and eating a number of lupins, on purpose, he persuaded him by numbers of arguments, that he had done no harm; for that it was not to be expected that a man should not indulge his natural inclinations and habits; and he comforted him by showing him that he, in a similar case, would certainly have behaved in a similar manner. And after that, he became a pupil of Crates, and a man of great eminence as a philosopher.

II. He burnt all his writings, as Hecaton tells us in the first book of his Apophthegms, and said:—

These are the phantoms of infernal dreams;

As if he meant that they were all nonsense. But some say that it was the notes which he had taken of the lectures of Theophrastus which he burnt, quoting the following verse:—

Vulcan, draw near, 'tis Thetis asks your aid.

III. He used to say that some things could be bought with money, as for instance a house; and some with time and industry, as education; that wealth was mischievous; if a man did not use it properly. IV. He died at a great age, having suffocated himself.

V. His pupils were Theomentus and Cleomenes, Demetrius of Alexandria, the son of Theombrotus, Timarchus of Alexandria, the son of Cleomenes, and Echecles, of Ephesus. Not but what Echecles was also a pupil of Theombrotus; and Menedemus, of whom we shall speak hereafter, was his pupil. Menippus, of Sinope, too, was a very eminent person in his school.

LIFE OF HIPPARCHIA.

I. Hippaechia, the sister of Metrocles, was charmed among others, by the doctrines of this school.

II. Both she and Metrocles were natives of Maronea. She fell in love with both the doctrines and manners of Crates, and could not be diverted from her regard for him, by either the wealth, or high birth, or personal beauty, of any of her suitors, but Crates was everything to her; and she threatened her parents to make away with herself, if she were not given in marriage to him. Crates accordingly, being entreated by her parents to dissuade her from this resolution, did all he Horn. IL 2. 395. Pope's version, 460. could; and at last, as he could not persuade her, he rose up, and placing all his furniture before her, he said, " This is the bridegroom whom you are choosing, and this is the whole of his property; consider these facts, for it will not be possible for you to become his partner, if you do not also apply yourself to the same studies, and conform to the same habits that he does." But the girl chose him; and assuming the same dress that he wore, went about with him as her husband, and appeared with him in public everywhere, and went to all entertainments in his company. III. And once when she went to sup with Lysimachus, she attacked Theodorus, who was surnamed the Atheist; proposing to him the following sophism; " What Theodorus could not be called wrong for doing, that same thing Hipparchia ought not to be called wrong for doing. But Theodorus does no wrong when he beats himself; therefore Hipparchia does no wrong when she beats Theodorus." He made no reply to what she said, but only pulled her clothes about; but Hipparchia was neither offended nor ashamed, as many a woman would have been; but when he said to her:—

" Who is the woman who has left the shuttle

So near the warp?"

" I, Theodorus, am that person," she replied; " but do I appear to you to have come to a wrong decision, if I devote that time to philosophy, which I otherwise should have spent at the loom?" And these and many other sayings are reported of this female philosopher.

IV. There is also a volume of letters of Crates t extant, in which he philosophizes most excellently; and in style is very little inferior to Plato. He also Wrote some tragedies, which are imbued with a very sublime spirit of philosophy, of which the following lines are a specimen:—

'Tis not one town, nor one poor single house, That is my country; but in every land

Each city and each dwelling seems to me,

A place for my reception ready made.

And he died at a great age, and was buried in Boeotia.

This line is from the Bacchae of Euripides, v. 1228. + From this last paragraph it is inferred by some critics, that originally the preceding memoirs of Crat33, Metrocles, and Hipparchia, formed only one chapter or book. LIFE OF MENIPPUS.

I. Menippus was also a Cynic, and a Phoenician by descent, a slave by birth, as Acbaicus tells us in his Ethics; and Diodes informs us that his master was a native of Pontus, of the name of Baton; but that subsequently, in consequence of his importunities and miserly habits, he became rich, and obtained the rights of citizenship at Corinth.

II. He never wrote anything serious; but his writings are full of ridiculous matter; and in some respects similar to those of Meleager, who was his contemporary. And Hermippus tells us that he was a man who lent money at daily interest, and that he was called a usurer; for he used to lend on nautical usury, and take security, so that he amassed a very great amount of riches. III. But at last he fell into a snare, and lost all his money, and in a fit of despair he hung himself, and so he died. And we have written a playful epigram on him:—

This man was a Syrian by birth, And a Cretan usurious hound,

As the name he was known by sets forth;

You've heard of him oft I'll be bound;

His name was Menippus—men entered his house,

And stole all his goods without leaving a louse,

When (from this the dog's nature you plainly may tell)

He hung himself up, and so went off to helL

IV. But some say that the books attributed to him are not really his work, but are the composition of Dionysius and Zopyrus the Colophonians, who wrote them out of joke, and then gave them to him as a man well able to dispose of them.

V. There were six persons of the name of Menippus; the first was the man who wrote a history of the Lydians, and made an abridgment of Xanthus; the second was this man of whom we have been speaking; the third was a sophist of Stratonice, a Carian by descent; the fourth was a statuary: the fifth and the sixth were painters, and they are both mentioned by Apollodorus, VI. The writings left by the Cynic amount to thirteen volumes; a Description of the Dead; a volume called Wills; a volume of Letters in which the Gods are introduced; treatises addressed to the Natural Philosophers, and Mathematicians, and Grammarians; one on the Generations of Epicurus, and on the Observance of the Twentieth Day by the philosophers of his school; and one or two other essays.

THE LIFE OF MENEDEMUS.

L Menedemtjs was a disciple of Celotes of Lampsacus.

II. He proceeded, as Hippobotus tells, to such a great degree of superstition, that he assumed the garb of a fury, and went about saying that he had come from hell to take notice of all who did wrong, in order that he might descend thither again and make his report to the deities who abode in that country. And this was his dress: a tunic of a dark colour reaching to his feet, and a purple girdle round his waist, an Arcadian hat on his head with the twelve signs of the zodiac embroidered on it, tragic buskins, a preposterously long beard, and an ashen staff in his hand. III. These then are the lives of each of the Cynics; and we shall also subjoin some of the doctrines which they all held in common, if indeed it is not an abuse of language to call that a sect of philosophy at all, instead of, as some contend it should be termed, a mere system of life.

They wished to abolish the whole system of logic and natural philosophy, like Aristo of Chios, and thought that men should study nothing but ethics; and what some people assert of Socrates was described by Diocles as a characteristic of Diogenes, for he said that his doctrine was, that a man ought to investigate—

Only the good and ill that taketh place
Within our houses.

They also discard all liberal studies." Accordingly, Antisthenes said that wise men only applied themselves to literature and learning for the sake of perverting others; they also wish to abolish geometry and music, and everything of that s kind. Accordingly, Diogenes said once to a person who was showing him a clock; " It is a very useful thing to save a man from being too late for supper. " And once when a man made an exhibition of musical skill before him, he said:—

" Cities are governed,, so are houses too,
By wisdom, not by harp-playing and whistling."

Their doctrine is, that the chief good of mankind is to live according to virtue, as Antisthenes says in his Hercules, in which they resemble the Stoics. For those two sects have a good deal in common with one another, on which account they themselves say that cynicism is a short road to virtue; and Zeno, the Cittiaean lived in the same manner.

They also teach that men ought to live simply, using only plain food in moderate quantities, wearing nothing but a cloak, and despising riches, and glory, and nobleness of birth; accordingly some of them feed upon nothing beyond herbs and cold water, living in any shelter that they can find, or in tubs as Diogenes did; for he used to say that it was the peculiar property of the Gods to want nothing, and that, therefore, when a man wished for nothing he was like the Gods.

Another of their doctrines is, that virtue is a thing which may be taught, as Antisthenes affirms in his Heraclides; and that when it has once been attained it can never be lost. They also say that the wise man deserves to be loved, and cannot commit error, and is a friend to every one who resembles him, and that he leaves nothing to fortune. And everything which is unconnected with either virtue or vice they call indifferent, agreeing in this with Aristo, the Chian.

These then were the Cynics; and now we must pass on to the Stoics, of which sect the founder was Zeno, who had been a disciple of Crates.
This a parody on two lines in the Antiope of Euripides.
JVwup y&p avSpbc tv filv ohcovvrat noXttc.
E5 o'oleoc e!c r av iroXtpov ia%vn fi-iya.
Which may be translated:—
Wisdom it is which regulates both cities,"
And private citizens, and makes their lot Secure and happy; nor is her influence Of less account in war.

BOOK VII.
LIFE OF ZENO.

I. Zeno was the son of Innaseas, or Demeas, and a native of Citium, in Cyprus, which is a Grecian city, partly occupied by a Phoenician colony, II. He had his head naturally bent on one side, as Timotheus, the Athenian, tells us, iu his work on Lives. And Apollonius, the Tyrian, says that he was thin, very tall, of a dark complexion; in reference to which some one once called him an Egyptian Clematis, as Chrysippus relates in the first volume of his Proverbs: he had fat, flabby, weak legs, on which account Perssus, in his Convivial Reminiscences, says that he used to refuse many invitations to supper; and he was very fond, as it is said, of figs both fresh and dried in the sun.

III. He was a pupil, as has been already stated, of Crates. After that, they say that he became a pupil of Stilpon and of Xenocrates, for ten years, as Timocrates relates in his Life of Dion. He is also said to have been a pupil of Polemo. But Hecaton, and Apollonius, of Tyre, in the first book of his essay on Zeno, say that when he consulted the oracle, as to what he ought to do to live in the most excellent manner, the God answered him that he ought to become of the same complexion as the dead, on which he inferred that he ought to apply himself to the reading of the books of the ancients. Accordingly, he attached himself to Crates in the following manner. Having purchased a quantity of purple from Phoenicia, he was shipwrecked close to the Piraeus; and when he had made his way from the coast as far as Athens, he sat down by a bookseller's stall, being now about thirty years of age. And as he took up the second book of Xenophon's Memorabilia and began to read it, he was delighted with it, and asked where such men as were described in that book lived; and as Crates happened very seasonably to pass at the moment, the bookseller pointed him out, and said, " Follow that man." From that time forth he hecame a pupil of Crates; but though he was in other respects very energetic in his application to philosophy, still he was too modest for the shamelessness of the Cynics. On which account, Crates, wishing to cure him of this false shame, gave him a jar of lentil porridge to carry through the Ceramicus; and when he saw that he was ashamed, and that he endeavoured to hide it, he struck the jar with his staff, and broke it; and, as Zeno fled away, and the lentil porridge ran all down bis legs, Crates called after him, " Why do you run away, my little Phoenician, you have done no harm?" For some time then he continued a pupil of Crates, and when he wrote his treatise entitled the Republic, some said, jokingly, that he had written it upon the tail of the dog. IV. And besides his Republic, he was the author also of the following works: —a treatise on a Life according to Nature; one on Appetite, or the Nature of Man; one on Passions; one on the Becoming; one on Law; one on the usual Education of the Greeks; one on Sight; one on the Whole; one on Signs; one on the Doctrines of the Pythagoreans; one on Things in General; one on Styles; five essays on Problems relating to Homer; one on the Bearing of the Poets. There is also an essay on Art by him, and two books of Solutions and Jests, and Reminiscences, and one called the Ethics of Crates. These are the books of which he was the author.

V. But at last he left Crates, and became the pupil of the philosophers whom I have mentioned before, and continued with them for twenty years. So that it is related that he said, " I now find that I made a prosperous voyage when I was wrecked." But some affirm that he made this speech in reference to Crates. Others say, that while he was staying at Athens he heard of a shipwreck, and said, " Fortune does well in having driven us on philosophy." But as some relate the affair, he was not wrecked at all, but sold all his cargo at Athens, and then turned to philosophy.

VI. And he used to walk up and down in the beautiful colonnade which is called the Priscanactium, and which is also called *iroirJXri,* from the paintings of Polygnotus, and there he delivered his discourses, wishing to make that spot tranquil; for in the time of the thirty, nearly fourteen hundred of the citizens had been murdered there by them. VII. Accordingly, for the future, men came thither to hear him, and from this his pupils were called Stoics, and so were his successors also, who had been at first called Zenonians, as Epicurus tells us in his Epistles. And before this time, the poets who frequented this colonnade *(eroa)* had been called Stoics, as we are informed by Eratosthenes, in the eighth book of his treatise on the Old Comedy; but now Zeno's pupils made the name more notorious. _ Now the Athenians had a great respect for Zeno, so that they gave him the keys of their walls, and they also honoured him with a golden crown, and a brazen statue; and this was also done by his own countrymen, who thought the statue of such a man an honour to their city. And the Cittiaeans, in the district of Sidon, also claimed him as their countryman. VIII. He was also much respected by Antigonus, who, whenever he came to Athens, used to attend his lectures, and was constantly inviting him to come to him. But he begged off himself, and sent Persaeus, one of his intimate friends, who was the son of Demetrius, and a Cittiaean by birth, and who flourished about the hundred and thirtieth olympiad, when Zeno was an old man. The letter of Antigonus to Zeno was as follows, and it is reported by Apollonius, the Syrian, in his essay on Zeno. KING ANTIGONUS TO ZENO THE PHILOSOPHEB, GBEETING.

" I think that in good fortune and glory I have the advantage of you; but in reason and education I am inferior to you, and also in that perfect happiness which you have attained to. On which account I have thought it good to address you, and invite you to come to me, being convinced that you will not refuse what is asked of you. Endeavour, therefore, by all means to come to me, considering this fact, that you will not be the instructor of me alone, but of all the Macedonians together. For he who instructs the ruler of the Macedonians, and who leads him in the path of virtue, evidently marshals all his subjects on the road to happiness. For as the ruler is, so is it natural that his subjects for the most part should be also."

And Zeno wrote him back the following answer.

ZERO TO KING ANTIGONUS, GREETING.

" I admire your desire for learning, as being a true object for the wishes of mankind, and one too that tends to their advantage. And the man who aims at the study of philosophy has a proper disregard for the popular kind of instruction which tends only to the corruption of the morals. And you, passing by the pleasure which is so much spoken of, which makes the minds of some young men effeminate, show plainly that you are inclined to noble pursuits, not merely by your nature, but also by your own deliberate choice. And a noble nature, when it has received even a slight degree of training, and which also meets with those who will teach it abundantly, proceeds without difficulty to a perfect attainment of virtue. But I now find my bodily health impaired by old age, for I am eighty years old: on which account I am unable to come to you. But I send you some of those who have studied with me, who in that learning which has reference to the soul, are in no respect inferior to me, and in their bodily vigour are greatly my superiors. And if you associate with them you will want nothing that can bear upon perfect happiness."

So he sent him Persaeus and Philonides, the Theban, both of whom are mentioned by Epicurus, in his letter to his brother Aristobulus, as being companions of Antigonus.

IX. And I have thought it worth while also to set down the decree of the Athenians concerning him; and it is couched in the following language.

"In the archonship of Arrhenides, in the fifth presidency of the tribe Acamantis, on the twenty-first day of the month Maimacterion, on the twenty-third day of the aforesaid presidency, in a duly convened assembly, Hippo, the son of Cratistoteles, of the borough of Xypetion, being one of the presidents, and the rest of the presidents, his colleagues, put the following decree to the vote. And the decree was proposed by Thrason, of Anacaea, the son of Thrason.

" Since Zeno the son of Iunaseas, the Cittiaean, has passed many years in the city, in the study of philosophy, being in all other respects a good man, and also exhorting all the young men who have sought his company to the practice of virtue, and encouraging them in the practice of temperance; making his own life a model to all men of the greatest excellence, since it has in every respect corresponded to the doctrines which he has taught; it has been determined by the people (and may the determination be fortunate), to praise Zeno, the son of

Innaseas, the Cittiaean, and to present him with a golden crown in accordance with the law, on account of his virtue and temperance, and to build him a tomb in the Ceramicus, at the public expense. And the people has appointed by its vote five men from among the citizens of Athens, who shall see to the making of the crown and the building of the tomb. And the scribe of the borough shall enrol the decree and engrave it on two pillars, and he shall be permitted to place one pillar in the Academy, and one in the Lyceum, And he who is appointed to superintend the work shall divide the expense that the pillars amount to, in such a way that every one may understand that the whole people of Athens honours good men both while they are living and after they are dead. And Thrason of Anacaea, Philocles of the Piraeus, Phsedrus of Anaphlystos, Medon of Acharnaes, Mecythus of Sypalyttas, and Dion of Paeania, are hereby appointed to superinteiM the building of the tomb." These then are the terms of the dec-fee.

X. But Antigonus, of Carystos, says, that Zeno himself never denied that he was a native of Cittium. For that when on one occasion, there was a citizen of that town who had contributed to the building of some baths, and was having his name engraved on the pillar, as the countryman of Zeno the philosopher, he bade them' add, " Of Cittium." XI. And at another time, when he had had a hollow covering made for some vessel, he carried it about for some money, in order to procure present relief for some difficulties which were distressing Crates his master. And they say that he, when he first arrived in, Greece, had more than a thousand talents, which he lent out at nautical usury.

XII. And he used to eat little loaves and honey, and to drink a small quantity of sweet smelling wine. XIII. He had very few youthful acquaintances of the male sex, and he did not cultivate them much, lest he should be thought to be a misogynist. And he dwelt in the same house with Persaeus; and once, when he brought in a female fluteplayer to him, he hastened to bring her back to him.

XIV. And he was, it is said, of a very accommodating temper; so much so, that Antigonus, the king, often came to dine with him, and often carried him off to dine with him, at the house of Aristocles the harp-player; but when he was there, he would presently steal away, XV. It is also said that he avoided a crowd with great care, so that he used to sit at the end of a bench, in order at all events to avoid being incommoded on one side. And he never used to walk with more than two or three companions. And he used at times to exact a piece of money from all who came to hear him, with a view of not being distressed by numbers; and this story is told by Cleanthes, in his treatise on Brazen Money. And when he was surrounded by any great crowd, he would point to a balustrade of wood at the end of the colonnade which surrounded an altar, and say, " That was once in the middle of this place, but it was placed apart because it was in people's way; and now, if you will only withdraw from the middle here, you too will incommode me much less." XVI. And when Demochares, the son of Laches, embraced him once, and said that he would tell Antigonus, or write to him of everything which he wanted, as he always did everything for him, Zeno, when he had heard him say this, avoided his company for the future. And it is said, that after the death of Zeno, Antigonus said, " What a spectacle have I lost." On which account he employed Thrason, their ambassador, to entreat of the Athenians to allow him to be buried in the Ceramicus. And when he was asked why he had such an admiration for him, he replied, " Because, though I gave him a great many important presents, he was never elated, and never humbled." XVII. He was a man of a very investigating spirit, and one who inquired very minutely into everything; in reference to which, Timon, in his Silli, speaks thus

I saw an aged woman of Phoenicia,
Hungry and covetous, in a proud obscurity,
Longing for everything. She had a basket
So full of holes that it retained nothing.

Likewise her mind was less than a simdapsus.

He used to study very carefully with Philo, the dialectician, and to argue with him at their mutual leisure; on which A sort of guitar or violin.

account he excited the wonder of the younger Zeno, no less than Diodorus his master. XVIII. There were also a lot of dirty beggars always about him, as Timon tells us, where he says:—

Till he collected a vast cloud of beggars,
Who were of all men in the world the poorest,
And the most worthless citizens of Athens.

And he himself was a man of a morose and bitter countenance, with a constantly frowning expression. He was very economical, and descended even to the meanness of the barbarians, under the pretence of economy.

XIX. If he reproved any one, he did it with brevity and without exaggeration, and as it were, at a distance. I allude, for instance, to the way in which he spoke of a man who took exceeding pains in setting himself off, for as he was crossing a gutter with great hesitation, he said, " He is right to look down upon the mud, for he cannot see himself in it." And when some Cynic one day said that he had no oil in his cruise, and asked him for some, he refused to give him any, but bade him go away and consider which of the two was the more impudent. He was very much in love with Chremonides; and once, when he and Cleanthes were both sitting by him, he got up; and as Cleanthes wondered at this, he said, " I hear from skilful physicians that the best thing for some tumours is rest." Once, when two people were sitting above him at table at a banquet, and the one next him kept kicking the other with his foot, he himself kicked him with his knee; and when he turned round upon him for doing so, he said, " "Why then do you think that your other neighbour is to be treated in this way by you? "

On one occasion he said to a man who was very fond of young boys, that " Schoolmasters who were always associating with boys had no more intellect than the boys themselves." He used also to say that the discourses of those men who were careful to avoid solecisms, and to adhere to the strictest rules of composition, were like Alexandrine money, they were pleasing to the eye and well-formed like the coni, but were nothing the better for that; but those who were not so particular he likened to the Attic tessedrachmas, which were struck at random and without any great nicety, and so he said that their discourses often outweighed the more polished styles of the others. And when Ariston, his disciple, had been holding forth a good deal without much wit, but still in some points with a good deal of readiness and confidence, he said to him, " It would be impossible for you to speak thus, if your father had not been drunk when he begat you;" and for the same reason he nicknamed him the chatterer, as he himself was very concise in his speeches. Once, when he was in company with an epicure who usually left nothing for his messmates, and when a large fish was set before him, he took it all as if he could eat the whole of it; and when the others looked at him with astonishment, he said, " What then do you think that your companions feel every day, if you cannot bear with my gluttony for one day? "

On one occasion, when a youth was asking him questions with a pertinacity unsuited to his age, he led him to a lookingglass and bade him look at himself, and then asked him whether such questions appeared suitable to the face he saw there. And when a man said before him once, that in most points he did not agree with the doctrines of Antisthenes, he quoted to him an apophthegm of Sophocles, and asked him whether he thought there was much sense in that, and when he said that he did not know, " Are you not then ashamed," said he, " to pick out and recollect anything bad which may have been said by Antisthenes, but not to regard or remember whatever is said that is good? " A man once said, that the sayings of the philosophers appeared to him very trivial; " You say true," replied Zeno, " and their syllables too ought to be short, if that is possible." When some one spoke to him of Polemo, and said that he proposed one question for discussion and then argued another, he became angry, and said, " At what value did he estimate the suhject that had been proposed?" And he said that a man who was to discuss a question ought to have a loud voice and great energy, like the actors, but not to open his mouth too wide, which those who speak a great deal but only talk nonsense usually do. And he used to say that there was no need for those who argued well to leave their hearers room to look about them, as good workmen do who want to have their work seen; but that, on the contrary, those who are listening to them ought to be so attentive to all that is said as to have no leisure to take notes.

Once when a young man was talking a great deal, he said, " Your ears have run down into your tongue." On one occasion a very handsome man was saying that a wise man did not appear to him likely to fall in love; " Then," said he, " I cannot imagine anything that will be more miserable than you good-looking fellows." He also used often to say that most philosophers were wise in great things, but ignorant of petty subjects and chance details; and he used to cite the saying of Caphesius, who, when one of his pupils was labouring hard to be able to blow very powerfully, gave him a slap, and said, that excellence did not depend upon greatness, but greatness on excellence. Once, when a young man was arguing very confidently, he said, " I should not like to say, O youth, all that occurs to me." And once, when a handsome and wealthy Rhodian, but one who had no other qualification, was pressing him to take him as a pupil, he, as he was not inclined to receive him, first of all made him sit on the dusty seats that he might dirt his cloak, then he put him down in the place of the poor that he might rub against their rags, and at last the young man went away. One of his sayings used to be, that vanity was the most unbecoming of all things, and especially so in the young. Another was, that one ought not to try and recollect the exact words and expressions of a discourse, but to fix all one's attention on the arrangement of the arguments, instead of treating it as if it were a piece of boiled meat, or some delicate eatable. He used also to say that young men ought to maintain the most scrupulous reserve in their walking, their gait, and their dress; and he was constantly quoting the lines of Euripides on Capaneus, that— His wealth was ample.
But yet no pride did mingle with his state,
Nor had he haughty thought, or arrogance,
More than the poorest man.

And one of his sayings used to be, that nothing was more unfriendly to the comprehension of the accurate sciences than poetry; and that there was nothing that we stood in so much need of as time. When he was asked what a friend was, he replied, " Another I." They say that he was once scourging a slave whom he had detected in theft; and when he said to him, " It was fated that I should steal;" he rejoined, " Yes, and that you should be beaten." He used to call beauty the flower of the voice; but some report this as if he had said that the voice is the flower of beauty. On one occasion, when he saw a slave belonging to one of his friends severely bruised, he said to his friend, " I see the footsteps of your anger." He once accosted a man who was all over unguents and perfumes, " Who is this who smells like a woman?" When Dionysius Metathemenus asked him why he was the only perssn whom he did.not correct, he replied, " Because I have no confidence in you." A young man was talking a great deal of nonsense, and he said to him, " This is the reason why we have two ears and only one mouth, that we may hear more and speak less."

Once, when he was at an entertainment and remained wholly silent, he was asked what the reason was; and so he bade the person who found fault with him tell the king that thee was a man in the room who knew how to hold his tongue; now the people who asked him this were ambassadors who had come from Ptolemy, and who wished to know what report they were to make of him to the king. He was once asked how he felt when people abused him, and he said, " As an ambassador feels when he is sent away without an answer." Apollonius of Tyre tells us, that when Crates dragged him by the cloak away from Stilpo, he said. " 0 Crates, the proper way to take hold of philosophers is by the ears; so now do you convince me and drag me by them; but if you use force towards me, my body may be with you, but my mind with Stilpo." XX. He used to devote a good deal of time to Diodorus, as we learn from Hippobotus: and he studied dialectics under him. And when he had made a good deal of progress he attached himself to Polemo because of his freedom from arrogance, so that it is reported that he said to him, " I am not ignorant, 0 Zeno, that you slip into the garden-door and steal my doctrines, and then clothe them in a Phoenician dress." When a dialectician once showed him seven species of dialectic argument in the mowing argument, he asked him how much he charged for them, and when he said "A hundred drachmas," he gave him two hundred, so exceedingly devoted was he to learning.

XXI. They say too, that he was the first who ever em The Greek is, *iv rip Sep/ Jovrt Xoyw*, a species of argument so called, because he who used it mowed or knocked down his adversariese.—Aldob. ployed the word duty (xafljjxox), and who wrote a treatise on the subject. And that he altered the lines of Hesiod thus:—

He is the best of all men who submits
To follow good advice; he too is good,
Who of himself perceives whate'er is fit..

For he said that that man who had the capacity to give a proper hearing to what was said, and to avail himself of it, was superior to him who comprehended everything by his own intellect; for that the one had only comprehension, but the one who took good advice had action also.

XXII. When he was asked why he, who was generally austere, relaxed at a dinner party, he said, " Lupins too are bitter, but when they are soaked they become sweet." And Hecaton, in the second book of his Apophthegms, says, that in entertainments of that kind, he used to indulge himself freely. And he used to say that it was better to trip with the feet, than with the tongue. And that goodness was attained by little and little, but was not itself a small thing. Some authors, however, attribute this saying to Socrates. XXIII. He was a person of great powers of abstinence and endurance; and of very simple habits, living on food which required no fire to dress it, and wearing a thin cloak, so that it was said of him:—

The cold of winter, and the ceaseless rain,
Come powerless against him; weak is the dart
Of the fierce summer sun, or fell disease,
To bend that iron frame. He stands apart,
In nought resembling the vast common crowd;
But, patient and unwearied, night and day,
Clings to his studies and philosophy.

The Greek in the text is:—

Ketvoc *fiiv iravapiOTOg og tv tiirovn iriBtfVUA,* 'E(T0X6c i' aw *Kclkhvoq* 5c *aireg reavra vor/ay.* The lines in Hesiod are:—

Ketvoc */tiv TTavapiarog* 3c *aiirbq iravra voyay*
'Eo-oXoe i *av Kaxiivog* 8c *ev tiirdvrt irlOfireu.*—Op. E. Di. 293.

That man is best, whose unassisted wit '
Perceives at once what in each case is fit.
And next to him, he surely is most wise,
Who willingly submits to good advice.

XXIV. And the comic poets, without intending it, praise him in their very attempts to turn him into ridicule. Philemon speaks thus of him in his play entitled the Philosophers:—

This man adopts a new philosophy,
He teaches to be hungry; nevertheless,
He gets disciples. Bread his only food,
His best desert dried figs; water his drink.

But some attribute these lines to Posidippus. And they have become almost a proverb. Accordingly it used to be said of him, " More temperate than Zeno the philosopher." Posidippus also writes thus in his Men Transported;—

So that for ten whole days he did appear
More temperate than Zeno's self.

XXV. For in reality he did surpass all men in this description of virtue, and in dignity of demeanour, and, by Jove, in happiness. For he lived niuety-eight years, and then died, without any disease, and continuing in good health to the last. But Persaeus, in his Ethical School, states that he died at the age of seventy-two, and that he came to Athens when he was twenty-two years old. But Apollonius says that he presided over his school for forty-eight years.

XXVI. And he died in the following manner. When he was going out of his school, he tripped, and broke one of his toes; and striking the ground with "his hand, he repeated the line out of the Niobe:—

I come: why call me so f

And immediately he strangled himself, and so he died. But the Athenians buried him in the Ceramicus, and honoured him with the decrees which I have mentioned before, bearing witness to his virtue. And Antipater, the Sidonian, wrote an inscription for him, which runs thus:—

Here Citthim's pride, wise Zeno, lies, who climb'd
The sumits of Olympus; but unmoved
By wicked thoughts ne'er strove to raise on Ossa
The pine-clad Pelion; nor did he emulate
Th' immortal toils of Hercules; but found
A new way for himself to th' highest heaven,
By virtue, temperance, and modesty.

And Zenodotus, the Stoic, a disciple of Diogenes, wrote another:—

You made contentment the chief rule of-life,
Despising haughty wealth, O God-like

Zeno.
With solemn look, and hoary brow serene,
You taught a manly doctrine; and didst found
By your deep wisdom, a great novel school,
Chaste parent of unfearing liberty.
And if your country was Phoenicia,
Why need we grieve, from that land Cadmus came,
Who gave to Greece her written books of wisdom.

And Athenseus, the Epigrammatic poet, speaks thus of all the Stoics in common:— 0, ye who've learnt the doctrines of the Porch,
And have committed to your books divine
The best of human learning; teaching men
That the mind's virtue is the only good.
And she it is who keeps the lives of men,
And cities, safer than high gates or walls.
But those who place their happiness in pleasure,
Are led by the least worthy of the Muses.

And we also have ourselves spoken of the manner of Zeno's death, in our collection of poems in all metres, in the following terms;—

Some say that Zeno, pride of Cittium, Died of old age, when weak and quite worn out;
Some say that famine's cruel tooth did slay him;
Some that he fell, and striking hard the ground,
Said, " See, I come, why call me thus impatiently?"

For some say that this was the way in which he died. And this is enough to say concerning his death.

XXVII. But Demetrius, the Magnesian, says, in his essay on People of the Same Name, that his father Innaseas often came to Athens, as he was a merchant, and that he used to bring back many of the books of the Socratic philosophers, to Zeno, while he was still only a boy; and that, from this circumstance, Zeno had already become talked of in his own country; and that in consequence of this he went to Athens, where he attached himself to Crates. And it seems, he adds, that it was he who first recommended a clear enunciation of principles, as the best remedy for error. He is said, too, to have been in the habit of swearing " By Capers," as Socrates swore " By the Dog." XXVIII. Some, indeed, among whom is Cassius the Sceptic, attack Zeno on many accounts, saying first of all that he denounced the general system of education in vogue at the time, as useless, which he did in the beginning of his Republic. And in the second place, that he used to call all who were not virtuous, adversaries, and enemies, and slaves, and unfriendly to one another, parents to their children, brethren to brethren, and kinsmen to kinsmen; and again, that in his Republic, he speaks of the virtuous as the only citizens, and friends, and relations, and free men, so that in the doctrine of the Stoic, even parents and their children are enemies; for they are not wise. Also, that he lays down the principle of the community of women both in his Republic and in a poem of two hundred verses, and teaches that neither temples nor courts of law, nor gymnasia, ought to be erected in a city; moreover, that he writes thus about money, " That he does not think that men ought to coin money either for purposes of traffic, or of travelling." Besides all this, he enjoins men and women to wear the same dress, and to leave no part of their person uncovered. XXIX. And that this treatise on the Republic is his work we are assured by Chrysippus, in his Republic. He also discussed amatory subjects in the beginning of that book of his which is entitled the Art of Love. And in his Conversations he writes in a similar manner.

Such are the charges made against him by Cassius, and also by Isidorus, of Pergamus, the orator, who says that all the unbecoming doctrines and assertions of the Stoics were cut out of their books by Athenodorus, the Stoic, who was the curator of the library at Pergamus. And that subsequently they were replaced, as Athenodorus was detected, and placed in a situation of great danger; and this is sufficient to say about those doctrines of his which were impugned.

XXX. There were eight different persons of the name of Zeno. The first was the Eleatic, whom we shall mention hereafter 5 the second was this man of whom we are now speaking; the third was a Rhodian, who wrote a history of his country in one book; the fourth was a historian who wrote an account of the expedition of Pyrrhus into Italy and Sicily; and also an epitome of the transactions between the Romans and Carthaginians; the fifth was a disciple of Chrysippus, who wrote very few books, but who left a great number of disciples; the sixth was a physician of Hesophila, a very shrewd man in intellect, but a very indifferent writer; the seventh was a grammarian, who, besides other writings, has left some epigrams behind him; the eighth was a Sidonian by descent, a philosopher of the Epicurean school, a deep thinker, and very clear writer. XXXI. The disciples of Zeno were very numerous. The most eminent were, first of all, Persaeus, of Cittium, the son of Demetrius, whom some call a friend of his, but others describe him as a servant and one of the amanuenses who were sent to him by Antigonus, to whose son, Halcymeus, he also acted as; tutor. And Antigonus once, wishing to make trial of him, caused some false news to be brought to him that his estate had been ravaged by the enemy; and as he began to look gloomy at this news, he said to him, " You see that wealth is not a matter of indifference."

The following works are attributed to him. One on Kingly Power; one entitled the Constitution of the Lacedaemonians; one on Marriage; one on Impiety; the Thyestes; an Essay on Love; a volume of Exhortations; one of Conversations; four of Apophthegms; one of Reminiscences; seven treatises, the Laws of Plato.

The next was Ariston, of Chios, the son of Miltiades, who was the first author of the doctrine of indifference; then Herillus, who called knowledge the chief good; then Dionysius, who transferred this description to pleasure: as, on account of the violent disease which he had in his eyes, he could not yet bring himself to call pain a thing indifferent. He was a native of Heraclea; there was also Sphaerus, of the Bosphorus; and Cleanthes, of Assos, the son of Phanias, who succeeded him in his school, and whom he used to liken to tablets of hard wax, which are written upon with difficulty, but which retain what is written upon them. And after Zeno's death, Sphserus became a pupil of Cleanthes. And we shall speak of him in our account of Cleanthes.

These also were all disciples of Zeno, as we are told by Hippobotus, namely:— Philonides, of Theles; Callippus, of Corinth; Posidonius, of Alexandria; Athenodorus, of Soli; and Zeno, a Sidonian.

XXXII. And I have thought it best to give a general account of all the Stoic doctrines in the life of Zeno, because he it was who was the founder of the sect.
He has written a great many books, of which I have already

T given a list, in which he has spoken as no other of the Stoics has. And his doctrines in general are these. But we will enumerate them briefly, as we have been in the habit of doing in the case of the other philosophers.

XXXIII. The Stoics divide reason according to philosophy, into three parts; an3 say that one part relates to natural philosophy, one to ethics, and one to logic. And Zeno, the Cittiaean, was the first who made this division, in his treatise on Reason; and he was followed in it by Chrysippus, in the first book of his treatise on Reason, and in the first book of his treatise on Natural Philosophy; and also by Apollodorus; and by Syllus, in the first book of his Introduction to the Doctrines of the Stoics; and by Eudromus, in his Ethical Elements; and by Diogenes, the Babylonian; and Posidorus. Now these divisions are called *topics* by Apollodorus, *species* by Chrysippus and Eudromus, and *genera* by all the rest. And they compare philosophy to an animal, likening logic to the bones and sinews, natural philosophy to the fleshy parts, and ethical philosophy to the soul. Again, they compare it to an egg; calling logic the shejl, and ethics the white, and natural philosophy the yolk. Also to a fertile field; in which logic is the fence which goes round it, ethics are the fruit, and natural philosophy the soil, or the fruit-trees. Again, they compare it to a city fortified by walls, and regulated by reason; and then, as some of them say, no one part is preferred to another, but they are all combined and united inseparably; and so they' treat of them all in combination. But others class logic first, natural philosophy second, and ethics third; as Zeno does in his treatise on Reason, and in this he is followed by Chrysippus, and Archidemus, and Eudromus.

For Diogenes of Ptolemais begins with ethics; but Apollodorus places ethics second; and Panaetius and Posidonius begin with natural philosophy, as Phanias, the friend of Posidonius asserts, in the first book of his treatise on the School of Posidonius.

But Cleanthes says, that there are six divisions of reason according to philosophy: dialectics, rhetoric, ethics, politics, physics, and theology; but others assert that these are not divisions of reason, but of philosophy itself; and this is the opinion advanced by Zeno, of Tarsus, among others.

XXXIV. Some again say, that the logical division is properly subdivided into two sciences, namely, rhetoric and dialectics; and some divide it also into definitive species, which is coversant with rules and tests; while others deny the propriety of this last division altogether, and argue that the object of rules and tests is the discovery of the truth; for it is in this division that they explain the differences of representations. They also argue that, on"the other side, the science of definitions has equally for its object the discovery of truth, since we only know things by the intervention of ideas. They also call rhetoric a science conversant about speaking well concerning matters which admit of a detailed narrative; and dialectics they call the science of arguing correctly in discussions which can be carried on by question and answer; on which account they define it thus: a knowledge of what is true, and false, and neither one thing nor the other.

Again, rhetoric itself they divide into three kinds; for one description they say is concerning about giving advice, another is forensic, and the third encomiastic; and it is also divided into several parts, one relating to the discovery of arguments, one to style, one to the arrangement of arguments, and the other to the delivery of the speech. And a rhetorical oration they divide into the exordium, the narration, the reply to the statements of the adverse party, and the peroration.

XXXV. Dialectics, they say, is divided into two parts; one of which has reference to the things signified, the other to the expression. That which has reference to the things signified or spoken of, they divide again into the topic of things conceived in the fancy, and into those of axioms, of perfect determinations, of predicaments, of things alike, whether upright or prostrate, of tropes, of syllogisms, and of sophisms, which are derived either from the voice or from the things. And these sophisms are of various kinds; there is the false one, the one which states facts, the negative, the sorites, and others like these; the imperfect one, the inexplicable one, the conclusive one, the veiled one, the horned one, the nobody, and the mower. In the second part of dialectics, that which has for its object the expression, they treat of written language, of the different parts of a discourse, of solecism and barbarism, of poetical forms of expression, of ambiguity, of a melodious voice, of music; and some even add definitions, divisions, and diction.

They say that the most useful of these parts is the consideration of syllogisms; for that they show us what are the things which are capable of demonstration, and that contributes much to the formation of our judgment, and their arrangement and memory give a scientific character to our knowledge. They define reasoning to be a system composed of assumptiona and conclusions; and syllogism is a syllogistic argument proceeding on them. Demonstration they define to be a method by which one proceeds from that which is more known to that which is less. Perception, again, is an impression produced on the mind, its name being appropriately borrowed from impressions on wax made by a seal; and perception they divide intoi comprehensible and incomprehensible: Comprehensible, which J they call the criterion of facts, and which is produced by a real I object, and is, therefore, at the same time conformable to that i object; Incomprehensible, which has no relation to any real. object, or else, if it has any such relation, does not correspond . to it, being but a vague and indistinct representation.

Dialectics itself they pronounce to be a necessary science, and a virtue which comprehends several other virtues under its species. And the disposition not to take up one side of an argument hastily, they defined to be a knowledge by which we are taught when we ought to agree to a statement, and when we ought to withhold our agreement. Discretion they consider to be a powerful reason, having reference to what is becoming, so as to prevent our yielding to an irrelevant argument. Irrefutability they define to be a power in an argument, which prevents one from being drawn from it to its opposite. Freedom from vanity, according to them, is a habit which refers the perceptions back to right reason.

Again, they define knowledge itself as an assertion or safe comprehension, or habit, which, in the perception of what is seen, never deviates from the truth. And they say further, that without dialectic speculation, the wise man cannot be free from all error in his reasoning. For that that is what distinguishes what is true from what is false, and which easily detects those arguments which are only plausible, and those which depend upon an ambiguity of language. And without dialectics they say it is not possible to ask or answer questions correctly. They also add, that precipitation in denials extends to those things which are done, so that those who have not properly exercised their perceptions fall into irregularity and thoughtlessness. Again, without dialectics, the wise man cannot be acute, and ingenious, and wary, and altogether dangerous as an arguer. For that it belongs to the same man to speak correctly and to reason correctly, and to discuss properly those subjects which are proposed to him, and to answer readily whatever questions are put to him, all which qualities belong to a man who is skilful in dialectics. This then is a brief summary of their opinions on logic.

XXXVI. And, that we may also enter into some more minute details respecting them, we will subjoin what refers to what they call their introductory science, as it is stated by Diocles, of Magnesia, in his Excursion of Philosophers, where he speaks as follows, and we will give his account word for word.

The Stoics have chosen to treat, in the first place, of perception and sensation, because the criterion by which the truth of facts is ascertained is a kind of perception, and because the judgment which expresses the belief, and the comprehension, and the understanding of a thing, a judgment which precedes all others, cannot exist without perception. For perception leads the way; and then thought, finding vent in expressions, explains in words the feelings which it derives from perception. But there is a difference between *paiTania* and *ipavra.sij.a.* For *pavraefuz,* is a conception of the intellect, such as takes place in sleep; but *pavraela* is an impression, *ruruiaig,* produced on the mind, that is to say, an alteration, *aXXolueig,* as Chrysippus states in the twelfth book of his treatise on the Soul. For we must not take this impression to resemble that made by a seal, since it is impossible to conceive that there should be many impressions made at the same time on the same thing. But *po.waaia* is understood to be that which is impressed, and formed, and imprinted by a real object, according to a real object, in such a way as it could not be by any other than a real object; and, according to their ideas of the *pavraela.1,* some are sensible, and some are not. Those they call sensible, which are derived by us from some one or more senses; and those they call not sensible, which emanate directly from the thought, as for instance, those which relate to incorporeal objects, or any others which are embraced by reason. Again, those which are sensible, are produced by areal object, which imposes itself on the intelligence, and compels its acquiescence; and there are also some others, which are simply apparent, mere shadows, which resemble those which are produced by real objects.

Again, these *pavrdetcci* are divided into rational and irrational; those which are rational belong to animals capable of reason; those which are irrational to animals destitute of reason. Those which are rational are thoughts; those which are irrational have no name; but are again subdivided into artificial and not artificial. At all events, an image is contemplated in a different light by a man skilful in art, from that in which it is viewed by a man ignorant of art.

By sensation, the Stoics understand a species of breath which proceeds from the dominant portion of the soul to the senses, whether it be a sensible perception, or an organic dispo sition, which, according to the notions of some of them, is crippled and vicious. They also call sensation the energy, or active exercise, of the sense. According to them, it is to sensation that we owe our comprehension of white and black, and rough and smooth: from reason, that we derive the notions which result from a demonstration, those for instance which have for their object the existence of Gods, and of; Divine Providence. For all our thoughts are formed either I by indirect perception, or by similarity, or analogy, or trans1 position, or combination, or opposition. By a direct percepI tion, we perceive those things which are the objects of sense;. by similarity, those which start from some point present to our senses; as, for instance, we form an idea of Socrates from his likeness. We draw our conclusions by analogy, adopting either an increased idea of the thing, as of Tityus, or the Cyclops; or a diminished idea, as of a pigmy. So, too, the idea of the centre of the world was one derived by analogy from what we perceived to be the case of the smaller spheres. We use transposition when we fancy eyes in a mans breast; combination, when we take in the idea of a Centaur; opposition, when we turn our thoughts to death. Some ideas we also derive from comparison, for instance, from a comparison of words and places.

There is also nature; as by nature we comprehend what is just and good. And privation, when for instance, we form a notion of a man without hands. Such are the doctrines of the Stoics, on the subject of phantasia, and sensation, and thought.

XXXVII. They say that the proper criterion of truth is the comprehension, *pairaaia*; that is to say, one which is derived from a real object, as Chrysippus asserts in the twelfth book of his Physics; and he is followed by Antipater and Apollodorus. For Boethius leaves a great many criteria, such as intellect, sensation, appetite, and knowledge; but Chrysippus dissents from his view, and in the first book of his treatise on Reason, says, that sensation and preconception are the only criteria. And preconception is, according to him, a comprehensive physical notion of general principles. But others of the earlier Stoics admit right reason as one criterion of the truth; for instance, this is the opinion of Posidouius, and is advanced by him in his essay on Criteria. XXXVIII. On the subject of logical speculation, there appears to be a great unanimity among the greater part of the Stoics, in beginning with the topic of the voice. Now voice is a percussion of the air; or, as Diogenes the Babylonian, defines it, in his essay on the Voice, a sensation peculiar to the hearing. The voice of a beast is a mere percussion of the air by some impetus: but the voice of a man is articulate, and is emitted by intellect, as Diogenes lays it down, and is not brought to perfection in a shorter period than fourteen years. And the voice is a body according to the Stoics; for so it is laid ijown by Archidemus, in his book on the Voice, and by Diogenes, and Antipater, and also by Chrysippus, in the second volume of his Physics. For everything which makes anything, is a body; and the voice makes something when it proceeds to those who hear from those who speak.

A word (Xff/s), again, is, according to Diogenes, a voice consisting of letters, as " Day." A sentence *(X6yog)* is a significant voice, sent out by the intellect, as for instance, " It is day;" but dialect is a peculiar style imprinted on the utterance of nations, according to their race; and causes varieties in the Greek language, being a sort of local habit, as for instance, the Attics say *DaXarra,* and the Ionians say jj/4£g»j. The elements of words are the twenty-four letters; and the word letter is used in a triple division of sense, meaning the element itself, the graphical sign of the element, and the name, as Alpha. There are seven vowels, a, s, Jj, /, «,«,«; six mutes, /3, y, d, x, it, T. But voice is different from a word, because voice is a sound; but a word is an articulate sound. And a word differs from a sentence, because a sentence is always significative of something, but a word by itself has no signification, as for instance, j8X/Vg/. But this is not the case with a sentence. Again, there is a difference between, speaking and pronouncing; the sounds are pronounced, but what are spoken are things which are capable of being spoken of.

XXXIX. Now of sentences there are five parts, as Diogenes tells us in his treatise on Voice; and he is followed by Chrysippus. There is the noun, the common noun, the verb, the conjunction, and the article. Antipater adds also quality, in his treatise upon Words and the things expressed by them. And a common noun *(irgotriyogla)* is, according to Diogenes, a part of a sentence signifying a common quality, as for instance, man, horse. But a noun is a part of a sentence signifying a peculiar quality, such as Diogenes, Socrates. A verb is a part of a sentence signifying an uncombined categorem, as Diogenes (o A/oysnjs) or, as others define it, an element of a sentence, devoid of case, signifying something compound in reference to some person or persons, as, " I write," " I say. " A conjunction is a part of a sentence destitute of case, uniting the divisions of the sentence. An article is an element of a sentence, having cases, defining the genders of nouns and their numbers; as o, *ri, rb, 61, al, ra.* XL. The excellences of a sentence are five,—good Greek, clearness, conciseness, siutableness, elegance. Good Greek *C'EXXriviefibg)* is a correct style, according to art, keeping aloof from any vulgar form of expression; clearness is a style which states that which is conceived in the mind in such a way that it is easily known: conciseness is a style which embraces all that is necessary to the clear explanation of the subject under discussion; suitableness is a style suited to the subject; elegance is a style which avoids all peculiarity of expression. Of the vices of a sentence, on the other hand, barbarism is a use of words contrary to that in vogue among the well-educated Greeks; solecism is a sentence incongruously put together. XLI. A poetical expression is, as Posidonius defines it in his introduction on Style, " A metrical or rhythmical diction, proceeding in preparation, and avoiding all resemblance to prose." For instance, " The vast and boundless earth," " Th' expanse of heaven," are rhythmical expressions; and poetry is a collection of poetical expressions signifying something, containing an imitation of divine and human beings. XLII. A definition is, as Antipater explains it in the first book of his treatise on Definitions, a sentence proceeding by analysis enunciated in such a way as to give a complete idea; or, as Chrysippus says in his treatise on Definitions, it is the explanation of an idea. Description is a sentence which, in a figurative manner, brings one to a knowledge of the subject, or it may be called a simpler kind of definition, expressing the power of a definition in plainer language. Genus is a comprehending of many ideas indissolubly connected, as animal; for this one expression comprehends all particular kinds of animals. An idea is an imagination of the mind which does not express actually anything real, or any quality, but only a *quasi* reality and a *quasi* quality; such, for instance, is the idea of a horse when a horse is not present. Species is that which is comprehended under genus, as man is comprehended under animal.

Again, that is the most general genus which, being a genus itself, has no other genus, as the existent. And that is the most special species, which being a species has no other species, as, for instance, Socrates.

XLIII. The division of genus is a dissection of it into the proximate species; as, for instance, " Of animals, some are rational, others irrational." Contrary division is the dissection of genus into species on the principle of the contrary; so as to be by a sort of negation; as, for instance, " Of existent things, some are good and some not good; " and, " Of things which are not good, some are bad and some indifferent." Partition is an arrangement of a genus with reference to place, as Crinis says, for instance, " Of goods, some have reference to the mind and some to the body." XLIV. Ambiguity (d/ipi/3oX/a) is an expression signifying two or more things having an ordinary or a peculiar meaning, according to the pronunciation, in such a way that more things than one may be understood by the very same expression. Take, for instance, the words auXjjrg/j Tcttwxs. For you may understand by them, a house has fallen down three times *(avXr)Tg!g Ti!rraxi)*, or, a female flute-player has fallen, taking aiXijrg/s as synonymous with aiX»jrg/'a. LV. Dialectics are, as Posidonius explains them, the science of what is true and false, and neither one or the other, and it is, as Chrysippus explains it, conversant aboutwords that signify and things that are signified; these then are the doctrines asserted by the Stoics in their speculations on the subject of the voice. XL VI. But in that part of dialectics which concerns things and ideas signified, they treat of propositions, of perfect enunciations, of judgments, of syllogisms, of imperfect enunciations, of attributes and deficiences, and of both direct and indirect categorems or predicaments. XLVII. And they say that enunciation is the manifestation of the ideal perception; and these enunciations the Stoics pronounce some to be perfect in themselves, and some to be defective; nowthose are defective, which furnish an incomplete sense, as for instance, "He writes." For then we ask further, "Who writes?" But those are perfect in themselves, which give a sense entirely complete, as for instance, " Socrates writes." Accordingly, in the defective enunciations, categorems are applied; but in those which are perfect in themselves, axioms, and syllogisms, and questions, and interrogations, are brought into play. Now a categorem is something which is predicated of something else, being either a thing which is added to one or more objects, according to the definition of Apollodorus, or else a defective enunciation added to the nominative case, for the purpose of forming a proposition.

Now of categorems, some are accidents. ... as for instance, " The sailing through a rock.".... And of categorems, some are direct, some indirect, and some neither one nor the other. Now those are correct, which are construed with one of the oblique cases, in such a manner as to produce a categorem, as for instance, "He hears, he sees, he converses." And those are indirect, which are construed with the passive voice, as for instance, " I am heard, I am seen."" Huerner thinks (as indeed is evident) that something is lost here; and proposes to read the sentence thus:—Twv *Si* rortiyoprjjuariDW rd *ftiv* £m *ov/jtflapaTa* (Iif *To irXtiv, olov* Scuicpdrijc irXeT. Tct *Si irapaovp. jiafiara it rb Sia irirpaq irXiiv.* With reference to which passage, Liddell and Scott, Gr. Eng. Lex. *voc. oififinfia,* thus speak: " *aiifijiafia....* as a philosophical term of the Stoics—raT-qyopijpa, a complete predicament such as is an intransitive ver': e. g. EwnrpaVic *irtpurarii*; while an imperfect verb was regarded as an incomplete predicament; e. g. Swicparct *fiiXti,* and called irapaau/a/ 3ajua, or *wupaKaTtyopjijla."*

And those which are neither one nor the other, are those which are construed in a neutral kind of manner, as for instance, "To think, to walk." And those are reciprocal, which are among the indirect ones, with out being indirect themselves. Those are effects, *ingyrifiaTa,* which are such words as, " He is shaved;" for then, the man who is shaved, implies himself.

The oblique cases, are the genitive, the dative, and the accusative.

XLVII1. An axiom, is that thing which is true, or false, or perfect in itself, being asserted, or denied positively, as far as depends upon itself; as Chrysippus explains it in his Dialectic Definitions; as for instance, "It is day," " Dion is walking." And it has received the name of axiom, *a%!ufia,* because it is either maintained, dg/oDra/, or repudiated. For the man who says, " It is day," appears to maintain the fact of its being day. If then it is day, the axiom put before one is true; but if it is not day, the axiom is false. And an axiom, a question, and an interrogation, differ from one another, and so does an imperative proposition from one which is adjurative, or imprecatory, or hypothetical, or appellative, or false. For that is an axiom which we utter, when we affirm anything positively, which is either true or false. And a question is a thing complete in itself, as also is an axiom, but which requires an answer, as for instance, "Is it day?" Now this is neither true nor false; but, as " It is day " is an axiom; so is, " Is it-day?'" a question. But an interrogation, *irve/ia,* is a thing to which it is not possible to make an answer symbolically, as in the case of a question, egcurjj/ia, saying merely " Yes," but we must reply, " He does live in this place."

The imperative proposition is a thing which we utter when we give an order, as for instance this:—

Do you now go to the sweet stream of Inachus.

The appellative proposition is one which is used in the case in which, when a man says anything, he must address somebody, as for instance:— Atrides, glorious king of men,

Most mighty Agamemnon.t

A false judgment is a proposition, which, while it has at the

This line is from the Inaehus of Sophocles (one of his lost plays). + Homer, Iliad II. 484.

same time the appearance of a real judgment, loses this character by the addition, and under the influence of, some particle, as for instance:

The Parthenon at least is beautiful. How like the herdsman is to Priam's sons.

There is also the dubitative proposition, which differs from the judgment, inasmuch as it is always uttered in the form of a doubt; as for instance:—

Are not, then, grief and life two kindred states?

But questions, and interrogations, and things like these, are neither true nor false, while judgments and propositions are necessarily one or the other.

Now of axioms, some are simple, and others are not simple; as Chrysippus, and Archedemus, and Athenodorus, and Antipater, and Crinis, agree in dividing them. Those are simple, which consist of an axiom or proposition, which is not ambiguous, (or of several axioms, or propositions of the same character,) as for instance the sentence, "It is day." And those are not simple, which consist of an axiom or proposition which is ambiguous, or of several axioms or propositions of that character. Of an axiom, or proposition, which is ambiguous, as "If it is day;" of several axioms, or propositions of that character, as, "If it is day, it is light." I And simple propositions are divided into the affirmative, the negative, the privative, the categorical, the definite, and the indefinite; those which are not simple, are divided into the combined, and the adjunctive, the connected and the disjunctive, and the causal and the augmentative, and the diminutive. That is an affirmative proposition, "It is not day." And the species of this is doubly affirmative. That again is doubly affirmative, which is affirmative of an affirmative, as for instance, "It is not not day;" for this amounts to, "It is day." That is a negative proposition, which consists of a negative particle and a categorem, as for instance, " No one is walking." That is a privative proposition which consists of a privative particle and an axiom according to power, as "This man is inhuman." That is a categorical proposition, which consists of a nominative case and a categorem, as for instance, " Dion is walking." That is a definite proposition, This line is from the Citharista of Menander. which consists of a demonstrative nominative case and a categorem, as for instance, " This man is walking." That is an indefinite one which consists of an indefinite particle, or of indefinite particles, as for instance, " Somebody is walking," " He is moving."

Of propositions which are not simple, the combined proposition is, as Chrysippus states, in his Dialectics, and Diogenes, too, in his Dialectic Art; that which is held together by the copulative conjunction " if." And this conjunction professes that the second member of the sentence follows the first, as for instance, " If it is day, it is light." That which is adjunctive is, as Crinis states in his Dialectic Art, an axiom which is made to depend on the conjunction " since " (ete/), beginning with an axiom and ending in an axiom,as for instance, "Since it is day, it is light." And this conjunction professes both that the second portion of the proposition follows the first, and the first is true. That is a connected proposition which is connected by some copulative conjunctions, as for instance, " It both is day, and it is light." That is a disjunctive proposition which is disconnected by the disjunctive conjunction, "or" *(ijroi,)* as for instance, " It is either day or night. " And this proposition professes that one or other of these propositions is false. That is a causal proposition which is connected by the word, "because;" as for instance, " Because it is day, it is light." For the first is, as it were, the cause of the second. That is au augmentative proposition, which explains the greater, which is construed with an augmentative particle, and which is placed between the two members of the proposition, as for instance, " It is rather day than night." The diminutive proposition is, in every respect, the exact contrary of the preceding one; as for instance, "It is less night than day." Again, at times, axioms or propositions are opposed to one another in respect of their truth and falsehood, when one is an express denial of the other; as for instance, " It is day," and, " It is not day."

Again, a conjunctive proposition is correct, when it is such that the opposite of the conclusion is contradictory of the premiss; as for instance, the proposition, "If it is day, it is light," is true; for, " It is not light," which is the opposite to the conclusion expressed, is contradictory to the premiss, " It is day." And a conjunctive proposition is incorrect, when it is such that the opposite of the conclusion is not inconsistent with the premiss, as for instance, " If it is day, Dion is walking." For the fact that Dion is not walking, is not contradictory of the premiss, " It is day."

An adjunctive proposition is correct, which begins with a true premiss, and ends in a consequence which follows of necessity, as for instance, " Since it is day, the sun is above the earth." But it is incorrect when it either begins with a false premiss, or ends with a consequence which does not follow properly; as for instance, " Since it is night, Dion is walking," for this may be said in the day-time.

A causal proposition is correct, when it begins with a true premiss, and ends in a consequence which necessarily follows from it, but yet does not have its premiss reciprocally consequent upon its conclusion; as for instance, " Because it is day, it is light." For the fact of its being light, is a necessary consequence of its being day; but the fact of its being day, is not necessarily a consequence of its being light. A causal proposition is incorrect, which either begins with a false premiss, or ends with a conclusion that does not follow from it, or which has a premiss which does not correspond to the conclusion; as for instance, " Because it is night, Dion is walking."

A proposition is persuasive, which leads to the assent of the mind, as for instance, " If she brought him forth, she is his mother." But still this is a falsehood, for a hen is not the mother of an egg. Again, there are some propositions which are possible, and some which are impossible; and some which are necessary, and some which are not necessary. That is possible, which is capable of being true, since external circumstances are no hindrance to its being true; as for instance, " Diocles lives." And that is impossible which is not capable of being true; as for instance, " The earth flies." That is necessary which, being true, is not capable of being false; or perhaps is intrinsically capable of being false, but still has external circumstances which hinder its being false, as for instance, " Virtue profits a man." That again, is not necessary, which is true, but which has a capacity of being false, though external circumstances offer no hiudrance to either alternative; as for instance, " Dion walks."

That is a reasonable or probable proposition, which has a great preponderance of opportunities in favour of its being true; as for instance, " I shall be alive to-morrow." And there are other different kinds of propositions and conversions of them, from true to false, and re-conversions again; concerning which we must speak at some length.

XLIX. An argument, as Crinis says, is that which is composed of a lemma or major premiss, an assumption or minor premiss, and a conclusion; as for instance this, " If it is day, it is light;" " But it is day, therefore it is light." For the lemma, or major premiss, is, " If it is day, it is light." The assumption, or minor premiss, is, "It is day." The conclusion follows, " Therefore it is light." The mode of a proposition is, as it were, a figure of an argument, as for instance, such ss this, " If it is the first, it is the second; but it is the first, therefore it is the second."

A conditional syllogism is that which is composed of both the preceding arguments; as for instance, " If Plato is alive, Plato breathes; but the first fact is so, therefore so is the second." And this conditional syllogism has been introduced for the sake, in long and complex sentences, of not being forced to repeat the assumption, as it was a long one, and also the conclusion; but of being able, instead, to content one's self with summing it up briefly thus, " The first case put is true, therefore so is the second."

Of arguments, some are conclusive, others are inconclusive. Those are inconclusive which are such, that the opposite of the conclusion drawn in them is not necessarily incompatible with the connection of the premisses. As for instance, such arguments as these, " If it is day, it is light; but it is day, therefore, Dion is walking." But of conclusive arguments, some are called properly by the kindred name conclusions, and some are called syllogistic arguments. Those then are syllogistic which are either such as do not admit of demonstration, or such as are brought to an indemonstrable conclusion, according to some one or more propositions; such for instance as the following: " If Dion walks, then Dion is in motion." Those are conclusive, which infer their conclusion specially, and not syllogistically; such for instance, as this, " The proposition it is both day and night is false. Now it is day; therefore, it is not night."

Those again, are unsyllogistic arguments which have an air of probability about them, and a resemblance to syllogistic ones, but which still do not lead to the deduction of proper conclusions. As for instance, " If Dion is a horse, Dion is an animal; but Dion is not a horse, therefore, Dion is not an animal."

Again, of arguments, some are true, and some are false. Those are true which deduce a conclusion from true premisses, as, for instance, " If virtue profits, then vice injures." And those are false which have some falsehood in their premisses, or which are inconclusive; as, for instance, " If it is day, it is light; but it is day, therefore, Dion is alive."

There are also arguments which are possible, and others which are impossible; some likewise which are necessary, and others which are not necessary. There are too, some which are not demonstrated from their not standing in need of demonstration, and these are laid down differently by different people; but Chrysippus enumerates five kinds, which serve as the foundation for every kind of argument; and which are assumed in conclusive arguments properly so called, and in syllogisms, and in modes.

The first kind that is not demonstrated, is that in which the whole argument consists of a conjunctive and an antecedent; and in which the first term repeats itself so as to form a sort of conjunctive proposition, and to bring forward as the conclusion the last term. As, for instance, " If the first be true, so is the second; but the first is true, therefore, so is the second." The second kind that is not demonstrated, is that which, by means of the conjunctive and the opposite of the conclusion, has a conclusion opposite to the first premiss. As, for instance, " If it be day, it is light; but it is night, therefore it is not day." For here the assumption arises from the opposite of the conclusion, and the conclusion from the opposite of the first term. The third kind that is not demonstrative, is that which, by a negative combination, and by one of the terms in the proposition, produces the contradictory of the remainder; as, for instance, " Plato is not dead and alive at the same time but Plato is dead; therefore, Plato is not alive. The fourth kind that is not demonstrative, is that which, by means of a disjunctive, and one of those terms which are in the disjunctive, has a conclusion opposite to what remains; as, for instance, " It is either the first, or the second; but it is the first; therefore, it is not the second." The fifth kind that is not demonstrative, is that in which the whole argument consists of a disjunctive proposition, and the opposite of one of the terms, aud then one makes the conclusion identical with the remainder; as, for instance, " It is either day or night; but it is not night; therefore it is. day."

According to the Stoics, truth follows upon truth, as " It is light," follows upon "It is day." And falsehood follows upon falsehood; as, " If it is false that it is night, it is also false that it is dark." Sometimes too, truth follows from falsehood; for instance, though it is false that " the earth flies," it is true that " there is the earth." But falsehood does never follow from truth; for, from the fact that " there is the earth," it does not follow " that the earth flies."

There are also some arguments which are perplexed, being veiled and escaping notice; or such as are called sorites, the horned one, or the nobody. That is a veiled argument which resembles the following one; " two are not a few, nor three, nor those, nor four, and so on to ten; but two are few; therefore, so are ten few."

The nobody is a conjunctive argument, and one that consists of the indefinite and the definite, and which has a minor premiss and a conclusion; as, for instance, " If any one is here, he is not in Rhodes."

L. Such then are the doctrines which the Stoics maintain on the subject of logic, in order as far as possible to establish their point that the logician is the only wise man. For they assert that all affairs are looked at by means of that speculation It would appear that there is a considerable hiatus here; for the instance following is a sorites, and not a specimen of the veiled argument. And there is no instance given of the concealed, or of the horned one. Still, the mere fact of the text being unintelligible, is far from proving that we have not got it as Diogenes wrote it; as though in the language of the writer in Smith's Biographical Dictionary, vol. i. pp. 1022, 1023, "the work contains a rich store of living features, which serve to illustrate the private life of the Greeks," it is equally clear that the author " was unequal to writing a history of Greek philosophy. His work in reality is nothing but a compilation of the most heterogeneous and often contradictory accounts The traces of carelessness and mistakes are very numerous; much in the work is confused, and there is also much that is quite absurd. And as far as philosophy itself is concerned, Diogenes very frequently did not know what he was talking about when he abridged the theories of the philosophers." oh proceeds by argument, including under this assertion Doth those that belong to natural and also those which belong to moral philosophy: for, say they, how else could one determine the exact value of nouns, or how else could one explain what laws are imposed upon such and such actions? Moreover, as there are two habits both incidental to virtue, the one considers what each existing thing is, and the other inquires what it is called. These then are the notions of the Stoics on the subject of logic.

LI. The ethical part of philosophy they divide into the topic of inclination, the topic of good and bad, the topic of the passious, the topic of virtue, the topic of the chief good, and of primary estimation, and of actions; the topic of what things are becoming, and of exhortation and dissuasion. And this division is the one laid down by Chrysippus, and Archedemus, and Zeno, of Tarsus, and Apollodorus, and Diogenes, and Antipater, and Posidonius. For Zeno, of Cittium, and Cleanthes, have, as being more ancient they were likely to, adopted a more simple method of treating these subjects. But these men divided logical and the natural philosophy. LII. They say that the first inclination which an animal has is to protect itself, as nature brings herself to take an interest in it from the beginning, as Chrysippus affirms in the first book of his treatise on Ends; where he says, that the first and dearest object to every animal is its own existence, and its consciousness of that existence. For that it is not natural for any animal to be alienated from itself, or even to be brought into such a state as to be indifferent to itself, being neither alienated from nor interested in itself. It remains, therefore, that we must assert that nature has bound the animal to itself by the greatest unanimity and affection; for by that means it repels all that is injurious, and attracts all that is akin to it and desirable. But as for what some people say, that the first inclination of animals is to pleasure, they say what is false. For they say that pleasure, if there be any such thing at all, is an accessory only, which, nature, having sought it out by itself, as well as those things which are adapted to its constitution, receives incidentally in the same manner as animals are pleased, and plants made to flourish.

Moreover, say they, nature makes no difference between animals and plants, when she regulates them so as to leave them without voluntary motion or sense; and some things too take place in ourselves in the same manner as in plants. But, as inclination in animals tends chiefly to the point of making them pursue what is appropriate to them, we may say that their inclinations are regulated by nature.. And as reason is given to rational animals according to a more perfect principle, it follows, that to live correctly according to reason, is properly predicated of those who live accordiug to nature. For nature is as it were the artist who produces the inclination.

LIII. On which account Zeno was the first writer who, in his treatise on the Nature of Man, said, that the chief good was confessedly to live according to nature; which is to live according to virtue, for nature leads us to this point. And in like manner Cleanthes speaks in his treatise on Pleasure, and so do Posidonius and Hecaton in their essays on Ends as the Chief Good. And again, to live according to virtue is the same thing as living according to one's experience of those things which happen by nature; as Ghrysippus explains it in the first book of his treatise on the Chief Good. For our individual natures are all parts of universal nature; on which account the chief good is to live in a manner corresponding to nature, and that means corresponding to ope's own nature and to universal nature; doing none of those things which the common law of mankind is in the habit of forbidding, and that common law is identical with that right reason which pervades everything, being the same with Jupiter, who is the regulator and chief manager of all existing things.

Again, this very thing is the virtue of the happy man and the perfect happiness of life when everything is done according to a harmony with the genius of each individual with reference to the will of the universal governor and manager of all things. Diogenes, accordingly, says expressly that the chief good is to act according to sound reason in our selection of things according to our nature. And Archidemus defines it to be living in the discharge of all becoming duties. Chrysippus again understands that the nature, in a manner corresponding to which we ought to live, is both the common nature, and also human nature in' particular; but Cleanthes will not admit of any other nature than the common one alone, as that to which people ought to live in a manner corresponding; and repudiates all mention of a particular nature. And he asserts that virtue is a disposition of the mind always consistent and always harmonious; that one ought to seek it out for its own sake, without being influenced by fear or hope by any external influence. Moreover, that it is in it that happiness consists, as producing in the soul the harmony of a life always consistent with itself; and that if a rational animal goes the wrong way, it is because it allows itself to be misled by the deceitful appearances of exterior things, or perhaps by the instigation of those who surround it; for nature herself never gives us any but good inclinations.

LIV. Now virtue is, to speak generally, a perfection in everything, as in the case of a statue; whether it is invisible as good health, or speculative as prudence. For Hecaton says, in the first book of his treatise on Virtues, that the scientific and speculative virtues are those which have a constitution arising from speculation and study, as, for instance, prudence and justice; and that those which are not speculative are those which are generally' viewed in their extension as a practical result or effect of the former; such for instance, as health and strength. Accordingly, temperance is one of the speculative virtues, and it happens that good health usually follows it, and is marshalled as it were beside it; in the same way as strength follows the proper structure of an arch.—And the unspeculative virtues derive their name from the fact of their not proceeding from any acquiescence reflected by intelligence; but they are derived from others, are only accessories, and are found even in worthless people, as in the case of good health, or courage. And Posidonius, in the first book of his treaties on Ethics, says that the great proof of the reality of virtue is that Socrates, and Diogenes, and Antisthenes, made great improvement; and the great proof of the reality of vice may be found in the fact of its being opposed to virtue.

Again, Chrysippus, in the first book of his treatise on the Chief Good, and Cleanthes, and also Posidonius in his Exhortations, and Hecaton, all agree that virtue may be taught. And that they are right, and that it may be taught, is plain from men becoming good after having been bad. On this account Panaetius teaches that there are two virtues, one speculative and the other practical; but others make three kinds, the logical, the natural, and the ethical. Posidonius divides virtue into four divisions; and Cleanthes, Chrysippus, and Antipater make the divisions more numerous still; for Apollophanes asserts that there is but one virtue, namely, prudence.

Among the virtues some are primitive and some are derived. The primitive ones are prudence, manly courage, justice, and temperance. And subordinate to these, as a kind of species contained in them, are magnanimity, continence, endurance, presence of mind, wisdom in council. And the Stoics define prudence as a knowledge of what is good, and bad, and indifferent; justice as a knowledge of what ought to be chosen, what ought to be avoided, and what is indifferent; magnanimity as a knowledge of engendering a lofty habit, superior to all such accidents as happen to all men indifferently, whether they be good or bad; continence they consider a disposition which never abandons right reason, or a habit which never yields to pleasure; endurance they call a knowledge or habit by which we understand what we ought to endure, what we ought not, and what is indifferent; presence of mind they define as a habit which is prompt at finding out what is suitable on a sudden emergency; and wisdom in counsel they think a knowledge which leads us to judge what we are to do, and how we are to do it, in order to act becomingly. And analogously, of vices too there are some which are primary, and some which are subordinate; as, for instance, folly, and cowardice, and injustice, and intemperance, are among the primary vices; incontinence, slowness, and folly in counsel among the subordinate ones. And the vices are ignorance of those things of which the virtues are the knowledge.

LV. Good, looked at in a general way, is some advantage, with the more particular distinction, being partly what is actually useful, partly what is not contrary to utility. On which account virtue itself, and the good which partakes of virtue are spoken of in a threefold view of the subject. First, as to what kind of good it is, and from what it ensues; as, for instance, in an action done according to virtue. Secondly, as to the agent, in the case of a good man who partakes of virtue. .j. t The third point of view is wanting; and those that are given appear to be ill selected. The French translator, following the hint of

At another time, they define the good in a peculiar manner, as being what is perfect according to the nature of a rational being as rational being. And, secondly, they say that it ia conformity to virtue, so that all actions which partake of virtue, and all good men, are themselves in some sense the good. And in the third place, they speak of its accessories, joy, and mirth, and things of that kind. In the same manner they speak of vices, which they divide into folly, cowardice, injustice, and things of that kind. And they consider that those things which partake of vices, and actions done according to vice, and bad men, are themselves in some sense the evil; and its accessories are despondency, and melancholy, and other things of that kind.

LVI. Again, of goods, some have reference to the mind, and some are external; and some neither have reference to the mind, nor are external. The goods having reference to the mind are virtues, and actions according to the virtues. The external goods are the having a virtuous country, a virtuous friend, and the happiness of one's country and friend. And those which are not external, and which have no reference to the mind, are such as a man's being virtuous and happy to himself. And reciprocally, of evils, some have reference to the mind, such as the vices and actions according to them; some are external, such as having a foolish country, or a foolish friend, or one's country or one's friend being unhappy. And those evils which are not external, and which have no reference to the mind, are such as a man's being worthless and unhappy to himself. LVII. Again, of goods, some are final, some are efficient, and some are both final and efficient. For instance, a friend, Huebner, gives the following passage from Sextus Empiricus (a physician of the Sceptic school, about B.C. 250), in his work against the Philosophers,'which he says may serve to rectify and complete the statement of Diogenes Laertius. "Good is said in one sense of that which produces the useful, or from which the useful results; that is, the good *par excellence,* virtue. For virtue is as it were the source from whioh all utility naturally flows. In another sense it is said of that which is accidentally the cause of utility; under this point of view we call good not only virtue, but also those actions which are conformable to virtue, for they are accidentally useful. In the third and last place, we call good everything that possibly can be useful, comprehending under this definition virtue, virtuous actions, friends, good men, the Gods, &c, &c." and the services done by him to one, are efficient goods; but courage, and prudence, and liberty, and delight, and mirth, and freedom from pain, and all kinds of actions done according to virtue, are final goods. There are too, as I said before, some goods which are both efficient and final; for inasmuch as they produce perfect happiness they are efficient, and inasmuch as they complete it by being themselves parts of it, they are final. And in the same way, of evils, some are final, and some efficient, and some partake of both natures. For instance, an enemy and the injuries done to one by him, are efficient evils; fear, meanness of condition, slavery, want of delight, depression of spirits, excessive grief, and all actions done according to vice, are final evils; and some partake of both characters, since, inasmuch as they produce perfect unhappiness, they are efficient; and inasmuch as they complete it in such a way as to become parts of it, they are final.

LVIII. Again, of the goods which have reference to the mind, some are habits, some are dispositions, and some are neither habits nor dispositions. Dispositions are virtues, habits are practices, and those which are neither habits nor dispositions are energies. And, speaking generally, the following may be called mixed goods: happiness in one's children, and a happy old age. But knowledge is a pure good. And some goods are continually present, such as virtue; and some are not always present, as joy, or taking a walk. LIX. But every good is expedient, and necessary, and profitable, and useful, and serviceable, and beautiful, and advantageous, and eligible, and just. Expedient, inasmuch as it brings us things, which by their happening to us do us good; necessary, inasmuch as it assists us in what we have need to be assisted; profitable, inasmuch as it repays all the care that is expended on it, and makes a return with interest to our great advantage; useful, inasmuch as it supplies us with what is of utility; serviceable, because it does us service which is much praised; beautiful, because it is in accurate proportion to the need we have of it, and to the service it does. Advantageous, inasmuch as it is of such a character as to confer advantage on us; eligible, because it is such that we may rationally choose it; and just, because it is in accordance with law, and is an efficient cause of union.

And they call the honourable the perfect good, because it has naturally all the numbers which are required by nature, and because it discloses a perfect harmony. Now, the species of this perfect good are four in number: justice, manly courage, temperance, and knowledge; for in these goods all beautiful actions have their accomplishment. And analogously, there are also four species of the disgraceful: injustice, and cowardice, and intemperauce, and folly. And the honourable is predicated in one sense, as making those who are possessed of it worthy of all praise; and in a second sense, it is used of what is well adapted by nature for its proper work; and in another sense, when it expresses that which adorns a man, as when we say that the wise man alone is good and honourable.

The Stoics also say, that the beautiful is the only good, as Hecaton says, in the third book of his treatise on Goods, and Chrysippus asserts the same principle in his essays on the Beautiful. And they say that this is virtue, and that which partakes of virtue; and this assertion is equal to the other, that everything good is beautiful, and that the good is an equivalent term to the beautiful, inasmuch as the one thing is exactly equal to the other. For since it is good, it is beautiful; and it is beautiful, therefore, it is good.

LX. But it seems that all goods are equal, and that every good is to be desired in the highest degree, and that it admits of no relaxation, and of no extension. Moreover, they divide all existing things into good, bad, and indifferent. The good are the virtues, prudence, justice, manly courage, temperance, and the rest of the like qualities. The bad are the contraries, folly, injustice,' and the like. Those are indifferent which are neither beneficial nor injurious, such as life, health, pleasure, beauty, strength, riches, a good reputation,-nobility of birth; and their contraries, death, disease, labour, disgrace, weakness, poverty, a bad reputation, baseness of birth, and the like; as Hecaton lays it down in the seventh book of his treatise on the Chief Good; and he is followed by Apollodorus, in his Ethics, and by Chrysippus. For they affirm that those things are not good but indifferent, though perhaps a little more near to one species than to the other.

For, as it is the property of the hot to warm and not to chill one, so it is the property of the good to benefit and not to injure one. Now, wealth and good health cannot be said to benefit any more than to injure any one: therefore, neither wealth nor good health are goods. Again, they say that-that thing is not good which it is possible to use both well and ill. But it is possible to make either a good or a bad use of wealth, or of health; therefore, wealth and good health are not goods. Posidonius, however, affirms that these things do come under the head of goods. But Hecaton, in the nineteenth book of his treatise on Goods, and Chrysippus, in his treatises on Pleasure, both deny that pleasure is a good. For they say that there are disgraceful pleasures, and that nothing disgraceful is good. And that to benefit a person is to move him or to keep him according to virtue, but to injure him is to move him or to keep him according to vice.

They also assert, that things indifferent are so spoken of in a twofold manner; firstly, those things are called so, which have no influence in producing either happiness or unhappiness; such for instance, as riches, glory, health, strength, and the like; for it is possible for a man to be happy without any of these things; and also, it is upon the character of the use that is made of them, that happiness or unhappiness depends. In another sense, those things are called indifferent, which do not exite any inclination or aversion, as for instance, the fact of a man's having an odd or an even number of hairs on his head, or his putting out or drawing back his finger; for it is not in this sense that the things previously mentioned are called indifferent, for they do excite inclination or aversion. On which account some of them are chosen, though there is equal reason for preferring or shunning all the others.

LXI. Again, of things indifferent, they call some preferred (goijjTiEva), and others rejected (dTocrgojjy/isva). Those are preferred, which have some proper value (af/av), and those are rejected, which have no value at all ctTaiav iyp-tra). And by the term proper value, they mean that quality of things, which causes them to concur in producing a well-regulated life; and in this sense, every good has a proper value. Again, they say that a thing has value, when in some point of view, it has a sort of intermediate power of aiding us to live conformably to nature; and under this class, we may range riches or good health, if they give any assistance to natural life. Again, value is predicated of the price which one gives for the attainment of an object, which some one, who has experience of)the object sought, fixes as its fair price; as if we were to say, for instance, that as some wheat was to be exchanged for barley, with a mule thrown in to make up the difference. Those goods then are preferred, which have a value, as in the case of the mental goods, ability, skill, improvement, and the like; and in the case of the corporeal goods, life, health, strength, a good constitution, soundness, beauty; and,in the case of external goods, riches, glory, nobility of birth, and the like.

Rejected things are, in the case of qualities of the mind, stupidity, unskilfulness, and the like; in the case of circumstances affecting the body, death, disease, weakness, a bad constitution, mutilation, disgrace, and the like; in the case of external circumstances, poverty, want of reputation, ignoble birth, and the like. But those qualities and circumstances which are indifferent, are neither preferred nor rejected. Again, of things preferred, some are preferred for their own sakes, some for the sake of other things, and some partly for their own sakes and partly for that of other things. Those which are preferred for their own sakes, are ability, improvement, and the like; those which are preferred for the sake of other things, are wealth, nobility of birth, and the like; those which are preferred partly for their own sake, and partly for that of something else, are strength, vigour of the senses, universal soundness, and the like; for they are preferred, for their own sakes, inasmuch as they are in accordance with nature; and for the sake of something else, inasmuch as they are productive of no small number of advantages; and the same is the case in the inverse ratio, with those things which are rejected.

LXII. Again, they say that that is duty, which is preferred, and which contains in itself reasonable arguments why we should prefer it; as for instance, its corresponding to the nature of life itself; and this argument extends to plants and animals, for even their nature is subject to the obligation of certain duties. And duty (rJ *xotSfixov*) had this name given to it by Zeno, in the first instance, its appellation being derived from its coming to, or according to some people, *ajrb rou xara rivag qxiiv;* and its effect is something kindred to the preparations made by nature. Now of the things done according to inclination, some are duties, and some are contrary to duty; and some are neither duties nor contrary to duty, Those are duties, which reason selects to do, as for instance, to honour one's parents, one's brothers, one's country, to gratify one's frieuds. Those actions are contrary to duty, which reason does not choose; as for instance, to neglect one's parents, to be indifferent to one's brothers, to shirk assisting one's friends, to be careless about the welfare of one's country, and so on. Those are neither duties, nor contrary to duty, which reason neither selects to do, nor, on the other hand, repudiates, such actions, for instance, as to pick up straw, to hold a pen, or a comb, or things of that sort.

Again, there are some duties which do not depend on circumstances, and some which do. These do not depend on circumstances, to take care of one's health, and of the sound state of one's senses, and the like. Those which do depend on circumstances, are the mutilation of one's members, the sacrificing of one's property, and so on. And the case of those actions which are contrary to duty, is similar. Again, of duties, some are always such, and some are not always. What is always a duty, is to live in accordance with virtue; but to ask questions, to give answers, to walk, and the like, are not always duties. And the same statement holds good with respect to acts contrary to duty.

There is also a class of intermediate duties, such as the duty of boys obeying their masters.

LXIII. The Stoics also say that the mind is divisible into eight parts; for that the five organs of sensation, and the vocal power, and the intellectual power, which is the mind itself, and the generative power, are all parts of the mind. But by error, there is produced a perversion which operates on the intellect, from which many perturbations arise, and many causes of inconstancy. And all perturbation is itself, according to Zeno, a movement of the mind, or superfluous inclination, which is irrational, and contrary to nature. Moreover, of the.'superior class of perturbations, as Hecaton says, in the second book of his treatise on the Passions, and as Zeno also says in his work on the Passions, there are four kinds, grief, fear, desire, and pleasure. And they consider that these perturbations are judgments, as Chrysippus contends in his work on the Passions; for covetousness is an opinion that money is a beautiful object, and in like manner drunkenness and intemperance, and other things of the sort, are judgments. And grief they define to be an irrational contraction of the mind, and it is divided into the following species, pity, envy, emulation, jealousy, pain, perturbation, sorrow, anguish, confusion. Pity is a grief over some one, on the ground of his being in undeserved distress. Envy is a grief, at the good fortune of another. Emulation is a grief at that belonging to some one else, which one desires one's self. Jealousy is a grief at another also having what one has one's self. Pain is a grief which weighs one down. Perturbation is grief which narrows one, and causes one to feel in a strait. Sorrow is a grief arising from deliberate thought, which endures for some time, and gradually increases. Anguish is a grief with'acute pain. Confusion is an irrational grief, which frets one, and prevents otfe from clearly discerning present circumstances'. But fear is the expectation of evil; and the following feelings are all classed under the head of fear: apprehension, hesitation, shame, perplexity, trepidation, and anxiety. Apprehension is a fear which produces alarm. Shame is a fear of discredit. Hesitation is a fear of coming activity. Perplexity is a fear, from the imagination of some unusual thing. Trepidation is a fear accompanied with an oppression of the voice. Anxiety is a fear of some uncertain event.

Again, desire is an irrational appetite; to which head, the following feelings are referrible: want, hatred, contentiousness, anger, love, enmity, rage. Want is a desire arising from our not having something or other, and is, as it were, separated from the thing, but is still stretching, and attracted towards it in vain. And hatred is a desire that it should be ill with some one, accompanied with a certain continual increase and extension. Contentiousness is a certain desire accompanied with deliberate choice. Anger is a desire of revenge, on a person who appears to have injured one in an unbecoming way. Love is a desire not conversant about a virtuous object, for it is an attempt to conciliate affection, because of some beauty which is seen. Enmity is a certain anger of long duration, and full of hatred, and it is a watchful passion, as is shown in the following lines:—

For though we deem the short-liv'd fury past,
'Tis sure the mighty will revenge at last.
Horn II. I. 81. Popes Version, 1.105.

But rage is anger at its commencement.

Again, pleasure is an irrational elation of the mind over something which appears to be desirable; and its different species are enjoyment, rejoicing at evil, delight, and extravagant joy. Enjoyment now, is a pleasure which charms the " mind through the ears. Rejoicing at evil *(imaixaxid)*, is a pleasure which arises at the misfortunes of others. Delight *(rig-ig.)* that is to say turning (rgl-vj//s), is a certain turning of the soul (fl-goT-giwrij *rig-urn)*, to softness. Extravagant joy is the dissolution of virtue. And as there are said to be some sicknesses (Kgiwffraj-a,)in the body, as, for instance, gout and arthritic disorders; so too are those diseases of the soul, such as a fondness for glory, or for pleasure, and other feelings of that sort. For an *auerri/ia.* is a disease accompanied with weakness; and a disease is an opinion of something which appears exceedingly desirable. And, as in the case of the body, there are illnesses to which people are especially liable, such ascolds or diarrhoea; so also are there propensities which the mind is under the influence of, such as enviousness, pitifulness, quarrelsomeness, and so on.

There are also three good dispositions of the mind; joy, caution, and will. And joy they say is the opposite of pleasure, since it is a rational elation of the mind; so caution is the opposite of fear, being a rational avoidance of anything, for the wise man will never be afraid, but he will act with caution; and will, they define as the opposite of desire, since it is a rational wish. As therefore some things fall under the class of the first perturbations, in the same manner do some things fall under the class of the first good dispositions. And accordingly, under the head of will, are classed goodwill, placidity, salutation, affection; and under the head of caution are ranged reverence and modesty; under the head of joy, we speak of delight, mirth, and good spirits.

LXIV. They say also, that the wise man is free from perturbations, because he has no strong propensities. But that this freedom from propensities also exists in the bad man, being, however, then quite another thing, inasmuch as it proceeds in him only from the hardness and unimpressibility of his nature. They also pronounce the wise man free from vanity, since he regards with equal eye what is glorious and what is inglorious. At the same time, they admit that there is another character devoid of vanity, who, however, is only reckoned one of the rash men, being in fact the bad man. They also say that all the virtuous men are austere, because they do never,, speak with reference to pleasure, nor do they listen to what is said by others with reference to pleasure. At the same time, they call another man austere too, using the term in nearly the same sense as they do when they speak of austere wine, which is used in compounding medicines, but not for drinking.

TheyWso pronounce the wise to be honest-hearted men, anxiouslyattending to those matters which may make them better, by means of some principle which conceals what is bad, and brings to light what is good. Nor is there any hypocrisy about them; for they cut off all pretence in their voice and appearance. They also keep aloof from business;

for they guard carefully against doing any thing contrary to their duty. They drink wine, but they do not get drunk; and they never yield to frenzy. Occasionally, extraordinary imaginations may obtain a momentary power over them, owing to some melancholy or trifling, arising not according to the principle of what is desirable, but contrary to nature. Nor, again, will the wise man feel grief; because grief is an irrational contraction of the soul, as Apollodorus defines it in his Ethics.

They are also,-as they say, godlike; for they have something in them which is as it were a God. But the bad man is an atheist. Now there are two kinds of atheists; one who speaks in a spirit of hostility to, and the other, who utterly disregards, the divine nature; but they admit that all bad men are not atheists in this last sense. The good, on the contrary, are pious; for they have a thorough acquaintance with the laws respecting the Gods. And piety is a knowledge of the proper reverence and worship due to the Gods. Moreover they sacrifice to the Gods, and keep themselves pure; for they avoid all offences having reference to the Gods, and the Gods admire them; for they are holy and just in all that concerns the Deity; and the wise men are the only priests; for they consider the matters relating to sacrifices, and the erection of temples, and purifications, and all other things which peculiarly concern the Gods. They also pronounce that men are bound to honour their parents, and their brethren, in the second place after the Gods. They also say that parental affection for one's children is natural to them, and is a feeling which does not exist in bad men. And they lay down the position that all offences are equal, as Chrysippus argues in the fourth book of his Ethic Questions, and so say Persaeus and Zeno. For if one thing that is true is not more true than another thing that is true, neither is one thing that is false more false than another thing that is false; so too, one deceit is not greater than another, nor one sin than another. For the man who is a hundred furlongs from Canopus, and the man who is only one, are both equally not in Canopus; and so too, he who commits a greater sin, and he who commits a less, are both equally not in the right path.

Heraclides of Tarsus, indeed, the friend of Antipater, of Tarsus, and Athenodorus, both assert that offences are not equal.

Again, the Stoics, as for instance, Chrysippus, in the first book of his work on Lives, say, that the wise man will take a part in the affairs of the state, if nothing hinders him. For that he will restrain vice, and excite men to virtue. Also, they say that he will marry, as Zeno says, in his Republic, and beget children. Moreover, that the wise man will never form mere opinions, that is to say, he will never agree to anything that is false; and that he will become a Cynic; for that Cynicism is a short path to virtue, as Apollodorus calls it in his Ethics; that he will even eat human flesh, if there should be occasion; that he is the only free man, and that the bad are slaves; for that freedom is a power of independent action, but slavery a deprivation of the same. That there is besides, another slavery, which consists in subjection, and a third which consists in possession and subjection; the contrary of which is masterhood, which is likewise bad.

And they say, that not only are the wise free, but that they are also kings, since kingly power is an irresponsible dominion, which can only exist in the case of the wise man, as Chrysippus says in his treatise on the Proper Application of his Terms made by Zeno; for he says that a ruler ought to give decisions on good and evil, and that none of the wicked understand these things. In the same way, they assert that they are the only people who are fit to be magistrates or judges, or orators, and that none of the bad are qualified for these tasks. Moreover, that they are free from all error, in consequence of their not being prone to any wrong actions. Also, that they are unconnected with injury, for that they never injure any one else, nor themselves. Also, that they are not pitiful, and that they never make allowance for any one; for that they do not relax the punishments appointed by law, since yielding, and pity, and mercifulness itself, never exist in any of their souls, so as to induce an affectation of kindness in respect of punishment; nor do they ever think any punishment too severe. Again, they say that the wise man never wonders at any of the things which appear extraordinary; as for instance, at the stories about Charon, or the ebbing of the tide, or the springs of hot water, or the bursting forth of flames. But, say they further, the wise man will not live in solitude; for he is by nature sociable and practical. Accordingly, he will take exercise for the sake of hardening and invigorating his body. And the wise man will pray, asking good things from the Gods, as Posidonius says in the first book of his treatise on Duties, and Hecaton says the same thing in the thirteenth book of his treatise on Extraordinary Things.

They also say, that friendship exists in the virtuous alone, on account of their resemblance to one another. And they describe friendship itself as a certain communiou of the things which concern life, since we use our friends as ourselves. And they assert that a friend is desirable for his own sake, and that a number of friends is a good; and that among the wicked there is no such thing as friendship, and that no wicked man can have a friend.

Again, they say that all the foolish are mad; for that they are not prudent, and that madness is equivalent to folly in every one of its actions; but that the wise man does everything properly, just as we say that Ismenias can play every piece of flute-music well. Also, they say that everything belongs to the wise man, for that the law has given them perfect and universal power; but some things also are said to belong to the wicked, just in the same manner as some things are said to belong to the unjust, or as a house is said to belong to a city in a different sense from that in which a thing belongs to the person who uses it.

LXV. And they say that virtues reciprocally follow one another, and that he who has one has all; for that the precepts of them all are common, as

Chrysippus affirms in the first book of his treatise on Laws; and Apollodorus, in his Natural Philosophy, according to the ancient system; and Hecaton, in the third book of his treatise on Virtues. For they say that the man who is endued with virtue, is able to consider and also to do what must be done. But what must be done must be chosen, and encountered, and distributed, and awaited; so that if the man does some things by deliberate choice, and some in a spirit of endurance, and some distributively, and some patiently; he is prudent, and courageous, and just, and temperate. And each of the virtues has a particular subject of its own, about which it is conversant; as, for instance, courage is conversant about the things which must be endured; prudence is conversant about what must be done and what must not, and what is of a neutral or indifferent character. And in like manner, the other virtues are conversant about their own peculiar subjects; and wisdom in counsel and shrewdness follow prudence; and good order and decorum follow temperance; and equality and goodness of judgment follow justice; and constancy and energy follow courage.

Another doctrine of the Stoics is, that there is nothing intermediate between virtue and vice; while the Peripatetics assert that there is a stage between virtue and vice, being an improvement on vice which has not yet arrived at virtue. For the Stoics say, that as a stick must be either straight or crooked, so a man must be either just or unjust, and cannot be more just than just, or more unjust than unjust; and that the same rule applies to all cases. Moreover, Chrysippus is of opinion that virtue can be lost, but Cleanthes affirms that it cannot; the one saying that it can be lost by drunkenness or melancholy, the other maintaining that it cannot be lost on account of the firm perceptions which it implants in men. They also pronounce it a proper object of choice; accordingly, we are ashamed of actions which we do improperly, while we are aware that what is honourable is the only good. Again, they affirm that it is of itself sufficient for happiness, as Zeno says, and he is followed in this assertion by Chrysippus in the first book of his treatise on Virtues, and by Hecaton in the second book of his treatise on Goods.

" For if," says he, " magnanimity be sufficient of itself to enable us to act in a manner superior to all other men; and if that is a part of virtue, then virtue is of itself sufficient for happiness, despising all things which seem troublesome to it." However, Panaetius and Posidonius do not admit that virtue has this sufficiency of itself, but say that there is also need of good health, and competency, and strength. And their opinion is that a man exercises virtue in everything, as Cleanthes asserts, for it cannot be lost; and the virtuous man on every occasion exercises his soul, which is in a state of perfection.

LXVI. Again, they say that justice exists by nature, and not because of any definition or principle; just as law does, or right reason, as Chrysippus tells us in his treatise on the Beautiful; and they think that one ought not to abandon philosophy on account of the different opiniqns prevailing among philosophers, since on this principle one would wholly quit life, as Posidonius argues in his Exhortatory Essays. Another doctrine of Chrysyppus is, that general learning is very useful.

And the School in general maintain that there are no obligations of justice binding on us with reference to other animals, on account of their dissimilarity to us, as Chrysippus asserts in the first book of his treatise on Justice, and the same opinion is maintained by Posidonius in the first book of his treatise on Duty. They say too, that the wise man will love those young men, who by their outward appearance, show a natural aptitude for virtue; and this opinion is advanced by Zeno, in his Republic, and by Chrysippus in the first book of his work on Lives, and by Apollodorus in his Ethics. And they describe love as an endeavour to benefit a friend on account of his visible beauty; and that it is an attribute not of acquaintanceship, but of friendship. Accordingly, that Thrasmides, although he had his mistress in his power, abstained from her, because he was hated by her. Love, therefore, according to them is a part of friendship, as Chrysippus asserts in his essay on Love; and it is not blameable. Moreover, beauty is the flower of virtue.

And as there are three kinds of lives; the theoretical, the practical, and the logical; they say that the last is the one which ought to be chosen. For that a logical, that is a rational, animal was made by nature on purpose for speculation and action. And they say that a wise man will very rationally take himself out of life, either for the sake of his country or of his friends, or if he be in bitter pain, or under the affliction of mutilation, or incurable disease. And they also teach that women ought to be in common among the wise, so that whoever meets with any one may enjoy her, and this doctrine is maintained by Zeno in his Republic, and by Chrysippus in his treatise on Polity, and by Diogenes the Cynic, and by Plato; and then, say they, we shall love all boys equally after the manner of fathers, and all suspicion on the ground of undue familiarity will be removed.

They affirm too, that the best of political constitutions is a mixed one, combined of democracy, and kingly power, and aristocracy. And they say many things of this sort, and more too, in their Ethical Dogmas, and they maintain them by suitable explanations and arguments. But this may be enough for us to say of their doctrines on this head by way of summary, and taking them in an elementary manner.

LXVII. They divide natural philosophy into the topics of bodies, and of principles, and of elements, and of GodSj. and of boundaries, and of place, and of the vacuum. And they make these divisions according to species; but according to genera they divide them into three topics, that of the world, that of the elements, and the third is that which reasons on causes. The topic about the world, they say, is subdivided into two parts. For that in one point of view, the mathematicians also have a share in it; and according to it it is that they prosecute their investigations into the nature of the fixed stars and the planets; as, for instance, whether the sun is of such a size as he appears to be, and similarly, whether the moon is; and in the same way they investigate the question of spherical motion, and others of the same character. The other point of view is that which is reserved exclusively for natural philosophers, according to which it is that the existence and substance of things are examined, for instance, whether the sun and the stars consist of matter and form, and whether the sun is born or not born, whether it is living or lifeless, corruptible or incorruptible, whether it is regulated by Providence, and other questions of this kind.

The topic which examines into causes they say is also divisible into two parts; and with reference to one of its considerations, the investigations of physicians partake of it; according to which it is that they investigate the dominant principle of the soul, and the things which exist in the soul, and seeds, and things of this kind. And its other division is claimed as belonging to them also by the mathematicians, as, for instance, how we see, what is the cause of our appearance being reflected in a mirror, how clouds are collected, how thunder is produced, and the rainbow, and the halo, and comets, and things of that kind.

LXVIII. They think that there are two general principles in the universe, the active and the passive. That the passive is matter, an existence without any distinctive quality. That the active is the reason which exists in the passive, that is to say, God. For that he, being eternal, and existing throughout all matter, makes everything. And Zeno, the Cittiaean, lays down this doctrine in his treatise on Essence, and so does Cleanthes in his essay on Atoms, Chrysippus in the first book of his Investigations in Natural Philosophy, towards the end, Archedemus in his work on Elements, and Posidonius in the second book of his treatise on Natural Philosophy. But they say that principles and elements differ from one another. For that the one had no generation or beginning, and will have no end; but that the elements may be destroyed by the operation of fire. Also, that the elements are bodies, but principles have no bodies and no forms, and elements too have forms.

Now a body, says Apollodorus in his Natural Philosophy, is extended in a threefold manner; in length, in breadth, in depth; and then it is called a solid body; and the superficies is the limit of the body having length and breadth alone, but not depth. But Posidonius, in the third book of his Heavenly Phaenomeua, will not allow a superficies either any substantial reality, or any intelligible existence. A line is the limit of a superficies, or length without breadth, or something which has, nothing but length. A point is the boundary of a line, and is the smallest of all symbols.

They also teach that God is unity, and that he is called Mind, and Fate, and Jupiter, and by many other names besides. And that, as he was in the beginning by himself, he turned into water the whole substance which pervaded the air; and as the seed is contained in the produce, so too, he being the seminal principle of the world, remained behind in moisture, making matter fit to be employed by himself in the production of those things which were to come after; and then, first of all, he made the four elements, fire, water, air, and earth. And Zeno speaks of these in his treatise on the Universe, and so does Chrysippus in the first book of his Physics, and so does Archedemus in some treatise on the Elements.

LXIX. Now an element is that out of which at first all things which are are produced, and into which all things are resolved at last. And the four elements are all equally an essence without any distinctive quality, namely, matter; but fire is the hot, water the moist, air the cold, and earth the dry —though this last quality is also common to the air. The fire is the highest, and that is called aether, in which first of all the sphere was generated in which the fixed stars are set, then that in which the planets revolve; after that the air, then the water; and the sediment as it were of all is the earth, which is placed in the centre of the rest.

LXX. They also speak of the world in a threefold sense; at one time meaning God himself, whom they call a being of a certain quality, having for his peculiar manifestation universal substance, a being imperishable, and who never had any generation, being the maker of the arrangement and order that we see; and who, after certain periods of time, absorbs all substance in himself, and then re-produces it from himself. And this arrangement of the stars they call the world, and so the third sense is one composed of both the preceding ones. And the world is a thing which is peculiarly of such and such a quality consisting of universal substance, as Posidonius affirms in his Meteorological Elements, being a system compounded of heaven and earth, and all the creatures which exist in them; or it may be called a system compounded of Gods and men, and of the things created on their account. And the heaven is the most remote circumference of the world, in which all the Divine Nature is situated.

Again, the world is inhabited and regulated according to intellect and providence, as Chrysippus says, in his works on Providence, and Posidonius in the thirteenth book of his treatise on Gods, since mind penetrates into every part of the world, just as the soul pervades us; but it is in a greater degree in some parts, and in a less degree in others. For instance, it penetrates as a habit, as, for instance, into the bones and sinews; and into some it penetrates as the mind does, for instance, into the dominant principle. And thus the whole world, being a living thing, endowed with a soul and with reason, has the aether as its dominant principle, as Antipater, of Tyre, says in the eighth book of his treatise on the World. But Chrysippus, in the first book of his essay on Providence, and Posidonius in his treatise on Gods, say that the heaven is the dominant principle of the world; and Cleanthes attributes this to the sun. Chrysippus, however, on this point contradicts himself; for he says in another place, that the most subtle portion of the aether, which is also called by the Stoics the first God, is what is infused in a sensible manner into all the beings which are in the air, and through every animal and every plant, and through the earth itself according to a certain habit; and that it is this which communicates to them the faculty of feeling.

They say too, that the world is one and also finite, having a spherical form. For that such a shape is the most convenient for motion, as Posidonius says, in the fifteenth book of his Discussions on Natural Philosophy, and so says Antipater also in his essay on the World. And on the outside there is diffused around it a boundless vacuum, which is incorporeal. And it is incorporeal inasmuch, as it is capable of being contained by bodies, but is not so. And that there is no such thing as a vacuum in the world, but that it is all closely united and compact; for that this condition is necessarily brought about by the concord and harmony which exist between the heavenly bodies and those of the earth. And Chrysippus mentions a vacuum in his essay on a Vacuum, and also in the first book of his treatise on the Physical Arts, and so does Apollophanes in his Natural Philosophy, and so does-Apollodorus, and so does Posidonius in the second book of his discourses on Natural Philosophy. And they say that these things are all incorporeal, and all alike. Moreover, that time is incorporeal, since it is an interval of the motion of the world. And that of time, the past and the future are both illimitable, but the present is limited. And they assert that the world is perishable, inasmuch as it was produced by reason, and is one of the things which are perceptible by the senses; and whatever has its parts perishable, must also be perishable in the whole. And the parts of the world are perishable, for they change into one another. Therefore, the whole world is perishable. And again, if anything admits of a change for the worse it is perishable; therefore, the world is perishable, for it can be dried up, and it can be covered with water.

Now the world was created when its substance was changed from fire to moisture, by the action of the air; and then its denser parts coagulated, and so the earth was made, and the thinner portions were evaporated and became air; and this being rarefied more and more, produced fire. And then, by the combination of all these elements, were produced plants and animals, and other kinds of things. Now Zeno speaks of the creation, and of the destruction of the world, in his treatise on the Universe, and so does Cleanthes, and so does Antipater, in the tenth book of his treatise on the World. But Panaetius asserts that the world is imperishable.

Again, that the world is an animal, and that it is endued with reason, and life, and intellect, is affirmed by Chrysippus, in the first volume of his treatise on Providence, and by Apollodorus in his Natural Philosophy, and by Posidonius; and that it is an animal in this sense, as being an essence endued with life, and with sensation. For that which is an animal, is better than that which is not an animal. But nothing is better than the world; therefore the world is an animal. And it is endued with life, as is plain from the fact of our own soul being as it were a fragment broken off from it. But Boethus denies that the world is an animal.

Again, that the world is one, is affirmed by Zeno, in his treatise on the Universe, and by Chrysippus, and by Apollodorus, in his Natural Philosophy, and by Posidonius, in the first book of his Discourses on Natural Philosophy. And by the term, the universe, according to Apollodorus, is understood both the world itself, and also the whole of the world itself, and of the exterior vacuum taken together. The world, then, is finite, and the vacuum infinite.

LXXI. Of the stars, those which are fixed are only moved in connection with the movements of the entire heaven; but the planets move according to their own peculiar and separate motions. And the sun takes an oblique path through the circle of the zodiac, and in the same manner also does the moon, which is of a winding form. And the sun is pure fire, as Posidonius asserts in the seventh book of his treatise on the Heavenly Bodies, and it is larger than the earth, as the same author informs us, in the sixteenth book of his Disclosures on Natural Philosophy. Also it is spherical, as he says in another place, being made on the same principle as the world is. Therefore it is fire, because it performs all the functions of fire. And it is larger than the earth, as is proved by the fact of the whole earth being illuminated by it, and also the whole heaven. Also the fact of the earth throwing a conical shadow, proves that the sun is greater than it; and the sun is seen in every part, because of its magnitude. But the moon is of a more earthy nature than the sun, inasmuch as it is nearer the earth.

Moreover, they say that all these fiery bodies, and all the other stars, receive nutriment; the sun from the vast sea, being a sort of intellectual appendage; and the moon from the fresh waters, being mingled with the air, and also near the earth, as Posidonius explains it in the sixth book of his Discourses on Natural Philosophy. And all the other stars derive their nourishment from the earth. They also consider that the stars are of a spherical figure, and that the earth is immovable. And that the moon has not a light of her own, but that she borrows it from the sun. And that the sun is eclipsed, when the moon runs in front of it on the side towards us, as Zeno describes in his work on the Universe; for when it comes across it in its passage, it conceals it, and again it reveals it; and this is a phenomenon easily seen in a basin of water. And the moon is eclipsed when it comes below the shadow of the earth, on which account this never happens, except at the time of the full moon; and although it is diametrically opposite to the sun every month, still it is not eclipsed every month, because when its motions are obliquely towards the sun, it does not find itself in the same place as the sun, being either a little more to the north, or a little more to the south. When therefore it is found in the same place with the sun, and with the other intermediate objects, then it takes as it were the diameter of the sun, and is eclipsed. And its place is along the line which runs between the crab and the scorpion, and the ram and the bull, as Posidonius tells us.

LXXII. They also say that God is an animal immortal, rational, perfect, and intellectual in his happiness, unsusceptible of any kind of evil, having a foreknowledge of the world and of all that is in the world; however, that he has not the figure of a man; and that he is the creator of the universe, and as it were, the Father of all things in common, and that a portion of him pervades everything, which is called hy different names, according to its powers; for they call him A/a as being the person *(di h)* everything is, and Zjjva, inasmuch as he is the cause of life, (rou *Zjjv),* or because he pervades life. And *'AOriva,* with reference to the extension of his dominant power over the aether *(iig ald'soa).* And "Hga, on account of his extension through the air *(tig* dlga). And *'Hpaierog,* on account of his pervading fire, which is the chief instrument of art; and *Tloeii&w,* as pervading moisture, and Aj,ajjr»jg, as pervading the earth (r»i). And in the same way, regarding some other of his peculiar attributes, they have given him other names.

The substance of God is asserted by Zeno to be the universal world, and the heaven; and Chrysippus agrees with this doctrine, in his eleventh book on the Gods; and so also does Posidonius, in the first book of his treatise on the same subject. Antipater, in the seventh book of his treatise on the World, says that his substance is aerial. And Boethus, in his treatise on Nature, calls the substance of God the sphere of the fixed stars.

LXXEII. And his nature they define to be, that which keeps the world together, and sometimes that which produces the things upon the earth. And nature is a habit which derives its movements from itself, perfecting and holding together all that arises out of it, according to the principles of production, in certain definite periods, and doing the same as the things from which it is separated. And it has for its object, suitableness and pleasure, as is plain from its having created man. LXXIV. But Chrysippus, in his treatise on Fate, and Posidonius, in the second book of his work on Fate, and Zeno, and Boethus, in the eleventh book of his treatise on Fate, say, that all things are produced by fate. And fate, It is hardly necessary to remark that 'A0t)va is the name of Minerva, not of Jupiter; "Hpa, of Juno; "Hatoroe, of Vulcan; *HoaeiSuiv,* of Neptune, and Aityxjjrijp, of Ceres. "Hnurroj is properly derived from *faivw,* to shine; *IlootiSwv* has some affinity with jro(o, to drink. *AiifitTt)p* is only a dialectic variation of Tij *firjTrjp* (s/'/iag/ilv»)), is a connected (s/go/isvij) cause of existing things, or the reason according to which the world is regulated. LXXV. They also say that divination has a universal existence, since Providence has; and they define it as an act on account of certain results, as Zeno and Chrysippus, in the second book of his treatise on Divination, and Athenodorus and Posidonius, in the twelfth book of his discourses on Natural Philosophy, and in the fifth book of his treatise on Divination, all agree in saying; for Panaetius denies that it has any certain foundation. LXXVI. And they say that the substance of all existing things is Primary Matter, as Chrysippus asserts in the first book of his Physics; and Zeno says the same. Now matter is that from which anything whatever is produced. And it is called by a twofold appellation, essence and matter; the one as relating to all things taken together, and the other to things in particular and separate. The one which relates to all things taken together, never becomes either greater or less; but the one relating to things in particular, does become greater or less, as the case may be. LXXVII. Body is, according to them, a substance and finite; as Antipater says, in the second book of his treatise on Substance; and Apollodorus, in his Natural Philosophy, agrees with him. It is also subject to change, as we learn from the same author; for if it were immutable, then the things which have been produced out of it would not have been produced; on which account he also says that it is infinitely divisible: but Chrysippus denies that it is infinite; for that nothing is infinite, which is divisible at all. LXXVIII. He admits, however, that it is infinitely divisible, and that its concretions take place over the whole of it, as he explains in the third book of his Physics, and not according to any circumference or juxtaposition; for a little wine when thrown into the sea, will keep its distinctness for a brief period, but after that, will be lost. LXXIX. They also say that there are some Daemones, who have a sympathy with mankind, being surveyors of all human affairs; and that there are heroes, which are the souls of virtuous men, which have left their bodies. LXXX. Of the things which take place in the air, they say that winter is the effect of the air above the earth being cooled, on account of the retirement of the sun to a greater distance than before; that spring is a good temperature of the air, according to the sun's approach towards us; that summer is the effect of the air above the earth being warmed by the approach of the sun towards the north; that autumn is caused by the retreat of the sun from us. to those places from which they flow. LXXXI. And the cause of the production of the winds is the sun, which evaporates the clouds. Moreover, the rainbow is the reflexion of the sun's rays from the moist clouds, or, as Posidouius explains it in his Meteorology, a manifestation of a section of the sun or moon, in a cloud suffused with dew; being hollow and continuous to the sight; so that it is reflected as in a mirror, under the appearance of a circle. And that comets, and bearded stars, and meteors, are fires which have an existence when the density of the air is borne upwards to the regions of the aether.

That a ray of light is a kindling of sudden fire, borne through the air with great rapidity, and displaying an appearance of length; that rain proceeds from the clouds, being a transformation of them into water, whenever the moisture which is caught up from the earth or from the sea, by the sun, is not able to be otherwise disposed of; for when it is solidified, it is then called hoarfrost. And hail is a cloud congealed, and subsequently dispersed by the wind. Snow is moisture from a congealed cloud, as Posidonius tells us in the eighth book of his discourse on Natural Philosophy. Lightning is a kindling of the clouds from their being rubbed together, or else broken asunder by the wind, as Zeno tells us in his treatise on the Universe; and thunder is the noise made by them on the occasion of their being rubbed together or broken asunder; and the thunderbolt is a sudden kindling which falls with great violence on the earth, from the clouds being rubbed together or broken asunder, or, as others say, it is a conversion of fiery air violently brought down to the earth. A typhon is a vast thunderbolt, violent and full of wind, or a smoky breath of a cloud broken asunder. A *irgtierrn* is a cloud There is a'hiatus in the text here. Casaubon supplies the meaning by a reference to Plutarch's Treatise on the opinions of the Philosophers, iii. 7, " that the winds are a flowing of the air, and that they have various names with reference to the countries from which they flow." rent by fire, with wind, into the hollows of the earth, or when the wind is pent up in the earth, as Posidonius says in his eighth book; and that sone of them are shakings, others rendings, others emissions of fire, and others, instances of violent fermentation.

LXXXII. They also think that the general arrangement of the world is in this fashion; that the earth is in the middle, occupying the place of the centre; next to which comes the water, of a spherical form; and having the same centre as the earth; so that the earth is in the water; and next to the water comes the air, which has also a spherical form. LXXXIII. And that there are five circles in the heaven; of which the first is the arctic circle, which is always visible; the second is the tropical summer circle; the third is the equinoctial circle; the fourth, the winter tropical circle; and the fifth the antarctic, which is not visible. And they are called parallel, because they do not incline to one another; they are drawn however around the same centre. But the zodiac is oblique, cutting the parallel circles. There are also five zones on the earth; the first is the northern one, placed under the arctic circle, uninhabitable by reason of the cold; The second is temperate; the third is uninhabitable because of the heat, and is called the torrid zone; the fourth is a temperate zone, on the other side of the torrid zone; the fifth is the southern zone, being also uninhabitable by reason of the cold.t LXXXIV. Another of their doctrines is that nature is an artificial fire tending by a regular road to production, which is a fiery kind of breath proceeding according to art. Also, that the soul is sensible, and that it is a spirit which is born with us; consequently it is a body and continues to exist after death; that nevertheless it is perishable. But that the soul of the universe is imperishable, and that the souls which exist in animals are only parts of that of the universe. But Zeno, the Cittiaean, and Antipater, in their treatise concerning the Something is evidently wanting here; probably some mention of an earthquake. t This is similar to Virgil's description.

Quinque tenent coelum zonae, quarum una cornsco

Semper Sole rubens, et torrida semper ab igni:

Quam circum extremae dextra Uevaque trahuntur,

Soul, and Posidonius also, all say that the soul is a warm spirit; for that by it we have our breath, and by it we are moved. Cleanthes, accordingly, asserts that all souls continue to exist till they are burnt up; but Chrysippus says that it is only the souls of the wise that endure. And they further teach that there are eight parts of the soul; the five senses, and the generative faculties, and voice, and reason. And we see because of a body of luminous air which extends from the organ of sight to the object in a conical form, as it is asserted by Chrysippus, in the second, book of his Natural Philosophy, and also by Apollodorus. And the apex of this cone is close to the eye, and its base is formed by the object which is seen; so that that which is seen is as it were reported to the eye by this continuous cone of air extended towards it like a staff. In the same way, we hear because the air between the speaker and the hearer is struck in a spherical manner; and is then agitated in waves, resembling the circular eddies which one sees in a cistern when a stone is dropped into it.

Sleep, they say, is produced by a relaxation of the aesthetic energies with reference to the dominant part of the soul. And the causes of the passions they explain to be the motions and conversions which take place in connection with this spirit or soul.

LXXXV. Seed, they define as a thing of a nature capable of producing other things of the same nature as the thing from which it has been separated. And the seed of man, which man emits, is, together with moisture, mixed up with the parts of the soul by that kind of mixture which corre

Coerulea glacie concrete atque imbribus atris. Has inter mediamque duae mortalibus aegris Munere eonoeasse Divum, et via secta per ambas, Obliquus qua se signorum verteret ordo.—Georq. I. 233. There is no part of Dryden's translation superior to that of this passage.

Five girdles bind the skies; the torrid zone

Glows with the passing and repassing sun;

Far on the right and left, th' extremes of heaven,

To frosts, and snows, and bitter blasts are given;

Betwixt the midst. And there the Gods assigned

Four habitable seats for human kind,

And cross their limits cut a sloping way,

Which the twelve signs in beauteous order sway. L 322.

sponds to the capacity of the parents. And Chrysippus says, in the second book of his Natural Philosophy, that it is a spirit according to substance; as is manifest from the seeds which are planted in the earth; and which, if they are old, do not germinate, because all their virtue has evaporated. And Sphaerus says, that seed proceeds from the entire body, and that that is how it is that it produces all the parts of the body.

They also say that the seed of the female is unproductive; for, as Sphaerus says, it is devoid of tone, and small in quantity, and watery.

LXXXVI. They also say that that is the dominant part of the soul which is its most excellent part; in which the imaginations and the desires are formed, and whence reason proceeds. And this place is in the heart.

These then are the doctrines on the subject of natural philosophy entertained by them, which it seems sufficient for us to detail, having regard to the due proportions of this book. And the following are the points in which some of them disagreed with the rest.

LIFE OF ARISTON. '

I. Aeiston the Bald, a native of Chios, surnamed the Scion, said, that the chief good was to live in perfect indifference to all those things which are of an intermediate character between virtue and vice; making not the slightest difference between them, but regarding them all on a footing of equality. For that the wise man resembles a good actor; who, whether he is filling the part of Agamemnon or Thersites, will perform them both equally well.

II. And he discarded altogether the topic of physics, and of logic, saying that the one was above us, and that the other had nothing to do with us; and that the only branch of philosophy with which we had any real concern was ethics. III. He also said that dialectic reasonings were like cobwebs; which," although they seem to be put together on principles of art, are utterly useless. IV. And he did not introduce many virtues into his scheme, as Zeno did; nor one virtue under a great many names, as the Megaric philosophers did; but defined virtue as consisting in behaving in a certain manner with reference to a certain thing.

V. And as he philosophized in this manner, and carried on ' his discussions in the Cynosarges, he got so much influence as to be called a founder of a sect. Accordingly, Miltiades, and Diphilus were called Arisfoneans.

VI. He was a man of very persuasive eloquence, and one who could adapt himself well to the humours of a multitude. On which account Timon says of him: —

And one who, from Ariston'a wily race, Traced his descent.

Diocles, the Magnesian, tells us that Ariston having fallen in with Polemo, passed over to his school, at a time when Zeno was lying ill with a long sickness. The Stoic doctrine to which he was most attached, was the one that the wise man is never guided by opinions. But Persaeus argued against this, and caused one of two twin brothers to place a deposit in his hands, and then caused the other to reclaim it; and thus he convicted him, as he was in doubt on this point, and there fore forced to act on opinion. He was a great enemy of Arcesilaus. And once, seeing a bull of a monstrous conformation, having a womb, he said, " Alas! here is an argument for Arcesilaus against the evidence of his senses." On another occasion, when a philosopher of the Academy said that he did not comprehend anything, he said to him, " Do not you even see the man who is sitting next to you?" And as he said that he did not, he said:—

Who then has blinded you, who's been so harsh,
As thus to rob you of your beaming eyes?

VII. The following works are attributed to him. Two books of Exhortatory Discourses; Dialogues on the Doctrines of Zeno; six books of Conversations; seven books of Discussions on Wisdom; Conversations on Love; Commentaries on Vain Glory; twenty-five books of Reminiscences; three books of Memorabilia; eleven books of Apophthegms; a volume against the Orators; a volume against the Rescripts of Alexinus; three treatises against the Dialecticians; four books of Letters to Cleanthes. But Panaetius and Sosicrates say, that his only genuine writings are his letters; and that all the rest are the works of Ariston the Peripatetic.

VIII. It is said that he, being bald, got a stroke of the sun, and so died. And we have written a jesting epigram on him in Scayon iambics, in the following terms:—

Why, O Ariston, being old and bald,
Did you allow the sun to roast your crown?
Thus, in an unbecoming search for warmth,
Against your will, you've found out chilly Hell.

IX. There was also another man of the name of Ariston; a native of Julii, one of the Peripatetic school. And another who was an Athenian musician. A fourth who was a tragic poet. A fifth, a native of Aloea, who wrote a treatise on the Oratorical Art. A sixth was a peripatetic Philosopher of Alexandria.

LIFE OF HERILLUS.

I. Herillus, a native of Carthage, said that the chief good was knowledge; that is to say, the always conducting one's self in such a way as to refer everything to the principle of living according to knowledge, and not been misled by ignorance. He also said that knowledge was a habit not departing from reason in the reception of perceptions.

On one occasion, he said that there was no such thing as a chief good, but that circumstances and events changed it, just as the same piece of brass might become a statue either of Alexander or of Socrates. And that besides the chief good or end (j-sxoj), there was a subordinate end (kmWs) different from it. And that those who were not wise aimed at the "'YirorfXlc, a name given by Herillus in Diogenes Laertius to a man's natural talents, *Sec,* which ought all to be subordinate to the attainment of the chief good."—L. E. S. *in* toe.

latter; but that only the wise man directed his views to the former. And all the things between virtue and vice he pronounced indifferent. II. His books contain but few lines, but they are full of power, and contain arguments in opposition to Zeno. III. It is said, that when he was a boy, many people were attached to him; and as Zeno wished to drive them away, he persuaded him to have his head shaved, which disgusted them all. IV. His books are these. One on Exercise; one on the Passions; one on Opinion; the Lawgiver; the Skilful Midwife; the Contradictory Teacher; the Preparer; the Director; the Mercury; the Medea; a book of Dialogues; a book of Ethical Propositions. LIFE OF DIONTSIUS

I. Dionysius, the Deserter, as he was called, asserted that pleasure was the chief good, from the circumstance of his being afflicted with a complaint in his eyes. For, as be suffered severely, he could not pronounce pain a thing indifferent.

II. He was the son of Theophantus, and a native of Heraclea. III. He was a pupil, as we are told by Diocles, first of all of Heraclides, his fellow citizen; after that of Alexinus, and Menedemus; and last of all of Zeno. And at first, as he was very devoted to learning, he tried his hand at all kinds of poetry. Afterwards, he attached himself to Aratus, whom he took for his model. Having left Zeno, he turned to the Cyrenaics, and became a frequenter of brothels, and in other respects indulged in luxury without disguise. IV. When he had lived near eighty years, he died of starvation.

V. The following books are attributed to him. Two books on Apathy; two on Exercise; four on Pleasure; one on .-Y

Riches, and Favours, and Revenge; one on the Use of Men; one on Good Fortune; one on Ancient Kings; one on Things which are Praised; one on Barbarian Customs.

These now are the chief men who differed from the Stoics. But the man who succeeded Zeno in his school was Cleanthes, whom we must now speak of.

LIFE OF CLEANTHES.

I. Cleanthes was a native of Assos, and the son of Phanias. He was originally a boxer, as we learn from Antisthenes, in his Successions. And he came to Athens, having but four drachmas, as some people say, and attaching himself to Zeno, he devoted himself to Philosophy in a most noble manner; and he adhered to the same doctrines as his master.

II. He was especially eminent for his industry, so that as he was a very poor man, he was forced to undertake mercenary employments, and he used to draw water in the gardens by night, and by day he used to exercise himself in philosophical discussions; on which account he was called Phreantles. They also say that he was on one occasion brought before a court of justice, to be compelled to give an account what his sources of income were from which he maintained himself in such good condition: and that then he was acquitted, having produced as his witness the gardener in whose garden he drew the water; and a woman who was a mealseller, in whose establishment he used to prepare the meal. And the judges of the Areopagus admired him, and voted that ten minae should be given to him; but Zeno forbade him to accept them.

They also say that Antigonus presented him three thousand drachmas. And once, when he was conducting some young men to some spectacle, it happened that the wind blew away his cloak, and it was then seen that he had nothing on under it; on which he was greatly applauded by the Athenians, From *Qpeap*, a well, and *avrXtu*, to draw water.

according to the account given by Demetrius, the Magnesian, in his essay on People of the same Name. And he was greatly admired by them on account of this circumstance.

They also say that Antigonus, who was a pupil of his, once asked him why he drew water; and that he made answer, "Do I do nothing beyond drawing water? Do I not also dig, and do I not water the land, and do all sorts of things for the sake of philosophy?" For Zeno used to accustom him to this, and used to require him to bring him an obol by way of tribute. And once he brought one of the pieces of money which he had collected in this way, into the middle of a company of his acquaintances, and said, " Cleanthes could maintain even another Cleanthes if he were to choose; but others who have plenty of means to support themselves, seek for necessaries from others; although they only study philosophy in a very lazy manner. " And, in reference to these habits of his, Cleanthes was called a second Heracles.

III. He was then very industrious; but he was not well endowed by nature, and was very slow in his intellect. On which account Timon says of him:—
What stately ram thus measures o'er the ground,
And master of the flock surveys them round?
What citizen of Assos, dull and cold,
Fond of long words, a mouth-piece, but not bold.T

And when he was ridiculed by his fellow pupils, he used to bear it patiently. IV. He did not even object to the name when he was called an ass; but only said that he was the only animal able to bear the burdens which Zeno put upon him. " And once, when he was reproached as a coward, he said, " That is the reason why I make but few mistakes." He used to say, in justification of his preference of his own way of life to that' of the rich, " That while they were playing at ball, he was earning money by digging hard and barren ground." And he very often used to blame himself. And once, Ariston heard him doing so, and said, " Who is it that you are reproaching?" The Greek used is *Snroipopa*; which was a term especially applied to the money which slaves let out to hire paid to their master.

T This is a parody on Horn. II. iii. 196. Pope's version, i. 260. The word sX/ioc means the mouth-piece of a flute.

and he replied, "An old man who has grey hair, but no hrains."

When some one once said to him, that Arcesilaus did not do what he ought, " Desist," he replied, " and do not blame him; for if he destroys duty as far as his words go, at all events he establishes it by his actions." Arcesilaus once said to him, " I never listen to flatterers. " " Yes," rejoined Cleanthes, " I flatter you, when I say that though you say one thing, you do another." When some one once asked him what lesson he ought to inculcate on his son, he replied, " The warning of Electra:"—

Silence, silence, gently step.

When a Lacedaemonian once said in his hearing, that labour was a good thing, he was delighted, and addressed him:—

Oh, early worth, a soul so wise and young
Proclaims you from the Bage Lycurgus sprung.

Hecaton tells us in his Apophthegms, that once when a young man said, " If a man who beats his stomach *yaerglfyi*, then a man who slaps his thigh

/i)jg/£s/," he replied, " Do you stick to your *diafirigifyi.*" But analogous words do not always indicate analogous facts. Once when he was conversing with a youth, he asked him if he felt; and as he said that he did, " Why is it then," said Cleanthes, " that I do not feel that you feel T

When Sositheus, the poet, said in the theatre where he was present:—

Men whom the folly of Cleanthes urges;

He continued in the same attitude; at which the hearers were surprised, and applauded him, but drove Sositheus away. And when he expressed his sorrow for having abused him in this manner, he answered him gently, saying, " That it would be a preposterous thing for Bacchus and Hercules to bear being ridiculed by the poets without any expression of anger, and for him to be indignant at any chance attack." He used also to say, " That the Peripatetics were in the same condidion as lyres, which though they utter sweet notes, do not Taken from the Orestes of Euripides, i. 140.

t This is parodied from Horn. Od. iv. 611. Pope's version,.!. 831. hear themselves." And it is said, that when he asserted that, on the principles of Zeno, one could judge of a man's character by his looks, some witty young men brought him a profligate fellow, having a hardy look from continual exercise in the fields, and requested him to tell" them his moral character; and he, having hesitated a little, bade the man depart; and, as he departed, he sneezed, " I have the fellow now," said Cleanthes, "he is a debauchee."

He said once to a man who was conversing with him by himself, " You are not talking to a bad man." And when some one reproached him with his old age, he rejoined, " I too wish to depart, but when I perceive myself to be in good health in every respect, and to be able to recite and read, I am content to remain." They say too, that he used I to write down all that he heard from Zeno on oyster shells, / and on the shoulder-blades of oxen, from want of money *to J* buy paper with.

V. And though he was of this character, and in such circumstances, he became so eminent, that, though Zeno had many other disciples of high reputation, he succeeded him as the president of his School.

VI. And he left behind him some excellent books, which are these. One on Time; two on Zeno's System of Natural Philosophy; four books of the Explanations of Heraclitus: one on Sensation; one on Art; one addressed to Democritus; one to Aristarchus; one to Herillus; two on Desire; one entitled Archaeology; one on the Gods; one on the Giants; one on Marriage; one on Poets; three on Duty; one on Good Counsel; one on Favour; one called Exhortatory; one on Virtues; one on Natural Ability; one on Gorgippus; one ' on Enviousness; one on Love; one on Freedom; one called the Art of Love; one on Honour; one ou Glory; The Statesman; one on Counsel; one on Laws; one on Deciding as a Judge; one on the Way of Life; three on Reason; one on the Chief Good; one on the Beautiful; one on Actions; one on Knowledge; one on Kingly Power; one on Friendship; one on Banquets; one on the Principle that Virtue is the same in Man and Woman *f* one on the Wise Man Employing Sophisms; one on Apophthegms; two books of Conversations; one on Pleasure; one on Properties; one on Doubtful Things; one on Dialectics; one on Modes; one on Categorems.

VII. These are his writings.

And he died in the following manner. His gums swelled very much; and, at the command of his physicians, he abstained from food for two days. And he got so well that his physicians allowed him to return to all his former habits; but he refused, and saying that he had now already gone part of the way, he abstained from food for the future, and so died; being, as some report, eighty years old, and having been a pupil of Zeno nineteen years. And we have written a playful epigram on him also, which runs thus:—

I praise Cleanthes, but praise Pluto more;

Who could not bear to see him grown so old,

So gave him rest at last among the dead,

Who'd drawn such loads of water while alive.

LIFE OF SPILERUS.

I. Spherus, a native of the Bosphorus, was, as we have said before, a pupil of Cleanthes after the death of Zeno.

II. And when he made a considerable advance in philosophy he went to Alexandria, to the court of Ptolemy Philopater. And once, when there was a discussion concerning the question whether a wise man would allow himself to be guided by opinion, and when Sphaerus affirmed that he would not, the king, wishing to refute him, ordered some pomegranates of wax to be set before him; and when Sphaerus was deceived by them, the king shouted that he had given his assent to a false perception. But Sphaerus answered very neatly, that he had not given his assent to the fact that they were pomegranates, but to the fact that it was probable that they might be pomegranates. And that a perception which could be comprehended differed from one that was only probable.

Once, when Innesistratus accused him of denying that

Ptolemy was a king, he said to him, " That Ptolemy was a man with such and such qualities, and a king." III. He wrote the following books. Two on the World; one on the Elements of Seed; one on Fortune; one on the Smallest Things; one on Atoms and Phantoms; one on the Senses; five Conversations about Heraclitus; one on Ethical Arrangement; one on Duty; one on Appetite; two on the Passions; one on Kingly Power; on the Lacedaemonian Constitution; three on Lycurgus and Socrates; one on Law; one on Divination; one volume of Dialogues on Love; one on the Eretrian Philosophers; one on Things Similar; one on Terms; one on Habits; three on Contradictions; one on Reason; one on Riches; one on Glory; one on Death; two on the Art of Dialectics; one on Categorems: one on Ambiguity; and a volume of Letters.

LIFE OF CHRYSIPPUS.

I. Chbysippus was the son of Apollonius, and a native of either Soli or Tarsus, as Alexander tells us in his Successions; and he was a pupil of Cleanthes. Previously he used to practise running as a public runner; then he became a pupil of Zeno or of Cleanthes, as Diocles and the generality of authors say, and while he was still living he abandoned him, and became a very eminent philosopher.

II. He was a man of great natural ability, and of great acuteness in every way, so that in many points he dissented This is referring to the Stoic doctrine ridiculed by Horace: Si dives qui sapiens est,
Et sutor bonus, et solus formosus, et est Bex
Cur optas quod habes?—Hor. Sat. i. 130.--
Which may be translated:— If every man is rich who's wise,
A cobbler too beyond all price;
A handsome man, and eke a king;
_.. Why thus your vows at random fling!
from Zeno, and also from Cleanthes, to whom he often used to say that he only wanted to be instructed in the dogmas of the school, and that he would discover the demonstrations for himself. But whenever he opposed him with any vehemence, he always repented, so that he used frequently to say:—

In most respects I am a happy man,
Excepting where Cleanthes is concerned;
For in that matter I am far from fortunate. —

And he had such a high reputation as a dialectician, that most people thought that if there were such a science as dialectics among the Gods; it would be in no respect different from that of Chrysippus. But though he was so eminently able in matter, he was not perfect in style.

III. He was industrious beyond all other men; as is plain from his writings; for he wrote more than seven hundred and five books. And he often wrote several books on the same subject, wishing to put down everything that occurred to him; and constantly correcting his previous assertions, and using a great abundance of testimonies. So that, as in one of his writings he had quoted very nearly the whole of the Medea of Euripides, and some one had his book in his hands; this latter, when he was asked what he had got there, made answer, " The Medea of Chrysippus." And Apollodorus, the Athenian, in his Collection of Dogmas, wishing to assert that what Epicurus had written out of his own head, and without any quotations to support his arguments, was a great deal more than all the books of Chrysippus, speaks thus (I give his exact words), " For if any one were to take away from the books of Chrysippus all the passages which he quotes from other authors, his paper would be left empty."
These are the words of Apollodorus; but the old woman who lived with him, as Dioles reports, used to say that he wrote five hundred lines every day. And Hecaton says, that he first applied himself to philosophy, when his patrimony had been confiscated, and seized for the royal treasury.

IV. He was slight in person, as is plain from his statue which is in the Ceramicus, which is nearly hidden by the equestrian statue near it; in reference to which circumstance, Carneades called him Cryxippus. He was once reproached From (cpiirrw, to hide, and 'i'mcog, a horse. by some one for not attending the lectures of Ariston, who was drawing a great crowd after him at the time; and he replied, " If I had attended to the multitude I should not have been a philosopher." And once, when he saw a dialectician pressing hard on Cleanthes, and proposing sophistical fallacies to him, he said, " Cease to drag that old man from more important business, and propose these questions to us who are young." At another time, when some one wishing to ask him something privately, was addressing him quietly, but when he saw a multitude approaching began to speak more energetically he said to him:—
Alas, my brother! now your eye is troubled;
You were quite sane just now; and yet how quickly
Have you succumbed to frenzy.
And at drinking parties he used to behave quietly, moving his legs about however, so that a female slave once said, " It is only the legs of Chrysippus that are drunk." And he had so high an opinion o.f himself, that once, when a man asked him, " To whom shall I entrust my son?" he said " To me, for if I thought that there was any one better than myself, I would have gone to him to teach me philosophy." In reference to which anecdote they report that people used to say of him:—

He has indeed a clear and subtle head,
The rest are forms of empty aether made.t
And also:—
For if Chrysippus had not lived and taught,
The Stoic school would surely have been nought.

VI. But at last, when Arcesilaus and Lacydes, as Sotion records in his eighth book, came to the Academy, he joined them in the study of philosophy; from which circumstance he got the habit of arguing for and against a custom, and discussed magnitudes and quantities, following the system of the Academics.

VII. Hermippus relates, that one day, when he was teaching in the Odeum, he was invited to a sacrifice by his pupils; These lines are from the Erestes of Euripides, v. 247. + This is a quotation from Homer, Od. x. 495. Pope's Version, 586. The Greek here is, olog iri-irvvTai. The line in Homer stands: .. oitp TrkirvvtrQai,—sc: irope irfpatQovHa , and, that drinking some sweet unmixed wine, he was seized with giddiness, and departed this life five days afterwards, when he had lived seventy-three years; dying in the hundred and forty-third olympiad, as Apollodorus says in his Chronicles. And we have written an epigram on him:—

Chrysippus drank with open mouth some wine;
Then became giddy, and so quickly died.
Too little reck'd he of the Porch's weal,
Or of his country's, or of his own dear life;
And so descended to the realms of Hell.
But some people say that he died of a fit of immoderate laughter. For that see-

ing his ass eating figs, he told his old woman to give the ass some unmixed wine to drink afterwards, and then laughed so violently that he died, VIII. He appears to have been a man of exceeding arrogance. Accordingly, though he wrote such numbers of books, he never dedicated one of them to any sovereign. And he was contented with one single old woman, as Demetrius tells us, in his People of the same Name. And when Ptolemy wrote to Gleanthes, begging him either to come to him himself or to send him some one, Sphaerus went to him, but Chrysippus slighted the invitation.

IX. However, he sent for the sons of his sister, Aristocrea and Philocrates, and educated them; and he was the first person who ventured to hold a school in the open air in the Lyceum, as the before mentioned Demetrius relates.

X. There was also another Chrysippus, a native of Cnidos, a physician, from whom Erasistratus testifies that he received great benefit. And another also who was a son of his, and the physician of Ptolemy; who, having had a false accusation brought against him, was apprehended and punished by being scourged. There was also a fourth who was a pupil of Erasistratus; and a fifth was an author of a work called Georgics.

XI. Now this philosopher used to delight in proposing questions of this sort. The person who reveals the mysteries to the uninitiated commits a sin; the heirophant reveals them to the uninitiated; therefore the hierophant commits sin? Another was, that which is not in the city, is also not in the house; but a well is not in the city, therefore, there is not a well in the house. Another was, there is a certain head; that head you have not got; there is then a a head that you have not "got; therefore, you have not got a head. Again, if a' man is in Megara, he is not in Athens; but there is a man in Megara, therefore, there is not a man in Athens. Again, if you say anything, what you say comes out of your mouth; but you say " a waggon," therefore a waggon comes out of your mouth. Another was, if you have not lost a thing, you have it; but you have not lost horns; therefore, you have horns. Though some attribute this sophism to Eubulides. XII. There are people who run Chrysippus down as having written a great deal that is very shameful and indecent. For in his treatise on the Ancient Natural Historians, he relates the story of Jupiter and Juno very indecently, devoting six hundred lines to what no one could repeat without polluting his mouth. For, as it is said, he composes this story, though he praises it as consisting of natural details, in a way more suitable to street walkers than to Goddesses; and not at all resembling the ideas which have been adopted or cited by writers in paintings. For they were found neither in Polemo, nor in Hypsicrates, nor in Antigonus, but were inserted by himself. And in bis treatise on Polity, he allows people to marry their mothers, or their daughters, or their sons. And he repeats this doctrine in his treatise on those things which are not desirable for their own sake, in the very opening of it. And in the third book of his treatise on Justice, he devotes a thousand lines to bidding people devour even the dead.

In the second book of his treatise on Life and Means of Support, where he is warning us to consider beforehand, how the wise man ought to provide himself with means, he says, " And yet why need he provide himself with means? for if it is for the sake of living, living at all is a matter of indifference; if it is for the sake of pleasure, that is a matter of indifference too; if it is for the sake of virtue, that is of itself sufficient for happiness. But the methods of providing one's self with means are ridiculous; for instance, some derive them from a king; and then it will be necessary to humour him. Some from friendship; and then friendship will become a thing to be bought with a price. Some from wisdom; and then wisdom will become mercenary; and these are the accusations which he brings."

But since he has written many books of high reputation, it has seemed good to me to give a catalogue of them, classifying them according to their subjects. They are the following:—

Books on Logic; Propositions; Logical Questions; a book of the Contemplations of the Philosopher; six books of Dialectic Terms addressed to Metrodorus; one on the Technical Terms used in Dialectics, addressed to Zeno; one called the Art of Dialectics, addressed to Aristagoras; four books of Probable Conjunctive Reasons, addressed to Dioscorides.

The first set of treatises on the Logical Topics, which concern things, contains: one essay on Propositions; one on those Propositions which are not simple; two on the Copulative Propositions, addressed to Athenades; three on Positive Propositions, addressed to Aristagoras; one on Definite Propositions, addressed to Athenodorus; one on Privative Propositions, addressed to Thearus; three on the Best Propositions, addressed to Dion; four on the Differences between Indefinite Propositions; two on those Propositions which are enunciated with a reference to time; two on Perfect Propositions.

The second set contains, one essay on a Disjunctive True Propositions, addressed to Gorgippides; four on a Conjunctive True Proposition, also addressed to Gorgippides; one called, the Sect, addressed to Gorgippides; one on the argument of Consequents; one on questions touched upon in the three preceding treatises, and now re-examined, this also is addressed to Gorgippides; one on what is Possible, addressed to Clitus; one on the treatise of Philo, on Signification; one on what it is that Falsehood consists in.

The third set contains, two treatises on Imperative Propositions; two on Interrogation; four on Examination; an epitome of the subject of Interrogation and Examination; four treatises on Answer; an abridgment on Answer; two essays on Investigation.

The fourth set contains ten books on Categorems, addressed to Metrodorus; one treatise on what is Direct and Indirect, addressed to Philarchus; one on Conjunctions, addressed to Apollonides; four on Categorems, addressed to Pasylus.

The fifth set contains, one treatise on the Five Cases; one on Things defined according to the Subject; two on Enunciation, addressed to Stesagoras; two on Appellative Nouns.

The next class of his writings refers to rules of Logic, with reference to words, and speech which consists of words.

The first set of these contains, six treatises on Singular and Plural Enunciations; five on Words, addressed to Sosigines and Alexander; four on the Inequality of Words, addressed to Dion; three on the Sorites which refer to Words; one on Solecisms in the Use of Words, addressed to Dionysius; one entitled Discourses, contrary to Customs; one entitled Diction, and addressed to Dionysius.

The second set contains, five treatises on the Elements of Speech and of Phrases; four on the Arrangement of Phrases; three on the Arrangement, and on the Elements of Phrases, addressed to Philip; one on the Elements of Discourse, addressed to Nicias; one on Correlatives.

The third set contains, two treatises against those who do not admit Division; four on Ambiguous Expressions, addressed to Apollos; one, Ambiguity in Modes; two on the Ambiguous Use of Figures, in Conjunctive Propositions; two on the essay on Ambiguous Expressions, by Panthorides;. five on the Introduction to the Ambiguous Expressions; one, being an abridgment of the Ambiguous Expressions, addressed to Epicrates; and a collection of instances to serve as an Introduction to the Ambiguous Expressions, in two books.

The next class" is on the subject of that part of logic which is conversant about reasonings and modes.

The first set of works in this class, contains, the Art of Reasoning and of Modes, in five books, addressed to Dioscorides; a treatise on Reasoning, in three books; one on the Structure of Modes, addressed to Stesagoras, in five books; a comparison of the Elements of Modes; a treatise on Reciprocal and Conjunctive Reasonings; an essay to Agatha, called also an essay on Problems, which follow one another; a treatise, proving that Syllogistic Propositions suppose one or more other terms; one on Conclusions, addressed to Aristagoras; one essay, proving that the same reasoning can affect several figures; one against those who deny that the same reasoning can be expressed by syllogism, and without syllogism, in two books; three treatises against those who attack the resolution of Syllogisms; one on the treatise on Modes, by Philo, addressed to Timostratus; two treatises on Logic, in one volume, addressed to Timocrates and Philomathes; one volume of questions on Reasonings and Modes.

The second set contains, one book of Conclusive Reasonings, addressed to Zeno; one on Primary Syllogisms, which are not demonstrative; one on the resolution of Syllogisms; one, in two books, on Captious Reasonings, addressed to Pasylus; one book of Considerations on Syllogisms; one book of Introductory Syllogisms, addressed to Zeno; three of Introductory Modes, addressed also to Zeno; five of False Figures of Syllogism; one of a Syllogistic Method, for the resolution of arguments, which are not demonstrative; one of Researches into the Modes, addressed to Zeno and Philomathes (but this appears to be an erroneous title).

The third set contains, one essay on Incidental Reasonings, addressed to Athenades (this again is an incorrect title); three books of Incidental Discourses on the Medium (another incorrect title); one essay on the Disjunctive Reasons of Aminias.

The fourth set contains, a treatise on Hypothesis, in three books, addressed to Meliager; a book of hypothetical reasonings on the Laws, addressed also to Meliager; two books of hypothethical reasoning to serve as an Introduction; two books of hypothetical reasonings on Theorems; a treatise in two books, being a resolution of the Hypothetical Reasonings of Hedylus; an essay, in three books, being a resolution of the Hypothetical Reasonings of Alexander (this is an incorrect title); two books of Expositions, addressed to Leodamas.

The fifth set contains, an introduction to Fallacy, addressed Aristocreon; an introduction to False Reasonings; a treatise in six books, on Fallacy, addressed to Aristocreon.

The sixth set contains, a treatise against those who believe Truth and Falsehood to be the same thing. One, in two books, against those who have recourse to division to resolve the Fallacy, addressed to Aristocreon; a demonstrative essay, to prove that it is not proper to divide indefinite terms; an essay, in three books, in answer to the objections against the non-division of Indefinite Terms, addressed to Pasylus; a solution, according to the principles of the ancients, addressed to Dioscorides; an essay on the Resolution of the Fallacy, addressed to Aristocreon, this is in three books; a resolution of the Hypothetical Arguments of Hedylus, in one book, addressed to Aristocreon and Apollos.

The seventh set contains, a treatise against those who contend that the premisses on the Fallacy, are false; a treatise on Negative Seasoning, addressed to Aristocreon, in two books; one book of Negative Reasonings, addressed to Gymnasias; two books of a treatise on Reasoning by Progression, addressed to Stesagoras; two books of Reasonings by Interrogation, and on the Arrest, addressed to Onetor; an essay, in two books, on the Corrected Argument, addressed to Aristobulus; another on the Non-apparent Argument, addressed to Athenades.

The eighth set contains, an essay on the Argument Oretis, in eight books, addressed to Menecrates; a treatise, in two books, on Arguments composed of a finite term, and an indefinite term, addressed to Pasylus; another essay on the Argument Outis, addressed to Epicrates.

The ninth set contains, two volumes of Sophisms, addressed to Heraclides, and Pollis; five volumes of Dialectic Arguments, which admit of no solution, addressed to Dioscorides; an essay, in one book, against the Method of Arcesilaus, addressed to Sphaerus.

The tenth set contains, a treatise in six books, against Custom, addressed to

Metrodorus; and another, in seven books, on Custom, addressed to Gorgippides.

There are, therefore, works on Logic, in the four grand classes which we have here enumerated, embracing various questions, without any connection with one another, to the number of thirty nine sets, amounting in the whole to three hundred and eleven treatises on Logic.

The next division comprises those works which have for their object, the explanation of Moral Ideas.

The first class of this division, contains an essay, giving a description of Reason, addressed to Theosphorus; a book of Ethical questions; three books of Principles, to serve as the foundation of Dogmas, addressed to Philomathes; two books of definitions of Good-breeding, addressed to Metrodorus; two books of definitions of the Bad, addressed to Metrodorus; The argument by progression is the sorites. "The arrest" is the method of encountering the sorites, by taking some particular point at which to stop the admissions required by the sorites.

two books of definitions of Neutral Things, addressed also to Metrodorus; seven books of definitions of Tbings, according to their genera, addressed to Metrodorus; and two books of Definitions, according to other systems, addressed to Metrodorus.

The second set contains, a treatise on Things Similar, in three books, addressed to Aristocles; an essay on Definitions, in seven books, addressed to Metrodorus.

The third set contains, a treatise, in seven books, on the Incorrect Objections made to Definitions, addressed to Laodamas; two books of Probable Arguments bearing on Definitions, addressed to Dioscorides; two books on Species and Genus, addressed to Gorgippides; one book on Divisions; two books on Contraries, addressed to Dionysius; a book of Probable Arguments relating to Divisions, and Genera, and Species; a book on Contraries.

The fourth set contains, a treatise, in seven books, on Etymologies, addressed to Diocles; another, in four books, on the same subject, addressed to the same person.

The fifth set contains, a treatise in two books, on Proverbs, addressed to Zenodotus; an essay on Poems, addressed to Philomathes; an essay, on How one Ought to Listen to Poems, in two books; an essay, in reply to Critics, addressed to Diodorus.

The next division refers to Ethics, looked at in a general point of view, and to the different systems arising out of them, and to the Virtues.

The first set contains, an essay against Pictures, addressed to Timonax; an essay on the Manner in which we express ourselves about, and form our Conceptions of, each separate thing; two books of Thoughts, addressed to Laodamas; an essay, in three books, on Conception, addressed to Pythonax; an essay, that the Wise Man is not Guided by Opinion;. an essay, in five books, on Comprehension, and Knowledge, and Ignorance; a treatise on Reason, in two books; a treatise on the Employment of Reason, addressed to Leptines.

The second set contains, a treatise, that the Ancient Philosophers approved of Logic, with Proofs to support the Arguments, in two books, addressed to Zeno; a treatise on Dialectics, in four books, addressed to Aristocreon; an answer to the Objections urged against Dialectics, in three books; an essay on Rhetoric, in four books, addressed to Dioscorides.

The third set contains, a treatise on Habit, in three books, addressed to Cleon; a treatise on Art and Want of Art, in four books, addressed to Aristocreon; a treatise, iu four books, on the Difference between the Virtues, addressed to Diodorus; a treatise, to show that all the Virtues are Equal; a treatise on the Virtues, in two books, addressed to Pollis.

The next division refers to Ethics, as relating to Good and Evil.

The first set contains, a treatise in ten books, on the Honourable, and on Pleasure, addressed to Aristocreon; a demonstration, that Pleasure is not the Chief Good of Man, in four books; a demonstration that Pleasure is not a Good at all, in four books; a treatise on what is said by...

The remainder of,the life.of Chrysippuaia lost. LIFE OF PYTHAGORAS.

I. Since we have now gone through the Ionian philosophy, which was derived from Thales, and the lives of the several illustrious men who were the chief ornaments of that school; we will now proceed to treat of the Italian School, which was founded by Pythagoras, the son of Mnesarchus, a seal engraver, aa he is recorded to have been by Hermippus; a native of Samos, or as Aristoxenus asserts, a Tyrrhenian, and a native of one of the islands which the Athenians occupied after they had driven out the Tyrrhenians. But some authors say that he was the son of Marmacus, the son of Hippasus, the son of Euthyphron, the son of Cleonymus, who was an exile from Phlias; and that Marmacus settled in Samos, and that from this circumstance Pythagoras was called a Samian. After that he migrated to Lesbos, having come to Pherecydes with letters of recommendation from Zoilus, his uncle. And having made three silver goblets, he carried them to Egypt as a present for each of the three priests. He had brothers, the eldest of whom was named Eunomus, the middle one Tyrrhenus, and a slave named Zamolxis, to whom the Getae sacrifice, believing him to be the same as Saturn, according to the account of Herodotus.

II. He was a pupil, as I have already mentioned, of Pherecydes, the Syrian; and after his death he came to ' Samos, and became a pupil of Hermodamas, the descendant of Creophylus, who was by this time an old man. III. And as he was a young man, and devoted to learning, he quitted his country, and got initiated into all the Grecian and barbarian sacred mysteries. Accordingly, he went to See Herod, iv. 93.

Egypt, on which occasion Polycrates gave him a letter of introduction to Amasis; and he learnt the Egyptian language, as Antipho tells us, in his treatise on those men who have been conspicuous for virtue, and he associated with the Chaldaeaus and with the Magi.

Afterwards he went to Crete, and in

company with Epimenides, he descended into the Idaean cave, (and in Egypt too, he entered into the holiest parts of their temples,) and learned all the most secret mysteries that relate to their Gods. Then he returned back again to Samos, and finding his country reduced under the absolute dominion of Polvcrates, he set sail, and fled to Crotona in Italy. And thereA having given laws to the Italians, he gained a very high) reputation, together with his scholars, who were about three! hundred in number, and governed the republic in a most excellent manner; so that the constitution was very nearly an aristocracy. J IV. Heraclides Ponticus says, that he was accustomed to speak of himself in this manner; that he had formerly been Ethalides, and had been accounted the son of Mercury; and that Mercury had desired him to select any gift he pleased except immortality. And that he accordingly hsd requested that, whether living or dead, he might preserve the memory of what had happened to him. While, therefore, he was alive, he recollected everything; and when he was dead, he retained the same memory. And at a subsequent period he passed into Euphorbus, and was wounded by Menelaus. And while he was Euphorbus, he used to say that he had formerly been iEthalides; and that he had received as a gift from Mercury the perpetual transmigration of his soul, so that it was constantly transmigrating and passing into whatever plants or animals it pleased; and he had also received the gift of knowing and recollecting all that his soul had suffered in hell, and what sufferings too are endured by the rest of the souls.

But after Euphorbus died, he said that his soul had passed into Hermotimus; and when he wished to convince people of this, he went into the territory of the Branchidae, and going into the temple of Apollo, he showed his shield which Menelaus had dedicated there as an offering. For he said that he, when he saile 1 from Troy,' had offered up his shield which was already getting worn out, to Apollo, and that nothing remained but the ivory face which was on it. And when Ilermotimus died, then he said that he had become Pyrrhus, a fisherman of Delos; and that he still recollected everything, how he had been formerly Ethalides, then Euphorbus, then Hermotimus, and then Pyrrhus. And when Pyrrhus died, he became Pythagoras, and still recollected all the circumstances that I have been mentioning.

V. Now, some people say that Pythagoras did not leave behind him a single book; but they talk foolishly; for Heraclitus, the natural philosopher, speaks plainly enough of him, saying, " Pythagoras, the son of Mnesarchus, was the most learned of all men in history; and having selected from these writings, he thus formed his own wisdom and extensive learning, and mischievous art. " And he speaks thus, because Pythagoras, in the beginning of his treatise on Natural Philosophy, writes in the following maner: " By the air which I breathe, and by the water which 1 drink, I will not endure to be blamed on account of this discourse."

And there are three volumes extant written by Pythagoras.

This resembles the account which Ovid puts into the mouth of Pythagoras, in the last book of his Metamorphoses, where he makes him say:—

Morte carent animae, semperque priore relicta
Sede, novis domibus habitant vivuutque receptae;
Ipse ego, nam memiui, Trojani tempora belli,
Panthorides Euphorbus eram, cui pectore quondam
Haesit in adverso gravis hasta minoris Atridae:
Aguovi Clypeum laevae gestamina nostrae
Nuper Abante'is templo Jononis in Argis.

Which may be translated:—

Death has no pow'r th' immortal soul to slay;
That, when its present body turns to clay,
Seeks a fresh home, and with unminish'd might
Inspires another frame with life and light.
So I myself, (well I the past recall)
When the fierce Greeks begirt Troy's holy wall,
Was brave Euphorbus; and in conflict drear,
Poured forth my blood beneath Atrides' spear:
The shield this arm did bear I lately saw
In J uno's shrine, a trophy of that war.

One on Education; one on Politics; and one on Natural Philosophy. But the treatise which is now extant under the name of Pythagoras is the work of Lysis, of Tarentum, a philosopher of the Pythagorean School, who fled to Thebes, and became the master of Epaminondas. And Heraclides, the son of Sarapion, in his Abridgment of Sotion, says that he wrote a poem in epic verse on the Universe; and besides that a sacred poem, which begins thus;—

Dear youths, I warn you cherish peace divine,
And in your hearts lay deep these words of mine.

A third about the Soul; a fourth on Piety; a fifth entitled Helothales, which was the name of the father of Epicharmus, of Cos; a sixth called Crotona, and other poems too. But the mystic discourse which is extant under his name, they say is really the work of Hippasus, having been composed with a view to bring Pythagoras into disrepute. There were also many other books composed by Aston, of Crotona, and attributed to Pythagoras.

Aristoxenus asserts that Pythagoras derived the greater part of his ethical doctrines from Themistoclea, the priestess at Delphi. And Ion, of Chios, in his Victories, says that he wrote some poems and attributed them to Orpheus. They also say that the poem called the Scopeadae is by him, which begins thus:—

Behave not shamelessly to any one.

VI. And Sosicrates, in his Successions, relates that he, having being asked by Leon, the tyrant of the Phliasians, who he was, replied, " A philosopher." And adds, that he used to compare life to a festival. " And as some people came to a festival to contend for the prizes, and others for the purposes of traffic, and the best as spectators; so also in life, the men of slavish dispositions," said he, " are born hunters after glory and covetousuess, but philosophers are seekers after truth." And thus he spoke on this subject. But in the three treatises above mentioned, the following principles are laid down by Pythagoras generally.

He forbids men to pray for anything in particular for themselves, because they do not know what is good for them. He calls drunkenness an expression identical with ruin, and rejects all superfluity, saying, " That no one ought to exceed the proper quantity of meat and drink. " And on the subject of venereal pleasures, he speaks thus:—" One ought to sacrifice to Venus in the winter, not in the summer; and in autumn and spring in a lesser degree. But the practice is pernicious at every season, and is never good for the health." And once, when he was asked when a man might indulge in the pleasures of love, he replied, " Whenever you wish to be weaker than yourself." VII. And he divides the life of man thus. A boy for twenty years; a young man (vsawirxos) for twenty years; a middle-aged man *(ndviag)* for twenty years; an old man for twenty years. And these different ages correspond proportionably to the seasons: boyhood answers to spring; youth to summer; middle age to autumn; and old age to winter. And he uses *nanaxog* here as equivalent to *fiiigdxiov,* and *nav'tag* as equivalent to avijg.

VIII. He was the first person, as Timaeus says, who asserted that the property of friends is common, and that friendship is equality. And his disciples used to put all their possessions together into one store, and use them in common; and for five years they kept silence, doing nothing but listen to discourses, and never once seeing Pythagoras, until they were approved; after that time they were admitted into his house, and allowed to see him. They also abstained from the use. of cypress coffins, because the sceptre of Jupiter was made of that wood, as Hermippus tells us in the second book of his account of Pythagoras.

IX. He is said to have been a man of the most dignified appearance, and his disciples adopted an opinion respecting him, that he was Apollo who had come from the Hyperboreans; and it is said, that once when he was stripped naked, he was seen to have a golden thigh. And there were many people who affirmed, that when he was crossing the river Nessus it addressed him by his name.

X. Timaeus, in the tenth book of his Histories, tells us, that he used to say that women who were married to men had the names of the Gods, being successively called virgins, then nymphs, and subsequently mothers.

XI. It was Pythagoras also who carried geometry to perfection, after Moeris had first found out the principles of the elements of that science, as Aristiclides tells us in the second book of his History of Alexander; and the part of the science to which Pythagoras applied himself above all others was arithmetic. He also discovered the numerical relation of sounds on a single string: he also studied medicine. And Apollodorus, the logician, records of him, that he sacrificed a hecatomb, when he had discovered that the square of the hypothenuse of a right-angled triangle is equal to the squares of the sides containing the right angle. And there is an epigram which is couched in the following terms:—

When the great Samian sage his noble problem found,
A hundred oxen dyed with their life-blood the ground.

XII. He is also said to have been the first man who trained athletes on meat; and Eurymenes was the first man, according to the statement of Phavorinus, in the third book of his Commentaries, who ever did submit to this diet, as before that time men used to train themselves on dry figs and moist cheese, and wheaten bread; as the same Phavorinus informs us in the eighth book of his Universal History. But some, authors state, that a trainer of the name of Pythagoras certainly did train his athletes on this system, but that it was not our philosopher; for that he even forbade men to kill animals at all, much less would have allowed his disciples to eat then, as having a right to live in common with mankind. And this was his pretext; but in reality, he prohibited the eating of animals, because he wished to train and accustom men to simplicity of life, so that all their food should be easily procurable, as it would be, if they ate only such things as required no fire to dress them, and if they drank plain water; for from this diet they would derive health of body and acuteness of intellect.

The only altar at which he worshipped was that of Apollo the Father, at Delos, which is at the back of the altar of Ceratinus, because wheat, and barley, and cheese-cakes are the only offerings laid upon it, being not dressed by fire; and no victim is ever slain there, as Aristotle tells us in his Constitution of the Delians. They say, too, that he was the first person who asserted that the soul went a necessary circle, being changed about and confined at different times in different bodies.

XIII. He was also the first'person who introduced measures and weights among the Greeks; as Aristoxenus the musician informs us. XIV. Parmenides, too, assures us, that he was the first person who asserted the identity of Hesperus and Lucifer. XV. And he was so greatly admired, that they used to say that his friends looked on all his sayings as the oracles of God. And he himself says in his writings, that he had come among men after having spent two hundred and seven years in the shades below. Therefore the Lucanians and the Peucetians, and the Messapians, and the Romans, flocked around him, coming with eagerness to hear his discourses; but until the time of Philolaus, there were no doctrines of Pythagoras ever divulged; and he was the first person who published the three celebrated books which Plato wrote to have purchased for him for a hundred minae. Nor were the number of his scholars who used to come to him by night fewer than six hundred. And if any of them had ever been permitted to see him, they wrote of it to their friends, as if they had gained some great advantage.

The people of Metapontum used to call his house the temple of Ceres; and the street leading to it they called the street of the Muses, as we are told by Phavorinus in his Universal History.

And the rest of the Pythagoreans used to say, according to the account given by Aristoxenus, in the tenth book of his Laws on Education, that his precepts ought not to be divulged to all the world; and Xenophilus, the Pythagorean, when he was asked what was the best way for a man to educate his son, said, "That he must first of all take care that he wasborn in a city which enjoyed good laws."

Pythagoras, too, formed many excellent men in Italy, by This passage has been interpreted in more ways than one. Casaubon thinks with great probability that there is a hiatus in the text. I have endeavoured to extract a meaning out of what remains. Compare Samuel ii. 16, 23. "And the counsel of Ahitophel, which he counselled in those days, was as if a man had enquired at the oracle of God; so was all the counsel of Ahitophel both with David and with Absalom." his precepts, and among them Zaleucus, and Charondas.f the lawgivers.

XVI. For he was very eminent for his power of attracting friendships; and among other things, if ever he heard that any one had any community of symbols with him, he at once made him a companion and a friend. XVII. Now, what he called his symbols were such as these. " Do not stir the fire with a sword." " Do not sit down on a bushel." " Do not devour your heart." " Do not aid men in discarding a burden, but in increasing one." " Always have your bed packed up." " Do not bear the image of a God on a ring." " Efface the traces of a pot in the ashes." " Do not wipe a seat with a lamp." " Do not make water in the sun Zaleucus was the celebrated lawgiver of the Epizephyrian Locrians, and is said-to have been originally a slave employed by a shepherd, and to have been set free and appointed lawgiver by the direction of an oracle, in consequence of his announcing some excellent laws, which he represented Minerva as having communicated to him in a dream. Diogenes, is wrong however, in calling him a disciple of Pythagoras (see Bentley on Phalaris), as he lived about a hundred years before his time; his true date being 660 B.C. The code of Zaleucus is stated to have been the first collection of written laws that the Greeks possessed. Their character was that of great severity. They have not come down to us. His death is said to have occurred thus. Among his laws was one forbidding any citizen to enter the senate house in arms, under the penalty of death. But in a sudden emergency, Zaleucus himself, in a moment of forgetfulness, transgressed his own law: on which he slew himself, declaring that he would vindicate his law. (Eustath. ad. II. i. p. 60). Diodorus, however, tells the same story of Charondas. t Charondas was a lawgiver of Catana, who legislated for his own city and the other towns of Challidian origin in Magna Grecia, such as Zancle, Naxos, Leontini, Eubaea, Mylae, Himera, Callipolis, and Rhegium. His laws have not been preserved to us, with the exception of a few judgments. They were probably in verse, for Athenaeus says that they were sung in Athens at banquets. Aristotle tells us that they were adapted to an aristocracy. It is much doubted whether it is really true that he was a disciple of Pythagoras, though we are not sure of his exact time, so that we cannot pronounce it as impossible as in the preceding case. He must have lived before the time of Anaxilaus, tyrant of Rhegium, who reigned from B.C. 494 to B.C. 476, because he abolished the laws of Charondas, which had previously been in force in that city. Diodorus gives a code of laws which he states that Charondas gave to the city of Thurii, which was not founded till B.C. 443, when he must certainly have been dead a long time. There is one law of his preserved by Stobaeus, which is probably authentic, since it is found in a fragment of Theophrastus; enacting that all buying and selling shall be transacted by ready money only. shine." " Do not walk in the main street." " Do not "offer your right hand lightly." " Do not cherish swallows under your roof." " Do not cherish birds with crooked talons." " Do not defile; and do not stand upon the parings of your nails, or the cuttings of your hair." "Avoid a sharp sword." "When you are travelling abroad, look not back at your own borders." Now the precept not to stir fire with a sword meant, not to provoke the anger or swelling pride of powerful men; not to violate the beam of the balance meant, not to transgress fairness and justice; not to sit on a bushel is to have an equal care for the present and for the future, for by the bushel is meant one's daily food. By not devouring one's heart, he intended to show that we ought not to waste away our souls with grief and sorrow. In the precept that a man when travelling abroad should not turn his eyes back, he recommended those who were departing from life not to be desirous to live, and not to be too much attracted by the pleasures here on earth. And the other symbols may be explained in a similar manner, that we may not be too prolix here. XVIII. And above all things, he used to prohibit the eating of the erythinus, and the melanurus; and also, he enjoined his disciples to abstain from the hearts of animals, and from beans. And Aristotle informs us, that he sometimes used also to add to these prohibitions paunches and mullet. And some authors assert that he himself used to be contented with honey and honeycomb, and bread, and that he never drank wine in the day time. And his desert was usually vegetables, either boiled or raw; and he very rarely ate fish. His dress was white, very clean, and his bed-clothes were also white, and woollen, for linen had not yet been introduced into that country. He was never known to have eaten too much, or to have drunk too much, or to indulge in the pleasures of love. He abstained wholly from laughter, and from all such indulgences as jests and idle stories. And when he was angry, he never chastised any one, whether slave or freeman. He used to call admonishing, feeding storks.

He used to practise divination, as far as auguries and auspices go, but not by means of burnt offerings, except only the burning of frankincense. And all the sacrifices which he offered consisted of inanimate things. But some, however, assert that he did sacrifice animals, limiting himself to cocks, and sucking kids, which are called *airaXioi,* but that he very rarely offered lambs. Aristoxenus, however, affirms that he permitted the eating of all other animals, and only abstained from oxen used in agriculture, and from rams.

XIX. The same author tells us, as I have already mentioned, that he received his doctrines from Themistoclea, at.Delphi. And Hieronymus says, that when he descended to the shades below, he saw the soul of Hesiod bound to a brazen pillar, and gnashing its teeth; and that of Homer suspended from a tree, and snakes around it, as a punishment for the things that they had said of the Gods. And that those people also were punished who refrained from commerce with their wives; and that on account of this he was greatly honoured by the people of Crotona.

But Axistippus, of Cyrene, in his Account of Natural Philosophers, says that Pythagoras derived his name from the fact of his speaking (ayogauE/v) truth no less than the God at Delphi (roD Tv-mov).

It is said that he used to admonish his disciples to repeat these lines to themselves whenever they returned home to their houses:—

In what have I transgreea'd? What have I done?
What that I should have done have I omitted?

And that he used to forbid them to offer victims to the Gods, ordering them to worship only at those altars which were unstained with blood. He forbade them also to swear by the Gods; saying, " That every man ought so to exercise himself, as to be worthy of belief without an oath." He also taught men that it behoved them to honour their elders, thinking that which was precedent in point of time more honourable; just as in the world, the rising of the sun was more so than the setting; in life, the beginning more so than the end; and in animals, production more so than destruction.

Another of his rules was that men should honour the Gods above the daemones, heroes above men; and of all men parents were entitled to the highest degree of reverence. Another, that people should associate with one another in such a way as not to make their friends enemies, but to render their enemies friends. Another was that they should think nothing exclusively their own. Another was to assist the law, and to make war upon lawlessness. Not to destroy or injure a cultivated tree, nor any animal either which does not injure men. That modesty and decorum consisted in never yielding to laughter, and yet not looking stern. He taught that men should avoid too much flesh, that they should in travelling let rest and exertion alternate; that they should exercise memory; that they should never say or do anything in anger; that they should not pay respect to every kind of divination; that they should use songs set to the lyre; and hy hymns to the Gods and to eminent men, display a reasonable gratitude to them.

He also forbade his disciples to eat beans, because, as they were flatulent, they greatly partook of animal properties he also said that men kept their stomachs in better order by avoiding them; and that such abstinence made the visions which appear in one's sleep gentle and free from agitation. Alexander also says, in his Successions of Philosophers, that_ he found the following dogmas also set down in the Commentaries of Pythagoras:—

That the monad was the beginning of everything. From the monad proceeds an indefinite duad, which is subordinate to the monad as to its cause. That from the monad and the indefinite duad proceed numbers. And from numbers signs. And from these last, lines of which plane figures consist. And from plane figures are derived solid bodies. And from solid bodies sensible bodies, of which last there are four elements; fire, water, earth, and air. And that the world, which is endued with life, and intellect, and which is of a spherical figure, having the earth, which is also spherical, and inhabited all over in its centre, results from a combination of these elements, and derives its motion from them; and also that there are antipodes, and that what is below, as respects us, is above in respect of them.

This doctrine is alluded to doubtfully by Virgil, Georg. L 247.

Illie, ut perhibent, aut intempesta silet nox
Semper, et obducta densantur nocte tenebrae;
Aut redit a nobis Aurora, diemque reducit;
Nosque ubi primus equis oriens afflavit anhelis,
Illic sera rubens accendit lumina Vesper.

Thus translated by Dryden, 1. 838:—

There, as they say, perpetual night is found,
In silence brooding o'er th' unhappy ground.

He also taught that light and darkness, and cold and heat, and dryness and moisture, were equally divided in the world; and that, while heat was predominant it was summer; while cold had the mastery it, was winter; when dryness prevailed it was spring; and when moisture preponderated, winter. And while all these qualities were on a level, then was the loveliest season of the year; of which the flourishing spring was the wholesome period, and the season of autumn the most pernicious one. Of the day, he said that the flourishing period was the morning, and the fading one the evening; on which account that also was the least healthy time.

Another of his theories was, that the air around the earth was immoveable, and pregnant with disease, and that everything in it was mortal; but that the upper air was in perpetual motion, and pure and salubrious; and that everything in that was immortal, and on that account divine. And that the sun, and the moon, and the stars, were all Gods; for in them the warm principle predominates which is the cause of life. And that the moon.derives its light from the sun. And that there is a relationship between men and the Gods, because men partake of the divine principle; on which account also, God exercises his providence for our advantage. Also, that fate is the cause of the arrangement of the world both generally and particularly. Moreover, that a ray from the sun penetrated both the cold aether and the dense aether; and they call the air (ag), the cold aether (vjwg&v aiQiga), and the sea and moisture they call the dense aether *iraypv aMega)*. And this ray descends into the depths, and in this way vivifies everything. And everything which partakes of the principle of heat lives, on which account also plants are animated beings; but that all living things have not necessarily souls. And that the soul is a something torn off from the aether, both warm and cold, from its partaking of the cold aether. And that the soul is something different from life. Also, that it is immortal, because that from which it has been detached is immortal.

Also, that animals are born from one another by seeds, and

Or when Aurora leaves our northern sphere,
She lights the downward heav'n and rises there:
And when on us she breathes the living light
Red Vesper kindles there the tapers of the night

that it is impossible for there to be any spontaneous production by the earth. And that seed is a drop from the brain which contains in itself a warm vapour; and that when this is applied to the womb, it transmits virtue, and moisture, and blood from the brain, from which flesh, and sinews, and bones, and hair, and the whole body are produced. And from the vapour is produced the soul, and also sensation. And that the infant first becomes a solid body at the end of forty days; but, according to the principles of harmony, it is not perfect till seven, or perhaps nine, or at most ten months, and then it is brought forth. And that it contains in itself all the principles of life, which are all connected together, and by their union and combination form a harmonious whole, each of them developing itself at the appointed time.

The senses in general, and especially the sight, are a vapour of excessive warmth, and on this account a man is said to see through air, and through water. For the hot principle is opposed by the cold one; since, if the vapour in the eyes were cold, it would have the same temperature as the air, and so would be dissipated. As it is, in some passages he calls the eyes the gatas of the sun. And he speaks in a similar manner of hearing, and of the other senses.

He also says that the soul of man is divided into three parts; into intuition (vovg), and reason (pg), and mind *(iv-fib;)*, and that the first and last divisions are found also in other animals, but that the middle one, reason, is only found in man. And that the chief abode of the soul is in those parts of the body which are between the heart and the brain. And that that portion of it which is in the heart is the mind *(qv/m;):* but that deliberation (vows), and reason *(p$v)*, reside iu the brain

Moreover, that the senses are drops from them; and that the reasoning sense is immortal, but the others are mortal. And that the soul is nourished by the blood; and that reasons are the winds of the soul. That it is invisible, and so are its reasons, since the aether itself is' invisible. That the links of the soul are the veins, and the arteries, and the nerves. But that when it is vigorous, and is by itself in a quiescent state, *vovg* appears, in a division like this, to be the deliberative part of the mind; *pii)v*, the rational part of the intellect: *Ovfide,* that part with which the passions are concerned. then its links are words and actions. That when it is cast forth upon the earth it wanders about, resembling the body. Moreover, that Mercury is the steward of *the* souls and that on this account he has the name of Conductor, and Commercial, and Infernal, since it is he who conducts the souls from their bodies, and from earth, and sea; and that he conducts the pure souls to the highest region, and that he does not allow the impure ones to approach them, nor to come near one another; but commits them to be bound in indissoluble fetters by the Furies. The Pythagoreans also assert, that the whole air is full of souls, and that these are those which are ac-

counted daemones, and heroes. Also, that it is by them that dreams are sent among men, and also the tokens of disease and health; these last too, being sent not only to men, but to sheep also, and other cattle. Also, that it is they who are concerned with purifications, and expiations, and all kinds of divination, and oracular predictions, and things of that kind.

They also say, that the most important privilege in man is, the being able to persuade his soul to either good or bad. And that men are happy when they have a good soul; yet, that they are never quiet, and that they never retain the same mind long. Also, that an oath is justice; and that on that account, Jupiter is called Jupiter of Oaths ("Ogx/oj). Also, that virtue" is harmony, and health, and universal good, and God; on which account everything owes its existence and consistency to har-mony. Also, that friendship is a harmonious equality.

Again, they teach that one ought not to pay equal honours to Gods and to heroes; but that one ought to honour the Gods at all times, extolling them with praises, clothed in white garments, and keeping one's body chaste; but that one ought not to pay such honour to the heroes till after midday. Also, that a state of purity is brought about by purifications, and washings, and sprinklings, and by a man's purifying himself from all funerals, or concubinage, or pollution of every kind, and by abstaining from all flesh that has either been killed or died of itself, and from mullets, and from melanuri, and from eggs, and from such animals as lay eggs, and from beans, and from other things which are prohibited by those who have the charge of the mysteries in the temples.

And Aristotle says, in his treatise on Beans, that Pythagoras enjoined his disciples to abstain from beans, either because they resemble some part of the human body, or because they are like the gates of hell (for they are the only plants without parts); or because they dry up other plants, or because they are representatives of universal nature, or because they are used in elections in oligarchical governments. He also forbade his disciples to pick up what fell from the table, for the sake of accustoming them not to eat immoderately, or else because such things belong to the dead.

But Aristophanes says, that what falls belongs to the heroes; saying, in his Heroes:—
Never taste the things which fall
From the table on the floor.

He also forbade his disciples to eat white poultry, because a cock of that oolour was sacred to Month, and was also a suppliant. He was also accounted a good animal; and he was sacred to the God Month, for he indicates the time.

The Pythagoreans were also forbidden to eat of all fish that were sacred; on the ground that the same animals ought not to be served up before both Gods and men, just as the same things do not belong to freemen and to slaves. Now, white is an indication of a good nature, and black of a bad one. Another of the precepts of Pythagoras was, that men ought not to break bread; because in ancient times friends used to assemble around one loaf, as they even now do among the barbarians. Nor would he allow men to divide bread which unites them. Some think that he laid down this rule in reference to the judgment which takes place in hell; some because this practice engenders timidity in war. According to others, what is alluded to is the Union, which presides over the government of the universe.

Another of his doctrines was, that of all solid figures the sphere was the most beautiful; and of all plane figures, the circle. That old age and all diminution were similar, and also increase and youth were identical. That health was the permanence of form, and disease the destruction of it. Of salt his opinion was, that it ought to be set before people as a reminder of justice; for salt preserves everything which it There is a great variety of suggestions as to the proper reading here. There is evidently some corruption in the text.
touches, and it is composed of the purest particles of water and sea.

These are the doctrines which Alexander asserts that he discovered in the Pythagorean treatises; and Aristotle gives a similar account of them.

XV. Timon, in his Silli, has not left unnoticed the dignified appearance of Pythagoras, when ho attacks him on other points. And his words are these:—
Pythagoras, who often teaches
Precepts of magic, and with speeches
Of long high-sounding diction draws,
From gaping crowds, a vain applause.

And respecting his having been different people at different times, Xenophanes adds his evidence in an elegiac poem which commences thus:—
Now I will on another subject touch,
And lead the way.

And the passage in which he mentions Pythagoras is as follows:— They say that once, as passing by he saw
A dog severely beaten, he did pity him,
And spoke as follows to the man who beat him:—
" Stop now, and beat him not; since in his body,
I Abides the soul of a dear friend of mine,
Whose voice I recognized as he was crying."

These are the words of Xenophanes. Cratinus also ridiculed him in his Pythagorean Woman; but in his Tarentines, he speaks thus:—
They are accustomed, if by chance they see
A private individual abroad,
To try what powers of argument he has, i
How he can speak and reason: and they bother him
With strange antithesis and forced conclusions,
Errors, comparisons, and magnitudes,
Till they have filled and quite perplex'd his mind.

And Innesimachus says in his Alcmaeon:—
As we do sacrifice to the Phoebus whom-
Pythagoras worships, never eating aught
Which has the breath of life.

Austophon says in his Pythagorean:— A. He said that when he did descend below
Among the shades in Hell, he there beheld
All men who e'er had died; and there he saw,
That the Pythagoreans differ'd much
From all the rest; for that with them alone
Did Pluto deign to eat, much honouring Their pious habits.
B. He's a civil God,
If he likes eating with such dirty fellows.

And again, in the same play he says:—
They eat
Nothing but herbs and vegetables, and drink
Pure water only. But their lice are such, Their cloaks so dirty, and their unwash'd scent
So rank, that no one of our younger men Will for a moment bear them.

XXI. Pythagoras died in this manner. When he was sitting with some of his companions in Milo's house, some one of those whom he did not think worthy of admission into it, was excited by envy to set fire to it. But some say that the people of Crotona themselves did this, being afraid lest he might aspire to the tyranny. And that Pythagoras was caught as he was trying to escape; and coming to a place full of beans, he stopped there, saying that it was better to be caught than to trample on the beans, and better to be slain than to speak; and so he was murdered by those who were pursuing him. And in this way, also, most of his companions were slain; being in number about forty; but that a very few did escape, among whom were Archippus, of Tarentum, and Lysis, whom I have mentioned before.

But Dicaearchus relates that Pythagoras died afterwards, having escaped as far as the temple of the Muses, at Metapontum, and that he died there of starvation, having abstained from food for forty days. And Heraclides says, in his abridgment of the life of Satyrus, that after he had buried Pherecydes in Delos, he returned to Italy, and finding there a superb banquet prepared at the house of Milo, of Cortona, he left Crotona, and went to Metapontum, and there put an end to his life by starvation, not wishing to live any longer. But Hermippus says, that when there was war between the people of Agrigentum and the Syracusans, Pythagoras went out with his usual companions, and took the part of the Agrigentines; aud as they were put to flight, he ran all round a field of beans, instead of crossing it, and so was slain by the Syracusans; and that the rest, being about five-and-thirty in number, were burnt at Tarentum, when they were trying to excite a sedition in the state against the principal magistrates.

Hermippus also relates another story about Pythagoras. For he says that when he was in Italy, he made a subterraneous apartment, and charged his mother to write an account of everything that took place, marking the time of each on a tablet, and then to send them down to him, until he came up again; and that his mother did so; and that Pythagoras came up again after a certain time, lean, and reduced to a skeleton; and that he came into the public assembly, and said that he had arrived from the shades below, and then he recited to them all that had happened during his absence. And they, being charmed by what he told them, wept and lamented, and believed that Pythagoras was a divine being; so that they even entrusted their wives to him, as likely to' learn some good from him; and that they too were called Pythagoreans. And this is the story of Hermippus.

XXII. And Pythagoras had a wife, whose name was Theano; the daughter of Brontinus, of Crotona. But some say that she was the wife of Brontinus, and only a pupil of Pythagoras. And he had a daughter named Damo, as Lysis mentions in his letter to Hipparchus; where he speaks thus of Pythagoras: "And many say that you philosophize in public, as Pythagoras also used to do; who, when he had entrusted his Commentaries to Damo, his daughter, charged her to divulge them to no person out of the house. And she, though she might have sold his discourses for much money, would not abandon them, for she thought poverty and obedience to her fathers injunctions more valuable than gold; and that too, though she was a woman."

He had also a son, named Telauges, who was the successor of his father in his school, and who, according to some authors, was the teacher of Empedocles. At least Hippobotus relates that Empedocles said:—

'Telauges, noble youth, whom in due time,
Theano bore to wise Pythagoras." *t*

But there is no book extant, which is the work of Telauges, though there are some extant, which are attributed to his mother Theano. And they tell a story of her, that once, when she was asked how long a woman ought to be absent from her husband to be pure, she said, the moment she leaves her own husband, she is pure; but she is never pure at all, after she leaves any one else. And she recommended a woman, who was going to her husband, to put off her modesty with her clothes, and when she left him, to resume it again with her clothes; and when she was asked, " What clothes?" she said, " Those which cause you to be called a woman." XXIII. Now Pythagoras, as Heraclides, the son of Sarapian, relates, died when he was eighty years of age; according to his own account of his age, but according to the common account, he was more than ninety. And we have written a sportive epigram on him, which is couched in the following terms:—

You're not the only man who has abstained
Prom living food, for so likewise have we;
And who, I'd like to know did ever taste
Food while alive, most sage Pythagoras?
When meat is boil'd, or roasted well and salted,
I don't think it can well be called living.
Which, therefore, without scruple then we eat it,
And call it no more living flesh, but meat.

And another, which runs thus:—

Pythagoras was'so wise a man, that he
Never eat meat himself, and called it sin.
And yet he gave good joints of beef to others.
So that I marvel at his principles;
Who others wronged, by teaching them to do
What he believed unholy for himself.

And another, as follows:—

Should you Phythagoras' doctrine wish to know,
Look on the centre of Euphorbus' shield.
For he asserts there lived a man of old,
And when he had no longer an existence,
He still could say that he had been alive,
Or else he would not still be living now.

And this one too:

Alas! alas! why did Pythagoras hold
Beans in such wondrous honour? Why, besides,
Did he thus die among his choice companions?
There was a field of beans; and so the sage,
Died in the common road of Agrigentum,
Rather than trample down his favourite beans.

XXIV. And he flourished about the sixtieth olympiad: and his system lasted for nine or ten generations. And the last of the Pythagoreans, whom Aristoxenus knew, were Xenophilus, the Chalcidean, from Thrace; and Phanton the Phliasian, and Echurates, and Diodes, and Polymnestus, who were also Phliasians, and they were disciples of Philolaus and Eurytus, of Tarentum.

XXV. And there were four men of the name of Pythagoras, about the same time, at no great distance from one another. One was a native of Crotona, a man who attained tyrannical power; the second was a Phliasian, a trainer of wrestlers, as some say; the third was a native of Zacynthus; the fourth was this our philosopher, to whom they say the mysteries of philosophy belong, in whose time that proverbial phrase, " Ipse dixit," was introduced into ordinary life. Some also affirm, that there was another man of the name of Pythagoras, a statuary of Rhodes; who is believed to have been the first discoverer of rhythm and proportion; and another was a Samian statuary; and another an orator, of no reputation; and another was a physician, who wrote a treatise on Squills; and also some essays on Homer; and another was a man, who wrote a history of the affairs of the Dorians, as we are told by Dionysius.

But Eratosthenes says, as Phavorinus quotes him, in the eighth book of his Universal History, that this philosopher, of whom we are speaking, was the first man who ever practised boxing in a scientific manner, in the forty-eighth olympiad, having his hair long, and being clothed in a purple robe; and that he was rejected from the competition among boys, and being ridiculed for his application, he immediately entered among the men, and came off victorious. And this statement is confirmed among other things, by the epigram which Theaetetus composed:—

Stranger, if e'er you knew Pythagoras,
Pythagoras, the man with flowing hair,
The celebrated boxer, erst of Samos;
I am Pythagoras. And if you ask
A citizen of Elis of my deeds,
You'll surely think he is relating fables.

Phavorinus says, that he employed definitions, on account of the mathematical subjects to which he applied himself. And that Socrates and those who were his pupils, did so still more; and that they were subsequently followed in this by Aristotle and the Stoics.

He too, was the first person, who ever gave the name of x.6tffits to the universe, and the first who called the earth round; though Theophrastus attributes this to Parmenides, and Zeno to Hesiod. They say too, that Cylon used to be a constant adversary of his, as Antidicus was of Socrates. And this epigram also used to be repeated, concerning Pythagoras the athlete: —

Pythagoras of Samos, son of Crates,
Came while a child to the Olympic games,
Eager to battle for the prize in boxing.

XXVI. There is a letter of this philosopher extant, which is couched in the following terms:— PYTHAGORAS TO ANAXIMENES.

"You too, my most excellent friend, if you were not superior to Pythagoras, in birth and reputation, would have migrated from Miletus and gone elsewhere. But now the reputation of your father keeps you back, which perhaps would have restrained me too, if I had been like Anaximenes. But if you, who are the most eminent man, abandon the cities, all their ornaments will be taken from them, and the Median power will be more dangerous to them. Nor is it always seasonable to be studying astronomy, but it is more honourable to exhibit a regard for one's country. And I myself am not always occupied about speculations of my own fancy, but I am busied also with the wars which the Italians are waging against one another.

But since we have now finished our account of Pythagoras, we must also speak of the most eminent of the Pythagoreans. After whom, we must mention those who are spoken of more promiscuously in connection with no particular school; and then we will connect the whole series of philosophers worth speaking of, till we arrive at Epicurus, as we have already promised.

Now Jelanges and Theano we have mentioned; and we must now speak of Empedocles, in the first place, for, according to some accounts, he was a pupil of Pythagoras.

LIFE OF EMPEDOCLES.

I. Empedocles, as Hippobotus relates, was the son of Meton, the son of Empedocles, and a citizen of Agrigentum. And Timaeus, in the fifteenth book of his Histories, gives the same account, adding that Empedocles, the grandfather of the poet, was also a most eminent man. And Hermippus tells the same story as Timaeus; and in the same spirit Heraclides, in his treatise on Diseases, relates that he was of an illustrious family, since his father bred a fine stud of horses. Erastothenes, in his List of the Conquerors at the Olympic Games, says, that the father of Meton gained the victory in the seventy-first olympiad, quoting Aristotle as his authority for the assertion.

But Apollodorus, the grammarian, in his Chronicles, says that he was the son of Meton; and Glaucus says that he came to Thurii when the city was only just completed. And then proceeding a little further, he adds:—

And some relate that he did flee from thence,
And came to Syracuse, and on their side
Did fight in horrid war against th' Athenians;
But those men seem to me completely wrong—
For by this time he must have been deceased,
Or very old, which is not much believed;
For Aristotle, and Heraclides too,
Say that he died at sixty years of age.

But certainly the person who got the victory with a single horse in the seventy-first olympiad was a namesake of this man, and that it is which deceived Apollodorus as to the age of this philosopher.

But Satyrus, in his Lives, asserts, that Empedocles was the son of Exaenetus, and that he also left a son who was named Exaenetus. And that in the same Olympiad, he himself gained the victory with the single horse; and his son, in wrestling, or, as Heraclides says in his Abridgment, in running. But I have found in the Commentaries of Phavorinus, that Empedocles sacrificed, and gave as a feast to the spectators of the games, an ox made of honey and flour, and that he had a brother named Callicratidas.

But Jelanges, the son of Pythagoras, in his letters to Philolaus, says that Empedocles was the son of Archinomus; and that he was a citizen of Agrigentum, he himself asserts at the beginning of his Purifications.

Friends, who the mighty citadel inhabit,
Which crowns the golden wave&;of Acragas.

And this is enough to say about his family.

II. Timaeus, in his ninth book, relates that he was a pupil of Pythagoras, saying that he was afterwards convicted of having divulged his doctrines, in the same way as Plato was, and therefore that he was forbidden from thenceforth to attend his school. And they say that

Pythagoras himself mentions him when he says:—

And in that band there was a learned man,
Of wondrous wisdom; one, who of all men
Had the profoundest wealth of intellect.

But some say that when the philosopher says this, he is referring to Parmenides.

Neanthes relates, that till the time of Philolaus and Empedocles, the Pythagoreans used to admit all persons indiscriminately into their school; but when Empedocles made their doctrines public by means of his poems, then they made a law to admit no Epic poet. And they say that the same thing happened to Plato; for that he oo was excluded from the school. But who was the teacher of the Pythagorean school that Empedocles was a pupil of, they do not say; for, as for the letter of Jelanges, in which he is stated to have been a pupil of Hippasus and Brontinus, that is not worthy of belief. But Theophrastus says that he was an imitator and a rival of Parmenides, in his poems, for that he too had delivered his opinions on natural philosophy in epic verse.

Hermippus, however, says that he was an imitator, not of Parmenides, but of Xenophanes with whom he lived; and that he imitated his epic style, and that it was at a, later period that he fell in with the Pythagoreans. But Alcidamas, in his Natural Philosophy, says, that Zeno and Empedoclea were pupils of Parmenides, about the same time; and that they subsequently seceded from him; and that Zeno adopted a philosophical system peculiar to himself; but that Empedocles became a pupil of Anaxagoras and Pythagoras, and that he imitated the pompous demeanour, and way of life, and gestures of the one, and the system of Natural Philosophy of the other.

III. And Aristotle, in his Sophist, says that Empedocles was the first person who invented rhetoric, and Zeno the first person who invented dialectics. And in his book on Poetry, he says, that Empedocles was a man of Homeric genius, and endowed with great power of language, and a great master of metaphor, and a man who employed all the successful artifices of poetry, and also that when he had written several poems, and among them one on the passage of the Hellespont, by Xerxes, and also the prooamium of a hymn to Apollo, his daughter subsequently burnt them, or, as Hieronymus says, his sister, burning, the prooemium unintentionally, but the Persian poem on purpose, because it was incomplete. And speaking generally, he says that he wrote tragedies and political treatises.

But Heraclides, the son of Sarapion, says that the tragedies were the work of some other Empedocles; and Hieronymus says that he had met with forty-three. Neanthes, too, affirms that when he was a young man, he wrote tragedies, and that he himself had subsequently met with them; and Satyrus, in his Lives, states that he was a physician, and also a most excellent orator. And accordingly, that Gorgias, of Leontini, was his pupil, a man of the greatest eminence as a rhetorician, and one who left behind him a treatise containing a complete system of the art; and who, as we are told by Apollodorus, in his Chronicles, lived to the age of a hundred and nine years.

IV. Satyrus tells us that he used to say that he had been present when Empedocles was practising magic; and that he professes this science, and many others too in his poems when he says:—

And all the drugs which can relieve disease,
Or soften the approach of age, shall be
Revealed to your inquiries; I do know them,
And I to you alone will them disclose.
You shall restrain the fierce unbridled winds,
Which, rushing o'er the earth, bow down the corn.
And crush the farmer's hopes. And when you will,
You shall recall them back to sweep the land:
Then you shall learn to dry the rainy clouds,
And bid warm summer cheer the heart of men.
Again, at your behest, the drought shall yield
To wholesome show'rs: when you give the word
Hell shall restore its dead.

V. And Timaeus,-in his eighteenth book, says, that this man was held in great esteem on many accounts; for that once, when the etesian gales were blowing violently, so as to injure the crops, he ordered some asses to be flayed, and some bladders to be made of their hides, and these he placed on the hills and high places to catch the wind. And so, when the wind ceased, he was called wind-forbidden (xwXuffavf/ias). And Heraclides, in his treatise on Diseases, says that he dictated to Pausanias the statement which he made about the dead woman. Now Pausanias, as both Aristippus and Satyrus agree, was much attached to him; and he dedicated to him the works which he wrote on Natural Philosophy, in the following terms:—

Hear, 0 Pausanias, son of wise Anchites.

He also wrote an epigram upon him:—

Gela, his native land, does boast the birth
Of wise Anchites' son, that great physician,
So fitly named Pausanias, from his skill;
A genuine son of Esculapius,
Who has stopped many men whom fell disease
Marked for its own, from treading those dark paths
Which lead to Proserpine's infernal realms.

The case of the dead woman above mentioned, Heraclides says, was something of this sort; that he kept her corpse for thirty days dead, and yet free from corruption; on which account he has called himself a physician and a prophet, taking it also from these verses:— From *irain),* to cause to cease, *avia,* sorrow.

Frienda who the mighty citadel inhabit,
Which crowns the golden waves of Acragas.
Votaries of noble actions, Hail to ye;
I, an immortal God, no longer mortal,

Now live among you well revered by all,
As is my due, crowned with holy fillets
And rosy garlands. And whene'er I come
To wealthy cities, then from men and women
Due honours meets me; and crowds follow me,
Seeking the way which leads to gainful glory.
Some ask for oracles, and some entreat,
For remedies against all kinds of sickness.

VII. And he says that Agrigentum was a very large city, since it had eight hundred thousand inhabitants: on which account Empedocles, seeing the people immersed in luxury, said, " The men of Agrigentum devote themselves wholly to luxury as if they were to die tomorrow, but they furnish their houses as if they were to live for ever." VIII. It is said that Cleomenes, the rhapsodist, sung tbis very poem, called the Purifications, at Olympia; at least this is the account given by Phavorirms, in his Commentaries.

IX. And Aristotle says, that he was a most liberal man, and far removed from anything like a domineering spirit; since he constantly refused the sovereign power when it was offered to him, as Xanthus assures us in his account of him, showing plainly that he preferred a simple style of living. And Timaeus tells the same story, giving at the same time the reason why he was so very popular. For he says that when on one occasion, he was invited to a banquet by one of the magistrates, the wine was carried about, but the supper was not served up. And as every one else kept silence, he, disapproving of what he saw, bade the servants bring in the supper; but the person who had invited him said that he was waiting for the secretary of the council. And when he came he was appointed master of the feast, at the instigation of the giver of it, and then he gave a plain intimation of his tyrannical inclinations, for he ordered all the guests to drink, and those who did not drink were to have the wine poured over their heads. Empedocles said nothing at the moment, but the next day he summoned them before the court, and procured the execution of both the entertainer and the master of the feast.

And this was the beginning of his political career. And at another time, when Acron, the physician, asked of the council a place where he might erect a monument to his father, on account of his eminence as a physician, Empedocles came forward and opposed any such grant, adducing many arguments on the ground of equality, and also putting the following question: —" And what elegy shall we inscribe upon it? Shall we say:—

"Aicpov tTjrpov'AKpwv' 'AKpnyavr-lvov irarpbg aicpov KpVTTTU KptjpvOS dlCpO£ ITClTpiSog aKpoTaTtg

But some give the second line thus:—
'AKporart/c Kopvipqg rti/i/3oc arpo£ icartx"

And others assert that it is the composition of Simonides.

But afterwards Empedocles abolished the assembly of a thousand, and established a council in which the magistrates were to hold office for three years, on such a footing that it ""V should consist not only of rich men, but of those who were favourers of the interests of the people. Timteus, however, in his first and second book (for he often mentions him), says that he appeared to entertain opinions adverse to a republic. And, as far as his poetry goes, any one may see that he was arrogant and self-satisfied. Accordingly, he says:— Hail to ye,
I, an immortal God, no Jonger mortal,
Now live among you:
And so on.

But when he went to the Olympic games he was considered a worthy object of general attention; so that there was no mention made of any one else in comparison of Empedocles.

X. Afterwards, indeed, when Agrigentum was settled, the descendants of his enemies opposed his return; on which account he retired to Peloponnesus, where he died. And Timon has not let even Empedocles escape, but satirises him in this style, saying:—

And then Empedocles, the honeyed speaker
Of soft forensic speeches; he did take
As many offices as he was able,
Creating magistrates who wanted helpers.

It is impossible to give the force of this epigram in any other language. It is a pun on 'Axpuiv, 'Aicpayag, and dicpoc. The last word But there are two accounts of the manner of his death.

XI. For Heraclides, relating the story about the dead woman, how Empedocles got great glory from sending away a dead woman restored to life, says that he celebrated a sacrifice in the field of Pisianax, and that some of his friends were invited, among whom was Pausanias. And then, after the banquet, they lay down, some going a little way off, and some lying under the trees close by in the field, and some wherever they happened to choose. But Empedocles himself remained in the place where he had been sitting. But when day broke, and they arose, he alone was not found. And when he was sought for, and the servants were examined and said that they did not know, one of them said, that at midnight he had heard a loud voice calling Empedocles; and that then he himself rose up and saw a great light from heaven, but nothing else. And as they were all amazed at what had taken place, Pausanias descended and sent some people to look for him; but afterwards he was commanded not to busy himself about the matter, as he was informed that what had happened was deserving of thankfulness, and that they behoved to sacrifice to Empedocles as to one who had become a God.

Hermippus says also, that a woman of the name of Panthea, a native of Agrigentum, who had been given over by the physicians, was cured by him, and that it was on this account that he celebrated a sacrifice; and that the guests invited were about eighty in number. But Hippobotus says that he rose up and went away as if he were going to mount Etna; and that when he arrived at the crater of fire he leaped in, and disappeared, wishing to establish a belief that he had become a God. But afterwards the truth was detected by one of his slippers having been dropped. For he used to wear slippers with brazen soles. Pausanias, however, contradicts this statement.

meaning not only *high, lofty,* but also *eminent, very skilful.* The plain English would be:—" The lofty height of a most eminent country conceals Acron, a skilful physician of Acragas, the son of a skilful father." The variation would be:—" A high tomb on a very high summit, conceals," &c. This story is mentioned by Horace:— Siculique poetae,
Narrabo interitum; deus immortalis haberi,
Dum cupit'Empedoeles ardentem frigidus tnam,
Insiluit. A P. 466.

But Diodorus, of Ephesus, writing about Anaximander, says that Empedocles imitated him; indulging in a tragic sort of pride, and wearing magnificent appareL And when a pestilence attacked the people of Selinus, by reason of the bad smells arising from the adjacent river, so that the men died and the women bore dead children, Empedocles'contrived a plan, and brought into the same channel two other rivers at his own expense; and so, by mixing their waters with that of the other river, he sweetened the stream. And as the pestilence was removed in this way, when the people of Selinus were on one occasion holding a festival on the bank of the river, Empedocles appeared among them; and they rising up, offered him adoration, and prayed to him as to a God. And he, wishing to confirm this idea which they had adopted of him, leaped into the fire.

But Timaeus contradicts all these stories; saying expressly, that he departed into Peloponnesus, and never returned at all, on which account the manner of his death is uncertain. And he especially denies the tale of Heraclides in his fourth book; for he says that Pisianax was a Syracusan, and had no field in the district of Agrigentum; but that Pausanias erected a monument in honour of his friend, since such a report had got about concerning him; and, as he was a rich man, made it a statue and little chapel, as one might erect to a God. " How then," adds Timaaus, " could he have leaped into a crater, of which, though they were in the neighbourhood, he had never made any mention? He died then in Peloponnesus; and there is nothing extraordinary in there being no tomb of his to be seen; for there are many other men who have no tomb visible." These are the words of Timaeus; and he adds further, " But Heraclides is altogether a man fond of strange stories, and one who would assert that a man had fallen from the moon."

Hippobotus says, that there was a clothed statue of Empe docles which lay formerly in Agrigentum, but which was afterwards placed in front of the Senate House of the Romans divested of its clothing, as the Romans had carried it off and erected it there. And there are traces of some inscriptions or reliefs still discernible on it.

Neanthes, of Cyzicus, who also wrote about the Pythagoreans, says, that when Meton was dead, the seeds of tyrannical power began to appear; and that then Empedocles persuaded the Agrigentines to desist from their factious disputes, and to establish political equality. And besides, as there were many of the female citizens destitute of dowry, he portioned them out of his own private fortune. And relying on these actions of his, he assumed a purple robe and wore a golden circlet on his hand, as Phavorinus relates in the first book of his Commentaries. He also wore slippers with brazen soles, and a Delphian garland. His hair was let grow very long, and he had boys to follow him; and he himself always preserved a solemn countenance, and a uniformly grave deportment. And he marched about in such style, that he seemed to all the citizens, who met him and who admired his deportment, to exhibit a sort of likeness to kingly power. And afterwards, it happened that as on the occasion of some festival he was going in a chariot to Messene, he was upset and broke his thigh; and he was taken ill in consequence, and so died, at the age of seventy-seven. And his tomb is in Megara.

But as to his age, Aristotle differs from this account of Neanthes; for he asserts that he died at sixty years of age; others again say, that he was a hundred and nine when he died. He flourished about the eighty-fourth olympiad. Demetrius, of Traezen, in his book against the Sophists, reports that, as the lines of Homer say:—

He now, self-murdered, from a beam depends,
And his mad soul to blackest hell descends.

But in the letter of Telauges, which has been mentioned before, it is said that he slipped down through old age, and fell into the sea, and so died.

And this is enough to say about his death.

There is also a jesting epigram of ours upon him, in our collection of Poems in all Metres, which runs thus:—

You too, Empedocles, essayed to purge
Your body in the rapid flames, and drank
The liquid fire from the restless crater;
I say not that you threw yourself at once
Into the stream of Etna's fiery flood.
But seeking to conceal yourself you fell,
And so you met with unintended death.
This is slightly parodied from Homer. Od. xi. 278. Pope's Version, 337.

And another:—

'Tis said the wise Empedoclea did fall
Out of his chariot, and so broke his thigh:
But if he leapt into the flames of Etna,
How could his tomb be shown in Megara?

XII. The following were some of his doctrines. He used to assert that there were four elements, fire, water, earth, and air. And that that is friendship by which they are united, and discord by which they are separated. And he speaks thus on this subject:—

Bright Jove, life-giving Juno, Pluto dark,
And Nestis, who fills mortal eyes with tears.

Meaning by Jove fire, by Juno the earth, by Pluto the air, and by Nestis water. And these things, says he, never cease alternating with one another; inasmuch as this arrangement is perpetual. Accordingly, he says subsequently:—

Sometimes in friendship bound they coalesce,
Sometimes they're parted by fell discord's hate.

And he asserts that the sun is a vast assemblage of fire, and that it is larger than the moon. And the moon is disk-shaped; and that the heaven itself is like crystal; and that the soul inhabits every kind of form of animals and plants. Accordingly, he thus expresses himself.

For once I was a boy, and once a girL
A bush, a bird, a fish who swims the sea,

XIII. His writings on Natural Philosophy and his Purifications extend to five thousand verses; and his Medical Poem to six hundred; and his Tragedies we have spoken of previously.

LIFE OF EPICHARMUS.

I. Epicharmus was a native of Cos, the son of Helothales; he also was a pupil of Pythagoras. When he was three months old he was brought to Megara, in Sicily, and from thence he came to Syracuse, as he himself tells us in his writings. And on his statue there is the following inscription.

As the bright sun excels the other stars,
As the sea far exceeds the river streams:
So does sage Epicharmus men surpass,
Whom hospitable Syracuse has crowned.

II. He has left behind him Commentaries in which he treats of natural philosophy, and delivers apophthegms, and discusses medicine. ' He has also added brief notes to many of his commentaries, in 'which he declares plainly that he is the author of the works.

III. He died at the age of ninety years.

LIFE OF ARCHYTAS.

I. Archytas was a native of Tarentum, and the son of Innesagoras; or, as Aristoxenus relates, of Histiaeus.

II. He also was a Pythagorean; and he it was who saved Plato's life by means of a letter, when he was in danger of being put to death by Dionysius. III. He was a man held in very general esteem on account of his universal virtue; and he was seven times appointed general of his countrymen, when no one else had ever held the office for more than one year, as the law forbade it to be held for a longer period. IV. Plato wrote his letters to him; as he had begun the correspondence by writing himself to Plato, which he did in the following manner:— ARCHYTAS TO PLATO, GREETING. " I am very glad that you have recovered from your delicate state of health; for you yourself have sent me word of your recovery, and Lamiscus gives the same account. I have been much occupied with some commentaries, and have been among the Lucanians, and have met with the descendants of Orellus. I have now in my possession, and I send to you the treatises on Law, and Kingly Power, and Piety, and the Creation of the Universe. As for the rest, I have not been able to find them, but whenever I do find any, I will send them to you."

B B

Thus wrote Archytas. And Plato sent him an answer in the following terms:—
PLATO TO ARCHYTAS, GREETING.

' I was exceedingly glad to receive the Commentaries which came from you, and I have admired their author in the greatest possible, degree; and he seems to us to be. a man worthy of his ancient ancestors. For they are said to have been originally natives of Myra; and to have been among the Trojans, whom Laomedon took with him, gallant men, as the story handed down by tradition attests. As for my Commentaries which you ask me for, they are not yet completed, but, such as they are I send them to you. And on the propriety of taking care of such things we are both agreed, so that I have no need to impress anything on you on that head. Farewell.
'

These then are the letters which these philososophers wrote to one another.

V. There were four people of the name of Archytas. The first, this man of whom we are speaking. The second was a Mytilenean, a musician. The third wrote a treatise on Agriculture. The fourth was an epigrammatic poet. Some writers also make mention of a fifth, who was an architect; and there is a book on mechanics extant which is attributed to him; which begins in this way:—

" This is what I heard from Teucer, the Carthaginian."

And concerning the musician, the following story is told: That once he was reproached for not making himself heard, and he replied, "My organ contends on my behalf, and speaks." VI. Aristoxenus says, that this Pythagorean was never once defeated while acting as general. But that as he was attacked by envy, he once gave up his command, and his army was immediately taken prisoner.

VII. He was the first person who applied mathematical principles to mechanics, and reduced them to a system; and the first also who gave a methodical impulse to descriptive geometry in seeking, in the sections of a demicylinder for a proportional mean, which should enable him to find the double of a given cube. He was also the first person who ever gave the geometrical measure of a cube, as Plato mentions in his Eepublic.

LIFE OF ALCM,EON.

I. Alcmjeon was a citizen of Crotona; he also was a pupil of Pythagoras. And the chief part of his writings are on medical subjects; but he also at times discusses points of natural philosophy, and asserts that the greater part of human affairs have two sides. He appears to have been the first person who wrote a treatise on Natural Philosophy, as Phavorinus affirms, in his Universal History; and he used to argue that the moon had the same nature for ever which she had at that moment.

II. He was the son of Pirithus, as he himself states at the beginning of his treatise, where he says, " Alcmaeou, of Crotona, the son of Pirithus, says this to Brontinus, and Leon, and Bathyllus. About things invisible, and things mortal, the Gods alone have a certain knowledge; but men may form conjectures...." And so on.

He used also to say that the soul was immortal, and that it was in a state of perpetual motion iu the same way as the sun.

LIFE OF HIPPASUS.

I. Hippasus was a citizen of Metapontum, and a pupil of Pythagoras.

II. He used to say that the time of the changes of the world was definite, and that the universe also was finite, and in a state of perpetual motion. III. Demetrius, in his treatise on People of the same Name, says that he left no writings behind him. IV. There were two people of the name of Hippasus; this man, and another who wrote an account of the Constitution of the Lacedaemonians, in five books. And he was himself a Lacedaemonian. LIFE OF PHILOLAUS.

I. Philolaus was a native of Crotona, and a pupil of Pythagoras, it was from him that Plato wrote to Dion to take care and purchase the books of Pythagoras.

II. And he died under suspicion of having designed to seize on the tyranuy; and we have written an epigram on him:—

I say that all men ought above all things
  To guard against suspicion. For, though. innocent,
  Still if you are suspected, you're unfortunate.
  And thus his native city of Crotona
  Slew Philolaus; for the jealous citizens
  Thought that his house betrayed a tyrant's purpose.

III. His theory was, that everything was produced by harmony and necessity. And he was the first person who affirmed that the earth moved in a circle; though some attribute the assertion of this principle to Icetas of Syracuse. IV. He wrote one book, which flermippus reports, on the authority of some unknown writer, that Plato the philosopher purchased when he was in Sicily (having come thither to the court of Dionysius), of the relations of Philolaus, for forty Alexandrian minae of silver; and that from this book he copied his Timaeus. But others say that Plato received it as a present, after having obtained his liberty for a young man, one of the disciples of Philolaus, who had been arrested by Dionysius. Demetrius, in his treatise on people of the same name, says that he was the first of the Pythagoreans who wrote a treatise on Natural Philosophy; and it begins thus:—

" But nature in the world has been composed of bodies infinite and finite, and so is the whole world and all that is in it. " LIFE OF EUDOXUS.

I. Eudoxus was the son of Eschines, and a native of Cnidos. He was an astronomer, a geometrician, a physician, and a lawgiver. In geometry he was a pupil of Archytas, and in medicine of Philistion, the Sicilian, as Callimachus relates in his Tablets; and Sotion, in his Successions, asserts that he was likewise a pupil of Plato; for that, when he was twenty-three years of age, and in very narrow circumstances, he came to Athens with Theomedon the physician, by whom he was chiefly supported, being attracted by the reputation of the Socratic school. Some say that his attachment to Theomedon was cemented by nearer ties. And when he had arrived at Pira3us, he went up to the city every day, and when he had heard the Sophists lecture he returned. And having spent two months there, he returned home again; and being again aided by the contributions of his friends, he set sail for Egypt, with Chrysippus the physician, bearing letters of introduction from Agesilaus to Nectanabis, and that he recommended him to the priests.

II. And having remained there a year and four months, he shaved his eyebrows after the manner of the Egyptian priests, and composed, as it is said, the treatise called the Octacteris. From thence he went to Cyzicus, and to the Propontis, in both of which places he lived as a Sophist; he also went to the court of Mansolus. And then, in this manner, he returned again to Athens, having a great many disciples with him, for the sake, as some say, of annoying Plato, because he had originally discarded him from his school. Some say, that when Plato gave an entertainment on one occasion, Eudoxus, as the guests were very numerous, introduced the fashion of sitting in a semicircle. Nichomachus, the son of Aristotle, affirms that he used to say, that pleasure was the good.

III. He was received in his own country with great honours, as the decree that was passed respecting him shows. He was also accounted very illustrious among the Greeks, having given laws to his own fellow citizens, as Hermippus tells us in the fourth book of his account of the Seven Wise Men; and having also written treatises on Astronomy and Geometry, and several other considerable works.

He had three daughters, Actis, Philtis, and Delphis. And Eratosthenes asserts, in his books addressed to Baton, that he also composed dialogues entitled Dialogues of Dogs; others say that these were written by some Egyptians, in their own language, and that Eudoxus translated them, and published them in Greece. One of his pupils was Chryeippus, of Cnidos, son of Erineus, who learnt of him all that he knew about the Gods, and the world, and the heavenly bodies; and who learnt medicine from Philistion the Sicilian. He also left some very admirable Reminiscences.

IV. He had a son of the name of Aristagoras, who was the teacher of Chrysippus, the son of Aethlius; be was the author of a work on Remedies for the Eyes, as speculations on natural philosophy had come very much under his notice.

V. There were three people of the name of Eudoxus. The first, this man of whom we are speaking; the second, a Rhodian, who wrote histories; the third, a Sicilist, a son of Agathocles, a comic poet, who gained three victories at the Dionysia in the city, and five at the Lenaea, as Apollodorus tells us in his Chronicles. We also find another, who was a physician of Cnidos, who is mentioned by this Eudoxus, in his Circuit of the World, where he says that he used to warn people to keep constantly exercising their limbs in every kind of exercise, and their senses too.

VI. The same author says, that the Cnidean Eudoxus flourished about the hundred and third olympiad; and that he was the inventor of the theory of crooked lines. And he died in his fifty-third year. But when he was in Egypt with Conuphis, of Heliopolis, Apis licked his garment; and so the priests said that he would be short-lived, but very illustrious, as it is reported by Phavorinus in his Commentaries. And we have written an epigram on him, that runs thus:—

'Tis said, that while at Memphis wise Eudoxus
Learnt his own fate from th' holy fair-horned bull;
He said indeed no word, bulls do not speak;
Nor had kind nature e'er calf Apis gifted
With an articulately speaking mouth.
But standing on one side he lick'd his cloak,
S'lowing by this most plainly—in brief time
You shall put off your life. So death came soon,
When he had just seen three and fifty times
The Pleiads rise to warn the mariners.

There were three festivals of Bacchus at Athens at which dramatic contests took place, the *AiovCma Kar'* aypouf, or, " in the fields;" the Aijvata or rd *iv* A'vaif, or "the marshes," a part of the city near the Acropolis, m which was situated the *Aqvaiov,* an enclosure

And instead of Eudoxus, they used to call him Endoxus, on account of the brilliancy of his reputation. And since we have gone through the illustrious Pythagoreans, we must now speak of the Promiscuous philosophers, as they call them. And we will first of all speak of Heraclitus.
dedicated to Bacchus; and the *ralv anrv,* " in the city," or *ra fiiyaka Atovvaia.* The comic contests usually took place at the second or Linaean festivals. Sometimes also at the Great Dionysia., t *Ivsoioq,* glorious. LIFE OF HEKACLITUS.

I. Heraclitus was the son of Blyson, or, as some say, of Heraceon. and a citizen of Ephesus. He flourished about the sixty-ninth olympiad.

II. He was above all men of a lofty and arrogant spirit, as is plain from his writings, in which he says, " Abundant learning does not form the mind; for if it did, it would have instructed Hesiod, and Pythagoras, and likewise Xenophanes, and Hecataeus. For the only piece of real wisdom is to know that idea, which by itself will govern everything on every occasion. He used to say, too, that Homer deserved to be expelled from the games and beaten, and Archilochus likewise. He used also to say, " It is more necessary to extinguish insolence, than to put out a fire." Another of his sayings was, " Thejpeople ought to fight for the lawasfortheir city." He also attacks the Ephesians for having bamshed his companion Hermodorus, when he says, " The Ephesians deserve to have all their youth put to death, and all those who are younger still banished from their city, inasmuch as they have banished Hermodorus, the best man among them, saying,
Let no one of us be pre-eminently goodj and if there be any such person, let him" go to another city and another people."

And when he was requested to make laws for them, he refused, because the city was already immersed in a thoroughly bad constitution. And having retired to the temple of Diana with his children, he began to play at dice; and when all the Ephesians flocked round him, he said, " You wretches, what are you wondering at? is it not better to do this, than to meddle with public affairs in your company?" III. And at last, becoming a complete misanthrope, he used to live, spending his time in walking aboutHfie mountains; feeding on grasses and plants, and in consequence of these habits, he was attacked by the dropsy, and so then he returned to the city, and asked the physicians, in a riddle, whether they were able to produce a drought after wet weather. And as they did not understand him, he shut himself up in a stable for oxen, and covered himself with cow-dung, hoping to cause the wet to evaporate from him, by the warmth that this produced. And as he did himself no go good in this way, he died, having lived seventy years; and we have written an epigram upon him which runs thus:—

I've often wondered much at Heraclitus,
That he should chose to live so miserably,
And die by such a miserable fate.
For fell disease did master all his body,
With water quenching all the light of his eyes,
And bringing darkness o'er his mind and body.

But Hermippus states, that what he asked the physicians was this, whether any one could draw off the water by depressing his intestines? and when they answered that they could not, he placed himself in the sun, and ordered his servants to plaster him over with cow-dung; and being stretched out in that way, on the second day he died, and was buried in the market-place. But Neanthes, of Cyzicus says, that as he could not tear off the cow-dung, he remained there, and on account of the alteration in his appearance, he was not discovered, and so was devoured by the dogs.

IV. And he was a wonderful person, from his boyhood, since, while he was young, he used to say that he knew nothing but when he had grown up, he then used to affirm that he knew everything. And he was no one's pupil, but he I used to say, that he himself had investigated every thing, and / had learned everything of himself. But Sotion relates, that jsome people affirmed that he had been a pupil of Xenophanes. And that Ariston, stated in his account of Heraclitus, that he was cured of the dropsy, and died of some other disease. And Hippobotus gives the same account.

V. There is a book of his extant, which is about nature generally, and it is divided into three discourses; one on the Universe; one on Politics; and one on Theology. And he deposited this book in the temple of Diana, as some authors report, having written it intentionally in an obscure style, in order that only those who were able men might comprehend it, and that it might not be exposed to ridicule at the hands of the common people. Timon attacks this man also, saying:— _. Among them came that cuckoo Heraclitus
The enigmatical obscure reviler
Of all the common people.

Theophrastus asserts, that it was out of melancholy that he left some of his works half finished, and wrote several, in completely different styles; and Antisthenes, in his Successions, adduces as a proof of his lofty spirit, the fact, that he yielded to his brother the title and privileges of royalty. And his book had so high a reputation, that a sect arose in consequence of it, who were called after his own name, Heracliteans.

VI. The following may be set down in a general manner as his main principles: that everything is created from fire, and is dissolved into fire; that everything happens according to destiny, and that all existing things are harmonized, and made to agree together by opposite tendencies; and that all things are full of souls and daemons. He also discussed all the passions which exist in the world, and used also to contend that the sun was of that precise magnitude of which he appears to be. One of his sayings too was, that no one, by whatever road he might travel, could ever possibly find out the boundaries of the soul, so deeply hidden are the principles which regulate it. He used also to call opinion_thfl. sacreddisease; and to say that eye-sight wasoffelHIeceived. OrnetImesTln his writings, he expresses himself with great brilliancy and clearness; so that even the most stupid man may easily understand him, and receive an elevation of soul from him. And his conciseness, and the dignity of his style, are incomparable.

In particulars, his doctrines are of this kind. That fire is an element, and that it is by the changes of fire that all things exist; being engendered sometimes by rarity, sometimes by density. But he explains nothing clearly. He also says, that everything is produced by contrariety, and that everything flows on like a river; that the universe is finite, According to Strabo, the descendants of Androclus, the founder of Ephesus (of which family Heraclitus came), bore the title of king, and had certain prerogatives and privileges attached to the title.

and that there is one world, and that that is produced from fire, and that the whole world is in its turn again consumed by fire at certain periods, and that all this happens according to fate. That of the contraries, that which leads to production is called war and contest, and that which leads to the conflagration is called harmony and peace; that change is the road leading upward, and the road leading downward; and that the whole world' exists according to it.

For that fire, when densified becomes liquid, and becoming concrete, becomes also water; again, that the water when concrete is turned to earth, and that this is the road down; again, that the earth itself becomes fused, from which water is produced, and from that everything else is produced; and then he refers almost everything to the evaporation which takes place from the, sea; and"this fsTthe road which leads upwards. Also, that there are evaporations, both from earth and sea, some of which are bright and clear, and some are dark; and that the fire is increased by the dark ones, and the moisture by the others. But what the_ space which surrounds us i Jie_4p-soexplain. He states, however, that there are vessels in it, turned with their hollow part towards us; in which all the bright evaporations are collected, and form flames, which are the stars; and that the brightest of these flames, and the hottest, is the light of the sun; for that all the other stars are farther off from the earth; and that on this account, they give less light and warmth; and that the moon is nearer the earth, but does not move through a pure space; the sun, on the other hand, is situated in a transparent space, and one free from all admixture, preserving a well proportioned distance from us, on which account it gives us more light and more heat. And that the sun and moon are eclipsed, when the before-mentioned vessels are turned upwards. And that the different phases of the moon take place every.month, as its vessel keeps gradually turning round. Moreover, that day and night, and months and years, and rains and winds, and things of that kind, all exist according to, and are caused by, the different evaporations.

For that the bright evaporation catching fire in the circle of the sun causes day, and the predominance of the opposite one causes night; and again, from the bright one the heat is increased so as to produce summer, and from the dark one the cold gains strength and produces winter; and he also explains the causes of the other phenomena in a corresponding manner.

But with respect to the earth, he does not explain at all of what character it is, nor does he do so in the case of the vessels; and these were his main doctrines.

VII. Now, what his opinion about Socrates was, and what expressions he used when he met with a treatise of his which Euripides brought him, according to the story told by Ariston, we have detailed in our account of Socrates. Seleucus, the grammarian, however, says that a man of the name of Croton, in his Diver, relates that it was a person of the name of Crates who first brought this book into Greece; and that he said that he wanted some Delian diver who would not be drowned in it. And the book is described under several titles; some calling it the Muses, some a treatise on Nature; but Diodotus calls it— A well compacted helm to lead a man
I Straight through the path of life.
Some call it a science of morals, the arrangement of the changes of unity and of everything.

VIII. They say that when he was asked why he preserved silence, he said, " That you may talk." IX. Darius was very desirous to enjoy his conversation; and wrote thus to him:— KING DARIUS, THK SON OF HTSTASPES, ADDRESSES HERACLTTUS, OF EPHESDS, THE WISE MAN, GREETING HIM.

" You have written a book on Natural Philosophy, difficult to understand and difficult to explain. Accordingly, if in some parts it is explained literally, it seems to disclose a very important theory concerning the universal world, and all that is contained in it, as they are placed in a state of most divine motion. But commonly, the mind is kept in suspense, so that those who have studied your work the most, are not able precisely to disentangle the exact meaning of your expressions. Therefore, king Darius, the son of Hystaspes wishes to enjoy the benefit of hearing you discourse, and of receiving some There ia probably some corruption in the text here.

Grecian instruction. Come, therefore, quickly to my sight,
and to my royal palace; for the Greeks, in general, do not accord to wise men the distinction which they deserve, and disregard the admirable expositions delivered by them, which are, however, worthy of being seriously listened to and studied; but with me you shall have every kind of distinction and honour, and you shall enjoy every day honourable and worthy conversation, and your pupils' life shall become /
virtuous, in accordance with your precepts." ',

HERACLITUS, OF EPHESUS, TO KING DARIUS, THE SON OF
HTSTASPES, GREETING.

" All the men that exist in the world, are far removed from truth and just dealings; but they are full of evil foolishness, which leads them to insatiable covetousness and vain-glorious ambition. I, however, forgetting all their worthlessness, and shunning satiety, and who wish to avoid all envy on the part of my countrymen, and all appearance of arrogance, will never come to Persia, since I am quite contented with a little, and live as best suits my own inclination."

X. This was the way in which the man behaved even to the king. And Demetrius, in his treatise on People of the same Name, says that he also despised the Athenians, among whom he had a very high reputation. And that though he was himself despised by the Ephesians, he nevertheless preferred his own home. Demetrius Phaleruus also mentions him in his Defence of Socrates.

XI. There were many people who undertook to interpret his book. For Antisthenes and Heraclides, Ponticus, and Cleanthes, and Sphaerus the Stoic; and besides them Pausanias, who was surnamed Heraclitistes, and Nicoraedes, and Dionysius, all did so. And of the grammarians, Diodotus undertook the same task; and he says that the subject of the book is not natural philosophy, but politics; and that all that is said in it about natural philosophy, is only by way of illustration. And Hieronymus tells us, that a man of the name of Scythenus, an iambic poet, attempted to render the book into verse. XII. There are many epigrams extant which were written upon him, and this is one of them:—

I who lie here am Heraelitus, spare me
Ye rude unlettered men: 'Twas not for you
That I did labour, but for wiser people.
One man may be to me a countless host.
And an unnumbered multitude be no one;
And this I still say in the shades below.

And there is another expressed thus:—

Be not too hasty, skimming o'er the book
Of Heraelitus; 'tis a difficult road,
For mist is there, and darkness hard to pierce.
But if you have a guide who knows his system,
Then everything is clearer than the sun.

XIII. There were five people of the name of Heraelitus. The first was this philosopher of ours. The second a lyric poet, who wrote a panegyrical hymn on the Twelve Gods. The third was an Elegiac poet, of Halicarnassus; on whom Callimachus wrote the following epigram:—

I heard, 0 Heraelitus, of your death,
And the news filled my eyes with mournful tears,
When I remembered all the happy hours
When we with talk beguiled the setting sun.
You now are dust; but still the honeyed voice
Of your sweet converse doth and will survive;
Nor can fell death, which all things else destroys,
Lay upon that bis ruthless conquering grasp.

The fourth was a Lesbian, who wrote a history of Macedonia. The fifth was a man who blended jest with earnest; and who, having been a harp-player, abandoned that profession for a serio-comic style of writing.

LIFE OF XENOPHANES.
I. Xenophanes was the son of Dexius, or, as Apollodorus says, of Orthomenes. He was a citizen of Colophon; and is praised by Timon. Accordingly, he says:—

Xenophanes, not much a slave to vanity,
The wise reprover of the tricks of Homer.

He, having been banished from his own country, lived at
Zande, in Sicily, and at Cataua.

II. And, according to the statements made by some people, he was a pupil of no one; but, as others say, he was a pupil of Boton the Athenian; or, as another account again affirms, of Archelaus. He was, if we may believe Sotion, a contemporary of Anaxemander.

III. He wrote poems in hexameter and in elegiac verse; and also he wrote iambics against Hesiod and Homer, attacking the things said in their poems about the Gods. He also used to recite his own poems. It is said likewise, that he argued against the opinions of Thales and Pythagoras, and that he also attacked Epimenides. He lived to an extreme old age; as he says somewhere himself:—

Threescore and seven long years are fully passed,
Since first my doctrines spread abroad through Greece:
And 'twixt that time and my first view of light
Six lustres more must added be to them:
If I am right at all about my age,
Lacking but eight years of a century.

His doctrine was, that there were four elements of existing things; and an infinite number of worlds, which were all unchangeable. He thought that the clouds were produced by the vapour which was borne upwards from the sun, and which lifted them up into the circumambient space. That the essence of God was of a spherical form, in no respect resembling man; that the universe could see, and that the universe could hear, but could not breathe; and that it was in all its parts intellect, and wisdom, and eternity. He was the first person who asserted that everything which is produced is perishable, and that the soul is a spirit. He used also to say that the many was inferior to unity. Also, that we ought to associate with tyrants either as little as possible, or else as pleasantly as possible.

When Empedocles said to him that the wise man was undiscoverable, he replied, " Very likely; for it takes a wise man to discover a wise man." And Sotion says, that he was the first person who asserted that everything is incomprehensible. But he is mistaken in this.

Xenophanes wrote a poem on the Founding of Colophon; and also, on the Colonisation of Elea, in Italy, consisting of two thousand verses. And he flourished about the sixtieth olympiad.

IV. Demetrius Phalereus, in his treatise on Old Age, and Phenaetius the Stoic, in his essay on Cheerfulness, relate that he buried his sons with his own hands, as Anaxagoras had also done. And he seems to have been detested by the Pythagoreans, Parmeniscus, and Orestades, as Phavorinus relates in the first book of his Commentaries.

V. There was also another Xenophanes. a native of Lesbos, and an iambic poet.

These are the Promiscuous or unattached philosophers.

LIFE OF PARMENIDES. "

I. Parmenides, the son of Pyres, and a citizen of Velia, was a pupil of Xenophanes. And Theophrastus, in his Abridgment, says that he was also a pupil of Anaximander. However, though he was a pupil of Xenophanes, he was not afterwards a follower of his; but he attached himself to Aminias, and Diochartes the Pythagorean, as Sotion relates, which last was a poor but honourable and virtuous man. And he it was whose follower he became, and after he was dead he erected a shrine, or *ypwov,* in his honour. And so Parmenides, who was of a noble family and possessed of considerable wealth, was induced, not by Xenophanes but by Aminias, to embrace the tranquil life of a philosopher.

II. He was the first person who asserted that the earth was of a spherical form; and that it was situated in the centre of the universe. He also taught that there were two elements, fire and earth; and that one of them occupies the place of the maker, the other that of the matter. He also used to teach that man was originally made out of clay; and that they were composed of two parts, the hot and the cold; of which, in fact, everything consists. Another of his doctrines was, that the mind and the soul were the same thing, as we are informed There is great obscurity and uncertainty of the text here. The reading translated is that of Huebner, *iripnpao8ai.* Some read *iri-irpavBai, he* seems to have abandoned the Pythagoreans. Others propose *TTttr-paxOai.* The French translator renders,—He had for enemies the Pythagoreans. by Theophrastus,' in his Natural Philosophy, when he enumerates the theories of nearly all the different philosophers.

He also used to say that philosophy was of a twofold character; one kind resting on certain truth, the other on opinion. On which account he says some wheie:

And 'twill be needful for you well to know,
The fearless heart of all-oonvincing truth:
Also the opinions, though less sure, of men,
Which rest upon no certain evidence.

III. Parmenides too philosophizes in his poems; as Hesiod and Xenophanes, and Empedocles used to. And he used to say that argument was the test of truth; and that the sensations were not trustworthy witnesses. Accordingly, he says:—

Let not the common usages of men
Persuade your better taught experience,
To trust to men's unsafe deceitful sight,
Or treacherous ears, or random speaking tongue:
Reason alone will prove the truth of facts.

On which account Timon says of him:—

The vigorous mind of wise Parmenides,
Who classes all the errors of the thoughts
Under vain phantasies.

Plato inscribed one of his dialogues with his name'—Parmenides, or an essay on Ideas. He flourished about the sixtyninth Olympiad. He appears to have been the first person who discovered that Hesperus and Lucifer were the same star, as Phavorinus records, in the fifth book of his Commentaries. Some, however, attribute this discovery to Pythagoras. And Callimachus asserts that the poem in which this doctrine is promulgated is not his work.

IV. He is said also to have given laws to his fellowcitizens, as Speusippus records, in his acconnt of the Philosophers. He was also the first employer of the question called the Achilles, as Phavorinus assures us in his Universal History.

V. There was also another Parmenides, an orator, who wrote a treatise on the art of Oratory.

See the account of Zeno the Cittiaean.
c c

LIFE OF MELISSUS.

I. Melissus was a Samian, and the son of Ithageses. He was a pupil of Parmenides; but he also had conversed with Heraclitus, when he recommended him to the Ephesians, who were unacquainted with him, as Hippocrates recommended Democritus to the people of Abdera.

II. He was a man greatly occupied in political affairs, and held in great esteem among his fellow citizens; on which account he was elected admiral. And he was admired still more on account of his private virtues. III. His doctrine was, that the Universe was infinite, unsusceptible of change, immoveable, and one, being always like to itself, and complete; and that there wa3 no such thing as real motion, but that there only appeared to be such. As respecting the Gods, too, he denied that there was any occasion to give a definition of them, for that there was no certain knowledge of them. IV. Apollodorus states that he flourished about the eightyfourth olympiad. LIFE OF ZENO, THE ELEATIC.

I. Zeno was a native of Velia. Apollodorus, in his Chronicles, says that he was by nature the son of Telentagoras, but by adoption the son of Parmenides.

II. Timon speaks thus of him and Melissus:—

Great is the strength, invincible the might
Of Zeno, skilled to argue on both sides
Of any question, th' universal critic;

And of Melissus too. They rose superior
To prejudice in general; only yielding
To very few.

And Zeno had been a pupil of Parmenides, and had been on other accounts greatly attached to him.

III. He was a tall man, as Plato tells us in his Parmenide3. and the same writer, in his Phaedrus, calls him also the Eleatic Palamedes. IV. Aristotle, in his Sophist, says that he was the inventor of dialectics, as Empedocles was of rhetoric. And he was a man of the greatest nobleness of spirit, both in philosophy and in politics. There are also many books extant, which are attributed to him, full of great learning and wisdom.

V. He, wishing to put an end to the power of Nearches, the trant (some, however, call the tyrant Diomedon), was arrested, as we are informed by Heraclides, in his abridgment of Satyrus. And when he was examined, as to his accomplices, and as to the arms which he was taking to Lipara, he named all the friends of the tyrant as his accomplices, wishing to make him feel himself alone. And then, after he hail mentioned some names, he said that he wished to whisper something privately to the tyrant; and when he came near him he bit him, and would not leave his hold till he was stabbed. And the same thing happened to Aristogiton, the tyrant slayer. But Demetrius, in his treatise on People of the same Name, says that it was his nose that he bit off.

Moreover, Antisthenes, in his Successions, says that after he had given him information against his friends, he was asked by the tyrant if there was any one else. And he replied, "Yes, you; the destruction of the city." And that he also said to the bystanders, " I marvel at your cowardice, if you submit to be slaves to the tyrant out of fear of such pains as I am now enduring." And at last he bit off his tongue and spit it at him; and the citizens immediately rushed forward, and slew the tyrant with stones. And this is the account that is given by almost every one.

But Hermippus says, that he was put into a mortar, and pounded to death. And we ourselves have written the following epigram on him:—

Your noble wish, 0 Zeno, was to slay
A cruel tyrant, freeing Elea
From the harsh bonds of shameful slavery,
But you were disappointed; for the tyrant
Pounded you in a mortar. I say wrong,
He only crushed your body, and not you.

VI. And Zeno was an excellent man in other respects: and he was also a despiser of great men in an equal decree with Heraclitus; for he, too, preferred the town which was formerly called Hyele, and afterwards Elea, being a colony of the Phocaeans, and his own native place, a poor city possessed of no other importance than the knowledge of how to raise virtuous citizens, to the pride of the Athenians; so that he did not often visit them, but spent his life at home.

VII. He, too, was the first man who asked the question called Achilles, though Phavorinus attributes its first use to Parmenides, aud several others. VIII. His chief doctrines were, that there were several worlds, and that there was no vacuum; that the nature of all things consisted of hot and cold, and dry and moist, these elements interchanging their substances with one another; that man was made out of the earth, and that his soul was a mixture of the before-named elements in such a way that no one of them predominated. IX. They say that when he was reproached, he was indignant; and that when some one blamed him, he replied, " If when I am reproached, I am not angered, then I shall not be pleased when I am praised. "

X. We have already said in our account of the Cittiaean, that there were eight Zenos; but this one flourished about the seventy-ninth olympiad.

LIFE OF LEUCIPPUS.

I. Leucippus was a native of Velia, but, as some say, of Abdera; and, as others report, of Melos.

II. He was a pupil of Zeno. And his principal doctrines were, that all things were infinite, and were interchanged with one another; and that the universe was a vacuum, and full of bodies; also that the worlds were produced by bodies falling into the vacuum, and becoming entangled with one another; and that the nature of the stars originated in motion, according to their increase; also, that the sun is borne round in a See the life of Parmepide. greater circle around the moon; that the earth is carried on revolving round the centre: and that its figure resembles a clrum; he "was the first philosopher who spoke, of atoms as principles. III. These are his doctrines in general; in particular detail, they are as follow: he says that the universe is infinite, as I have already mentioned; that of it, one part is a plenum, and the other a vacuum. He also says that the elements, and the worlds which are derived from them, are infinite, and are dissolved again into them; and that the worlds are produced in this manner: That many bodies, of various kinds and shapes, are borne by amputation from the-infinite, into a vast vacuum; and then, they being collected together, produce one vortex; according to which they, dashing against one another, and whirling about in every direction, are separated in such a way that like attaches itself to like.

But as they are all of equal weight, when by reason of their number they are no longer able to whirl about, the thin ones depart into the outer vacuum, as if they bounded through, and the others remain behind, and becoming entangled with one another, run together, and produce a sort of spherical shaped figure.

This subsists as a kind of membrane; containing within itself bodies of every kind; and as these are whirled about so as to revolve according to the resistence of the centre, the circumambient membrane becomes thin, since bodies are without ceasing, uniting according to the impulse given by the vortex; and in this way the earth is produced, since these bodies which have once been brought to the centre remain there.

On the other side, there is produced another enveloping membrane, which increases incessantly by the accretion of exterior bodies; and which, as it is itself animated by a circular movement, drags with it, and adds to itself, everything it meets with; some of these bodies thus enveloped re-unite again and form compounds, which are at first moist and clayey, but soon becoming dry, and being drawn on in the universal movement of the circular vortex, they catch fire, and constitute the substance of the stars. The orbit of the sun is the most distant one; that of the moon is the nearest to the earth; and between the two are the orbits of the other stars.

All the stars are set on fire by the rapidity of their own motion; and the sun is set on fire by the stars; the moon has only a slight quantity of fire; the sun and the moon are eclipsed in... in consequence of the inclination of the earth towards the south. In the north it always snows, and those districts are cold, and are often frozen.

The sun is eclipsed but seldom; but the moon frequently, because her orbits are unequal.

Leucippus admits also, that the production of worlds, their increase, their diminution, and their destruction, depend on a certain necessity. the character of which he does not precisely sx-plaTrT—r_—.-.

LIFE OF DEMOCRITUS.

I. Democritus was the son of Hegesistratus, but as some say, of Athenocrites, and, according to other accounts, of Damasippus. He was a native of Abdera, or, as it is stated by some authors, a citizen of Miletus.

II. He was a pupil of some of the Magi and Chaldaeans, whom Xerxes had left with his father as teachers, when he had been hospitably received by him, as Herodotus informs us;+ and from these men he, while still a boy, learned the principles of astronomy and theology. Afterwards, his father entrusted him to Leucippus, and to Anaxagoras, as some authors assert, who was forty years older than he. And Phavorinus, in his Universal History, says that Democritus said of Anaxagoras, that his opinions about the sun and moon were not his own, but were old theories, and that he had stolen them. And that he used_also to pull to pieces his assertions about _Jhe composition of the world, and ahoutjakidj as he was hostile to him, because he had declined to admit him as a pupil. How then can he have been a pupil of his, as some assert? And There is evidently a considerable gap in the text here. + As there is no such passage in Herodotus, Valchenaer conjectures that we ought here to read Metrodorus. Demetrius in his treatise on People of the same Name, and Antisthenes in his Successions, both affirm that he travelled to Egypt to see the priests there, and to learn mathematics of them; and that he proceeded further to the Chaldeans, and penetrated into Persia, and went as far as the Persian Gulf. Some also say that he made acquaintance with the Gymnosophists in India, and that he went to Ethiopia. ' III. He was one of three brothers who divided their patrimony among them; and the most common story is, that he took the smaller portion, as it was in money, because he required money for the purpose of travelling; though his brothers suspected him of entertaining some treacherous design. And Demetrius says, that his share amounted to more than a hundred talents, and that he spent the whole of it.

IV. He also says, that he was so industrious a man, that he cut off for himself a small portion of the garden which surrounded his house, in which there was a small cottage, and shut himself up in it. And on one occasion, when his father brought him an ox to sacrifice, and fastened it there, he for a long time did not discover it, until his father having roused him, on the pretext of the sacrifice, told him what he had done with the ox.

V. He further asserts, that it is well known that he went to Athens, and as he despised glory, he did not desire to be known; and that he became acquainted with Socrates, without Socrates knowing who he was. " For I came," says he, " to Athens, and no one knew me." " If," says Thrasylus, " the Rivals is really the work, of Plato, then Democritus must be the anonymous interlocutor, who is introduced in that dialogue, besides iEnopides and Anaxagoras, the one I mean who, in the conversation with Socrates, is arguing about philosophy, and whom the philosopher tells, that a philosopher resembles a conqueror in the Pentathlum." And he was veritably a master of five branches of philosophy. For he was thoroughly acquainted with physics, and ethics, and mathematics, and the whole encyclic system, and indeed he was thoroughly experienced and skilful in every kind of art. He it was who was the author of the saying, " Speech is the shadow of action." But Demetrius Phalereus, in-his Defence of Socrates, affirms that he never came to Athens at all. And that is a still stranger circumstance than any, if he despised so important a city, not wishing to derive glory from the place in which he was, but preferring rather himself to invest the place with glory.

VI. And it is evident from his writings, what sort of man he was. " He seems," says Thrasylus, " to have been also an admirer of the Pythagoreans." And he mentions Pythagoras himself, speaking of him with admiration, in the treatise which is inscribed with his name. And he appears to have derived all his doctrines from him to such a degree, that one would have thought that he had been his pupil, if the difference of time did not prevent it. At all events, Glaucus, of Rhegium, who was a contemporary of his, affirms that he was a pupil of some of the Pythagorean school.

And Apollodoms, of Cyzicus, says that he was intimate with Philolaus; " He used to practise himself," says Antisthenes, " in testing perceptions in various manners; sometimes retiring into solitary places, and spending his time even among tombs." VII. And he further adds, that when he returned from his travels, he lived in a most humble manner; like a man who had spent all his property, and that on account of his poverty, he was supported by his brother Damasus. But when he had foretold some future event, which happened as he had predicted, and had in consequence become famous, he was for all the rest of his life thought worthy of almost divine honours by the generality of people. And as there was a law, that a man who had squandered the whole of his patrimony, should not be allowed funeral rites in his country, Antisthenes says, that he, being aware of this law, and not wishing to be exposed to the calumnies of those who envied him, and would be glad to accuse him, recited to the people his work called the Great World," which is far superior to all his other writings, and that as a reward for it he was presented with five hundred talents; and not only that, but he also had some brazen statues erected in his honour. And when he died, he was buried at the public expense; after having attained the age of more than a hundred years. But Demetrius says, that it was his relations who read the Great World, and that they were presented with a hundred talents only; and Hippobotus coincides in this statement.

VIII. And Aristoxenus, in his Historic Commentaries, says that Plato wished to bum all the writings of Democritus that he was able to collect; but that Amyclas and Cleinias, the Pythagoreans, prevented him, as it would do no good; for that copies of his books were already in many hands. And it is plain that that was the case; for Plato, who mentions nearly all the ancient philosophers, nowhere speaks of Democritus; not even in those passages where he has occasion to contradict his theories, evidently, because he said that if he did, he would be showing his disagreement with the best of all philosophers; a man whom even Timon praises in the following terms:—

Like that Democritus, wisest of men,

Sage ruler of his speech; profound converser,

Whose works I love to read among the first.

IX. But he was, according to the statement made by himself in the Little World, a youth when Anaxagoras was an old man, being forty years younger than he was. And he says, that he composed the Little World seven hundred and thirty years after the capture of Troy. And he must have been born, according to the account given by Apollodorus in his Chronicles, in the eightieth olympiad; but, as Thrasylus says, in his work entitled the Events, which took place before the reading of the books of Democritus, in the third year of the seventy-seventh olympiad, being, as it is there stated, one year older than Socrates. He must therefore have been a contemporary of Archelaus, the pupil of Anaxagoras, and of Enopides, for he makes mention of this letter. He also speaks of the theories of Parmenides and Zeno, on the subject of the One, as they were the men of the highest reputation in histories, and he also speaks of Protagoras of Abdera, who confessedly lived at the same time as Socrates.

X. Athenodorus tells us, in the eighth book of his Conversations, that once, when Hippocrates came to see him, he ordered some milk to be brought; and that, when he saw the milk, he said that it was the milk of a black goat, with her first kid; on which Hippocrates marvelled at his accurate knowledge. Also, as a young girl came with Hippocrates, on the first day, he saluted her thus, " Good morning, my maid; but on the next day, " Good morning, woman;" for, indeed, she had ceased to be a maid during the night.

XI. And Hermippus relates, that Democritus dfed in the following manner: he was exceedingly old, and appeared at the point of death; and his sister was lamenting that he would die during the festival of the Thesmophoria, and so prevent her from discharging her duties to the Goddess; and so he bade her be of good cheer, and desired her to bring him hot loaves every day. And, by applying these to his nostrils, he kept himself alive even over the festival. But when the days of the festival were passed (and it lasted three days), then he expired, without any pain, as Hipparchus assures us, having lived a hundred and nine years. And we have written an epigram upon him in our collection of poems in every metre, which runs thus:—

What man was e'er so wise, who ever did

So great a deed as this Democritus?

Who kept off death, though present for three days,

And entertained him with hot steam of bread.

Such was the life of this man.

XII. Now his principal doctrines were these. That atoms and the vacuum were the beginning of the universe; and that everything else existed only in opinion. That the worlds were infinite, created, and perishable. But that nothing was created out of nothing, and that nothiug was destroyed so as to become nothing. That the atoms were infinite both in magnitude and number, and were borne about through the universe in endless revolutions. And that thus they produced all the combinations that exist; fire, water, air, and earth; for that all these things are only combinations of certain atoms; which combinations are incapable of being affected by external cir The Thesmophoria was a festival in honour of Ceres, celebrated in various parts of Greece; and only by married women; though girls might perform some of the ceremonies. Herodotus says, that it was introduced into Greece from Egypt, by the daughters of Danaus. The Attic Thesmophoria lasted probably three days, and began on the eleventh day of the month Pyanession; the first day was called *avoSoc,* or *ica9oSo(,* from the women going in procession to Eleusis; the second *vr)dTtia,* or fasting; the third was called *xaWiyivtia,* as on that day Ceres was invoked under that name, and it was the day of merriment of the festival. cumstances, and are unchangeable by reason of their solidity. Also, that the sun and the moon are formed by such revolutions and round bodies; and in like manner the soul is produced; and that the soul and the mind are identical: that we see by the falling of visions across our sight; and that everything that happens, happens of necessity. Motion, being the cause of the production of everything, which hejadlsnecessitv. The chief good he asserts to be cheerfulness; which, however, he does not consider the same as pleasure; as some people, who have misunderstood him, have fancied that he meant; but he understands by cheerfulness, a condition according to which the soul lives calmly and steadily, being disturbed by no fear, or superstition, or other passion. He calls this state *tbiv/ita,* and *tiiierii,* and several other names.

Everything which is made he looks upon as depending for its existence on opinion; but atoms and the vacuum he believes exist by nature. These' were his principal opinions. XIII. Of his books, Thrasylus has given a regular catalogue, in the same way that he has arranged the works of Plato, dividing them into four classes.

Now these are his ethical works. The Pythagoras; a treatise on the Disposition of the Wise Man; an essay on those in the Shades Below; the Tritogeneia (this is so called because from Minerva three things are derived which hold together all human affairs); a treatise on Manly Courage or Valour; the Horn of Amalthea; an essay on Cheerfulness; a volume of Ethical Commentaries. A treatise entitled, For Cheerfulness, *iviarii*) is not found.

These are his writings on natural philosophy. The Great World (which Theophrastus asserts trf be the work of Leucippus); the Little World; the Cosmography; a treatise on the Planets; the first book on Nature; two books on the Nature of Man, or on Flesh; an essay on the Mind; one on the Senses (some people join these two together in one volume, which they entitle, on the Soul); a treatise on Juices; one on Colours; one on the Different Figures; one on the Changes of Figures; the Cratynteria (that is to say, an essay, approving of what has been said in preceding ones); a treatise on Phaenomenon, or on Providence; three books on Pestilences, or Pestilential Evils; a book of Difficulties. These are his books on natural philosophy.

His miscellaneous works are these. Heavenly Causes; Aerial Causes; Causes affecting Plane Surfaces: Causes referring to Fire, and to what is in Fire; Causes affecting Voices; Causes affecting Seeds, and Plants, and Fruits: three books of Causes affecting Animals; Miscellaneous Causes; a treatise on the Magnet. These are his miscellaneous works.

His mathematical writings are the following. A treatise on the Difference of Opinion, or on the Contact of the Circle and the Sphere; one on Geometry; one on Numbers; one on Incommensurable Lines, and Solids, in two books: a volume called Explanations; the Great Year, or the Astronomical Calendar; a discussion on the Clepsydra; the Map of the Heavens; Geography; Polography; Artmography, or a discussion on Rays of Light. These are his mathematical works.

His works on music are the following. A treatise on Rythm and Harmony; one on Poetry; one on the beauty of Epic Poems; one on Euphonious and Discordant Letters; one on Homer, or on Propriety of Diction and Dialects; one on Song, one on Words; the Onomasticon. These are his musical works.

The following are his works on art. Prognostics; a treatise on the Way of Living, called also Diaetetics, or the Opinions of a Physician; Causes relating to Unfavourable and Favourable Opportunities; a treatise on Agriculture, called also the Georgic; one on Painting; Tactics, and Fighting in heavy Armour. These are his works on such subjects.

Some authors also give a list of some separate treatises which they collect from his Commentaries. A treatise on the Sacred Letters seen at Babylon; another on the Sacred Letters seen at Meroe; the Voyage round the Ocean; a treatise on History; a Chaldaic Discourse; a Phrygian Discourse; a treatise on Fever; an essay on those who are attacked with Cough after illness; the Principles of Laws; Things made by Hand, or Problems.

As to the other books which some writers ascribed to him, some are merely extracts from his other writings, and some are confessedly the work of others. And this is a sufficient account of his writings.

Namely, reasoning well, expressing one's self well, and acting well. XIV. There were six people of the name of Democritus. The first was this man of whom we are speaking; the second was a musician of Chios, who lived about the same time; the third was a sculptor who is mentioned by Antigonus; the fourth is a man who wrote a treatise on the Temple at Ephesus, and on the city of Samothrace; the fifth was an epigrammatic poet, of great' perspicuity and elegance; the sixth was a citizen of Pergamus, who wrote a treatise on Oratory. LIFE OF PROTAGORAS.

I. Pbotagobas was the son of Artemon, or, as Apollodorus says (which account is corroborated by Deinon, in his History of Persia), of Maeander. He was a native of Abdera, as Heraclides Ponticus tell us, in his treatise on Laws; and the same authority informs us that he made laws for the Thurians. But, according to the statement of Eupolis, in his Flatterers, he was a native of Teos; for he says:—

Within youll find Protagoras, of Teos.

He, and Prodicas of Ceos, used to levy contributions for giving their lectures; and Plato, in his Protagoras, says that Prodicas had a very powerful voice. II. Protagoras was a pupil of Democritus. And he was surnamed Wisdom, as Phavorinus informs us in his Universal History. III. He was the first person who asserted that in every question there were two sides to the argument exactly opposite to one another. And he used to employ them in his arguments, being the first person who did so. But he began something in this manner: " Man is the measure of all things: of those things which exist as he is; and of those things which do not exist as he is not." And he used to say that nothing else was soul except the senses, as Plato says, in the Theaetetus; and that everything was true. And another of his treatises he begins in this way: " Concerning the Gods, I am not able to know to a certainty whether they exist or whether they do not. For there are many things which prevent one from knowing, especially the obscurity of the subject, and the shortness of the life of man." And on account of this beginning of his treatise, he was banished by the Athenians. And they burnt his books in the marketplace, calling them in by the public crier, and compelling all who possessed them to surrender them.

He was the first person who demanded payment of his pupils; fixing his charge at a hundred minae. He was also the first person who gave a precise definition of the parts of time; and who explained the value of opportunity, and who instituted contests of argument, and who armed the disputants with the weapon of sophism. He it was too who first left facts out of consideration, and fastened his arguments on words; and who was the parent of the present superficial and futile kinds of discussion. On which account Timon says of him:—

Protagoras, that slippery arguer, I
In disputatious contests fully skilled.

He too, it was, who first invented that sort of argument which is called the Socratic, and who first employed the reasonings of Antisthenes, which attempt to establish the point that they cannot be contradicted; as Plato tells us in his Euthydemus. He was also the first person who practised regular discussions on set subjects, as Artemidorus, the dialectician, tells us in his treatise against Chrysippus. He was also the original inventor of the porter's pad for men to carry their burdens on, as we are assured by Aristotle, in his book on Education; for he himself was a porter, as Epicurus says somewhere or other. And it was in this way that he became highly thought of by Democritus, who saw him as he was tying up some sticks.

He was also the first person who divided discourse into four parts; entreaty, interrogation, answer, and injunction: though some writers make the parts seven; narration, interrogation, answer, injunction, promise, entreaty, and invocation; and these he called the foundations of discourse: but Allidomas says that there are four divisions of discourse; affirmation, denial, interrogation, and invocation.

V. The first of his works that he ever read in public was the treatise on the Gods, the beginning of which we have quoted above, and he read this at Athens in the house of Euripides, or, as some say, in that of Megaclides; others say that he read it in the Lyceum; his pupil, Archagoras, the son of Theodotus, giving him the aid of his voice. His accuser was Pythodorus, the son of Polyzelus, one of the four hundred; but Aristotle calls him Evathlus.

VI. The writings of his which are still extant are these: a treatise on the Art of Contention; one on Wrestling; one on Mathematics; one on a Republic; one on Ambition; one on Virtues; one on the Original Condition of Man; one on those in the Shades Below; one on the Things which are not done properly by Men; one volume of Precepts; one essay entitled Justice in Pleading for Hire; two books of Contradictions.

These are his books.

Plato also addressed a dialogue to him.

VII. Philochorus relates that, as he was sailing to Sicily his ship was wrecked, and that this circumstance is alluded to by Euripides in his Ixion; and some say that he died on his journey, being about ninety years old. But Apollodorus states his age at seventy years, and says that he was a sophist forty years, and that he flourished about the eighty-fourth Olympiad. There is an epigram upon him written by myself, in the following terms:—

I hear accounts of you, Protagoras,
That, travelling far from Athens, on the road,
You, an old man, and quite infirm, did die.
For Cecrops' city drove you forth to exile;
But you, though 'scaping dread Minerva's might,
Could not escape the outspread arms of Pluto.

VIII. It is said that once, when he demanded of Evathlus his pupil payment for his lessons, Evathlus said to him, " But I have never been victorious in an argument;" and he rejoined, " But if I gain my cause, then I should naturally receive the fruits of my victory, and so would you obtain the fruits of yours."

IX. There was also another Protagoras, an astronomer, on whom Euphorion wrote an elegy; and a third also, who was a philosopher of the Stoic sect. LIFE OF DIOGENES, OF APOLLONIA.

I. Diogenes was a native of Apollonia, and the son of Apollothemis, a natural philosopher of high reputation; and he was, as Antisthenes reports, a pupil of Anaximenes. He was also a contemporary of Anaxagoras, and Demetrius Phalereus says, in his Defence of Socrates, that he was very unpopular at Athens, and even in some danger of his life.

II. The following were his principal doctrines; that the air was an element; that the worlds were infinite, and that the vacuum also was infuite; that the air, as it was condensed, and as it was rarified, was the productive cause of the worlds; that nothing can be produced out of nothing; and that nothing can be destroyed so as to become nothing; that the earth is round, firmly planted in the middle of the universe, having acquired its situation from the circumvolutions of the hot principle around it, and its consistency from the cold.

The first words of his treatise are:—

"It appears to me that he who begins any treatise ought to lay down principles about which there can be no dispute, and that his exposition of them ought to be simple and dignified." LIFE OF ANAXARCHUS.

I. Anaxarchus was a native of Abdera. He was a pupil of Diogenes, of Smyrna; but, as some say, of Metrodorus, of Chios; who said that he was not even sure that he knew nothing; and Metrodorus waa a pupil of Nessus, of Chios; though others assert that he was a disciple of Democritus.

II. Anaxarchus too enjoyed the intimacy of Alexander, and flourished about the hundred and tenth olympiad, He had for an enemy Nicocreon, the tyrant of Cyprus. And on one occasion, when Alexander, at a banquet, asked him what he This is thus embodied by Lucretius:—

Nam nihil e nihilo, in nihilum nil poase reverti.

thought of the entertainment, he is said to have replied, " 0 king, everything is provided very sumptuously; and the only thing wanting is to have the head of some satrap served up;" hinting at Nicocreon. And Nicocreon did not forget his grudge against him for this; but after the death of the king, when Anaxarchus, who was making a voyage, was driven against his will into Cyprus, he took him and put him in a mortar, and commanded him to be pounded to death with iron pestles. And then they say that he, disregarding this punishment, uttered that celebrated saying, " Beat the bag of Anaxarchus, but you will not beat Anaxarchus himself." And then, when Nicocreon commanded that his tongue should be cut out, it is said that he bit it off, and spit it at him. And we have written an epigram upon him in the following terms:—

Beat more and more; you're beating but a bag;
Beat, Anaxarchus is in heav'n with Jove.
Hereafter Proserpine will rack your bones,
And say, Thus perish, you accursed beater.

III. Anaxarchus, on account of the evenness of his temper and the tranquillity of his life, was called the Happy. And he was a man to whom it was very easy to reprove men and bring them to temperance. Accordingly, he produced an alteration in Alexander who thought himself a God, for when he saw the blood flowing from some wound that he had received, he pointed to him with his finger, and said, " This is blood, and not:—
" Such stream as issues from a wounded God;
Pure emanation, uncorrupted flood,
Unlike our gross, diseas'd, terrestrial blood."

But Plutarch says that it was Alexander himself who quoted these lines to his friends.

They also tell a story that Anaxarchus once drank to him, and then showed the goblet, and said:—

Shall any mortal hand dare wound a God?
Horn. IL v. 340. Pope's version, 422.
LIFE OF PYRRHO.

I. Pyrrho was a citizen of Elis, and the son of Pleistarchus, as Diocles informs us, and, as Apollodorus in his Chronicles asserts, he was originally a painter.

II. And he was a pupil of Bryson, the son of Stilpon, as we are told by Alexander in his Chronicles. After that he attached himself to Anaxarchus, and attended him everywhere; so that he even went as far as the Gymuosophists, in India, and the Magi. " III. Owing to which circumstance, he seems to have taken a noble line in philosophy, introducing the doctrine of incomprehensibility, and of the necessity of suspending qnes_judgment, as we learn from Ascanius, of Abdera! For he used to say that nothing was honourable, or disgraceful, or just, or unjust. And on the same principle he asserted that there was no such thing as downright truth; but that men did everything in consequence of custom and law. For that nothing was any more this than that. And "his life corresponded to his principles; for he never shunned anything, and never guarded against anything; encountering everything, even waggons for instance, and precipices, and dogs, and everything of that sort; committing nothing whatever to his senses. So that he used to be saved, as Antigonus the Carystian tells us, by his friends who accompanied him. And iEnesidemus says that he studied philosophy on the principle of suspending his judgment on all points, without however, on any occasion acting in an imprudent manner, or doing anything without due consideration. And he lived to nearly ninety years of age. IV. And Antigonus, of Carystus, in his account of Pyrrho, mentions the following circumstances respecting him; that he was originally a person of no reputation, but a poor man, and a painter; and that a picture of some camp-bearers, of very moderate execution, was preserved in the Gymnasium at Elis, which was his work; and that he used to walk out into the fields and seek solitary places, very rarely appearing to his family at home; and that he did this in consequence of having heard some Indian reproaching Anaxarchus for never teaching any one else any good, but for devoting all his time to paying court to princes in palaces. He relates of him too, that he always maintained the same demeanour, so that if any one left him in the middle of his delivery of a discourse, he remained and continued what he was saying; although, when a young man, he was of a very excitable temperament. Often too, says Antigonus, he would go away for a time, without telling any pne beforehand, and taking any chance persons whom he chose for his companions. And once, when Anaxarchus had fallen into a pond, he passed by without assisting him; and when some one blamed him for tbs, Anaxarchus himself praised his indifference and absence of all emotion.

On one occasion he was detected talking to himself, and when he was asked the reason, he said that he was studying how to be good. In his investigations he was never despised by any one, because he always spoke explicitly and straight to the question that had been put to him. On which account Nausiphanes was charmed by him even when he was quite young. And he used to say that he should like to be endowed with the disposition of Pyrrho, without losing his own power of eloquence. And he said too, that Epicurus, who admired the conversation and manners of Pyrrho, was frequently asking him about him.

V. He was so greatly honoured by his country, that he was appointed a priest; and on his account all the philosophers were exempted from taxation. He had a great many imitators of his impassiveness; in reference to which Timon speaks thus of him in his Python, and in his Silli:—

Now, you old man, you Pyrrho, how could you
Find an escape from all the slavish doctrines
And vain imaginations of the Sophists?
How did you free yourself from all the bonds
Of sly chicane, and artful deep persuasion?
How came you to neglect what sort of breeze
Blows round your Greece, and what's the origin
And end of everything?

And again, in his Images, he says:—

These things, my heart, 0 Pyrrho, longs to hear,
How you enjoy such ease of life and quiet,
The only man as happy as a God.

And the Athenians presented him with the freedom of their city, as Diocles tells us, because he had slain Cotys,

146 • The lives and opinions of eminent philosophers • Diogenes Laertius

the Thracian.

VI. He also lived in a most blameless manner with his sister, who was a midwife, as Eratosthenes relates, in his treatise on Riches and Poverty; so that he himself used to carry poultry, and pigs too if he could get any, into the marketplace and sell them. And he used to clean all the furniture of the house without expressing any annoyance. And it is said that he carried his indifference so far that he even washed a pig. And once, when he was very angry about something connected with his sister (and her name was Philista), and some one took him up, he said, " The display of my indifference does not depend on a woman. " On another occasion, when he was driven back by a dog which was attacking him, he said to some one who blamed him for being discomposed, " That it was a difficult thing entirely to put off humanity; but that a man ought to strive with all his power to counteract circumstances with his actions if possible, and at all events with his reason." They also tell a story that once, when some medicines of a consuming tendency, and some cutting and cautery was applied to him for some wound, that he never even contracted his brow. And Timon intimates his disposition plainly enough in the letters which he wrote to Python. Moreover, Philo. the Athenian, who was a friend of his, said that he was especially fond of Democritus; and next to him of Homer; whom he admired greatly, and was continually saying:—

But as the race of falling leaves decay,
Such is the fate of man.

He used also, as it is said, to compare men to wasps, and flies, and birds, and to quote the following lines:—

Die then, my friend, what boots it to deplore?
The great, the good Patroclus is no more.
He, far thy better, was foredoom'd to die;
And thou, doest thou bewail mortality?
t

And so he would quote anything that bore on the uncertainty and emptiness and fickleness of the affairs of man. Posidonius tells the following anecdote about him: that when some people who were sailing with him were looking gloomy because II. vi. 146. t II. xxL 106. Pope's version, 115.

of a storm, he kept a calm countenance, and comforted their minds, exhibiting himself on deck eating a pig, and saying that it became a wise man to preserve an untroubled spirit in that manner, Memenius is the only writer who asserts that he used to deliver positive dogmas. VII. He had many emiagjit &sciples, and among them Eurylochus, of whom the following detective characteristic is related; for, they say, that he was once worked up to such a pitch of rage that he took up a spit with the meat on it, and chased the cook as far as the market-place. And once in Elis he was so harassed by some people who put questions to him in the middle of his discourses, that he threw down his cloak and swam across the Alpheus. He was the greatest possible enemy to the Sophists, as Timon tells us. But Philo, on the contrary, was very fond of arguing; on which account Timon speaks of him thus:—

Avoiding men to study all devoted,
He ponders with himself; and never heeds
The glory or disputes which harass Philo.

Besides these disciples, Pyrrho also had Hecateus of Abdera. and Timon the Phliasian, who wrote the, Silli, and whom we shall speak of hereafter; and also Nausiphanes, of Teos, who, I as some say, was the master of Epianus.

VIII. All these men were called Pyrrhoneans from their. master; and also doubters, and sceptics, and ephjxstics, or I suspenders of their judgment, and investigators, from their principles. And their philosophy was called investigatory, from their investigating or seeking the truth on all sides; and sceptical from their being always doubting *(axivrofiai),* and never finding; and ephectic, from the disposition which they encouraged after investigation, I mean the suspending of their j udgment *(im%fi);* and doubting, because they asserted that the dogmatic philosophers only doubted, and that they did the same. And they were called Pyrrhoneans from Pyrrho himself.

But Theodosius, in his Chapters on Scepticism, contends, that we ought not to call the Pyrrhonean school sceptical; for since, says he, the motion and agitation of the mind in each individual is incomprehensible to others, we are unable to know what was the disposition of Pyrrho; and if we do not know it we ought not to be called Pyrrhoneans. He also adds that Pyrrho was not the original inventor of Scepticism, and that he had no particular dogma of any kind; and that, consequently, it can only be called Pyrrhonism from some similarity. Some say that Homer was the original founder of this school; since he at different times gives different accounts of the same circumstance, as much as any one else ever did; and since he never dogmatizes definitively respecting affirmation; they also say that the maxims of the seven wise men were sceptical; such as that, "Seek nothing in excess," and that, "Suretyship is near calamity;" which shows that calamity follows a man who has given positive and certain surety; they also argue that Archilochus and Euripides were Sceptics; and Archilochus speaks thus:—

And now, 0 Glaucus, son of Leptines,
Such is the mind of mortal man, which changes
With every day that Jupiter doth send.

And Euripides says:—

Why then do men assert that wretched mortals
Are with true wisdom gifted; for on you
We all depend; and we doeverything,
Which pleases you.

Moreover, Xenophanes, and Zeno the Eleatic, and Democritus were also Sceptics; of whom Xenophanes speaks thus:—

And no man knows distinctly anything,
And no man ever will.

And Zeno endeavours to put an end to the doctrine of motion by J saying: " The object moved does not move either in the place in i which it is, or in that in which it is not." Democritus, too, discards the qualities, where he

says: what is cold is cold in opinion, and what is hot is hot in opinion; but atoms and the vacuum exist in reality. And again he says: " But we know nothing really; for truth lies in the bottom." Plato, too, following them, attributes the knowledge of the truth to the Gods and *i*
to the sons of the Gods, and leaves men only the investigation
of probability. And Euripides says:—

Who now can tell whether to live may not
Be properly to die. And whether that
Which men do call to die, may not in truth
Be but the entrance into real life?

And Empedocles speaks thus:—

These things are not perceptible to sight,
Nor to the ears, nor comprehensible
To human intellect.

And in a preceding passage he says:—

Believing nothing, but such circumstances
As have befallen each.

Heraclitus, too, says, " Let us not form conjectures at random, about things of the greatest importance." And Hippocrates delivers his opinion in a very doubtful manner, such as becomes a man; and before them all Homer has said:—

Long in the field of words we may contend,
Reproach is infinite and knows no end.

And immediately after:—

Armed, or with truth or falsehood, right or wrong.
(So voluble a weapon is the tongue),
Wounded we wound, and neither side can fail,
For every man has equal strength to rail:

Intimating the equal vigour and antethetical force of words. And the Sceptics persevered in overthrowing all the dogmas of every sect, while they themselves asserted nothing dogmatically; and contented themselves with expressing the opinions of others, without affirming anything themselves, not even that they did affirm nothing; so that even discarded all positive denial; for to say, " We affirm nothing," was to affirm something. " But we," said they, " enunciate the doctrines of others, to prove our own perfect indifference; it is just as if we were to express the same thing by a simple sign." So these words, " We affirm nothing," indicate the absence of all affirmation, just as other propositions, such as, " Not more one thing than another," or, " Every reason has a corresponding reason opposed to it," and all such maxims indicate a similar idea. But the phrase, "Not more one thing," &e.,has sometimes an affirmative sense, indicating the equality of certain things, as for instance, in this sentence, " A pirate is not worse than a liar." But by the sceptics this is said not positively, but negatively, as for instance, where the speaker contests a point Homer, II. xx. 248. Pope's version, 294.
and says, "It was not Scylla, any more than it was Chimaera." And the word " more," itself, is sometimes used to indicate a comparison, as when we say, " That honey is more sweet than grapes. " And at other times it is used positively, and at the same time negatively, as when we say, " Virtue profits us more than hurts us;" for in this phrase we intimate that virtue does profit, and does not hurt us. But the Sceptics abolish the whole expression, "Not more than it;" saying, that "Prudence has not existence, any more than it has no existence. " Accordingly, then, expression, as Timon says in his Python, indicates nothing more than an absence of all affirmation, or of all assent of the judgment.

Also the expression, " Every reason has a corresponding reason," &c., does in the same manner indicate the suspension of the judgment; for if, while the facts are different, the expressions are equipollent, it follows that a man must be quite ignorant of the real truth.

Besides this, to this assertion there is a contrary assertion opposed, which, after having destroyed all others, turns itself against itself, and destroys itself, resembling, as it were, those cathartic medicines which, after they have cleansed the stomach, then discharge themselves, and are got rid of. And so the dogmatic philosophers say, that all these reasonings are so far from overturning the authority of reason that they confirm it. To this the Sceptics reply, that they only employ reason as an instrument, because it is impossible to overturn the authority of reason, without employing reason; just as if we assert that there is no such thing as space, we must employ the word "space," but that not dogmatically, but demonstratively; and if we assert that nothing exists according to necessity, it is unavoidable that we must use the word "necessity." The same principle of interpretation did they adopt; for they affirmed that facts are not by nature such as they appear to be, but that they only seem such; and they said, that what they doubt is not what they think, for their thoughts are evident to themselves, but the reality of the things which are only made known to them by their sensations.

The Pyrrhonean system, then, is a simple explanation of appearances, or of notions of every kind, by means of which, comparing one thing with another, one arrives at the conelusion, that there is nothing in all these notions, but contradiction and confusion; as iEnesidemus says in his Introduction to Pyrrhonism. As to the contradictions which are found in those speculations, when they have pointed out in what way each fact is convincing, they then, by the same means, take away all belief from it; for they say that we regard as certain, those things which always produce similar impressions on the senses, those which are the offspring of habit, or which are established by the laws, and those too which give pleasure or excite wonder. And they prove that the reasons opposite to those on which our assent is founded are entitled to equal belief.

IX. The difficulties which they suggest, relating to the agreement subsisting between what appears to the senses, and what is comprehended by the intellect, divide themselves into ten modes of argument, according to which the subject and object of our knowledge is incessantly changing. And these ten modes Phyrrho lays down in the following manner.

The first relates to the difference which one remarks between the sentiments of animals in respect of pleasure, and pain, and what is injurious, and what is advantageous; and from this we conclude, that the same objects do not always produce the same impressions; and that the fact of this difference ought to be a reason with us for suspending our judgment. For there are some animals which are produced without any sexual connexion, as those which live in the fire, and the Arabian Phoenix, and worms. Others again are engendered by copulation, as men and others of that kind; and some are composed in one way, and others in another; on which account they also differ in their senses, as for instance, hawks are very keen-sighted; dogs have a most acute scent. It is plain, therefore, that the things seen produce different impressions on those animals which differ in their power of sight. So, too, young branches are eagerly eaten by the goat, but are bitter to mankind; and hemlock is nutritious for the quail, but deadly to man; and pigs eat their own dung, but a horse does not.

The second mode refers to the nature and idiosyncracies of men. According to Demophon, the steward of Alexander used to feel warm in the shade, and to shiver in the sun. And Andron, the Argive, as Aristotle tells us, travelled through the dry parts of Libya, without once drinking. Again, one man is fond of medicine, another of farming, another of commerce; and the same pursuits are good for one man, and injurious to another; on which account, we ought to suspend our opinions.

The third mode, is that which has for its object the difference of the organs of sense. Accordingly, an apple presents itself to the sight as yellow, to the taste as sweet, to the smell as fragrant; and the same form is seen, in very different lights, according to the differences of mirrors. It follows, therefore, that what is seen is just as likely to be something else as the reality.

The fourth refers to the dispositions of the subject, and the changes in general to which it is liable. Such as health, sickness, sleep, waking, joy, grief, youth, old age, courage, fear, want, abundance, hatred, friendship, warmth, cold, easiness of breathing, oppression of the respiratory organs, and so on. The objects, therefore, appear different to us according to the disposition of the moment; for, even madmen are not in a state contrary to nature. For, why are we to say that of them more than of ourselves? For we too look at the sun as if it stood still. Theon, of Tithora, the Stoic, used to walk about in his sleep; and a slave of Pericles' used, when in the same state, to walk on the top of the house.

The fifth mode is conversant with laws, and established customs, and belief in mythical traditions, and the conventions of art, and dogmatical opinions. This mode embraces all that relates to vice, and to honesty; to the true, and to'the false; to the good, and to the bad; to the Gods, and to the production, and destruction of all visible objects. Accordingly, the same action is just in the case of some people, and unjust in that of others. And good in the case of some, and bad in that of others. On this principle we see that the Persians do not think it unnatural for a man to marry his daughter; but among the Greeks it is unlawful. Again, the Massagetae, as Eudoxus tells us in the first book of his Travels over the World, have their women in common; but the Greeks do not. And the Cilicians delight in piracy, but the Greeks avoid it. So again, different nations worship different Gods; and some believe in the providence of God, and others do not. The Egyptians embalm their dead, and then bury them; the Eomans burn them; the Paeonians throw them into the lakes. All these considerations show that we ought to suspend our judgment.

The sixth mode has reference to the promiscuousness and confusion of objects; according to which nothing is seen by us simply and by itself; but in combination either with air, or with light, or with moisture, or with solidity, or heat, or cold, or motion, or evaporation or some other power. Accordingly, purple exhibits a different hue in the sun, and in the moon, and in a lamp. And our own complexions appear different when seen at noonday and at sunset. And a stone which one cannot lift in the air, is easily displaced in the water, either because it is heavy itself and is made light by the water, or because it is light in itself and is made heavy by the air. So that we cannot positively know the peculiar qualities of anything, just as we cannot discover oil in ointment.

The seventh mode has reference to distances, and position, and space, and to the objects which are in space. In this mode one establishes the fact that objects which we believe to be large, sometimes appear small; that those which we believe to be square, sometimes appear round; that those which we fancy even, appear full of projections; those which we think straight, seem bent; and those which we believe to be colour less, appear of quite a different complexion. Accordingly, the sun, on account of its distance from us, appears small. The mountains too, at a distance, appear airy masses and smooth, but when beheld close, they are rough. Again, the sun has one appearance at his rise, and quite a different one at midday. And the same body looks very different in a wood from what it does on plain ground. So too, the appearance of an object changes according to its position as regards us; for instance, the neck of a dove varies as it turns. Since then, it is impossible to view these things irrespectively of place and position, it is clear that their real nature is not known.

The eighth mode has respect to the magnitudes or quantities of things; or to the heat or coldness, or to the speed or slow There is too remarkable a similarity in this to Campbell's lines:—

'Tis distance lends enchantment to the view,
And robes the mountains in their azure hue:
to allow one to pass it over without pointing it out.
ness, or to the paleness or variety of colour of the subject. For instance, a moderate quantity of wine when taken invigorates, but an excessive quantity weakens. And the same is tbe case with

food, and other similar things.

The ninth depends upon the frequency, or rarity, or strangeness of the thing under consideration. For instance, earthquakes excite no wonder among those nations with whom they are of frequent occurrence; nor does the sun, because he is seen every day.

The ninth mode is called by Phavorinus, the eighth, and by Sextus and Enesidemus, the tenth; and Sextus calls the tenth the eighth, which Phavorinus reckons the tenth as the ninth in order.

The tenth mode refers to the comparison between one thing and another; as, for instance, between what is light and what is heavy; between what is strong and what is weak; between what is greater and what is less; what is above and what is below. For instance, that which is on the right, is not on the right intrinsically aud by nature, but it is looked upon as such in consequence of its relation to something else; and if that other thing be transposed, then it will no longer be on the right. In the same way, a man is spoken of as a father, or brother, or relation to some one else; and day is called so in relation to the sun: and everything has its distinctive name in relation to human thought: therefore, those things which are known in relation to others, are unknown of themselves.

And these are the ten modes.

X. But Agrippa adds five other modes to them. One derived from the disagreement of opinions; another from the necessity of proceeding *ad infinitum* from one reasoning to another; a third from relation; a fourth from hypothesis; and the last from the reciprocal nature of proofs.

That which refers to the disagreement of opinions, shows that all the questions which philosophers propose to themselves, or which people in general discuss, are full of uncertainty and contradiction.

That which is derived from the necessity of proceeding incessantly from one reasoning to another, demonstrates that it is impossible for a man ever, in his researches, to arrive at undeniable truth; since one truth is only to be established by another truth; and so on, *ad infinitum.*

The mode which is derived from relation rests on the doctrine that no object is ever perceived independently and entirely by itself, but always in its relation to something else; so that it is impossible to know its nature correctly.

That which depends on hypothesis is directed against those arguers who pretend that it is necessary to accept the principles of things taken absolutely, and that one must place one's faith in them without any examination, which is an absurdity; for one may just as well lay down the opposite principles.

The fifth mode, that one namely which arises from the reciprocal nature of proofs, is capable of application whenever the proof of the truth which we are looking for supposes, as a necessary preliminary, our belief in that truth; for instance, if, after we have proved the porosity of bodies by their evaporations, we return and prove the evaporations by the porosity.

XI. These Sceptics then deny the existence of any demon-5 stration, of any test of truth, of any signs, or causes, or motion, or learning, and of anything as intrinsically or naturally good j or bad. For every demonstration, say they, depends either on things which demonstrate themselves, or on principles which are indemonstrable. If on things which demonstrate themselves, then these things themselves require demonstration; and so on *ad infinitum*. If on principles which are indemonstrable, then, the very moment that either the sum total of these principles, or even one single one of them, is incorrectly urged, the whole demonstration falls instantly to pieces. But if any one supposes, they add, that there are principles which require no demonstration, that man deceives himself strangely, not seeing that it is necessary for him in the first place to establish this point, that they contain their proof in themselves. For a man cannot prove that there are four elements, because there are four elements.

Besides, if particular proofs are denied in a complex demonstration, it must follow that the whole demonstration is also incorrect. Again, if we are to know that an argument is really a demonstrative proof, we must have a test of truth; and in order to establish a test, we require a demonstrative proof; and these two things must be devoid of every kind of certainty, since they bear reciprocally the one on the other.

How then is any one to arrive at certainty about obscure matters, if one is ignorant even how one ought to attempt to prove them? For what oue is desirous to understand is not what the appearance of things is, but what their nature and essence is.

They show, too, that the dogmatic philosophers act with great simplicity; for that the conclusions which they draw from their hypothetical principles, are not scientific truths but mere suppositions; and that, in the same manner, one might establish the most improbable propositions. They also say that those who pretend that one ought not to judge of things by the circumstances which surround them, or by their accessories, but that one ought to take their nature itself as one's guide, do not perceive that, while they pretend to give the precise measure and definition of everything, if the objects present such and such an appearance, that depends solely on their position and relative arrangement. They conclude from thence, that it is necessary to say that everything is true, or that everything is false. For if certain things only are true, how is one to recognize them. Evidently it will not be the senses which judge in that case of the objects of sensation, for all appearances are equal to the senses; nor will it be the intellect, for the same reason. But besides these two faculties, there does not appear to be any other test or criterion at all. So, say they, if we desire to arrive at any certainty with respect to any object which comes under either sense or intellect, we must first establish those opinions which are laid down previously as bearing on those objects. For some people have denied this doctrine, and others have overturned that; it is therefore indispensable that they should be judged of either by the senses or by the intellect. And the authority of each of these faculties is contested; it is therefore impossible to form a positive judgment of the operations of the senses and of the intellect; and if the contest between the different opinions, compels us to a neutrality, then the measure which appeared proper to apply to the appreciation of all those objects is at the same time put an end to, and one must fix a similar valuation on everything.

Perhaps our opponent will say, " Are then appearances trustworthy or deceitful? " We answer that, if they are " Diogenes here appears (though he gives no intimation of his doing so,) to be transcribing the reasonings of some one of the Sceptics." *French Trand.* trustworthy, the other side has nothing to object to those to whom the contrary appearance presents itself. For, as he who says that such and such a thing appears to him is trustworthy, so also is he who says that the contrary appears to him. And if appearances are deceitful, then they do not deserve any confidence when they assert what appears to them to be true. / "We are not bound then to believe that a thing is true, merely because it obtains assent. For all men do not yield to the same reasons; and even the same individual does not always see things in the same light. Persuasion often depends on external cir cumstances, on the authority of the speaker, on his ability, on the elegance of his language, on habit, or even on pleasure.

They also, by this train of reasoning, suppress the criterion of truth. Either the criterion has been decided on, or it has not. And if it has not, it does not deserve any confidence, and it cannot be of any use at all in aiding us to discern truth from falsehood. If, on the other hand, it has been decided on, it then enters into the class of particular things which require a criterion, and in that case to judge and to be judged amount to the same thing; the criterion which judges is itself judged of by something else, that again by a third criterion, and so on *ad infinitum.* Add to this, say they, the fact that people are not even agreed as to the nature of the criterion of truth; some say that man is the criterion, others that it is the senses which are so: one set places reason in the van, another class rely upon cataleptic perception.

As to man himself, he disagrees both with himself and with / others, as the diversity of laws and customs proves. The senses are deceivers, and reason disagrees with itself. Cataleptic perception is judged of by the intellect, and the intellect changes in various manners; accordingly, we can never find any positive criterion, and in consequence, truth itself wholly eludes our search.

They also affirm that there are no such things as signs; for if there are signs, they argue they must be such as are apprehended either by the senses or by the intellect. Now, there are none which are apprehended by the senses, for everything which is apprehended by the senses is general, while a sign is something particular. Moreover, any object which is apprehended by the senses has an existence of its own, while signs are only relative. Again, signs are not apprehended by the intellect, for in that case they would be either the visible manifestation of a visible thing, or the invisible manifestation of an invisible thing, oV the invisible sign of a visible thing: or the visible sign of an invisible thing. But none of all these cases are possible; there are therefore no such things as signs at all.

There is therefore no such thing as a visible sign of a visible thing; for that which is visible has no need of a sign. Nor, again, is there any invisible sign of an invisible thing; for when anything is manifested by means of another thing, it must become visible. On the same principle there is no invisible sign of a visible object; for that which aids in the perception of something else must be visible. Lastly, there is no visible manifestation of an invisible thing; for as a sign is something wholly relative, it must be perceived in that of which it is the sign; and that is not the case. It follows, therefore, that none of those things which are not visible in themselves admit of being perceived; for one considers signs as things which aid in the perception of that which is not evident by itself.

They also wholly discard, and, as far as depends on them, overturn the idea of any cause, by means of this same train of reasoning. Cause is something relative. It is relative to that of which it is the cause. But that which is relative is only conceived, and has no real existence. The idea of a cause then is a pure conception; for, inasmuch as it is a cause, it must be a cause of something; otherwise it would be no cause at all. In the same way as a father cannot be a father, unless there exists some being in respect of whom one gives him the title of father; so too a cause stands on the same ground. For, Supposing that nothing exists relatively to which a cause can be spoken of; then, as there is no production, or destruction, or anything of that sort, there can likewise be no cause. However, let us admit that there are such things as causes. In that case then, either a body must be the cause of a body, or that which is incorporeal must be the cause of that, which is incorporeal. Now, neither of these cases is possible; (therefore, there is no such thing as cause. In fact, one body cannot be-the cause of another body, since both bodies must have the same nature; and if it be said that one is the cause, inasmuch as it is a body, then the other must be a cause for the same reason. And in that case one would have two reciprocal causes; two agents' without any passive subject.

Again, one incorporeal thing cannot be the cause of another incorporeal thing for the same reason. Also, an incorporeal thing cannot be the cause of a body, because nothing that is incorporeal can produce a body. Nor, on the other hand, can a body be the cause of anything incorporeal, because in every production there must be some passive subject matter; but, as what is incorporeal is by its own nature protected from being a passive subject, it cannot be the object of any productive power. There is, therefore, no such thing as any cause at all. From all which it follows, that the first principles of all things have no reality; for such a principle, if it did exist, must be both the agent and the efficient cause.

Again, there is no such thing as motion. For whatever is moved, is moved either in the place in which it is, or in that in which it is not. It certainly is not moved in the place in which it is, and it is impossible that it should be moved in the place in which it is not; therefore, there is no such thing as motion at all.

They also denied the existence of all learning. If, said they, anything is taught, then either that which does exist is taught in its existence or that which does not exist is taught in its non-existence; but that which does exist is not taught in its existence (for the nature of all existent things is visible to all men, and is known by all men); nor is that which does not exist, taught in its non-existence, for nothing can happen to that which does not exist, so that to be taught cannot happen to it.

Nor again, say they, is there any such thing as production. For that which is, is not produced, for it exists already; nor that which is not, for that does not exist at all. And that which has no being nor existence at all, cannot be produced.

Another of their doctrines is, that there is no such thing as any natural good, or natural evil. For if there be any natural good, or natural evil, then it must be good to everyone, or evil to everyone; just as snow is cold to everyone. But there i., no such thing as one general good or evil which is common to all beings; therefore, there is no such thing as any natural good, or natural evil. For either one must pronounce every

E E thing good which is thought so by anyone whatever, or one must say that it does not follow that everything which is thought good is good. Now, we cannot say that everything which is thought good is good, since the same thing is thought good by one person (as, for instance, pleasure is thought good by Epicurus) and evil by another (as it is thought evil by Antisthenes); and on this principle the same thing will be both good and evil. If, again, we assert that it does not follow that everything which is thought good is good, then we must distinguish between the different opinions; which it is not possible to do by reason of the equality of the reasons adduced in support of them. It follows that we cannot recognize anything as good by nature.

And we may also take a view of the whole of their system by the writings which some of them have left behind them. JPyrrho himself has_left_nothing; but his friends Timon, and lEnesidemus, and Numemus, and Nausiphanes, and others of that class have left books. And the dogmatical philosophers arguing against them, say that they also adopt spurious and pronounce positive dogmas. For where they think that they are refuting others they are convicted, for in the very act of refutation, they assert positively and dogmatize. For when they say that they define nothing, and that every argument has an opposite argument; they do here give a positive definition, and assert a possitive dogma. But they reply to these objectors; as to the things which happen to us as men, we admit the truth of what you say; for we certainly do know that it is day, and that we are alive; and we admit that we know many other of the phaenomena of life. But with respect to those things as to which the dogmatic philosophers make positive assertions, saying that they are comprehended, we suspend our judgment on the ground of their being uncertain; and we know nothing but the passions; for we confess that we see, and we are aware that we comprehend that such a thing is the fact; but we do not know how we jsee, or how we comprehend. Also, we state in the way of narrative, that this appears white, without asserting positively that it really is so. And with respect to the assertion, ''We define nothing," and other sentences of that sort, we do not pronounce them as dogmas. For to say that is a different kind of statement from paying that the world is spherical; for the one fact is not evident, while the other statements are mere admissions. While, therefore, we say that we define nothing, we do

Again, the dogmatic philosophers say that the Sceptics overthrow all life, when they deny everything of which life consists. But the Sceptics say that they are mistaken; for they do not deny that they see, but that they do not know how it is that they see. For, say they, we assert what is actually the fact, but we do not describe its character. Again, we feel that fire burns, but we suspend our judgment as to whether it has a burning nature. Also, we see whether a person moves, and that a man dies; but how these things happen we know not. Therefore, say they, we only resist the uncertain deductions which are put by the side of evident facts. For when we say that an image has projections, we only state plainly what is evident; but when we say that it has not projections, we no longer say what appears evident, but something else. On which account Timon, in his Python, says that Pyrrho does not destroy the authority of custom. And in his Images he speaks thus:—

And in his treatise on the Senses, he says, " The reason why a thing is sweet I do not declare, but I confess that the fact of sweetness is evident." So too. iEnesidemus, in the first book of his Pyrrhoneari Discourses, says that Pyrrho defines nothing dogmatically, on account of the possibility of contradiction, but that he is guided by what is evident. And he says the same thing in his book against Wisdom, and in his treatise on Investigation.

In like manner, Zeuxis, a friend of iEnesidemus, in his treatise on Twofold Arguments, and Antiochus, of Laodicea, and Apellas, in his Agrippa, all declare nothing beyond what is evident. The criterion therefore, among the Sceptics, is that which is evident; as iEnesidemus also says; and Epicurus says the same thing.

But Democritus says, that there is no test whatever of appearances, and also that they are not criteria of truth. Moreover, the dogmatic philosophers attack the criterion derived

But what is evidently seen prevails, Wherever it may be.

from appearances, and say that the same objects present at times different appearances; so that a town presents at one time a square, and at another a round appearance; and. that consequently, if the

Sceptic does not discriminate between different appearances, he does nothing at all. If, on the contrary, he determines in favour of either, then, say they, he no longer attaches equal value to all appearances. The Sceptics reply to this, that in the presence of different appearances, they content themselves with saying that there are many appearances, and that it is precisely because things present themselves under different characters, that they affirm the existence of appearances.

Lastly, the Sceptics say, that the chief good is the suspension of the judgment which tranquillity of mind follows, like its shadow, as Timon and Enesidemus say; for that we need not choose these things, or avoid those, which all depend on ourselves: but as to those things which do not depend upon us, but upon necessity, such as hunger, thirst, and pain, those we cannot avoid; for it is not possible to put an end to them by reason.

But when the dogmatic philosophers object that the Sceptic, on his principles, will not refuse to kill his own father, if he is ordered to do so; so that they answer, that they can live very well without disquieting themselves about the' speculations of the dogmatic philosophers; but, suspending their judgment in all matters which do not refer to living and the preservation of life. Accordingly, say they, we avoid some things, and we seek others, following custom in that; and we obey the laws.

Some authors have asserted, that the chief good of the Stoics is impassibility; others say that it is mildness and tranquillity.

LIFE OF TIMON.

I. Apoixonides, of Nicaea, a philosopher of our school, in the first book of his Commentaries on the Silli, which he dedicated to Tiberius Caesar, says that Timon was the son of

Timarchus, and a Phliasian by birth. And then, when he was young, he studied dancing, and afterwards he renounced that study, and went to Megara to Stilpo. And having spent some time there, he returned home again and married. Then he came with his wife to Elis, to see Pyrrho, and there he remained while his children were born; the elder of whom, he called Xanthus, and taught him medicine, and left him his successor in his sect of philosophy. And he was a man of considerable eminence, as Sotion tells us in his eleventh book. Afterwards, being in difficulty as to bis means, he departed to the Hellespont and the Propontis; and living at Chalcedon as a Sophist, he earned a very high reputation and great popularity; from thence he departed, after having made a considerable fortune, and went to Athens, and remained there till his death, going across once for a short time to Thebes. He was also acquainted with king Antigonus, and with Ptolemy Philadelphus, as he himself testifies in his Iambics.

II. He was, says Antigonus, fond of drinking, and he at times occupied himself with works quite inconsistent with philosophy; for he wrote lyric and epic poems, and tragedies and satiric dramas, and thirty comedies, and sixty tragedies and Silli, and amatory poems. There are works of his also enumerated in a regular catalogue, extending to twenty thousand verses, which are mentioned by Antigonus, of Garystos, who also wrote his life. Of the Silli, there are three volumes; in which he attacks every one as if he were a Sceptic, and especially he lampoons the dogmatic philosophers under the form of parodies. The first volumeTof these Silli contain a long uninterrupted narration; but the second and third are in the form of dialogues. He is represented in them, as interrogating Xenophanes, the Colophonian, about every thing, and he utters a long continued discourse; in his second book he speaks of the more ancient philosophers; and in his third of the more modern ones; on which account some people have given the last book the name of the epilogue.

But the first book contains the same subjects, with this difference, that in that it is all confined to one single person; and its first line begins thus:—

Come hither, all you over-busy Sophists.

III. He died when he was nearly ninety years old, as Antigonus tells us; and Sotion, in his eleventh book, makes the same statement. I have heard it said that he had only one eye, and, indeed, he used to call himself Cyclops. IV. There was also another Timon, the misanthrope.

V. Now this philosopher was very fond of a garden, and also of solitude, as we are told by Antigonus. Accordingly it is reported, that Hieronymus, the Peripatetic, said of him, as among the Scythians, both they who fly, and they who pursue shoot with the bow, so in the case of the philosophers, those who pursue and those who fly both hunt for pupils, as Timon for instance.

VI. He was a man of very acute perceptions, and very quick at seeing the ridiculous side of any question: he was also very fond of learning, and a very clever man at devising plots for poets, and at composing dramas. And he used to associate with himself, in the composition of his tragedies, two other poets, named Alexander and Homer; and whenever he was disturbed by his maidservants or by the dogs, he paid no attention to them, studying above all things to live in tranquillity. They tell a story, that Aratus asked him how he could procure an entire and correct copy of Homer's poetry, and he answered, " If he could fall in with an old manuscript which had never been corrected. " And all his works used to lie about at random, and at times half eaten by mice; so that once when he was reading them to Zopyrus, the orator, and unrolling a volume, he read whatever passages came first, and when he got to the middle of the book he found a great gap, which he had not previously perceived, so very indifferent was he about such matters.

His constitution was so vigorous, that he could easily go without his dinner. And they say, that once when he saw Arcesilaus passing through the forum of the Cercipes, he said, "What are you doing here, where we freemen are?" And he used constantly to quote to those who invoked the testimony of their intellects to judge of the senses:—

Attagas and Numeniue are met.

And this jesting manner was habitual with him. Accord That is to say, the harmony between intellect and the senses will not last long. Attagas and Numenius were two notorious brigands.
ingly he once said to a man, who was surprised at everything, " Why do you not wonder that we three men have only four eyes between us?" for he himself had only one eye, no more had Dioscorides, his pupil; but the man to whom he was speaking had his sight unimpaired. On another occasion, he was asked by Arcesilaus, why he had come from Thebes, and he said, " To laugh at you all when I see you face to face." But though he attacked Arcesilaus in his Silli, he has praised him in the book entitled the Funeral Banquet of Arcesilaus.. VII. He had no successor, as Menodotus tells us; but his j school ceased, till Ptolemy the Cyrenean re-established it. According to the account given to us by Hippobotus and Sotion, he had as pupils, Dioscorides of Cyprus, and Nilolochus of Rhodes, and Euphranor of Seleucia, and Pracylus of the Troas, who was a man of such constancy of mind that, as Phylarchus relates in his History, he allowed himself to be punished as a traitor wholly undeservedly, not uttering one word of complaint against his fellow citizens; and Euphranor had for his pupil, Eubulus, of Alexandria, who was the master of Ptolemy, who was the master of Sarpedon and Heraclides. And Heraclides was the master of iEnesidemus, of Cnossus, who wrote eight books of Pyrrhonean discourses; he was also the master of Xeuxippus Polites, who was the master of Zeuxis Gonicpus, who was the master of Antiochus, of Laodicea, in Lycia. Antiochus again, was the master of Menodotus, of Nicomedia, a skilful physician, and of Theodos, of Laodicea; and Menodotus was the master of Herodotus, of Tarsus, the son of Arieus; Herodotus was the master of Sextus Empiricus, who left ten books of Sceptic Maxims, and other excellent works; and Sextus was the master of Saturninus Cythenas, who was also an empiric. 424 BOOK X. LIFE OF EPICURUS.

I. Epicures was an Athenian, and the son of Neocles and Chterestrate, of the burgh of Gargettus, and of the family of the Philaidie, as Metrodorus tells us in his treatise on Nobility of Birth. Some writers, and among them Heraclides, in his Abridgment of Sotion, say, that as the Athenians had Colonis and Samos, he was brought up there, and came to Athens in I his eighteenth year, while Xenoorates was president of the Academy, and Aristotle at Chalcis. But after the death of Alexander, the Macedonian, when the Athenians were driven out of Samos by Perdiccas, Epicurus went to Colophon to his father.
II. And when he had spent some time there, and collected some disciples, he again returned to Athens, in the time of Anaxicrates, and for some time studied philosophy, mingling with the rest of the philosophers; but subsequently, he some how or other established the school which was called after his name; and he used to say, that he began to study philosophy, when he was fourteen years of age; but Apollodorus, the Epicurean, in the first book of his account of the life of Epicurus, sa3s, that he came to the study of philosophy, having conceived a great contempt for the grammarians, because they could not explain to him the statements in Hesiod respecting Chaos.
But Hermippus tells us, that he himself was a teacher of grammar, and that afterwards, having met with the books of Democritus, he applied himself with zeal to philosophy, on which account Timon says of him.—
The last of all the natural philosophers,
And the most shameless too, did come from Samos,
A grammar teacher, and the most ill-bred
And most unmanageable of mankind.
And he had for his companions in his philosophical studies, his three brothers, Neocles, Chseredemus, and Aristobulus, who were excited by his exhortations, as Philodemus, the Epicurean, relates in the tenth book of the Classification of Philosophers. He had also a slave, whose name was Inus, as Myronianus tells us in his Similar Historical Chapters.
III. But Diotimus, the Stoic, was very hostile to him, and calumniated him in a most bitter manner, publishing fifty obscene letters, and attributing them to Epicurus, and also giving him the credit of the letters, which generally go under the name of Chrysippus. And Posidonius, the Stoic, and Nicolaus, and Sotion, in the twelfth of these books, which are entitled the Refutations of Diocles, of which there are altogether twenty-four volumes, and Dionysius, of Halicarnassus, have also attacked him with great severity; for they say that he used to accompany his mother when she went about the small cottages, performing purifications, and that he used to read the formula, and that he used also to keep a school with his father at very low terms. Also, that he, as well as as one of his brothers, was a most profligate man in his morals, and that he used to live with Leontium, the courtesan. Moreover, that he claimed the books of Democritus on Atoms, and that of Aristippus on Pleasure, as his own; and that he was not a legitimate citizen; and this last fact is asserted also by Timocrates, and by Herodotus, in his treatise on the Youth of Epicurus.
They also say that he used to flatter Mithras, the steward of Lysimachus, in a disgraceful manner, calling him in his letters Paean, and King; and also that he flattered Idomeneus, and Herodotus, and Timocrates who had revealed all his secret practices, and that he flattered them on this very account. And iu his letters to Leontium, he says, " O king Apollo, my dear Leontium, what transports of joy did I feel when I read your charming letter." And to Themista, the wife of Leontius, he writes, " I am ready and prepared, if you do not come to me, to roll myself to wherever you and Themista invite me." And he addresses Pythocles, a beautiful youth, thus, " I will sit quiet," says he, " awaiting your longed for and god-like approach." And at another time, writing to Themista, he says, " That he had determined to make his way with her," as Theodorus tells us in the fourth book of his treatises

against Epicurus,

He also wrote to many other courtesans, and especially to Leontium, with whom Metrodorus also was in love. And in his treatise on the Chief Good, he writes thus, " For I do not know what I can consider good, if I put out of sight the pleasures which arise from favours, and those which are derived from amatory pleasures, and from music, and from the contemplation of beauty." And in his letter to Pythocles, he writes, " And, my dear boy, avoid all sorts of education."

Epictetus also attacks him as a most debauched man, and reproaches him most vehemently, and so does Timocrates, the brother of Metrodorus, in his treatise entitled the Merry Guests, and this Timocrates had been a disciple in his school, though he afterwards abandoned it; and he says that he used to vomit twice a day, in consequence of his intemperance; and that he himself had great difficulty in escaping'from this nocturnal philosophy, and that mystic kind of re-union. He also accuses Epicurus of shameful ignorance in his reasoning, and still more especially in all matters relating to the conduct of life. And says that he was in a pitiable state of health, so that he could not for many years rise up from his sofa; and that he used to spend a tninae a day on his eating, as he himself states in his letter to Leontium, and in that to the philosophers at Mitylene. He also says that many courtesans used to live with him and Metrodorus; and among them Marmaricem, and Hedea, and Erotium, and Nicidium.

IV. And in the thirty-seven books which he wrote about natural philosgjhy, they"say that he says a great many things of the same kind over and over again, and that in them he writes in contradiction of other philosophers, and especially of Nausiphanes, and speaks as follows, word for word: " But if any one else ever was afflicted in such a manner, then certainly this man had a continual labour, striving to bring forth the sophistical boastfulness of his mouth, like many other slaves." And Epicurus also speaks of Nausiphanes in his letters, in the following terms: " These things led him on to such arrogance of mind, that he abused me and called me a schoolmaster." He used also to call him Lungs, and Blockhead, and Humbug, and Fornicator. And he used to call Plato's followers Flatterers of Dionysius, but Plato himself he called Golden. Aristotle he called a debauchee and a glutton, saying that he ' joined the army after he had squandered his patrimony, and sold drags. He used also to call Protagoras a porter, and the secretary of Democritus, and to say that he taught boys their letters in the streets. Heraclitus, he called a disturber; Democritus, he nicnamed Lerocr/tys; and Antidorus, Saenidorus;f c The Cynics he called enemies of Greece; and the Dialecticians he charged with being eaten up with envy. Pyrrho, he said, was ignorant and unlearned.,.

V. But these men who say this are all wrong, for there are plenty of witnesses of the unsurpassable kindness of the man / to every body; both his own country which honoured him with/ brazen statues, and his friend who were so numerous that they could not be contained in whole cities; and all his acquaintances who were bound to him by nothing but the charms of his doctrine, none of whom ever deserted him, except Metrodorus, the son of Stratoniceus, who went over to Carneades, probably because he was not able to bear with equanimity the unapproachable excellence of Epicurus. Also, the perpetual succession of his school, which, when every other school decayed, continued without any falling off, and produced a countless number of philosophers, succeeding one another without any interruption. We may also speak here of his gratitude towards his parents, and his beneficence to his brothers, and his gentleness to his servants (as is plain from his will, and from the fact too, that they united with him in his philosophical studies, and the most eminent of them was the one whom I have mentioned already, named Inus); and his universal philanthropy towards all men.

His piety towards the Gods, and his affection for his country. was quite unspeakable; though, from an excess_of-modesty, he avoided affairs of state. And though he lived when very difficult times oppressed Greece, he still remained in his own country, only going two or three times across to Ionia to see his friends, who used to throng to him from all quarters, and to live with him in his garden, as we are told by Apollodorus. (This garden he bought for eighty minae.) VI. And Diocles, in the third book of his Excursion, says That is "trifler," from epivw, to judge; and *Xtjpog,* nonsensical talk.

t That is, flattering for gifts; from *aaivui,* to wag the tail as a dog, to caress; and *Suipov,* a gift. that they all lived in the most simple and economical manner;

" They were content," says he, " with a small cup of light wine, and all the rest of their drink was water." He also Hells us that Epicurus would not allow his followers to throw Itheir property into a common stock, as Pythagoras did, who I said that the possessions of friends were held in common.

For he said that such a doctrine as that was suited rather for those who distrusted one another; and that those who distrusted one another were not friends. But he himself in his letters, says that he is content with water and plain hread, and adds, "Send me some Cytherean cheese, that if I wish to have a feast, I may have the means." This was the real character of the man who laid down the doctrine that pleasure was the chief good; whom Athenaeus thus mentions in an epigram:— 0 men, you labour for pernicious ends;

And out of eager avarice, begin

Quarrels and wars. And yet the wealth of nature

Fixes a narrow limit for desires,

Though empty judgment is insatiable.

This lesson the wise child of Neocles

Had learnt by heart, instructed by the Muses,

Or at the sacred shrine of Delphi's God.

And as we advance further, we shall learn tins fact from his dogmas, and his apophthegms.

VII. Of all the ancient philosophers he

was, as we are told by Diocles, most attached to Anaxagoras (although in some points he argued against him); ahd" to Archelaus, the master of Socrates. And he used, Diocles adds, to accustom his pupils to preserve his writings in their memory. Apollodorus, in his Chronicles, asserts that he was a pupil of Nausiphanes, and Praxiphanes; but he himself does not mention this; but says in his letter to Euridicus, that he had been his own instructor. He also agreed with Hermarchus in not admitting that Leucippus deserved to be called a philosopher; though some authors, among whom his Apollodorus, speak of him as the master of Democritus. Demetrius, the Magnesian, says that he was a pupil of Xenocrates also. VIII. He uses in his works plain language with respect to anything he is speaking of, for which Aristophanes, the grammarian, blames him, on the ground of that style being vulgar., But he was such an admirer of perspicuity, that even in his treatise on Rhetoric, he aims at and recommends nothing but clearness of expression. And in his letters, instead of the usual civil expressions, " Greeting," " Farewell," and so on, he substitutes, " May you act well," "May you live virtuously," and expressions of that sort. /Some of his biographers assert that it was he who composed the treatise entitled the Canon, in imitation of the Tripod of Nausiphanes, whose pupil they j say that he was, and add that he was also a pupil of Pamphilus, " the Platonist, at Samosy IX. They further tell us that he began to study philosophy at twelve years of age, and that he presided over his school thirty-two years. And he was born as we are told by Apollodorus, in his Chronicles, in the third year of the hundred and ninth olympiad, in the archonship of Sosigenes, on the seventh day of the month Gamelion, seven years after the death of Plato. And when he was thirty-two years of age, he first set up his school at Mitylene, and after that at Lampsacus; and when he had spent five years in these two cities, he came to Athens; and he died there in the second year of the hundred and twenty-seventh olympiad, in the archonship of Pytharatus, when he had lived seventy-two years. And Hermarchus, the son of Agemarchus, and a citizen of Mitylene, succeeded him in his school.

He died of the stone, as Hermarchus mentions in his letters, after having been ill a fortnight; and at the end of the fortnight, Hermippus says that he went into a brazen bath, properly tempered with warm water, aud asked for a cup of pure wine and drank it; and having recommended his friends to remember his doctrines, he expired. And there is an epigram of ours on him, couched in the following language:—

Now, fare-ye-well, remember all my words;
This was the dying charge of Epicurus:
Then to the bath he went, and drank some wine,
And sank beneath the cold embrace of Pluto.

Such was the life of the man, and such was his death.

X. And he made his will in the following terms:—

" According to this my will, I give all my possessions to Amynomachus, of Bate, the son of Philocrates, and to Timocrates, of Potamos, the son of Demetrius; according to the deed of gift to each, which is deposited in the temple of Cybele; on condition that they make over my garden and all that is attached to it to Hermarchus, of Mitylene, the son of Agemarchus; and to those who study philosophy with him, and to whomsoever Hermarchus leaves as his successors in his school, that they may abide and dwell in it, in the study and practice of philosophy; and I give it also to all those who philosophize according to my doctrines, that they may, to the best of their ability, maintain my school which exists in my garden, in concert with Amynomachus and Timocrates; and I enjoin their heirs to do the same in the most perfect and secure manner that they can; so that they also may maintain my garden, as those also shall to whom my immediate sucessors hand it down. As for the house in Melita, that Amynomachus and Timocrates shall allow Hermarchus that he may live in it during his life, together with all his companions in philosophy.

" Out of the income which is derived from that property, which is here bequeathed by me to Amynomachus and Timocrates, I will that they, consulting with Hermarchus, shall arrange in the best manner possible the offerings to the manes in honour of the memory of my father, and mother, and brothers, and myself, and that my birth-day may be kept as it has been in the habit of being kept, on the tenth day of the month Gamelion; and that the re-union of all the philosophers of our school, established in honour of Metrodorus and myself, may take place on the twentieth day of every month. They shall also celebrate, as I have been in the habit of doing myself, the day consecrated to my brothers, in the month Poseideon; and the day consecrated to the memory of Polyaenus, in the month Metageitnion.

" Amynomachus and Timocrates, shall be the guardians of Epicurus, the son of Metrodorus, and of the son of Polyaeitus, as long as they study philosophy under, and live with.'Hermarchus. In the same,way also, they shall be the guardians of the daughter of Metrodorus, and when she is of marriageable age, they shall give her to whomsoever Hermarchus shall select of his companions in philosophy, provided she is well behaved and obedient to Hermarchus. And Amynomachus and Timocrates shall, out of my income, give them such a sum for their support as shall appear sufficient year by year, after due consultation with Hermarchus. And they shall associate Hermarchus with themselves in the management of my revenues, in order that everything may be done with the approval of that man who has grown old with me in the study of philosophy, and who is now left as the president of all those who have studied philosophy with us. And as for the dowry for the girl when she is come to marriageable age, let Amynomachus and Timocrates arrange that, taking for the purpose such a sum from my property as shall seem to them, in conjunction with Hermarchus, to be reasonable. And let them also take care of Nicanor, as we ourselves have done; in order that all those who have studied philosophy with us, and who have assisted us with their means, and who have shown great friendship for us, and who have chosen to grow old with us in the study of philosophy, may never be in want of anything as far as our power to prevent it may extend.

" I further enjoin them to give all my books to Hermarchus; and, if anything should happen to Hermarchus before the children of Metrodorus are grown up, then I desire that Amynomachus and Timocrates, shall take care that, provided they are well behaved, they shall have everything that is necessary for them, as far as the estate which I leave behind me shall allow such things to be furnished to them. And the same men shall also take care of everything else that I have enjoined; so that it may all be fulfilled, as far as the case may permit.

" Of my slaves, I hereby emancipate Inus, and Nicias, and Lycon: I also give Phaidrium her freedom."

And when he was at the point of death, he wrote the following letter to Idomeneus:—

" We have written this letter to you on a happy day to us, which is also the last day of our life. For stranguryjhas attacked me, and also a dysentery, so violent tha£.iiothing can be added to the violence of my sufferings.-i'But the cheerfulness of my mind, which arises from the recollection of all my philosophical contemplations, counterbalances all these afflictions. And I beg you to take care of the children of Metrodorus, in a manner worthy of the devotion shown by the youth to me, and to philosophy."

Such then as I have given it, was his will.

XI. He had a great number of pupils, of whom the most eminent were Metrodorus, the Athenian, and Timocrates, and Sandes, of Lampsacus; who, from.the time that he first became acquainted with him, never left him, except once when he went home for six months; after which he returned to him. And he was a virtuous man in every respect, as Epicurus tells us in his Fundamental Principles. And he also bears witness to his virtue in the third book of his Timocrates. And being a man of this character, he gave his sister Bates in marriage to ldomeneus; and he himself had Leontium, the Attic courtesan, for his concubine. He was very unmoved at all disturbances, and even at death: as Epicurus tells us, in the first book of his Metrodorus. He is said to have died seven years before Epicurus himself, in the fifty-third year of his age. And Epicurus himself, in the will which I have given above, gives many charges about the guardianship of his children, showing by this that he had been dead some time. He also had a brother whom I have mentioned before, of the name of Timocrates, a trifling, silly man.

The writings of Metrodorus are these. Three books addressed to the Physicians; one essay on the Sensations; one addressed to Timocrates; one on Magnanimity; one on the Illness of Epicurus; one addressed to the Dialecticians; one against the Nine Sophists; one on the Road to Wisdom; one on Chance; one on Riches; one against Democritus; one on Nobility of Birth.

XII. Likewise Polyaenus, of Lampsacus, the son of Athenodorus, was a man of mild and friendly manners, as Philodemus particularly assures us. XIII. And his successor ws Jlermarchus, of Mitylene', the son of Agemarchus, a poor man; and his favourite pursuit was rhetoric. And the following excellent works of his are extant. Twenty-two books of letters about Empedocles; an essay on Mathematics; A treatise against Plato; another against Aristotle. And he died of paralysis, being a most eminent man. XIV. There was also Leontius, of Lampsacus, and his wife Themista, to whom Epicurus wrote. XV. There were also Colotes and ldomeneus; and these also were natives of Lampsacus. And among the most eminent philosophers of the school of Epicurus, were Pgh?stratus, who succeeded Hermarchus, and Dionysius who succeedeTTnm, and Basilides who succeeded him. Likewise Apollodorus, who was nicknamed the tyrant of the gardenszjifforugaroos), was a very eminent man, and wrote more thanjour hundred books. And there were the two Ptolemies ofATexarr(Ma, Ptolemy the Black, and Ptolemy the Fair. And Zeno, of Sidon, a pupil of Apollodorus, a very voluminous author; and Demetrius, who was surnamed the Lacedaemonian; and Diogenes, of Tarsus, who wrote the Select Dialogues; and Orion, and others whom the genuine Epicureans call Sophists. XVI. There were also three other persons of the name of Epicurus; first, the son of Leonteus and Themista; secondly, a native of Magnesia; and lastly, a Gladiator. XVII. And Epicurus was a most voluminous author, exceeding_all men in the number of his books; for there are more than three hundred volumes of them: and in the whole 1 of them there is not one citation from other sources, but they I are filled wholly with the sentiments of Epicurus himself. In ' the quantity of his writings he was rivalled by Chrysippus, as Carneades asserts, who calls him a parasite of the books of Epicurus; for if ever this latter wrote anything, Chrysippus immediately set his heart on writing a book of equal size; and in this way he often wrote the same thing over again; putting down whatever came into his head; and he published it all without any corrections, by reason of his haste. And he quotes such numbers of testimonies from other authors, that his books are entirely filled with them alone; as one may find also in the works of Aristotle and Zeno.

Such then, and so numerous are the works of Epicurus; the chief of which are the following. Thirty-seven treatises on Natural Philosophy; one on Atoms, and the Vacuum; one on Love; an abridgment of the Arguments employed against the Natural Philosophers; Doubts in Contradiction of the Doctrines of the Megarians; Fundamental Propositions; a treatise on Choice and Avoidance; another on the Chief Good; another on the Criterion, called also the Canon; the Chseridemus, a treatise on the Gods; one on Piety; the Hegesiana; four essays on Lives; one on Just Dealing; the Neocles; one essay addressed to Themista; the Banquet; the Euryloehus; one essay addressed to Metrodorus; one on Seeing; one on the Angle in an Atom; one on Touch; one on Fate; Opinions on the Passions; one treatise addressed to Timocrates; Prognostics; Exhortations; a treatise on Spectres; one on Perceptions; the Aristobulus; an essay on Music; one on Justice and the other Virtues; one on Gifts and Gratitude; the Polymedes; the Timocrates, a treatise in three books; the Metrodorus, in five books; the Antidorus, in two books; Opinions about the South Winds; a treatise addressed to Mithras; the Callistolas; an essay on Kingly Power; the Anaximenes; Letters.

XVIII. And I will endeavour to give an abridgment of the doctrines contained in these works, as it may be agreeable, I quoting three letters of his, in which he has made a sort of epitome of all his philosophy. I will also give his fundamental and peculiar opinions, and any apophthegms which he uttered which appear worthy of being selected. So that you may be thoroughly acquainted with the man, and may also judge that I understand him.

Now the first letter is one that he wrote to Herodotus, on the subject of Natural Philosophy; the second is one that he wrote to Pythocles, which is about the Heavenly Bodies; the third is addressed to Menaeceus, and in that there are contained the discussions about lives.

We must now begin with the first, after having said a little by way of preface concerning the divisions of philosophy which he adopted.

XIX. Now he divides philosophy into three parts. The canonical, the physical, and the ethical. The canonical, which serves as an introduction to science, is contained in the single treatise which iscalled the Tanon. The physical embraces the whole range of speculation on subjects of natural philosophy, and is contained in the thirty-seven books on nature, and in the letters again it is discussed in an elementary manner. The ethical contains the discussions on Choice and Avoidance; i and is comprised in the books about lives, and in some of the Letters, and in the treatise on the Chief Good. Accordingly, most people are in the habit of combining the canonical division with the physical; and then they designate the whole under the names of the criterion of the truth, and a discussion on principles, and elements. And they say that the physical division is conversant about production, and destruction, and nature; and that the ethical division has reference to the objects of choice and avoidance, and lives, and the chief good of mankind. XX. Dialectics they wholly reject as superfluous. For they say that the correspondence of words with things is sufficient for the natural philosopher, so as to enable him to advance with certainty in the study of nature.

Now, in the Canon, Epicurus says that the criteria of truth are the senses, and the preconceptions, and the passions. But the Epicureans, in general, add also the perceptive impressions of the intellect. And he says the same thing in his Abridgment, which he addresses to Herodotus, and also in his Fundamental Principles. For, says he, the senses are devoid of reason, nor are they capable of receiving any impressions of memory. For they are not by themselves the cause of anyj motion, and when they have received any impression from any external cause, then they can add nothing to it, nor can they subtract anything from it. Moreover, they are out of the reach of any control; for one sensation cannot judge of another which resembles itself; for they have all an equal value. Nor can one judge of another which is different from itself; since their objects are not identical. In a word, one sensation cannot control another, since the effects of all of them influence us equally. Again, the reason cannot pronounce ou the senses; i for we have already said that all reasoning has the senses for its foundation. Reality and the evidence of sensation establish the certainty of the senses; for the impressions of sight and I hearing are just as real, just as evident, as pain.

It follows from these considerations that we ought to judges of things which are obscure by their analogy to those which we perceive directly. In fact, every notion proceeds from the senses, either directly, or in consequence of some analogy, or proportion, or combination. Reasoning having always a share in these last operations. The visions of insanity and of sleep have a real object, for they act upon us; and that which has no reality can produce no action.

XXI. By preconception, the Epicureans mean a sort of comprehension as it were, or right opinion, or notion, or general idea which exists in us; or, in other words, the jjecollg£tkin_ of an external object often perceived anteriorly. Such for instance, is this idea: " Man is a being of such and such a nature." At the same moment that we utter the word man, we conceive the figure of a man, in virtue of a preconception which we owe to the preceding operations of the senses. Therefore, the first notion which each word awakens in us is a correct one; in fact, we could not seek for anything if we had not previously some notion of it. To enable us to affirm that what we see at a distance is a horse or an ox, we must have some preconception in our minds which makes us acquainted with the form of a horse and an ox. We could not give names to things, if we had not a preliminary notion of what the things were. XXII. These preconceptions then furnish us with certainty. And with respect to judgments, their certainty depends on our referring them to some previous notion, of itself certain, in virtue of which we affirm such and such a judgment; for instance, " How do we know whether this thing is a man?"

The Epicureans call opinion (5o£a) also supposition *(MXis)*. And say that it is at times true, and at times_false; for that, if it is supported by testimony, and not contradicted by testimony, then it is true; but if it is not supported by testimony, and is contradicted by testimony, then it is false. On which account they have introduced the expression of " waiting," as if, before pronouncing that a thing seen is a tower, we must wait till we come near, and learn what it looks like when we are near it.

XXIII. They say that there are two passions, pleasure'and pain, which affect everything alive. And that the one is natural, and the other foreign to our nature; with reference to which all objects of choice and avoidance are judged of. They say also, that there are two kinds of investigation; the one about facts, the other about mere words. And this is as far as an elementary sketch can go— their doctrine about division, and about the criterion. XXIV. Let us now go to the letter:— EPICURUS TO HERODOTUS, WISHING HE MAY DO WELL.

" For those, 0 Herodotus, who are not able accurately to comprehend all the things which I have written about nature, nor to investigate those larger books which I have composed on the subject, I have made an abridgment of the whole discussion on this question, as far as I thought sufficient to enable them to recollect accurately the most fundamental points; that so, on all grave occasions, they might be able to assist themselves on the most important and undeniable principles; in proportion as they devoted themselves to speculations on natural philosophy. And_ here it is necessary for those who have tnade sufficient progress in their view of the general question, to recollect the principles laid down as elements of the whole discussion; for we have still greater need of a correct notion of the whole, than we have even of an accurate under standing of the details. We must, therefore, give preference to the former knowledge, and lay up in our memory those principles on which we may rest, in order to arrive at an exact perception of things, and at a certain knowledge of particular objects.

" Now one has arrived at that point when one has thoroughly embraced the conceptions, .nd, if I may so express myself, the most essential forms, and when one has impressed them adequately on one's senses. For this clear and precise know-/y ledge of the whole, taken together, necessarily facilitates one's / particular perceptions, when one has brought one's ideas back to the elements and simple terms: In short, a veritable synthesis, comprising the entire circle of the phaenomena of the universe, ought to be able to resume in itself, and in a few words, all the particular facts which have been previously studied. This method being useful even to those who are already familiarised with the laws of the universe, I recommend them, while still pursuing without intermissionCjhe study of nature, which contributes more than anything else to " the tranquillity and happiness of life,Vo make a concise statement or summary of their opinions " i

" First of all, then, Herodotu's, one must determine with., exactness the notion comprehended.under each separateword7" in order to be able to refer to it, as to a certain criterion, the conceptions which emanate from ourselves, the ulterior researches and the difficulties; otherwise the judgment has no foundation. One goes on from demonstration to demonstration *ad infinitum;* or else one gains nothing beyond mere words. In fact, it is absolutely necessary that in every word we should perceive directly, and without the assistance of any demonstration, the fundamental notion which it expresses, if we wish to

I have any foundation to which we may refer our researches, our difficulties, and our personal judgments, whatever in other respects may be the criterion which we adopt, whether we take as our standard the impressions produced 6n"buF"senses, or the actual impression in general; or whether we cling to the idea by itself, or to any other criterion.

" We must also note carefully the impres«ojis_jvhich we receive in.the presence of objects, in order to bring ourselves back to that point in the circumstances in which it is necessary to suspend the judgment, or even when the question is about things, the evidence of which is not immediately perceived.

" When these foundations are once laid we may pass to the study of those things, the evidence of whjch is not immediate.. And, first of all, we must admit that nothingrTcome of that which does not exist; for, were the fact otherwise, then every thing would be produced from everything, and there would be no need of any seed. And if that which disappeared were so absolutely destroyed as to become non-existent, then every thing would soon perish, as the things with which they would be dissolved would have no existence. But, in truth, the universal whole always was such as jfc_now_is, andalways will be such. For thFre is nothing into which it can change; for there is nothing beyond this universal whole which can penetrate into it, and produce any change in it." (And Epicurus establishes the same principles at the beginning of the great Abridgment; and in the first book of his treatise on Nature.) " Now the universal whole is a body; for our senses bear us witness in every case that bodies have a real existence; and the evidence of the senses, as I have said before, ought to be the rule of our reasonings about everything which is not directly perceived. Otherwise, if that which we call the vacuum, or space, or intangible nature, had not a real existence, there would be nothing on which the bodies could be contained, or across which they could move, as we see that they really do move. Let us add to this reflection that one cannot conceive, either in virtue of perception, or of any analogy founded on perception, any general quality pe This sentence is a remark"of Diogenes himself. There are several more of his observations in parentheses as we proceed.

culiar to all beings which is not either an attribute, or an accident of the body, or of the vacuum." (The same principles are laid down in the first, and fourteenth, and fifteenth book of the treatise on Nature; and also in the Great Abridgment.)

' Now, of bodies, some are combinations, and some the elements out of which these combinations are formed. These last are indivisible, and protected from every kind of transformation; otherwise everything would be resolved into nonexistence. Theyjixist by their _own force, in the midst of the dissolution of the combined bodies, being absolutely.full, and as such offering nojtiandle for destruction to take hold of. It follows, therefore, as a matter of absolute necessity, that the principles of things must be corporeal, indivisible elements.

" The universe is infinite. For that which is finite has an extreme, and that which has an extreme is looked at m relation to something else. Consequently, that which has not an extreme, has no boundary; and if it has no boundary, it must be infinite, and not terminated by any limit. The universe then is infinite, both with reference to the quantity of bodies of which it is made up, and to the magnitude of the vacuum; for if the vacuum were infinite, the bodies being finite, then, the bodies would not be able to rest in any place; they would be transported about, scattered across the infinite vacuum for want of any power to steady themselves, or to keep one another in their places by mutual repulsion. If, on the other hand, the vacuum were finite, the bodies being infinite, then the bodies clearly could never be contained in the vacuum.

"Again: the atoms which form the bodies, these full elements from which the combined bodies come, and into which they resolve themselves, assume' an incalculable variety of forms, for the numerous differences which the bodies present cannot possibly result from an aggregate of the same forms. Each variety of forms contains an infinity of atoms, but there is not for that reason an infinity of atoms; it is only the number of them which is beyond all calculation. " (Epicurus adds, a little lower down, that divisibility, *ad infinitum,* is impossible; for, says he, the only things which change are the qualities; unless, indeed, one wishes to proceed from division to division, till one arrives absolutely at infinite littleness.)

" The atoms are in a continual state of motion." (He says, farther on, that they move with an equal rapidity from all eternity, since the vacuum offers no more resistance to the lightest than it does to the heaviest.)

"Among the atoms, some are separated by great distances, others come very near to one another in the formation of combined bodies, or at times are enveloped by others which are combining; but in this latter case they, nevertheless, preserve their own peculiar motion, thanks to the nature of the vacuum, which separates the one from the other, and yet offers them no resistance. The solidity which they possess causes them, while knocking against one another, to re-act the one upon the other; till at last the repeated shocks bring on the dissolution of the combined body; and for all this there is no external cause, the atoms and the vacuum being the only causes."

' (He says, further on, that the atoms have no peculiar quality /of their own, except from magnitude and weight-As to colour, he says in the twelfth book of his Principia, that it varies according to the position of the atoms. Moreover, he does not attribute to the atoms any kind of dimensions; and, accordingly, no atom has ever been perceived by the senses; but this expression, if people only recollect what is here said, will by itself offer to the thoughts a sufficient image of the nature of things.)

" But, again, the worlds also are infinite, whether they resemble this one of ours or whether they are different from it For, as the atoms are, as to their number, infinite, as I have proved above, they necessarily move about at immense distances; for besides, this infinite multitude of atoms, of which the world is formed, or by which it is produced, could not be entirely absorbed by one single world, nor even by any worlds, the number of which was limited, whether we suppose them like this world of ours, or different from it. There is, therefore, no fact inconsistent with an infinity of worlds.

" Moreover, there are images resembling, as far as their form goes, the solid bodies which we see, but which differ materially from them in the thinness of their substance. In fact it is not impossible but that there may be in space some secretions of this kind, and an aptitude to form surfaces without depth, and of an extreme thinness; or else that from the solids there may emanate some particles which preserve the connection, the disposition, and the motion which they had in the body. I give the name of images to these representations; and, indeed, their movement through the vacuum taking place, without meeting any obstacle or hindrance, perfects all imaginable extent in an inconceivable moment of time; for it is the meeting of obstacles, or the absence of obstacles, which pro- duces the rapidity or the slowness of their motion. At all events, a body in motion does not find itself, at any moment imaginable, in two places at the same time; that is quite inconceivable. From whatever point of infinity it arrives at some appreciable moment, and whatever may be the spot in its course in which we perceive its motion, it has evidently quitted that spot at the" moment of our thought; for this motion which, as we have admitted up to this point, encounters no obstacle to its rapidity, is wholly in the same condition as that the rapidity of which is diminished by the shock of some resistance.

"It is useful, also, to retain this principle, and to know that the images have an incomparable thinness; which fact indeed is in no respect contradicted by sensible appearances. From which it follows that their rapidity also is incomparable; for they find everywhere an easy passage, and besides, their infinite smallness causes them to experience no shock, or at all events to experience but a very slight one, while an infinite multitude of elements very soon encounter some resistance.

" One must not forget that the production of images is simultaneous witlπThe TnougKt / imagesffEsTnnd are continually flowing ott in aninsen-j sible mannexjndeed. because they are immediatelx-ieplaced. They preserve for a long time the same disposition, and the same arrangement that the atoms do in the solid body, although, notwithstanding, their form may be sometimes altered. The direct production of images in space is equally instantaneous, because these images are only light substances destitute of depth.

" But there are other manners in which natures of this kind are produced; for there is nothing in all this which at all contradicts the senses, if one only considers in what way the senses are exercised, and if one is inclined to explain the relation which is established between external objects and ourselves. Also, one must admit that something passes from external objects intojis in order to produce in us sight and the knowledge of forms; for it is difficult.to conceive that external objects can affect us through the medium of the air which is between us and them, or by means of rays, whatever emissions proceed from us to them, so as to give us an impression of their form and colour. This phenomenon, on the contrary, is perfectly explained, if we admit that certain images of the same colour, of the same shape, and of a proportionate magnitude pass from these objects to us, and so arrive at being seen and comprehended. These images are animated by an exceeding rapidity, and, as on the other side, the solid object forming a compact mass, and comprising a vast quantity of atoms, emits always the same quantity of particles, the vision is conHnued, and only produces iu us55e single geri oepfimwMcfr-preserves always the same reKUBfiTTcTthe object. Tivery conception, every sensibleeTceptioir which bears upon the form or the other attributes of these images, is only the same form of the solid perceived directly, either in virtue of a sort of actual and continued condensation of the image, or in consequence of the traces which it has left in us.

"Error and false judgments always depend upon the supposition that a preconceived idea will be confirmed, or at all events will not be overturned, by, evidence. Then, when it is not confirmed, we form our judgment in virtue of a sort of initiation of the thoughts connected, it is true with the perception, and with a direct representation; but still connected also with a conception peculiar to ourselves, which is the parent of error. In fact the representations which intelligence reflects like a mirror, whether one perceives them in a dream, or by any other conceptions of the intellect, or of any other of the criteria, can never resemble the objects that one calls real and true, unless there were objects of this kind perceived directly. And, on the other side, error could not be possible, *I* if we did not receive some other motion also, a sort of initiative *I* of intelligence connected; it is true with direct representation, but going beyond that representative. These conceptions being connected with the direct perception which produces the representation, but going beyond it, in consequence of a motion peculiar to the individual thought, produces error when it is not confirmed by evidence/or when it is contradicted by evidence: but when it is confirmed, or when it is not contradicted by evidence, then it produces truth.

'' We must carefully preserve these principles in order not to reject the authority of the faculties which perceive truth directly; and not, on the other hand, to allow what is false to be established with equal firmness, so as to throw everything into confusion.

" Moreoy_ejJhearing is produced,by some sort of current proceeding_from spmetEhg. thaxsneaks, or sounds, or roars", or in ariy"manner causes any odLoiLau current is_ diffused-intQ.,,sfflall bodies resembling one another iri _tlifii_-pal! which, preserving not only some kind of relation between one another, but even a sort of particular identity witE We object_from which they emanate, puts us, very f'requentlyTi or at least causes us to become awareoi the existence ot some external circumstance. If these currents did not carry with them some sort of sympathy, then there would be no such perception. We must not therefore think that it is the air which receives a certain form, under the action of the voice or of some other sound. For it is utterly impossible that the voice should act in this manner on the air. But the percussion j)roduced in us when we, by the utterance of a voice, cause a disengagement of certain particles, constituie_a-Ia reirrp.nl jesgmgEg a light, whisper, and prepares an acawstic feeling for us.

We must admit that the case of smelling is the same as that of hearing. There would be no sense of smell.i£_there did not emanate from mostnjDjetsTreTtarn particlesj:apable ofjroducjngjnmipre"ssion on the smejl. One"cIass being ill-suited to the organ7and consequently producing"a"diserdered state of i%"ihe other being suited to it, and causing it no distress.

" One must also allow, that the atoms possess no one of the qualities of sensible objects, except form, weight, magnitude, and anything else is unavoidably inherent iii form; in fact, every quality is changeable, but the atoms are necessarily unchangeable; for it is impossible but that in the dissolution of combined bodies, there must be something which continues solid and indestructible, of such a kind, that it will not change either into what does not exist, or out of what does not exist; but that it results either from a simple displacement of parts, which is the most usual case, or from the addition or subtraction of certain particles. It follows from that, that that which does not admit of any change in itself, is imperishable, participates in no respect in the nature of changeable things, and in a word, has its dimensions and forms immutably determined. And this is proved plainly enough, because even in the transformations which take place under our eyes, in consequence of the retrenchment of certain parts, we can still recognise the form of these constituent parts; while those qualities, which are not constituent parts, do not remain like the form, but perish in the dissolution of the combination. The attributes which we have indicated, suffice to explain all the differences of combined bodies; for rt'we must inevitably leave something indestructible, lest everyMtiiing should resolve itself into non-existence.

"However, one must not believe that every kind of magnitude exists in atoms, lest we find ourselves contradicted by phaenomena. But we must admit that there are atoms of different magnitude, because, as that is the case, it is then more easy to explain the impressions and sensations; at all events, I repeat, it is not necessary for the purpose of explaining the differences of the qualities, to attribute to atoms every kind of magnitude.

" We must not suppose either, that an atom can become visible to us; for, first of all, one does not see that that is the case, and besides, one cannot even conceive, how an atom is to become visible; besides, we must not believe, that in a finite body there are particles of every sort, infinite in number; consequently, one must not only reject the doctrine of inj finite divisibility in parcels smaller and smaller, lest we should I be reducing everything to nothing, and find ourselves forced to I admit, that in a mass composed of a crowd of elements, existence can reduce itself to non-existence. But one cannot even suppose that a finite object can be susceptible of transformations *ad infinitum,* or even of transformation into smaller objects than itself; for when once one has said that there are in an object particles of every kind, infinite in number, there is absolutely no means whatever of imagining that this object can have only a finite magnitude; in fact, it is evident that these particles, infinite in number, have some kind of dimen sion or other, and whatever this dimension may be in other respects, the objects which are composed of it will have an infinite magnitude; in presenting forms which are determined, and limits which are perceived by the senses, one conceives, easily, without its being necessary to study this last question directly, that this would be the consequence of the contrary supposition, and that consequently, one must come to look at every object as infinite.

" One must also admit, that the most minute particle perceptible to the sense, is neither absolutely like the objects which are susceptible of transformation, nor absolutely different from them, It has some characteristics in common with the object which admit of transformation, but it also differs from them, inasmuch as it does not allow any distinct parts to be discerned in it. When then, in virtue of these common characteristics, and of this resemblance, we wish to form an idea of the smallest particle perceptible by the senses, in taking the objects which change for our terms of comparison, it is necessary that we should seize on some characteristic common to these different objects. In this way, we examine them successively, from the first to the last, not by themselves, nor as composed of parts in juxtaposition, but only in their extent; in other words, we consider the magnitudes by themselves, and in an abstract manner, inasmuch as they measure, the greater a greater extent, and the smaller a smaller extent. This analogy applies to the atom, as far as we consider it as having the «mifHp«t dimenHifl" pnggjhlp. Evidently by its minuteness, it differs from all sensible objects, still this analogy is applicable to it; in a word, we establish by this comparison, that the atom really has some extent, but we exclude all considerable dimensions, for the sake of only investing it with the smallest proportions.

This is the argument in its completed form: " We can only form an idea of an atom by analogy, and analogy demonstrates to us that it is not of infinite littleness. In fact, let us compare it to the smallest particles recognisable by sense, and then let us endeavour to form an idea of these last. To do this we must take a term of comparison in complex objects, which are composed of various parts. Abstracting from these all other characteristics but that of extent, we see that these objects have dimensions, some greater and some less, measuring a'n extent which is greater or less as the case may be. The smallest sensible particle will then have its dimensions; it will measure the smallest pos

" We must also admit, in taking for our guide, the reasoning which discourses to us things which are invisible to the senses, that the most minute magnitudes, those which are not compound magnitudes, and which from the limit of sensible extent, are the first measure of the other magnitudes which are only called greater or less in their relation to the others. For these relations which they maintain with these particles, which are not subject to transformation, suffice to give them this characteristic of first measure. But they cannot, like atoms, qnmhinft _themselves, and form compound bodies in virtue of any motion belonging to themselves.

" Moreover, we must not say (while speaking of the infinite), that such or such a point is the highest point of it, or the lowest. For height and lowness must not be predicated of the infinite. We know, in reality, that if, wishing to determine the infinite, we conceive a point above our head, this point, whatever it may be, will never appear to us to have the character in question: otherwise, that which would be situated above the point so conceived as the limit of the infinite, would be at the same moment, and by virtue of its relation to the same point, both high and low; and this is impossible to imagine.

" It follows that thought can only conceive that one single movement of transference, from low to high, *ad infinitum;* and one single movement from high to low. From low to high, when even the object in motion, going from us to the places situated above our heads, meets ten thousand times with the feet of those who are above us; and from high to low, when in the same way it advances towards the heads of those who are below us. For these two movements, looked at by themselves and in their whole, are conceived as really opposed the one to the other, in their progress towards the infinite.

" Moreover, all jhe«toms are necessarily animated by the same_jupidity, when tEey move acrbssThe vacuum, or when no obstacle thwarts them. For why should heavy atoms have a more rapid movement than those which are small and fight, since in no quarter do they encounter any obstacle? Why, on sible sensible extent, that is to say, it will not be infinitely small. Applying this analogy to an atom, one comes to conceive it as measuring the smallest extent possible, but not as having no extent at all, which was what Epicurus wished to prove."—*French Translator.* the other hand, should the small atoms have arapidity superior to that of the large ones, since both the one and the other find everywhere an easy passage, from the very moment that no obstacle intervenes to thwart their movements? Movement from low to high, horizontal movement to and fro, in virtue of the rechorocaljDejcussion-of-the atoms, movement downwards, in virtue of their weight, will be all equal, for in I whatever sense the atom moves, it must have a movement as rapid as the thought, till the moment when it is repelled, in virtue of some external cause, or of its own proper weight, by the shock of some object which resists it.

" Again, even in the compound bodies, one atom does not move more rapidly than another. In fact, if one only looks at the continued movement of an atom which takes place in an indivisible moment of time, the briefest possible, they all have a movement equally rapid. At the same time, an atom has not, in any moment perceptible to the intelligence, a continued movement in the same direction; but rather a series of oscillating movements from which there results, in the last t analysis, a continued movement perceptible to the' senses.

If then, one were to suppose, in virtue of a reasoning on things invisible, that, in the intervals of time accessible to thought, the atoms have a continued movement one would deceive one's self, for that which is conceived by the thought is true as well as that which is directly perceived.

" Let us now return to the study of the affections, and of the sensations; for this will be the best method of proving that the soul is a bodily substance composed of slight particles, diffused over all the members of the body, and presenting a I / great analogy to a sort of spirit, having an admixture of heat, *V* resemblingлIFone time one, and at "another time thej)ther_of those two jmnclplesl There exists inTt a special part, endowed with ah" extreme mobility, in consequence of the exceeding slightness of the elements which compose it, and also in reference to its more immediate sympathy with the rest of the body. That it is which the faculties of the soul sufficiently prove, and the passions, and the mobility of its nature, and the thoughts, and, in a word, everything, the privation of which is death. We must admit that it is in the soul mosLaspecially that the principle oT¥ensatioii"T5gides. " AfTthe same time, it wOTtldTioTrpossess this power if it were not enveloped by the

I rest of the body which communicates it to it, and in its. turn / receives it from irrTutonIy in a certain measure; for there are certain affectTons"oTthe soul of which it is not capableT"

" It is on that account that, when the soul departs, the body is no longer possessed of sensation; for it has not this power, (that of sensation namely) in itself; but, on the other hand, this power can only manifest_itself in the soul through the medjujiLJifjthe-body. The souh reflecting the manifestations which are accomplished in the substance which environs it, realises in itself, in a virtue or power which belongs to it, the sensible affections, and immediately communicates them to the body in virtue of the reciprocal bonds of sympathy which unite it to the body; that is the reason why the destruction of a part of the body does not draw after it a cessation of all feeling in the soul while it resides in the body, provided that the senses still preserve some energy; although, nevertheless, the dissolution of the corporeal covering, or even of any one of its O portions, may smaetimes bring on with it the destruction of the soul.

" The rest of the body, on the other hand, even when it remains, either as a whole, or in any part, loses all feeling by the dispersion of that aggregate of atoms, whatever it may be, that forms the soul. When the entire combination of the body " is dissolved, then the soul too is dissolved, and ceases to retain those faculties which were previously inherent in it, and especially the power of motion; so that sensation perishes equally as far as the soul is concerned; for it is impossible to imagine that it still feels, from the moment when it is no longer in the same conditions of existence, and no longer possesses the same movements of existence in reference to the same organic system; from the moment, in short, when the things which cover and surround it are no longer such, that it retains in them the same movements as before.

(Epicurus expresses the same ideas in other works, and adds that the soul is composed of atoms of the most perfect lightness and roundness; atoms wholly different from those of fire. He distinguishes in it the irrational part which is diffused over the whole body, from the rational part which has its seat in the chest, as is proved by the emotions of fear and joy. He adds that sleep is produced when the parts of the soul diffused over the whole of the body concentre themselves, or when they disperse and escape by the pores of the body; for particles emanate from all bodies.)

" It must also be observed, that I use the word incorporeal *(aaui/iarog)* in the usual acceptation of the word, to express that which is in itself conceived as such. Now, nothing can I be conceived in itself as incorporeal except the vacuum; but the vacuum cannot be either passive or active; it is only the condition and the place of movement. Accordingly, thej who pretend_that the soul is incorporeal, utter words destitute of sense; for, if it had this character, it w6uld not be able either to dMtuTIw'jE as it is, we see plainly enough that it is liable to both these circumstances.

" Let us then apply all these reasonings to the affections and sensations, recollecting the ideas which we laid down at the i beginning, and then we shall see clearly that these general *jt*principles contain an exact solution of all the particular cases. '

" As to forms, and hues, and magnitudes, and weight, and the other qualities which one looks upon as attributes, whether it be of every body, or of those bodies only which are visible and perceived by the senses, this is the point of view under which they ought to be considered: they are not particular substances, having a peculiar existence of. their own, for that cannot be conceived; nor can one say any more.that i&ejUl &ve v no reality at all. They are not incorporeal substances inherent in the body, nor are they parts of the body. But they constitute by their union the eternal substance and the essence of the entire body. We must not fancy, however, that the body is composed of them, as an aggregate is formed of particles of the smallest dimensions of atoms or magnitudes, whatever they may be, smaller than the compound body itself; they only constitute by their union, I repeat, the eternal substance of the body. Each of these attributes has ideas and particular perceptions which correspond to it; but they cannot be per-j ceived independently of the whole subject taken entirely; the union of all these perceptions forms the idea of the body. Bodies often possess other attributes which are not eternally inherent in them, but which, nevertheless, cannot be ranged among the incorporeal and invisible things. Accordingly, it is sufficient to express the general idea of the movement of transference to enable us to conceive in a moment certain distinct qualities, and those combined beings, which, being o G taken in their totality, receive the name of bodies; and the necessary and eternal attributes without which the body cannot be conceived.

" There are certain conceptions corresponding to these attributes; but, nevertheless, they cannot be known abstractedly, and independently of some subjects; and further, inasmuch as they are not attributes necessarily inherent in the idea of :i . body, one can only conceive them in the moment in which they are visible; they are realities nevertheless; and one must not refuse them being an existence merely because they have neither the characteristic of the compound beings to which we give the name of bodies, nor that of the eternal attributes. We should be equally deceived if we were to suppose that they have a separate and independent existence; for that is true neither of them nor of the eternal attributes. They are, as one sees plainly, accidents of the body; accidents which do not of necessity make any part of its nature; which cannot be considered as independent substances, but still to each of which sensation gives the peculiar character under which it appears to us.

" Another important question is that of time. Here we cannot apply any more the method of examination to which we submit other objects, which we study with reference to a given subject; and which we refer to the preconceptions which exist in ourselves. We must seize, by analogy, and going round the whole circle of things comprised under this general denomination of time—we must seize, I say—that essential character which causes us to say that a time is long or short. It is not necessary for that purpose to seek for any new forms of expression as preferable to those which are in common use; we may content ourselves with those by which time is usually indicated. Nor need we, as certain philosophers do, affirm any particular attribute of time, for that would be to suppose that its essence is the same as that of this attribute. It is sufficient too seek for the ingredients of which this particular nature which we call time is composed, and for the means by which it is measured. For this we have no need of demonstration; a simple exposition is sufficient. It is, in fact, evident, that we speak of time as composed of days and nights, and parts of days and nights; passiveness and impassibility, movement and repose, are equally comprised in time. In 6hort, it is evident that in connection with these different states, we conceive a particular property to which we give the name of time.

(Epicurus lays down the same principles in the second book of his treatise on Nature, and in his great Abridgment.)

" It is from the infinite that the worlds are derived, and all the finite aggregates which present numerous analogies with the things which we observe under our own eyes. Each of these objects, great and small, has been separated from the infinite by a movement peculiar to itself. On the other hand, all these bodies will be successively destroyed, some more, and others less rapidly; some under the influence of one cause, and others because of the agency of some other. (It is evident, after this, that Epicurus regards the worlds as perishable, since he admits that their parts are capable of transformation. He also says in other places, that the earth rests suspended in the air.)

" We must not believe that the worlds have of necessity all one identical form. (He says, in fact, in the twelfth book of his treatise on the World, that the worlds differ from one another; some being spherical, other elliptical, and others of other shapes.)

" Nevertheless, there are not worlds of every possible form and shape.

" Let us also beware of thinking that animals are derived from the infinite; for there is no one who can prove that the germs from which animals are born, and plants, and all the other objects which we contemplate, have been brought from the exterior in such a world, and that this same work! would not have been able to produce them of itself. This remark applies particularly to the earth.

" Again, we must admit that in many and various respects, nature isl both instructed and constrained by circumstances themselves; and that reason subsequently makes perfect and enriches with additional discoveries the things which it has borrowed from nature; in some cases rapidly, and in others more slowly. And in some cases according to periods and times greater than those which proceed from the infinite; in other cases according to those which are smaller. So, originally it was only in virtue of express agreements that one gave names to things. But men whose ideas and passions varied according to their respective nations, formed these names of their own accord, uttering divers sounds produced by each passion, or by each idea, following the differences of the situations and of the peoples. At a later period one established in each nation, in a uniform manner, particular terms intended to render the relations more easy, and language more concise. Educated men introduced the notion of things not discoverable by the senses, and appropriated words to them when they found themselves under the necessity of uttering their thoughts; after this, other men, guided in every point by reason, interpreted these words in the same sense.

" As to the heavenly phaenomena, such as the motion and course of the stars, the eclipses, their rising and setting, and all other appearances of the sarue kind, we mu4t__b£ware of thinking that they are produced by any particular being which has regulated, or whose business it is to regulate, for the future, the order of the world, a being immortal and perfectly happy; for the cares and anxieties, the benevolence and the anger, far from being compatible with felicity, are, on the contrary, the consequence of weakness, of fear, and of the want which a thing has of something else. We must not fancy either that these globes of fire, which roll on in space, enjoy a perfect happiness, and give themselves, with reflection and wisdom, the motions which they possess. But we must respect the established notions on this subject, provided, "Z. nevertheless, that they do not all contradict the respect due to truth; for nothing is more calculated to trouble the soul — than this strife of contradictory notions and principles. We must therefore admit that from the first movement impressed on the heavenly bodies since the organization of the world there is derived a sort oijgcessity which regulates their course to this day.

" Let us be well assured that it is to physiology that it belongs to determine 'the causes of the most elevated phsenomena, and that happiness consists, above all things, in the science of the heavenly things and their nature, and in the knowledge of analogous phaenomena which may aid us in the comprehension of the ethics. These heavenly phaenomena admit of several explanations; they have no reason of a necessary character, and one may explain them in different manners. In a word, they have no relation—a moment's consideration will prove this by itself—with those imperishable and happy natures which admit of no division and of no confusion. As for the theoretical knowledge of the rising and setting of the stars, of the movement of the sun between the tropics, of the eclipses, and all other similar phsenomena, that is utterly useless, as far as any influence upon happiness that it can have. Moreover, those who, though possessed of this knowledge, are ignorant of nature, and of the most probable causes of the phaenomena, are no more protected from fear than if they were in the most complete ignorance; they even experience the most lively fears, for the trouble, with which the knowledge of which they are possessed inspires them, can find no issue; and is not dissipated by a clear perception of the reasons of these phaenomena.

"As to us, we find many explanations of the motions of the sun, of the rising and setting of the stars, of the eclipses and similar phaenomena, just as well as of the more particular phsenomena. And one must not think that this method of explanation is not sufficient to procure happiness and tranquillity. Let us content ourselves with examining how it is that similar phsenomena are brought about under our own eyes, and let us apply these observations to the heavenly objects and to everything which is not known but indirectly. Let us despise those people who are unable to distinguish facts susceptible of different explanations from others which can only exist and be explained in one single way. Let us disdain those men who do not know, by means of the different images which result from distance, how to give an account of the different appearances of things; who, in a word, are ignorant what are the objects which can excite any trouble in us. If, then, we know that such a phaenomenon can be brought about in the same manner as another given phsenomenon of the same character which does not inspire us with any apprehension; and if, on the other hand, we know that it can take place in many different manners, we shall not be more troubled at the sight of it than if we knew the real cause of it.

" We must also recollect that that which principally contributes to trouble the spirit of men is the persuasion which they cherish that the stars are beings imperishable and perfectly happy, and that then one's thoughts and actions are in contradiction to the will of these superior beings; they also, being deluded by these fables, apprehend an eternity of evils, they fear the insensibility of death, as that could affect them. What do I say? It is not even belief, but inconsiderateness and blindness which govern them in every thing, to such a degree that, not calculating these fears, they are just as much troubled as if they had really faith in these vain phantoms. And the real freedom from this kind of trouble consists in being emancipated from all these things, and in preserving the recollection of all the principles which we have established, especially of the most essential of them. Accordingly, it is well to pay a scrupulous attention to existing phaenomena and to the sensations, to the general sensations for general things, and to the particular sensations for particular things. In a word, we must take note of this, the immediate evidence with which each of these judicial faculties furnishes us; for, if we attend to these points, namely, whence confusion and fear arise, we shall divine the causes correctly, and we shall deliver ourselves from those feelings, tracing back the heavenly phsBnomena to their causes, and also all the others which present themselves at every step, and inspire the common people with extreme terror.

" This, Herodotus, is a kind of summary and abridgment of the whole question of natural philosophy. Bo that, if this reasoning be allowed to be valid, and be preserved carefully in the memory, the man who allows himself to be influenced by it, even though he may not descend to a profound study of its details, will have a great superiority of character over other men. He will personally discover a great number of truths which I have myself set forth in my entire work; and these truths being stored in his memory, will be a constant assistance to him. By means of these principles, those who have descended into the details, and have studied the question sufficiently, will be able, in bringing in all their particular knowledge to bear on the general subject, to run over without difficulty almost the entire circle of the natural philosophy; those, on the other hand, who are not yet arrived at perfection, and who have not been able to hear me lecture on these subjects, will be able in their minds to run over the main of the essential notions, and to derive assistance from them for the tranquillity and happiness of life."

This then is his letter on physics.

XXV. About the heavenly bodies he writes thus:— EPICUKUS TO PYTHOCLES, WISHING HE MAT DO WELL.

"Cleon has brought me'your letter, in which you continue to evince towards me an affection worthy of the friendship which I have for you. You devote all your care, you tell me, to engraving in your memory thos3 ideas which contribute to the happiness of life; and you entreat me at the same time to send you a simple abridgment and abstract of my ideas on the heavenly phaenomena, in order that you may without difficulty' preserve the recollection of them. For, say you, what I have written on this subject in my other works is difficult to recollect, even with continual study.

"I willingly yield to your desire, and I have good hope, that in fulfilling what you ask, I shall be useful too to many others, especially to those who are as yet novices in the real knowledge of nature, and to those to whom the perplexities and the ordinary affairs of life leave but little leisure. Be careful then to seize on those precepts thoroughly, engrave them deeply in your memory, and meditate on them with the abridgment addressed to Herodotus, which l also send you.

"Know then, that it is with the knowledge of the heavenly phaenomena, both with those which are spoken of in contact with one another, and of those which have a spontaneous existence, as wjthjevery other.-science; it has no other aim but that freedom from anxiety, and that calmness which is derived from a firm belief.

"Itis not good to desire what is impossible, and to endeavour to enunciate a uniform theory about everything; accordingly, we ought not here to adopt the method, which we have followed in our researches into Ethics, or in the solution of problems of natural philosophy. We there said, for instance; that there are no other things, except bodies and the vacuum, that the atoms are the principles of things, and so of the rest. In a word, we gave a precise and simple explanation of every fact, conformable to appearances.

"We cannot act in the same way with respect to the heavenly phenomena; these productions may depend upon several different causes, and we may give many different explanations on this subject, equally agreeing with the impressions of the senses. Besides, it is not here a question about reasoning on new principles, and of laying down, *a priori,* rules for the interpretation of nature; the only guides for us to follow are the appearances_themselves; for that which we have in view is not a set of systems and vain opinions, but much rather a life exempt from every jrind_ of disojiietude.

"The heavenly phaenomena do not inspire those who give different explanations of them, conformable with appearances, instead of explaining them by hypothesis, with any alarm. But if, abandoning hypothesis, one at the same time renounces the attempt to explain them by means of analogies founded on appearances, then one is placing one's self altogether at a distance from the science of nature, in order to fall Into fables.

"It is possible that the heavenly phsenomena may present some apparent characters which appear to assimilate them to those phaenomena which we see taking place around ourselves, without there being any real analogy at the bottom. For the heavenly phsenomena may depend for their production on many different causes; nevertheless, we must observe the appearances presented by each, and we must distinguish the different circumstances which attach to them, and which can be explained in different manners by means of analogous phaenomena which arise under our eyes.

"The world is a collection of things embraced by the heaven, containing the stars, the earth, and all visible objects. This collection, separated from the infinite, is terminated by an extremity, which is either rare, or dense, or revolving, or in a state of repose, or of a round, or triangular, or of some shape or other in fact, for it may be of any shape, the dissolution of which must bring the destruction of everything which they embrace. In fact, it can take place in every sort of way, since there is not one of those things which are seen which testifies against this world in which we cannot detect any extremity; and that such worlds are infinite in number is easily seen, and also that such a world can exist both in the world and in the lh%ra%ii«ij,m, as we call the space between the worlds, being a huge space made up of plenum and vacuum, but not, as some philosophers pretend, an immensity of space absolutely empty. This production of a world may be explained thus: seeds suitably appropriated to such an end may emanate either from one or from several worlds, or from the space that separates them; they flow towards a particular point where they become collected together and organized; after that, other germs come to unite them together in such a way as to form a durable whole, a basis, a nucleus to which all successive additions unite themselves.

"One must not content one's self in this question with saying, as one of the natural philosophers has done, that there is a re-union of the elements, or a violent motion in the vacuum under the influence of necessity, and that the body which is thus produced increases until it comes to crash against some other; for this doctrine is contrary to appearances.

"The sun, the niooTTr aTid the other stars, were originally formed separately, and were afterwards comprehended in the entire total of the world. All the other objects which our world comprises, for instance, the earth and the sea, were also formed spontaneously, and subsequently gained size by the addition and violent movement of light substances, composed of elements of fire and air, or even of these two principles at once. This explanation, moreover, is in accordance with the impressions of the senses.

"As to the magnitude of the sun and of the other stars, it is, as far as we are concerned, such as it appears to us to be. (This same doctriue is reproduced, and occurs again in the eleventh book of his treatise on Nature; where he says, " If the distance has made it lose its size, *d fortiori,* it would take away its brilliancy; for colour has not, any more than size, the property of traversing distance without alteration.")

" But, considered by itself, the sun may be a little greater or a little smaller than it appears; or it may be just such as it looks; for that is exactly the case with the fires of common occurrence among men, which are perceived by the senses at a distance. Besides, all the difficulties on this subject will be easily explained if one attends to the clear evidence of the perceptions, as I have shown in my books about Nature.

" The rising and setting of the sun, of the moon, and of the stars, may depend on the fact of their becoming lighted up, and extinguished alternately, and in the order which we behold. One may also give other reasons for this phsenomenon, which are not contradicted by any sensible appearances; accordingly, one might explain them by the passage of the stars above and below the earth, for the impressions of the senses agree also with this supposition.

" As to their motion, one may make that depend on the circular movement of the entire heaven. One may also suppose that the stars move, while the heaven itself is immoveable; for there is nothing to prevent the idea that originally, before the formation of the world, they may have received, by the appointment of fate, an impulse from east to west, and that now their movement continues in consequence of their heat, as the fire naturally proceeds onwards in order to seek the aliment which suits it.

" The intertropical movements of the sun and moon may depend, either on the obliquity impressed by fate on the heaven at certain determined epochs, or on the resistance of the air, or on the fact that these ignited bodies stand in need of being nourished by a matter suitable to their nature, and that this matter fails them; or finally, they may depend on the fact of their having originally received an impulse which compels them to move as they do describing a sort of spiral figure. The sensible evidence does not in the least contradict these different suppositions, and all those of the same kind which one can form, having always a due regard to what is possible, and bringing back each phaenomenon to its analogous appearances in sensible facts, without disquieting one's self about the miserable speculations of the astronomers.

" The evacuations and subsequent replenishings of the moon may depend either on a conversion of this body, or on the different forms which the air when in a fiery state can adopt, or perhaps to the interposition of another body, or lastly, to some one of the causes by which one gives account of the analogous phaenomena which pass under our eyes. Provided, however, that one does not obstinately adopt an exclusive mode of explanation; and that, for want of knowing what is possible for a man to explain, and what is inaccessible to his intelligence; one does not throw one's self into interminable speculations.

" It may also be possibly the case that the moon has a light of her own, or that she reflects that of the sun. For we see around us many objects which are luminous of themselves, and many others which have only a borrowed light. In a word, one will not be arrested by any of the celestial phaenomena, provided that one always recollects that there are many explanations possible; that one examines the principles and reasons which agree with this mode of explanation, and that one does not proceed in accounting for the facts which do not agree with this method, to suffer one's self to be foolishly carried away, and to propose a separate explanation for each phaenomenon, sometimes in one way, and sometimes in another.

" The appearance of a face in the orb of the moon, may depend either on a displacement of its parts, or on the interposition of some obstacle, or on any other cause capable of accounting for such an appearance. For one must not neglect to apply this same method to all the heavenly phaenomena; for, from the moment when one comes to any point of contradiction to the evidence of the senses, it will be impossible to possess perfect tranquillity and happiness.

" The eclipses of the sun and moon may depend either on the fact that these stars extinguish themselves, a phaenomenon which we often see produced under our eyes, or on the fact of other bodies, the earth, the heaven, or something else of the same kind interposing, between them and us. Besides, we must compare the different modes of explanation appropriate to phaenomena, and recollect that it is not impossible that many causes may at one and the same time concur in their production. (He says the same thing in the twelfth book of his treatise on Nature; and adds that the eclipses of the sun arise from the fact that it penetrates into the shade of the moon, to quit it again presently; and the eclipses of the moon from the fact of its entering into the shade of the earth. We also find the same doctrine asserted by Diogenes, the Epicurean, in the first book of his Select Opinions.)

' The regularandperiodical march of these phaenomena has nothing in it that oifght to surprise us, if we only attend to the analogous facts which take place under our eyes. Above all things let us beware of making the Deity interpose here, for that being we ought to suppose exempt from all occupation and perfectly happy; otherwise we shall be only giving vain explanations of the heavenly phaenomena, as has happened already to a crowd of authors. Not being able to recognize what is really possible, they have fallen into vain theories, in supposing that for all phaenomena there was but one single mode of production, and in rejecting all other explanations which are founded on probability; they have adopted the most unreasonable opinions, for want of placing in the front the study of the heavenly phaenomena, and of sensible facts, which ought to serve to explain the first.

" The differences in the length of nights and days may arise from the fact that the passage of the sun above the earth is more or less rapid; and more or less slow, according to the length of the regions which it has to pass through. Or, again, to the fact that certain regions are passed through more rapidly than others, as is seen to be the case by our own eyes, in those things to which we can compare the heavenly phaenomena. As to those who on this point admit only one explanation as possible, they put themselves in opposition to facts, and lose sight of the bounds set to human knowledge

" The prognostics which are derived from the stars may, like those which we borrow from animals, arise from a simple Coincidence. They may also have other causes, for example, some change in the air; for these two suppositions both harmonize equally with facts; but it is impossible to distinguish in what case one is to attribute them to the one cause or to the other.

" The clouds may be formed either by the air condensed under the pressure of the winds, or by the agency of atoms set apart for that end, or by emanations from the earth and waters, or by other causes. For there are a great number which are all equally able to produce this effect. When the clouds clash with one another, or undergo any transformation, they produce showers; and the long rains are caused by the motion of the clouds when moved from places suitable to them through the air, when a more violent inundation than usual takes place, from collections of some masses calculated to produce these effects.

" Thunder possibly arises from the movement of the winds revolving in the cavities of the clouds; of which we may see an image in vessels in our own daily use. It may also arise from the noise of fire acted upon by the wind in them, and from the tearings and ruptures of the clouds when they have received a sort of crystaline consistency. In a word, experience drawn from our senses, teaches us that all these phaenomena, and that one in particular, may be produced in many different manners.

" One may also assign different causes to the lightning; either the shock and collision of the clouds produce a fiery appearance, which is followed by lightning; or the lighting up of the clouds by the winds, produces this luminous appearance; or the mutual pressure of the clouds, or that of the wind against them, disengages the lightning. Or, one might say, that the interception of the light diffused from the stars, arrested for a time in the bosom of the clouds, is driven from them subsequently by their own movements, and by those of the winds, and so escapes from their sides; that the lightning is an extremely subtile light that evaporates from the clouds; that the clouds which carry the thunder are collected masses of fire; that the lightning arises from the motion of the fire, or from the conflagration of the wind, in consequence of the rapidity and continuousness of its motion. One may also attribute the luminous appearance of lightning to the rupture of the clouds under the action of the winds, or to the fall of inflammable atoms. Lastly, one may easily find a number of other explanations, if one applies to sensible facts, in order to search out the analogies which they present to the heavenly phaenomena.

" Lightning precedes thunder, either because it is produced at the same moment that the wind falls on the cloud, while the noise is only heard at the instant when the wind has penetrated into the bosom of the cloud; or, perhaps, the two phaenomena being simultaneous, the lightning arrives among us more rapidly than the noise of the thunderbolt, as is in fact remarked in other cases when we see at a distance the clash of two objects.

" The thunderbolt may be produced either by a violent condensation of the winds, or by their rapid motion and conflagration. It may arise from the fact of the winds meeting in places which are too dense, in consequence of the accumulation of clouds, and then a portion of the current detaches itself and proceeds fowards the lower situations; or else it may be caused by the fire which is contained in the bosom of the clouds precipitating itself downwards. As one may suppose that an immense quantity of fire being accumulated in the clouds dilates, violently bursting the substance which; envelops it, because the resistance of the centre hinders it from proceeding further. This effect is especially produced in the neighbourhood of high mountains; and, accordingly, they are very frequently struck with the thunderbolts. In short, one may give a number of explanations of the thunderbolt; but we ought, above all things, to be on our guard against fables, and this one will easily be, if one follows faithfully the sensible phaenomena in the explanation of these things, which are not perceived, except indirectly.

"Hurricanes (rg»9r?gfs) may be caused either by the presence of a cloud, which a violent wind sets in motion and precipitates with a spiral movement towards the lower regions, or by a violent gust which bears a cloud into the neighbourhood of some other current, or else by the mere agitation of the wind by itself, when air is brought together from the higher regions and compressed without being able to escape on either side, in consequence of the resistance of the air which surrounds it; when the hurricane descends towards the earth, then there result whirlwinds in proportion to the rapidity of the wind that has produced them; and this phaenomenon extends over the sea also.

" Earthquakes may arise from the wind penetrating into the interior of the earth, or from the earth itself receiving incessantly the addition of exterior particles, and being in incessant motion as to its constituent atoms, being in consequence disposed to a general vibration. That which permits the wind to penetrate is the fact that falls take place in the interior, or that the air being impressed by the winds insinuates itself into the subterraneous caverns. The movement which numberless falls and the re-action of the earth communicate to the earth, when this motion meets bodies of greater resistance and solidity, is sufficient to explain the earthquakes. One might, however, give an account of them in several other ways.

" Winds are caused, either by the successive and regular addition of some foreign matter, or else by the re-union of a great quantity of water; and the differences ofthe wind6 may arise from the fact that some portions of this same matter fall into the numerous cavities.of the earth, and are divided there.

″Hail is produced by an energetic condensation acting on the ethereal particles which the cold embraces in every direction; or, in consequence of a less violent condensation acting however on aqueous particles, and accompanied by division, in such a manner as to produce, at the same time, the re-union of certain elements and of the collective masses; or by the rupture of some dense and compact mass which would explain at the same time, the numerousness of the particles and their individual hardness. As to the spherical form of the hail, one may easily account for that by admitting that the shocks which it receives in every direction make all the angles disappear, or else that at the moment when the different fragments are formed, each of them is equally embraced on all sides by aqueous or ethereal particles.

" Snow may be produced by a light vapour full of moisture which the clouds allow to escape by passages intended for that end, when they are pressed, in a corresponding manner, by other clouds, and set in motion by the wind. Subsequently, these vapours become condensed in their progress under the action of the cold which surrounds the clouds in the lower regions. It may also be the case that this phenomenon is produced by clouds of a slight density as they become condensed. In this case the snow which escapes from the clouds would be the result of the contact, or approximation of the aqueous particles, which in a still more condensed state produce hail. This effect is most especially produced in the air. Snow, again, may result from the collection of clouds previously condensed and solidified; or from a whole army of other causes. '

" Dew proceeds from a re-union of particles contained in the air calculated to produce this moist substance. These particles may be also brought from places which are moist or covered with, water (for in those places, above all 'others, it is that dew is abundant). These then re-unite, again resume their aqueous form, and fall down. The same phaenomenon takes place in other cases before our own eyes under many analogies.

" Hoar-frost is dew congealed by the influence of the cold air that surrounds it.

" Ice is formed either by the detrition of round atoms contained in the water, and the re-union at scalene and acute angles of the atoms which exist in the water, or by an addition from without of these latter particles, which, penetrating into the water, solidify it by driving away an equal amount of round atoms.

" The rainbow may be produced by the reflection of the solar rays on the moist air; or it may arise from a particular property of light and air, in virtue of which these particular appearances of colour are formed, either because the shades which we perceive result directly from this property, or because, on the contrary, it only produces one single shade, which, reflecting itself on the nearest portions of the air, communicates to them the tints which we observe. As to the circular form of the rainbow, that depends either on the fact of the sight perceiving an equal distance in every direction, or the fact of the atoms taking this form when re-uniting in the air; or it may be caused by its detaching from the air which moves towards the moon, certain atoms which, being re-united in the clouds, give rise to this circular appearance.

" The lunar halo arises from the fact of the air, which moves towards the moon from all quarters, uniformly intercepting the rays emitted by this star, in such a way as to form around it a sort of circular cloud which partially veils it. It may also arise from the fact of the moon uniformly rejecting from all quarters, the air which surrounds it, in such a manner as to produce this circular and opaque covering. And perhaps this opaqueness may be caused by some particles which some current brings from without; perhaps also, the heat communicates to the moon the property of emitting by the pores in its surface, the particles by which this effect is produced.

" Comets arise either from the fact, that in the circumstances already stated, there are partial conflagrations in certain points of the heaven; or, that at certain periods, the heaven has above our heads a particular movement which causes them to appear. It may also be the case, that being themselves endowed with a peculiar movement, they advance at the end of certain periods of time, and in consequence of particular circumstances, towards the places which we inhabit. The opposite reasons explain their disappearance.

" Certain stars return to the same point in accomplishing their revolutions; and this arises, not only as has been sometimes believed, from the fact of the pole of the world, around which they move, being immoveable, but also from the fact that the gyrations of the air which surrounds them, hinder them from deviations like the wandering stars. Perhaps also, this may be caused by the fact, that except in the route in which they move, and in which we perceive them, they do not find any material suitable to their nature. One may also explain this phaenomenon in many other manners, reasoning according to sensible facts; thus, it is possible that certain stars may be wandering because that is the nature of their movements, and, for the same reason, others may be immoveable. It is also possible, that the same necessity which has originally given them their circular movement, may have.»mpelled some to 'follow their orbit regularly, and have iiubjected others to an irregular progress; we may also suppose iat the uniform character of the centre which certain stars traverse favour their regular march, and their return to a certain; and that in the case of others, on the contrary, the differences of the centre produce the changes which we observe. Besides, to assign one single cause to all these phaenomena, when the experience of our senses suggests us several, is folly. It is the conduct of ignorant astronomers covetous of a vain knowledge, who, assigning imaginary causes to facts, wish to leave wholly to the Deity the care of the government of the universe.

" Some stars appear to be left behind by others in their progress; this arises either from the fact of their having a slower motion, though traversing the same circle; or, because, though they are drawn on by the same propelling power, they have, nevertheless, a movement proper to themselves in a contrary direction; or it may be caused by the fact that, though all are placed in the same sphere of movement, still some have more space to traverse, and others less. To give one uniform and positive explanation of all these facts, is not consistent with the conduct of any people but those who love to flash prodigies in the eyes of the multitude.

" Falling stars may be particles detached from the stars, or fragments resulting from their collision; they may also be produced by the fall of substances which are set on fire by the action of the wind; by the re-union of inflammable atoms which are made to come together so as to produce this effect by a sort of reciprocal attraction; or else by the movement which is produced in consequence of the re-union of atoms in the very place where they meet. It may also happen that the light vapours re-unite and become condensed under the form of clouds, that they then take fire in consequence of their rotatory motion, and that, bursting the obstacles which surround them, they proceed towards the places whither the force by which they are animated drags them. In short, this phaenomenon also may admit of a great number of explanations.

" The presages which are drawn from certain animals arise from a fortuitous concourse of circumstances; for there is no necessary connection between certain animals and winter. They do not produce it; nor is there any divine nature sitting aloft watching the exits of these animals, and then accomplishing signs of this kind. Nor can such folly as this occur to any being who is even moderately comfortable, much less to one which is possessed of perfect happiness.

" Imprint all these precepts in your memory, O Pythocles, and so you will easily escape fables, and it will be easy for you to discover other truths analogous to these. Above all, apply yourself to the study of general principles, of the infinite, and of questions of this kind, and to the investigation of the different criteria and of the passions, and to the study of the chief good, with a view to which we prosecute all our researches. When these questions are once resolved, all particular difficulties will be made plain to you. As to those who will not apply themselves to these principles, they will neither be able to give a good explanation of these same questions, nor to reach that end to which all our researches tend." XXVI. Such are his sentiments on the heavenly phaenomena, But concerning the rules of life, and how we ought to choose some things, and avoid others, he writes thus. But first of all, let us go through the opinions which he held, and his disciples held about the wise man.

He said that injuries existed among men, either in consequence of hatred, or of envy, or of contempt, all which the wise man overcomes by reason. Also, that a man who has once been wise can never receive the contrary disposition, nor can he of his own accord invent such a state of thiugs as that he should be subjected to the dominion of the passions; nor can he hinder himself in his progress towards wisdom. That the wise man, however, cannot exist in every state of body, nor in every nation. That even if the wise man were to be put to the torture, he would still be happy. That the wise man will only feel gratitude to his friends, but to them equally whether they are present or absent. Nor will he groan and howl when he is put to the torture. Nor will he marry a wife whom the laws forbid, as Diogenes says, in his epitome of the Ethical Maxims of Epicurus. He will punish his servants, but also pity them, and show indulgence to any that are virtuous. They do not think that the wise man will ever be in love, nor that he will be anxious about his burial, nor that love is a passion inspired by the Gods, as Diogenes says in his twelfth book. They also assert that he will be indifferent to the study of oratory. Marriage, say they, is never any good to a man, and we must be quite content if it does no harm and the wise man—will never many or beget children, as , Epicurus himself lays it down, in Hs "Doubts andIn His treatises on JNatufK Stilt;Tinder certain circumstances of life, he will forsake these rules and marry. Nor will he ever indulge in drunkenness, says Epicurus, in his Banquet, nor will he entangle himself in affairs of state (as he says in his «/ first book on Lives). Nor will he become a tyrant. Nor will he become a Cynic (as he says in his second book about Lives). Nor a beggar. And even, though he should lose his eyes, he will still partake of life (as he says in the same book).

The wise man will be subject to grief, as Diogenes says, in the fifth book of his Select Opinions; he will also not object to go to law. He will leave books and memorials of himself behind him, but he will not be fond of frequenting assemblies. J He will take care of his property, and provide for the future. He will like being in the country, he will resist fortune, and will grieve none of his friends. He will show a regard for a fair reputation to such an extent as to avoid being despised; and he will find more pleasure than other men in speculations.

All faults are not equal. Health is good for some people, but a matter of indifference to others. Courage is a quality which does not exist by nature, but which is engendered by a consideration of what is suitable. Friendship is caused by one's wants; but it must be begun on our side. For we sow the earth; and friendship arises from a community of, and participation in, pleasures. Happiness must be understood in two senses; the highest happiness, such as is that of God, which admits of no increase; and another kind, whichjadmfts of the addition or abstraction of pleasures. The wise man may.raise statues if it suits his inclination, if it does not it does not dignify. The wise man is the only person who can converse correctly about music and poetry; and he can realise poems, but not become a poet.

It is possible for one wise man to be wiser than another. The wise man will also, if he is in need, earn money, but only J by his wisdom; he will propitiate an absolute ruler when occasion requires, and will humour him for the sake of correcting his habits; he will have a school, but not on such a system as to draw a crowd about him; he will also recite in a multitude, but that will be against his inclination; he will pronounce dogmas, and will express no doubts; he will be the same man asleep and awake; and he will be willing even to die for a friend.

These are the Epicurean doctrines.

XXVII. We must now proceed to his letter:— EPICUBUS TO MENCEDS GREETING.

" Let no one delay to study philosophy while he is young, and when he is old let him not become weary of the study; for no man can ever find the time unsuitable or too late to study the health of his soul. And he who asserts either that it is not yet time to philosophize, or that the hour is passed, is like a man who should say that the time is not yet come to be happy, or that it is too late. So that both young and old should study philosophy, the one in order that, when he is old, he may be young in good things through the pleasing recollection of the past; and the other in order that he may be at the same time both young and old, in consequence of his absence of fear for the future.

" It is right then for a man to consider the things which produce happiness, since, if happiness is present, we have everything, and when it is absent, we do everything with a view to possess it. Now, what I have constantly recommended to you, these things I would have you do and practise, considering them to be the elements of living well. First of all, believe that God is a being incorruptible and happy, as the common *l* opinion of the world about God dictates; and attach to your idea of him nothing which is inconsistent with incorruptibility or with happiness; and think that he is invested with everything which is able to preserve to him this happiness, in conjunction with incorruptibility. For there are Gods; for our knowledge of them is jjdistinct. But they are not of the character which people in general attribute to them; for they do not pay a respect to them which accords with the ideas that they entertain of them. And that man is not impious who discards the Gods believed in by the many, but he who applies to the Gods the opinions entertained of them by the many. For the assertions of the many about the Gods are noJ_anticipations *(irgoXj-/iig)*, but false opinions (woxıj/ And in consequence of these, the greatest evils whicn befall wicked men, and the benefits which are conferred on the good, are all attributed to the Gods; for they connect all their ideas of them with a comparison of human virtues, and everything which is different from human qualities, they regard as incompatible with the divine nature)

" Accustom yourself also to think death a matter with whicbri we are not at all concerned, since all good and all evil is in sensation, and since death is only the privation of sensation.J On which account, the correct knowledge of the fact that death is no concern of ours, makes the mortality of life pleasant to us, inasmuch as it sets forth no illimitable time, but relieves us for the longing for immortality. *I For* there is nothing terrible in living to a man who rightly comprehends that there is nothing terrible in ceasing to live I so that he was a silly man who said that he feared death, not because it would grieve him when it was present, but because it did grieve him while it was future. For it is very absurd that that which does not distress a man when it is present, should afflict him when only expected. Therefore, the most formidable of all evils, death, is nothing to us, since, when we exist, death is not present to us; and when death is present, then we have no existence. It is no concern then either of the living or of the dead; since to the one it has no existence, and the other class has no existence itself. But people in general, at times flee from death as the greatest of evils, and at times wish for it as a rest from the evils in life. Nor is the not living a thing feared, since living is not connected with it: nor does the wise man think not living an evil; but, just as he chooses food, not preferring that which is most abundant, but that which is nicest; so too, he enjoys time, not measuring it as to whether it is of the greatest length, but as to whether it is most agreeable. And he who enjoins a young man to live well, and an old man to die well, is a simpleton, not only because of the constantly delightful nature of life, but also because the care to live well is identical with the care to die well. And he was still more wrong who said:—

" TU well to taste of life, and then when born
To pass with quickness to the shades below.

" For if this really was his opinion why did he not quit life? for it was easily in his power to do so, if it really was his belief. But if he was joking, then he was talking foolishly in a case where it ought not to be allowed; and, we must recollect, that the future is not our own, nor, on the other hand, is it wholly not our own, I mean so that we can never altogether await it with a feeling of certainty that it will be, nor altogether despair of it as what will never be. And we must consider that some of the passions are natural, and some empty; and of the«natural ones some are necessary, and some merely natural. And of the necessary one's some are necessary to happiness, and others, with regard to the exemption of the body, from trouble; and others with respect to living itself; for a correct theory, with regard to these things, can refer all choice and avoidance to the health of the body and the freedom from disquietude of the soul. Since this is the end of living happily; for it is for the sake of this that we do everything, wishing to avoid grief and fear; and when once this is the case, with respect to us, then the storm of the soul is, as I may say, put an end to; since the animal is unable to go as if to something deficient, and to seek something different from that by which the good of the soul and body will be perfected.

" For then we have need of pleasure when we grieve, because pleasure is not present; but when we do not grieve, then we have no need of pleasure; and on this account, we affirm, that pleasure is the beginning and end of living happily; for we have recognized this as the first good, being connate with us; and with reference to it, it is that we begin every choice and avoidance; and to this wejcome as if we judged of all good by passion as the standard; and, since this is the first good and connate with us, on this account we do not choose every pleasure, but at times we pass over many pleasures when any difficulty is likely to ensue from them; and we think many This is a quotation from Theognia.

pains better than pleasures, when a greater pleasure follows them, if we endure the pain for a time.

" Every pleasure is therefore a good on account of its own nature, but it does not follow that every pleasure is worthy of being chosen; just as every pain is an evil, and yet every pain must not be avoided. But it is right to estimate all these things by the measurement and view of what is suitable and unsuitable; for at times we may feel the good as an evil, and at times, on the contrary, we may feel the evil as good. And, we think, contentment a great good, not in order that we may never have but a little, but in order that, if we have not much, we may make use of a little, being genuinely persuaded that those men enjoy luxury most completely who are the best able to do without it; and that everything which is naturaL-ie-easily provided, and what is useless is not easily procured. lAnd simple flavours give as much pleasure as costly fare, when everything that can give pain, and every feeling of want, is removed! and corn and water give the most extreme pleasure when any one in need eats them. To accustom one's self, therefore, to simple and inexpensive habits is a great ingredient in the perfecting of health, and makes a man free from hesitation with respect to the necessary uses of life. And when we, on certain occasions, fall in with more sumptuous fare, it makes us in a better disposition towards it, and renders us fearless with respect to fortune. WhenJjierefore. we say_ that pleasure is a chief good, we are not speaking of the pleasures of the debauched man, or those which lie in sensual enjoyment, as some think who are ignorant, and who do not entertain our opinions, or else interpret them perversely; but we mean the freedom of the *body* from pain, and_of_jhji nnnl frnm uunfutiiu-uT" FoFilTisfnot continued drmldngs"and revels, or the enjoyment of female society, or feasts of fish and other such things, 'as a costly table supplies, that make life pleasant, but sober contemplation, which examines into the 'reasons for all choice and avoidance, and which puts to flight the vain opinions from which the greater part of the confusion arises which troubles the soul.

" Now, the beginning and the greatest good of all these things is prudence, on which account prdencejssojnething moie_iaIuable than even philosophy, inasmuch asjiU the_atter vktues-ptu-jgJKm it, teaching us that it is not possible to live pleasantly unless one also lives prudently, and honourably. 1 and justly; and that one cannot live prudently, and honestly, and justly, without living pleasantly); for the virtues are connate with living agreeably, and living agreeably is inseparable from the virtues. Since, who can you think better than that man who has holy opinions respecting the Gods, and who is utterly fearless with respect to death, and who has properly contemplated the end of nature, and who comprehends that the chief good is easily perfected and easily provided; and the greatest evil lasts but a short period, and causes but brief pain. And who has no belief in necessity, which is set up by some as the mistress of all things, but he refers some things to fortune, some to ourselves, because necessity is an irresponsible power, and because he sees that fortune is unstable, while our own will is free; andjthis freedom constitutes, in our case, a responsibility which makes us encounter blame and praise. Since it would be better to follow the fables about the Gods than to be a slave to the fate of the natural philosopher; for the fables which are told give us a sketch, as if we could avert the wrath of God by paying him honour; but the other presents us with necessity who is. inexorable.

" And he, not thinking fortune a goddess, as the generality esteem her (for nothing is done at random by a God), nor a cause which no man can rely on, for he thinks that good or evil is not given by her to men so as to make them live happily, but that the principles of great goods or great evils are supplied by her; thinking it better to be unfortunate in accordance with reason, than to be fortunate irrationally; for that those actions which are judged to be the best, are rightly done in consequence of reason.

".Do you then study these precepts, and those which are akin to them, by all means day and night, pondering on them by yourself, and discussing them with any one like yourself, and then you will never be disturbed by either sleeping or waking fancies, but you will liye-like a God among men: for a man living amid immortal Gods, is in no resjjgctT like a mortal beirrgri --In other works, he discards divination; and also in his *i* Little Epitome. And he says divination has no existence; but, if it has any, still we should think that what happeris according to it is nothing to us.

These are his sentiments about the things which concern the life of man, and he has discussed them at greater length elsewhere.

XXVIII. Now, he differs with the Cyrenaics about pleasure. For they do not admit that to be pleasure which exists as a condition, but place it wholly in motion. He, however, admits both kinds to be pleasure, namely, that of the soul, and that of the body, as he says in his treatise on Choice and Avoidance; and also in his work on the Chief Good; and in the first book of his treatise on Lives, and in his Letter against the Mitylenian Philosophers. And in the same spirit, Diogenes, in the seventeenth book of his Select Discourses, and Metrodorus, in his Timocrates, speak thus. ",But when pleasure is understood, I mean both that which exiifs"irr" motion, and that which is a state...." And Epicurus, in Ks-treatise "on Choice, speaks thus: " Now, freedom from disquietude, and freedom from pain, are states of pleasure; bat joy and cheerfulness are beheld in motion and energy." XXIX. For they make out the pains of the body to be worse than those of the mind; accordingly, those who do wrong, are punished in the body. But he consid ers the pains of the soul the wqrst; forJb-jrtLjthe flesh is only sensible to present affliction, but the soul feels the past, the present, and the future. Therefore, in the same manner, he"c6ntehds that the pleasures of the soul are greater than those of the body; and he uses as a proof that pleasure is the chief good, the fact that all animals from the moment of their birth are delighted with pleasure, and are offended with pain by their natural instinct, and without the. employment of reason. Therefore, ' too, we, of our own inclination, flee from pain; so that Hercules, when devoured by his poisoned tunic, cries out:—

Shouting and groaning, and the rocks around

Re-echoed his sad wails, the mountain heights "

Of Locrian lands, and sad Eubaea's hills., XXXAnd we choose the virtues for the sake of pleasure, t/ and not on their own account; just as we seek the skill of thTphysician for the sake of health, as Diogenes says, in the From the Trachinae of Sophocles, 1784. twentieth book of his Select Discourses, where he also calls virtue a way of passing one's life *diayoiyij)*. But__Elgicurus says, that virtue alone is inseparable from pleasure, butthat every thing else may be.separated from it as mortal. XXXI. Let us, however, now add the finishing stroke, as one may say, to this whole treatise, and to the life of the philosopher; giving some of his fundamental maxims, and closing the whole work with them, taking that for our en "'which is the beginning of happiness. 1. " That which is happy and imperishable, neither has trouble itself, nor does it cause it to anything; so that it is not subject to the feelings of either anger or gratitude; for these feelings only exist in what is weak. (In other passages he says that the Gods are speculated on by reason, some existing according to number, and others according to some similarity of form, arising from the continual flowing on of similar images, perfected for this very purpose in human form.) / 2. " Death is nothing to us; for that which is dissolved is v devoid of sensation, and that which is devoid of sensation is nothing to us. 3. " The limit of the greatness of the pleasures is the v removal of everything which can give pain. And where pleasure is, as long as it lasts, that which gives pain, or that which feels pain, or both of them, are absent. *4* 4. " Pain does not abide continuously in the flesh, but in its extremity it is present only a very short time. That pain which only just exceeds the pleasure in the flesh, does not last many days. But long diseases have in them more that is pleasant than painful to the flesh. 5. " It is not possible to live pleasantly without living J prudently, and honourably, and justly; nor to live prudently, and honourably, and justly, without living pleasantly. But he to whom it does not happen to live prudently, honourably, and justly, cannot possibly live pleasantly. 6. " For the sake of feeling confidence and security with regard to men, and not with reference to the nature of government and kingly power being a good, some men have wished to be eminent and powerful, in order that others might attain this feeling by their means; thinking that so they would secure safety as for as men are concerned. So that, if the life of such men is safe, they have attained to the nature of good; but if it is not safe, then they have failed in obtaining that for the sake of which they originally desired power according to the order of nature. 7. " No pleasure is intrinsically bad: but the efficient causes of some pleasures bring with them a great many per-" turbations of pleasure. 8. " If every pleasure were condensed, if one may so say, and if each lasted long, and affected the whole body, or the essential parts of it, then there would be no difference between one pleasure and another. 9. " If those things which make the pleasures of debauched men, put an end to the fears of the mind, and to those which arise about the heavenly bodies, and death, and pain; and if they taught us what ought to be the limit of our desires, we should have no pretence for blaming those who wholly devote themselves to pleasure, and who never feel any pain or grief (which is the chief evil) from any quarter. 10. " If apprehensions relating to the heavenly bodies did not disturb us, and if the terrors of death have no concern with us, and if we had the courage to contemplate the boundaries of pain and of the desires, we should have no need of physiological studies. 11. "It would not be possible for a person to banish all fear about those things which are called most essential, unless he knew what is the nature of the universe, or if he had any idea that the fables told about it could be true; and therefore, it is, that a person cannot enjoy unmixed pleasure without physiological knowledge.

'12. " It would be no good for a man to secure himself safety as far as men are concerned, while in a state of apprehension as to all the heavenly bodies, and those under the earth, and in short, all those in the infinite.

13. Irresistible power and great wealth may, up to a certain point, give us security as far as men are concerned; but the security of men in general depends upon _the-tranquillity of their souls, and their freedom from ambition. There ia some hopeless corruption in the text here. Nor has any one succeeded in making it intelligible. The French translator divides it into two maxims. 14. ' The riches of nature are defined and easily procurable; but vain desires are insatiable. 15. " The wise man is but little favoured by fortune; but *J* his reason procures him the greatest and most valuable goods, and these he does enjoy, and will enjoy the whole of his life. 16. " The just man is.the freest of all men from disquietude; but the unjust man is a perpetual prey to it. 17. " Pleasure in the flesh is not increased, when once the pain arising from want is removed; it is only diversified. 18. " The most perfect happiness of the soul depends on these reflections, and on opinions of a similar character on all those questions which cause the greatest alarm to the mind. *i/* 19. " Infinite and finite time both have equal pleasure, if any one measures its limits by reason. 20. "If e flesh could experience boundless pleasure, it would want to dispose of eternity. *Jil* " But

reason, enabling us to conceive the end and /oissolution of the body, and liberating us from the fears *I* relative to eternity, procures for us all the happiness of which I life is capable, so completely that we have no further occasion To include eternity in our desires. In this disposition of mind, man is happy even when his troubles engage him to quit life; and to die thus, is for him only to interrupt a life of happiness. 22. " He who is acquainted with the limits of life knows, that that which removes the pain which arises from want, and which makes the whole of life perfect, is easily procurable; so that he has no need of those things which can only be attained with trouble. 23. " But as to the subsisting end, we ought to consider it with all the clearness and evidence which we refer to whatever we think and believe; otherwise, all things will be full of confusion and uncertainty of judgment. 24. " If you resist all the senses, you will not even have anything left to which you can refer, or by which you may-be able to judge of the falsehood of the senses which you condemn. 25. " If you simply discard one sense, and do not'distinguish between the different elements of the judgment, so as to know There in some great corruption here again. The French translator takes 19, 20, and 21 all as one. on the one hand, the induction which goes beyond the actual sensation, or, on the other, the actual and immediate notion; the affections, and all the conceptions of the mind which lean directly on the sensible representation, you will be imputing trouble into the other sense, and destroying in that quarter every species of criterion. 26. " If you allow equal authority to the ideas, which, being only inductive, require to be verified, and to those which bear about them an immediate certainty, you will not escape error; for you will be confounding doubtful opinions with those which are not doubtful, and true judgments with those of a different character. 27. " If, on every occasion, we do not refer every one of our actions to the chief end of nature, if we turn aside from that to seek or avoid some other object, there will be a want of agreement between our words and our actions.. 28. " Of all the things which wisdom provides for the hap-,/piness of the whole life, by far the most important is the acquisition of friendship. 29. " The same opinion encourages man to trust that no evil will be everlasting, or even of 'long duration; as it sees that, in the space of life allotted to us, the protection of friendship is most sure and trustworthy. 30. " Of the desires, some are natural and necessary, some natural, but not necessary, and some are neither natural nor necessary, but owe their existence to vain opinions. '. (Epicurus thinks that those are natural and necessary which. put an end to pains, as drink when one is thirsty; and that those are natural but not necessary which only diversify plea-, , sure, but do not remove pain, such as expensive food; and that these are neither natural nor necessary, which are such as crowns, or the erection of Statues.) .31. " Those desires which do not lead to pain, if they are not satisfied, are not necessary. It is easy to impose silence on them when they appear difficult to gratify, or likely to produce injury. 32. "When the natural desires, the failing to satisfy which is, nevertheless, not painful, are violent and obstinate, it is a proof that there is an admixture of vain opinion in them; for then energy does not arise from their own nature, but from the vain opinions of men. i!3, " Natural justice is a covenant of what is suitable, leading men to avoid injuring one another, and being injured. j4. " Those animals which are unable to enter into an argument of this nature, or to guard against doing or sustaining mutual injury, have no such thing as justice or injustice. And the case is the same with those nations, the members of which are either unwilling or unable to enter into a covenant to respect their mutual interests. 35. "Justice has no independent existence; it results from mutual contracts, and establishes itself wherever there is a mutual engagement to guard against doing or sustaining mutual injury. 36. " Injustice is not intrinsically bad; it has this character only because there is joined with it a fear of not escaping those who are appointed to punish actions marked with that character. 37. " It is not possible for a man who secretly does anything in contravention of the agreement which men have made with one another, to guard against doing, or sustaining mutual injury, to believe that he shall always escape notice, even if he have escaped notice already ten thousand times; for, till his death, it is uncertain whether he will not be detected. 38. " In a general point of view, justice is the same thing to every o; for there is something advantageous in mutual society. Nevertheless, the difference of place, and divers other cirodnistances, make justice vary. 39. " From the moment that a thing declared just by the law is generally recognized as useful for the mutual relations of men, it becomes really just, whether it is universally regarded as such or not. 40. " But if, on the contrary, a thing established by law is not really useful for the social relations, then it is not just; and if that which was just, inasmuch as it was useful, loses this character, after having been for some time considered so, it is not less true that, during that time, it was really just, at least for those who do not perplex themselves about vain words, but who prefer, in every case, examining and judging for themselves. 41. " When, without any fresh circumstances arising, a thing which has been declared just in practice does not agree with the impressions of reason, that is a proof that the thing was not really just. In the same way, when in consequence of new circumstances, a thing which has been pronounced just does not any longer appear to agree with utility, the thing which was just, inasmuch as it was useful to the social ra- tions and intercourse of mankind, ceases to be just the moment when it ceases to be useful. 42. " He who desires to live tranquilly without having any thing to fear from other men, ought to make himself friends; those whom he cannot make friends of, he should, at least, arvoid rendering enemies; and if that is not in his power, he should, as far as possible, avoid all intercourse with them, and keep them aloof, as far as it is for his interest to do so. 43. "The happiest men are they who have arrived at the point of having nothing to fear from those who surround them. Such men live with one another most agreeably, having the firmest grounds of confidence in one another, enjoying the advantages of friendship in all their fulness, and not lamenting, as a pitiable circumstance, the premature death of their friends." .

V LONDON:
J. HADDON AND SON, PRINTERS, CASTLE STREET, FINSBURY. INDEX.

The Roman numerals refer to the sections, theArabic figures to the pages.
-ieschines, a rhetorician, vii. 80.
calumniated, iii. 79.
lectured at Athens, iv. 80.
son of a sausage seller, i. 79.
   Alemon, Crotona, his view of the soul, 371.
Anacharsis, inventions of, ii. 48.
letter to Croesus, 49.
received by Solon, iii. 47.
return to Scythia, iv. 47.
sayings of, v. 47.
one of the wise, 46.
   Anaxagoras, called Mind, i. 59.
epigrams on, x. 62.
first prose writer, viii. 61,
opinions of, iii. 59.
prosecuted for impiety, ix. 61.
   Anaxakchus, called Happy, iii. 401.
intimate with Alexander, 400.
Nicocreon, his enemy, 401.
   Anaximander, the astronomer, 57.
   Anaximenes, letters to Pythagoras, 58.
   Antisthenes, doctrines of, v. 220.
founds a manly Stoic school, viii. 221.
love of life, x. 223.
pupil of Gorgias, ii. 217,
sayings of, iv. 218.
writings of, ix. 222.
   Arcesilads, a favourite of Eumenes and Hierocles, xiv. 168.
an admirer of Plato, viii. 165.
   Arcesilaus, a poet,iv. 164,
axiomatic and free-spoken, x. 165.
death from excess, x. 170.
disliked talkativeness, 166.
founder of the Middle Academy, ii. 163.

goes to Crantor, iii. 163.
letterto Thaumasias,xix. 170.
. liberal with money, xiii. 167.
vices of, xvi. 168.
ARCHELAtTS, 62.
a natural philosopher, ii. 62.
opinions on heat and cold, &c. iii. 63.
— production of animals, iii. 63.
Archttas, general at Tarentum, 369.
letter to Plato and reply, iv. 369.
mathematician, vii. 370.
Aristippus, a favourite of Dionysius, iii. 81.
opinions of, on pain and pleasure, 90.
retorts, iv. 82.
school of philosophy, viii. 89.
sycophancy, iv. 82.
teaches for money, ii. 81.
wealth, iv. 82.
writings, vi. 88.
Ariston, the bald, called Scion, i. 318.
an eloquent philosopher, vi. 319.
his writings, vii. 319,
Aristotle, apophthegms, xi. 187.
I I
   Aristotle, death from poison, vii. 182.
hymn to Hermias, 183.
leaves Plato, iv. 181.
lived in Philip's court, vi. 182.
opinions, criterion of truth, 192.
   — friendship, 192.
God, 193.
   — philosophy, 191.
Plato's most eminent pupil, ii. 18).
peripatetic, why so called, iv. 181.
scheme for early waking, x. 186.
school at Athens, vii. 182.
will of, ix. 185.
writings, many, xii. 189.
   Amicereans, their opinions, x. 92.
   Bias, the wise, 38.
declines the tripod, i. 38.
death of, in court, iv. 39.
eloquent and just as a lawyer, iii. 39.
a poet, v. 39.
sayings of, v. 39.
stratagem to save Priam, his native city, ii. 39.
   Bion, apophthegms of, iii. 172.

change of school?, iv. 173.
fear of death, x. 175.
fond of theatre, v. 174.
poverty of, i. 171.
selfishness of, ix. 174.
   Carneades, his letters, viii. 178.
well read in Stoic lore, ii. 177.
industry of, iii. 178.
his fear of death, vii. 178.
   Cedes, the Theban, 105.
   Charondas, account of, *note,* 345.
   Clido, the wise one of, 32.
brief in speech, v. 34.
death of, through joy, v. 34.
letter to Periander, v. 34.
opinion as to Cythera, iv. 33.
saying about suretyship, v. 34.
sayings of, ii. 33.
   Chbysippus, his abilities, ii. 327.
his books, xii. 331.
his industry, iii. 328.
his questions, xi. 330.
a pupil of Cleanthes, i. 327.
his self-esteem, iv. 329.
said to be an indecent writer, xii. 331.
   Cleanthes, a boxer, 322.
books of, ii. 325.
called an ass, iv. 323.
poor and industrious, ii. 322.
slow of intellect, iii. 323.
starved himself, vii. 326.
wrote on oyster shells, &c. for want of paper, iv. 323.
Ci Eobulus, one of the wise men, 41.
apophthegms of, iv. 42.
letter to Solon, vi. 43.
   Clitomachus, disciple and successor of Carneades, 179.
   Crantor. a poet, vi. 162.
a pupil of Polemo, iii. 161.
retires to temple of yEsculapius. iv. 161.
   Crates, a pupil of Polemo, 160.
lived with Crantor, iii. 160.
writings of, and disciples, iv. 161.
   Crates, a Theban cynic, 249.
his disposal of property, iv. 250.
his jesting with death, x. 252.
his indifference to public opinion, viii. 252.
his sayings, ix. 282.
   Crito, the Athenian, 103.
   Cynics, doctrines of, iii. 257.
discard liberal studies, 257.

prefer ethics to logic, 257.
simplicity in living, 258.
virtue, the chief good, 258. may be taught, 258.
    Cyrenaies, a sect of the school of Arislippus, viii. 89.
    Demetrius, governor of Athens, ii. 209.
honoured and envied, viii. 209.
    Demstrius, his reported blindness and restoration of sight, vii. 209.
statues erected to him, ii. 09.
sayings of, x. 211.
writings of, ix. 210.
Democritus, pupil of the magi, 390.
death, xi. 390.
disregard of glory, v. 391.
of wealth, vii. 392.
doctrines of, xii. 394.
lowly life, vii. 392.
    Plato's dislike of him, viii. 393.
sagacity, stories of, x. 394.
writings of, xiii. 395.
Dialectics, the Stoics' doctrine of, xxxv. 275.
Diogenes, accounts of his death, xi. 246.
anecdotes of him, vi. 228.
cynical sayings, 226.
lived in a cask, 225.
money changer, 224.
corrupted by him, i. 224.
neglect of music, vii. 245.
persuader, a skilful, x. 245.
poverty of, reconciled to, iii. 224.
pride and haughtiness of, iv. 225.
pupil of Antisthenes, ii. 224.
sold as a slave, ix. 245.
writings of. xii. 247.
    Diogenes of Apollonia, 400.
his chief doctrines, ii. 400.
    Dionysjus, a pupil of Zeno, 321.
writings of, v. 321.
    Druids, account of, *note* 3.
    Egyptian philosophy, vii. 9.
    Empedocles, accused of pride, xi. 366.
doctrines of, xii. 368.
inventor of rhetoric, iii. 361.
liberality of, ix. 363.
pacifies the Arigentines, xi. 366.
political career, ix. 363.
retires to Peloponnesus, x. 364.
story of his wonder working, xi 365.

    Empedocles, why called, wind-forbidder, v. 362.
    Epicharmus, inscription on his statue, 368.
    Epicurus, an Athenian, 424.
his character, v. 427.
criteria of truth, 435.
said to be debauched, iii. 426.
rejected dialectics, 435.
Diotimus, a Stoic, opposes him, iii. 425.
doctrines, his, on affections, 447.
. atoms, 439.
clouds,thunder,
    &c. 460.
comets, 464.
faults among
men, 467-forms and attributes, 449.
— grief, 467.
— heaven's phenomena, 452, 458.
  — injuries among
men, 466.
— meteorological,
461.
opinion and
supposition, 436. passions, pleasure, and pain, 436.
' pleasure, 471, 473.
——. —— production of
things, 441.
self-production,
451.
stars, 464.
study of philosophy, 468.
  — universe, 439.
flattered Mithras, iii. 425.
fundamental maxims of, xxxi. 474.
letter of, to Herodotus, xxiv.436
.—.— Menfficeus, xxvii 468.
. Pythocles, xxv. 455.
manner of his death, ix. 429.
plain language, his, viii. 428.
pupils, his, xi. 431.
    Epicurus, virtue, why to be chosen, v,,xxs. 473.'
luminous writings, xvii. 483.
will, his last, x. 429.
writings on natural philosophy, iv. 426.
youthful student, a, ix. 429.
    Epimenides, one of the wise men, 50.

built a temple at Athens, vi. 52.
honoured as a deity, xi. 53.
letter to Solon, ix. 52.
long life, his, story of, iv. 51.
long sleep, his, story of, ii. 50.
poems, and other writings, v. 51.
stays the plague at Athens, iii. 51.
    Ethical philosophy, what, xiii. 12, subdivisions, xiii. 12.
    Epoxides, his followers, iv. 97. '
opinions, ii. 97.
protector of Socrates, i. 97.
    Endoxus, astronomer, geometrician, and lawgiver, 373.
inventor of theory of crooked lines, vi. 374.
writings of, iii. 373.
    Fate, Stoics' view of, lxxiv. 318.
    Gynosophistae, what and who, i. 3.
    God, Stoics' view of, lxxii. 312.
    Hegesiaci, a sect of the school of Aristippus, their opinions, ix. 91.
    Heeaclides, a Peripatetic, Pythagorean, and Platonist, by turns, ii. 213.
remarkable attempt to deceive at his death, ii. 215.
surnamed Pompicus from his dress and size, iii. 213.
writings of, iv. 213.
    Heraclitus, book on nature, v. 377.
epigrams on him, xii. 381.
esteemed by Darius Hystaspes, letters between them, ix. 380.
lofty and arrogant, 376. '.
misanthropic, iii. 376.
i Hippaechia, a female philosopher, in love with Crates the Cynic, 254.
    Her contest with Theodoras, iii. 255.
    Hippasus, a disciple of Pythagoras, 371.
    Ionian school of philosophy, x. 10.
    Italian school of philosophy, x. 10.
    " Know thyself," the apophthegm, xiii. 21.
    Lacydes, founder of the New Academy, i. 176.
his death from excess, vi. 177.
his industry, ii. 176.
    Ledcippus, his chief dAtrines, ii. 388.
pupil of Zeno theTlleatic, 388.

Lvcon, an eloquent instructor of youth, i. 205.
delicacy in dress, iii. 206.
favourite of Eumenes and Attalus, iv. 206.
his will, ix. 206.

Magi, what and who, *note,* 3.
MELissus, his doctrine of universe, 386.
Menedembs, his banquets, xv. 110.
his character, vi. 107.
his death, xviii. 112.
despised Plato, &c, xi. 109.
disciple of Phsedo, 105.
endangered by his free speech, iv. 107.
friend of Antigonus, xvii. 111.
invention and readiness, xii. 109.
regardlessness of appearances, v. 107.
severe and rigid, iii. 106.
sent to Megara, but deserts, ii. 105.
thought highly of by his countrymen, xvi. 111.

Menedemtjs, a superstitious Cynic, 267.

Menippus, a Cynic, 253.
hangs himself, iii. 256.

Menippus, writer of low ridicule, ii. 256.
writings, vi. 256.
Metrooles, pupil of Crates the tnie, 253.,
destroys himself, 254.
Mind, Stoics, doctrine of, lxxiii. 299.
Monimus. feigned madness, i. 248.
a pupil of Diogenes, 248.
Myson, one of the wise men, 49. '
Natural philosophy, what so called, xiii. I.
Stoics' account of, lxvii. 307.
Orpheus, not a philosopher, iv. 7.
Onesicritus, a pupil of Diogenes, 249.

Parmehides, %rst 'to speak of the earth as" a sphere, ii. 384.
philosophized in poems, iii. 385.
Periandek, one of the wise men, his domestic crimes, 43.
his letter to Procles, viii. 46.
—— to the wise men, vii. 45.
from Thrasybulus, ix. 46.

sayings of, v. 45.
wish to conceal his grave, iii. 44.
Ph.zedo, founder of the Eliac school, 96.

Pherecydes, one of the wise men, 53.
epigrams on, vii. 55.
first writer on natural philosophy, ii. 54.
grave of, at Ephesus, iv. 54.
letter to Theales, viii. 56.
makes a sun-dial, vi. 55.
Philolacs, a pupil of Pythagoras, 372.
aims at regal power, ii. 372.
book, his one, iv. 372.
first to describe the earth's movement in a circle, iii. 372.
Philosophers, names of their sects, xii. 11.
who did not write, xi. 11.
Philosophy, arose among Greeks, iii. 6.

Philosophy, divisions of, xiii. 11.
earliest study of, i. 3.
two schools of, x. 10.
various kinds of, xi. 11.
Pisisiratus, his letter to Solon, vi. 20.

Pittacts, onc of the wise men, 35.
advice about marrying, viii. 37.
death of, vi. 36.
forbearance of, iii. 35.
a general and soldier, i. 35.
honoured by his country, ii. 35.
lameness of, ix. 33.
letter to Crcesus, x. 38.
a poet, v. 36.
sayings of, iv. 36.
Plato, academy, his, ix. 115.
account of his opinions, by Alcinus, 117.
aided by Epicharmus, a comic poet, xii. 116.
attachments, xxiii. 123.
to writings of Sophron, 119.
birth and early abode, ii. 113.
danger from Dionysius, xv. 120.
defends Chabrias, xviii. 121.
descent of, i. 113.
dialogues of, xxxv. 133.
disciples of, xxxi. 129.
disliked Aristippus, 126.
disliked by Xenophon, xxiv. 125.

education, his, v. 114.
epigrams on his tomb, 128.
epistles, his, xxxvi. 134.
marks in his books, xxxix. 136.
method of his argument, xxxii. 129.
opinions on arts, beauty, 144.
beneficence, 146.
contraries, 149.
discourse, 143.
entities divisible and undivisible, ISO.
independent and relative, 150.
end of affairs, 146.
friendships, 141.
God and matter, 137.
good and evil, 1 40.
Plato, good counsel, 150.
good laws and lawlessness, 148.
the good, 148.
good things, 149.
happiness, 147.
justice, 142.
knowledge, 142.
law, 143.
medical science, 143.
music, 143.
noble birth, 144.
philanthropy, 147.
political constitutions, 141.
power, 147.
rhetoric, 145.
rule, 145.
V the soul, 144.
things existing, 148.
virtue perfect, 144.
voice, 150.
opinions on his writings, xxv. 126.
refuses appointments from Arcadia and Thebes, xvii. 121.
ridiculed, xxii. 121.
Socrates' dream of him, vii. 114.
system, his, made difficult on purpose, xxxviii. 135.
theory of ideas, 118.
valiant soldier, a, x. 115.
visits Sicily, volcanoes, xiv. 119.
what he taught, xix. 122.
where he first taught, viii. 114.
will, his last. xxx. 127.
Polemo, his calmness, iv. 158.
epigram, viii. 160.
fond of Sophocles, vii. 159.
imitated Xenocrates, vi. 159.

intemperate and profligate, 158.
much honoured, iv. 158.
rigorous system of morals, iv. 158.
 Potamo and his school, xiv. 13.
 Potter's wheel, invented by Anacharsis,
viii. 48.
 PitoTiGoKAS, method of arguing, his,
iii. 397.
taught at a fixed price, 398.
works, his, v. 398.
wrecked in his way to Sicily, vii. 399.
 Ptrrho, originally a painter, 402.
account of him, by Antigonus.
. 402.
arguing, ten modes of, ix. 409.
arguing, five others added by
Agrippa, x. 412.
attached to Anaxarchus, ii. 402.
certainty not attainable, 414.
disciples, vii 405.
called Sceptics from their
doubting every thing, viii. 405.
eloquent, 403.
fortitude and economy, vi. 404.
good, natural, or natural evil,
none, 417.
honoured by his country, 403.
impassiveness, vi. 404.
learning, no such thing, 417.
left no writings, 418.
motion, none, 417.
production, none, 417.
signs, invisible of visible things,
416.
signs, visible of visible things,
none, 415.
system learned from his disciples,
418.
travelled to India, 402.
 Pythagoras, accounted a son of
Mercury, iv. 339.
his works, v. 340
community of property with
friends, viii. 342.
division of life, vii. 342.
doctrine of monads, xix. 348.
founder of Italian philosophy, i. 338.
geometrician, xi. 342.
greatly admired, xv. 342.
initiated into mysteries, iii. 338.
introduced weights and measures
to Greece, xiii. 344.

letter to Anaximenes, xxvi. 358.
manner of his death, xxi. 354.
opinions on nature, xix. 349.
practised divination, xviii. 346.
precepts, vi. 341.
as to worship, xix. 347.
prohibition as to food, xviii. 346.
ridiculed by Timon, xv. 353.
 Pythagoras, symbols, his, xvii. 345.
wife and son, xxii. 355.
worship of Apollo, xii. 343,.
Schools of philosophy, xiii. 12.
Seven wise men, the, xiv. 21.
Simias, the Theban, 105,
Simon, the Athenian leather cutter,
104.
 Socrates, an artificer, 64.
character, his, viii. 66.
contests, his, xxv. 74.
counsels and sayings, xvi. 69.
daemon warnings, xvi. 6!).
executed for opinions, the first
philosopher who was, v. 64.
lamented by the Athenians,
xxiii. 73.
persuasive power, xii. 68.
ransoms Phsedo, and teaches him
philosophy, xiv. 68.
school, his, xxvi. 74.
saves Xenophon's life, vii. 65.
serves in Xenophon's army, vii.
65.
slaves, would not have, xiii. 68.
wives, his, xvii. 70.
 Solon, the wise, life of, 23.
apophthegms, his, xvi. 30.
counsels, his, xii. 29.
death of, xv. 29.
escapes from Athens, iv. 25.
excite Athens against Salamis,
ii. 23.
inscription on his statue, xv. 29.
laws as to debts, i. 23.
laws, vii. 26.
letter to Crcesus, xx. 52.
Epimenides, xviii. 30.
Periander, xvii. 30.
Pisistratus, xix. 31.
means of preventing injustice,
x. 28.
opposes Pisistratus, iii. 24.
poems, his, xiii. 29.
taught time by moon, xi. 28.
 Speusippus, a basket-maker, vi. 152.
commentaries, his, xi. 153.

passionate and voluptuous, 152.
 Speusippus, Plato's successor, 152.
puts an end to his life, ix. 153.
Spherds, at Alexandria, 326.
his books, iii. 327.
Stars, Stoics, doctrine of, Ixxi. 311.
 Stilpo, his acuteness, ii. 100.
his dialogues, viii. 102.
his end, x. 103.
opinions on statues, v. 101.
politician, a, iii. 100.
rejects theory of species, vii. 102.
his simplicity, vi. 101.
visits Ptolemy Soter, iv. 101.
Stoics, doctrines of, xxxiii. 274.
 Strato, the natural philosopher, ii.
202.
 Ptolemv Philadelphus, his pupil,
iii. 202.
successor of Theophrastus, 202.
will, his last, vii. 203.
writings, his, iv. 203.
 Thales, the wise, astronomical science
studied and taught by him, ii. 14.
death of, xii. 20.
letter to Pherecvdes, xv. 22.
Solon, xvi. 22.
sayings of, ix. 18.
star-gazing and falling into *the*
ditch, viii. 18.
tripod awarded to him, vii. 16.
views of the soul, his, iii. 15.
Theodoreans, their opinions, xi. 93.
Theodorus, a disciple of Aristippus.
xv. 94.
banished for his opinions, xvi.
95.
 Theophrastus, Aristotle's pupil and
friend, 194.
character of, iv. 194.
name, symbolic, vi. 195.
will, his last, xiv. 200.
writings, his, xiii. 196.
Thesmopheria, what, *note,* 394.
Timon, of Phliasis, 420.
acuteness of, ii. 422.
delighted in a garden, v. 422.
V S
Timon, fond of drinking, ii. 421.
a jester, vi. 422.
his pupils, vii. 423.
 Virtue and vice, Stoics' doctrine of,
lxv. 304.
 Water, the principle of all things, vi.
IS.

Wise man, the Stoics', lxiv. 301.
Wise men, the, who, ix. 10.
   Xenocrates, accidental death, xii. 157.
a grave and solemn man, iii. 154.
hahit of meditation, viii. 156.
kind to a sparrow, vi. 156.
pupil of Plato, 154.
self-denial of, v. 155.
sold for his taxes, x. 157.
writings, his, ix. 156.
   Xenophanes, banished, 382,
buried his sons with his own hands, iv. 38 4.
doctrines, his, iii. 383.
wrote poems, iii. 383.
   Xenophon, banished by the Athenians, vii. 76.
called the Attic muse, xiv. 78.
conduct on death of his son, x. 77.
escape to Corinth, ix. 77.
first writer of memorabilia, iii. 75.
follower of Socrates, ii. 75.
   Xenophon, friend of Cyrus, v. 75.
love of Clinias, iv. 75.
writings, his, xiii. 78.
   Zaleneus, account of, *note,* 345.
   Zeno, the Stoic, his abstinence, &c, xxiii. 269.
admires Diodorus, xx. 266.
anecdotes of him, xix. 266.
Antigonus respects him, viii. 261.
Athenians crown him, ix. 263.
disciples and works, xxxi. 273.
doctrines, xxxii. 273.,
kills himself, xxvi. 270.
lectures in the Stoa or porch, vii. 261.
manner of reproving, xix. 265.
personal appearance, ii. 259.
pupil of Crates, iii. 259.
retiring disposition, xv. 264.
republic, his, xxviii. 271.
turn for investigation, xvii. 264.
his vices, xiii. 263.
writes about duty, xxi. 269.
writings, iv. 260.
   Zeno, the Eleatic, adopted son of Parmenides, 386.
arrested for treason against Nearches, v. 387.
chief doctrines, viii. 388.
invented dialectics, iv. 387.
pounded to death in a mortar, v. 387.
   Zoroaster, his philosophy, *note,* 5.